This book about Contemporary Arab Christian Theology *by Najib George Awad is a welcome correction of many prejudices in the Western view of their Christian coreligionists in the Middle East. We have a long history of not taking the theological contributions of our Christian brothers and sisters seriously. A theologian from Syria, Awad has worked with theological and philosophical acumen in different Western contexts, and he has developed a trustworthy voice in the ecumenical and interreligious theological landscape.*

Prof. Wilhelmus Valkenberg, Ordinary Professor of Religion and Culture, The Catholic University of America, Washington DC, USA

Contemporary Arab Christian Theology *is an in-depth and comprehensive study of the intellectual production of Arab-speaking Christian theologians in the Middle East in the last four decades. Najib Awad's book is an essential reading for anyone interested to understand the vibrancy, diversity, and relevance of Christian thought in a context marked by a Muslim majority, political conflicts, and economic crises.*

Rev. Dr. Mitri Raheb, President of Dar al-Kalima University, Bethlehem, Palestine

An important book that shows us the entire wealth and intellectual brilliance of Christian Arabic theology – in all its complexity, variety, and richness.

Prof. Dr. Klaus von Stosch, Professor of Systematic Theology, Director of the International Center for Comparative Theology and Social Issues, University of Bonn, Germany

This study from Najib George Awad presents a long overdue discussion of Christian Arab Theologies, in a way that takes the reader to the heart of the existential challenges and possibilities of theology as such, and thus also of theology by Arab Christians. Despite growing attention to Christians in and from the Middle East, their theologies have only superficially been engaged with. Language barriers may have played a role here, though also Western preoccupation with the socio-political position of these Christians might have prevented a closer look at their creative contribution to theology, in the past and the present. Awad convincingly shows that it is the loss of Christian theology if we continue to ignore this.

Prof. Heleen Murre-van den Berg, professor of Global Christianity, Radboud University, Holland

I0895801

This timely volume offers a Western audience an encounter with the much-neglected world of Arab Eastern Christians, whose voices both preceded and accompanied those of the Islamic majority of the territories of Syria, Lebanon, Iraq, Palestine, Jordan and Egypt. Opening up to the reader the complex history of these Christian communities, it depicts their theological heritage, as well as their theological reflection on contemporary struggles. The book seeks for a liberative potential through a hermeneutics of present life conditions, in conversation with the specific spiritual and intellectual legacy of Arab Eastern Christians who have lived in proximity with Islam for centuries. The book, written by someone from that context, makes an important contribution to the socio-political, cultural, and interreligious situation of the Arab Christian world, and allows non-Arabic speakers access to a wealthy textual tradition.

Prof. Ivana Noble, Professor of Ecumenical Theology,
Protestant Theological Faculty, Charles University, Czech Republic

Arab Christians have been an important part of the world Christian movement since the first day of Pentecost. Yet, today, most Western Christians continue to assume that all Arabs are Muslim. In the last thirty years there has been a great deal of Western scholarly activity engaging medieval Arab Christian theology, examining the indigenous Arab Christian theological discourse in response to Islam. Yet, there is an almost complete lack of Western interest in contemporary Arab theological thought and discourse. Of course, one reason for this lacuna is due to language. Few Western theologians have Arabic language skills, and few Arab theologians regularly write for Western audiences. In this landmark study, George Najib Awad provides a much-needed introduction to the lively and vibrant Arab Christian "reasoning and discourse" from within. Arab Christian theological reflection does need to be recognized for its ongoing creativity and does need to be included in surveys of contemporary World Christianity. We can thank Professor Awad for this important groundbreaking contribution.

Rev. Prof. David D. Grafton,
Professor of Islamic Studies and Christian-Muslim Relations,
Director of the Duncan Black Macdonald Center,
Hartford International University, CT USA

CONTEMPORARY ISSUES IN MISSION THEOLOGY

Contemporary Arabic Christian Theology

Series Preface

We live in a glocal world in which the global and local are co-dependant, informing and enriching each other. Mission theology, reflecting the wonderful diversity of the global church, sparkles with multi-coloured riches. At the same time, the church needs continued reflection on the overarching issues that arise from broader regional and global canvasses. This series is concerned with the latter, addressing cutting edge themes in global mission theology by leading scholars.

Series Editors

CONTEMPORARY ISSUES IN MISSION THEOLOGY

Contemporary Arabic Christian Theology

An Introduction to Its Identity, History, and Trends of Reasoning

Najib George Awad

First published 2024 by Regnum Books International

Regnum is an imprint of the Oxford Centre for Mission Studies
St. Philip and St. James Church
Woodstock Road
Oxford, OX2 6HR, UK
www.regnumbooks.net

British Library Cataloguing in Publication Data
A catalogue record for this book is available from the British Library

ISBN: 979-8-8898-3869-2
eBook ISBN: 979-8-8898-3870-8

Typeset by Words by Design

Cover image © Robin Schreiner www.unsplash.com

The publication of this volume is made possible through the
financial assistance of Evangelische Mission Weltweit

Distributed by Fortress Press in the US, Canada, India, and Brazil

Dedication

To the spirit and memory of the late friend and intellectual mentor,
Professor Christoph Schwöbel,
whose invitation in 2020 was the inspirational spark that
originated this project.

In most venerating regards and collegiality to all
the Arab-Eastern theologians,
my struggle-mates on the road of the Golgotha
of being a Christian voice in a tormented, dark sphere
like our homeland.

Contents

Introduction

In 2018, I was invited by the editors-in-chief of *St. Andrews Encyclopedia of Theology* to contribute a 10,000 word-long entry on Arabic Christian theology. I spent the ensuing years, in the heart of the coronavirus crisis, researching this theme and trying to produce the requested text. The long entry I produced at the end of that first-stage journey was published in the *Encyclopedia* in 2023.[1] Yet, I soon realised that my story with the subject of that entry was not going to end there. My journey toward achieving this goal opened my eyes widely to the fact that the international, intellectual, and academic (though not the public, political, and the cultural) interest in the theological productions of the Arab-Eastern Christian communities which exist today in the Arab Middle East and Northern Africa is noticeably marginal. There is hardly any considerable or serious attention to the theological trends of reasoning and the discourses these Christians produce today to express their belief systems and their religious rationales; this is if the Western academic world is aware that these Christians do still produce theological reasoning in the first place. Therefore, I was motivated to resume my research on this subject and to extensively expand my examination of it in depth, breadth, and span. I decided to produce a monograph on it in the near future.

What strongly inspired me to make this decision and embark on fulfilling this goal was what my initial work on the short entry for the *St. Andrews Encyclopedia* had invited me to realise. The Arabic-speaking communities are a stark example of a numerical minority in the context of today's Middle East. However, this community is deeply rooted and profoundly inherent (at least, this is how it tends to perceive itself) in the historical, socio-cultural, and civilisational textile of the human existence in this region. Usually, in the Western academic and scholarly circles, the Arabic-speaking Christian communities are not studied as collective human entities in the present sphere of existence in the Arab world. They are, rather, either approached as a small, insignificant community at the verge of rapid extinction, or they are reduced to a mere civilisational and religious relic-like *inheritance* from the far past of the existence of Christianity in the so-called Middle East, which became a Muslim-majority location almost thousand years ago. The Arabic-speaking Christians are looked at as groups of people who only strive to guarantee survival and avoid total extinction in their homeland, despite their surrounding, predominantly Muslim, life-setting.

---

[1] Najib George Awad, "Arab Christian Theology," in *St. Andrews Encyclopedia of Theology*, Brendan N. Wolfe et al. (eds.), www.saet.ac.uk/Christianity/ArabicChristianTheology [accessed 1.5.2023].

The above presumptions notwithstanding, the Arabic-speaking Christians are very lively, vibrant, and active groups of Middle Easterners in the present *Sitz im Leben* of that geographical context, despite their numerical and existential weaknesses and limitations. They are not only active in confronting the multi-faceted challenging conditions the Arab world's populations face and strive to overcome. They are not, that is, only tangibly present and functional on the praxical level of existence. They are also, and more interestingly, quite active in the difficult quests of that region's life on the *intellectual* and *discursive* levels as well. The Arabic-speaking Christians in today's Middle East are not at all intellectually stagnant; they are not theologically in *stasis*. Contrary to what the considerable portion of scholars and academics in the Western world might think or imagine, the Arabic-speaking Christians of today are not different from their ancestors, who, during the early centuries of Islam or the late antiquity era, were quite active and strongly contributive to the intellectual, cultural, theological, and philosophical life and movements that permeated the Muslim world, and they co-created with the Muslims (and the Jews) the Arab-Islamic civilisation. It is to be seriously questioned the conjecture that the contemporary Arabic-speaking Christians are totally obsessed with their existential, daily-life survival and politically-hinged status; so much so that occupations like 'thinking,' 'reasoning,' 'writing,' 'interpreting,' 'creating knowledge,' 'constructing opinions,' or 'composing discourses,' especially in relation to their religious faith and reasoning, are deemed by them mere 'mental gymnastics,' 'intellectual luxury,' 'inconsequential entertainment,' 'secondary, or even tertiary, interests.'

Far from the above being the case, in fact. The Arabic-speaking Christians in today's Middle East are quite active intellectually, especially on the level of developing religious thought about their life conditions, their self-perception, their relation to, and role in, their *Sitz im Leben*, and their reflections on the future. The theologians, thinkers, and intellectuals of the Christian communities in the Arab Middle East never quit pondering these matters and dimensions relating to the theoretical and religious-theological levels of interpretation and relatedness. It is just the case that in the Western world, the predominant majority of those who are aware of the existence of Christians in the Middle East, or who are interested in studying the Arab world or Eastern Christianity, do not have enough, if any, knowledge about the Arabic-speaking Christians' present intellectual and textual productions and discourses about the complex situation in that region.

Western knowledge-seekers are recently more and more exposed to the intellectual productions of the Arabic-speaking *Muslims* who come from the Middle East. There is today a huge amount of literature in almost all Western languages on the Arabic-speaking Middle Eastern Muslims and Islam, composed either by Arab-Muslims who still live in the Middle East, or those among them who reside in the West for the purposes of studying, working, immigration, asylum-seeking, or even refuge. However, the Western intellectual world has lost any direct or attentive contact with the intellectual and literary productions and contributions of the Arabic-speaking Christians and their contemporary theological discourses. The literature and discursive creativity of these Arabs, at least regarding theology, remain rather overshadowed by the interest in the religious thought of the contemporary Arab-Muslim circles of reasoning. They remain imprisoned in their Arabic language textuality without being translated into foreign languages, or they end up suffering from marginalisation and degradation because the Arabic-speaking Christian immigrants or students who live, study, and reside in the Western countries do not care to introduce their indigenous people's intellectual (especially theological) contributions to the world. Maybe this is due to the fact that, in their educational experience in the departments of theology and religious studies in universities and theological seminaries in the Western academic world, these theology students from among the Arab Christians realise that none of their curricula includes any kind of exposition to any theological voice or discourse written in Arabic or produced recently in their homeland. This gives them the impression (as it did give me one day when I was a theology student in the UK and scholar in Germany) that the only reliable, qualified, and referential theological reasoning is the one that is produced in the Western world.[2] Given my personal first-hand connectedness to Western theological and religious academia, and given my personal knowledge of the experiences of dozens of Arabic-speaking Christians who studied theology in the West, I am no longer surprised when I hear many of my academic colleagues and friends relating their and their students' frustration at not being able to obtain any substantial knowledge or understanding of the Arabic-speaking Christians' rational stances, intellectual views, and discourses on the major radical crises their homeland seems to be perpetually tormented by. Many of them also ask me why the Arabic-speaking Christian scholars and academics, whether inside or outside the Western academic world, do not write to introduce the Western intellectual world to the contemporary religious and theological contributions of the Arabic-speaking Christians in the Arab world, so that students and readers in the Western context can learn where Christianity is intellectually in the Middle East today?

It is because of such expressed shortages and requests that I aspired to develop this introductory study. In this book, I endeavour to shed light on the contemporary intellectual contributions of the Arabic-speaking Christians that exist today in the heart of that part of the world. I want to introduce Western readers and knowledge-seekers in general to the trends of thought and various discourses these Christians started to produce from the beginning of the eighties of the last century and which they are still echoing in the twenty-first century. This study does not aim at presenting an exhaustive, detailed description of every single Christian theological discourse one could find in the Arab world during the twentieth century. Such a task is valuable and needed, yet it requires a whole, multi-volume textual production by itself. This study focuses, instead, on the very latest and prevailing Christian theological discourses and trends of

[2] As a professional academic, I applied a couple of times for a temporary visiting professorship in World Christianity at some academic schools of divinity at American and European universities, proposing to teach during my professorship residence courses on Arabic-Eastern Christianity. My proposals were turned down and other candidates who offered teaching about Far Asian, African, or Latin American Christianity were invited instead.

reasoning that were produced during the past two decades of the twentieth century, up to the first two decades of the twenty-first. These four-decades-long histories in the contemporary Christian theological biography of the Arab world are loaded with all forms of pivotal historical changes and events that shaped the life, the worldviews, and the existential stances of the Middle Eastern people (Christian, Muslims, Jews, non-religious, etc.) in a radical manner. This is an era that drove the Arab-Eastern Christians to reflect on key aspects of their existence from frank theological perspectives. They pursued this in a manner, and from dimensions, they had not delved into before. So, when we speak about *contemporary* Arab-Eastern theology, what is meant is literally the most recent trends of theological reasoning one might find in the literature that has been produced by the members of this minor religious community and its ecclesial affiliates.

Those who have the chance to read this monograph will realise that the various intellectual discourses of the present Arabic-speaking Christian intellectuals and authors are all predominantly religious/theological in nature and concern. The reason behind this is that these Christians do still root their life and rotate all the aspects of their existence in that region around the ecclesial and religious presence and manifestation of their Christian self-perception and identity. This is not exceptional or unusual in the specific context called 'the Middle East' or 'the Arab world.' The Muslim majority presence in that context found all its living, existence, self-awareness, identity, and relatedness to the internal and external others, let alone its alterity, on its religious belief and worldview. Islam for the Muslims of the region is factually 'religion and worldliness' (*dīn wa-dunya*) on all levels of human existence, not just the one that is related to politics and state-rule – that is, not just on the level of the belief that Islam is 'religion and state' (*dīn wa-dawlah*). Be that as it may, any intellectual discourse, any cultural reasoning, any socio-political hermeneutics of the human reality and condition that are conducted by the Muslim-majority inhabitants of that region will be deeply baptised in religious water; profoundly rooted in the soil of theological reasoning; explicitly or implicitly shaped by religious *Weltanschauung* and theologically constituted *Kultur*. In the heart of such a context, it is not a surprise that the Christians in the Arab world tend today to strictly and primarily produce intellectual discourses and interpretations of their existence and worldviews that are religious and theological in nature and perspectives.

In the light of the above, this study aims to look at the trends of religious reasoning and discourses which the Arabic-speaking Christians have developed in their contemporary living context. Some of the questions the study will directly or indirectly offer proposed answers to are: how do the Arabophone Christians relate their Christianity to their living indigenous context in the Middle East since the eighties of the past century up till today? How do they perceive their Christian identity in relation to the major changes and challenges that have recently characterised their Muslim-majority context, and how do they perceive who they are in the light of the socio-political, cultural, interreligious, and contextual challenges and components of the broader Muslim-majority context they strive to continue existing in today? How are the Arabophone

Christians' religious and theological discourses similar to, and different from, other Christian religious and theological discourses in other parts of the world? What makes this Christian intellectual discourse 'Arab' and 'Middle Eastern' in its content, methodologies, perspectives, interpretations, and syntheses? What are the determining characteristics of these Arabophone religious hermeneutics in terms of their recent life conditions and challenges, and what are these characteristics' positive and negative ramifications and implications?

It is the hope of this introductory study to be able to open a window for overlooking this Christianity on its own terms, from its indigenous perspectives, and from within its original, very contemporary context. It is the hope that such a survey and analysis of Arabophone Christianity will enable the Western academic, intellectual, and public circles of idea-creators and decision-makers alike to perceive the worldview, the mind, and the self-perception of these Christians free from presumptions, prejudices, and pre-tailored imaginations and agendas. It is also the ambition that such a from-within understanding of the intellectual mind of the Arabophone Christians will offer ideas and interpretations that will be useful for developing *a posteriori* a potential understanding of the Arabophone Christian immigrants and refugees in the Western countries and how they try to relate to the living contexts of their hosting societies. This research introduces the intellectual and academic worlds to the minds and voices of communities that are not only almost disappearing inside their homeland, but also cast in the shadows and hardly known in their expatriation lands as well.

The monograph will start first with a clarification of how the phrase 'Arab-Eastern Christianity' is used in this study, what does it *not* connote, and what it exactly designates in the ensuing chapters. This chapter can be considered the conceptual foundation of the entire study, as it unpacks the notional and hermeneutical dimensions which the study stems from and the ones it tries to avoid, to exceed, or even to correct.

The second chapter will offer a brief historical narration of the life of Arab-Eastern Christianity and its role in the Muslim-majority context that became definitive of the identity of the Middle East from the seventh century onwards. This, rather brief historiographical sketch will place the theological reasoning of the Arabic-speaking Christians today within the historiological framework of the existence and life-conditions of the particular Christian communities that lived in the countries of the Fertile Crescent (which includes today the Arabic states of Syria, Lebanon, Iraq, Palestine, and Jordan), in addition to Egypt. It is in these countries specifically that the Arab-Eastern Christians existed historically and in which they continue to exist today. Due to economic and life-circumstantial factors, many Christians from these countries emigrated to the countries of the Arab Gulf (Kingdom of Saudi Arabia, United Arab Emirates, Qatar, Kuwait, Oman, and Bahrin) and they have been settling there since the second half of the twentieth century. These Christians do have their own religious presence and churches freely existing and practising in the Gulf countries. However, one does not yet find any theological literature coming out of these new residential havens. It is the hope that the production of Christian theological literature coming from the Christian residents in the Gulf countries will witness birth in the coming future.

The third chapter will touch upon the question of how Arab-Eastern Christianity is read in the relevant Western scholarship. This chapter can be considered a methodological base upon which the foundational approach to Arab-Eastern Christianity is constructed in this entire book. The chapter argues principally that one of the challenges that faces the developing of a genuine from-within reading and understanding of certain religious or historical traditions in general, and of Arab-Eastern Christianity in particular, lies in the epistemological reductionism that is practised in modern academy. In this epistemology, one can trace the marks of an intellectual totalitarianism, which scholars sometimes assume in their attempts at defining all the modes of knowledge and evaluating and charting them in relation to one another. This totalitarianism manifests itself in the readiness of scholars to exclude and re-configure a large swathe of historical data for the purpose of making them fit into a preconceived, pre-tailored narrative. In this chapter, I shall touch upon the Western scholarly approaches to the Arabic-speaking Christian tradition and demonstrate that their reading and interpretation of the historical context of these Christians' interreligious co-existence with Islam, as well as this scholarship's reading of these Christians' intellectual and theological values and worth, both stem from a preconceived application of an epistemological strategy shaped after manipulating and selectively dealing with how the Christians and the Muslims co-existed during the early Islamic period in the Arab-Eastern context and then over-projecting the conclusions on this old existence onto the present living context of the Christians in the Arab world. I shall be proposing a different, far more genuinely intrinsic, and *ad intra* reading of the Christian and Muslim co-existence and intellectual interreligious correlation in the Arab-Eastern *Sitz im Leben*. This proposed reading will become the foundation of my reading of the present theological trends of reasoning of this Christianity in the ensuing chapters.

The fourth and fifth chapters of the monograph will directly touch upon the theological heritage of Arab-Eastern Christianity in the past and in the present. Chapter four will offer a brief display of the original, oldest Arab-Eastern theological traditions that the Arabic-speaking Christians developed at the dawn of the Islamic empire in their homeland. It will display the constitutive, defining trends, methods, and focuses that characterised the theological discourses (*Kalām*) which the Arabic-speaking Christians created for the first time in history to relate to Islam and to cross-pollinate with the Muslims intellectually, religiously, and culturally. Visiting this earliest theological experiment will, hopefully, invite readers to grab the chance to compare and to contrast this antique Arabic theological reasoning with the most contemporary theological trends of discoursing and reasoning one can find in the context of the Arab-Eastern Christianity of today.

The central and main bulk of this book is going to be chapter five. In this long and detailed chapter, I present selected major trends of theological reasoning that are characteristic of how the Arab-Eastern Christians think theologically about their recent, specific living conditions and contextual situations. This chapter does not simply speak about every piece of writing composed by an Arabic-speaking Christian which one can find in the Arabic libraries and bookshops today. There are so many Christian authors in the Arab world who keep producing a plethora of writings on faith-based and spirituality subjects that are either mimicking what one finds in the Western theological library, Arabising the theological discourses that were developed outside the Arab world, or simply conveying purely spiritualist, homiletical religious reflections that lack any serious, rational, critical, or analytical engagement with human and divine realities. I try in this book to avoid such literature, despite my recognition of its contextual usefulness and responsive value to particular, private religious and intellectual needs present in Arab-Eastern life-settings. In this chapter, I try to focus, instead, on theological discourses and orientations that engage seriously, rationally, and hermeneutically with the down-to-earth existential and contextual challenges and enquiries which the Arab-Eastern Christians grabble with from webs of meaning, methods of reasoning, and strategies of interpretation that are uniquely expressive of their particular existential conditions and *Sitz im Leben.* I end up, therefore, highlighting the very specific trends of theological reasoning on the following themes, which I believe are uniquely symptomatic of the situations, conditions, experiences, and visions of these particular Christians and their existential framework: the principle of liberation; the method of contextualisation; the issue of 'the land'; the *habitus* of protectionism and self-protectionism; the centrality of cultural belongingness; interreligious relations; interrelational co-existence; and the issue of women's rights and role.

The last chapter of this study will offer an encompassing critical assessment of the trends of theological reasoning that have been exposed in chapter five. The goal here is just to shed light on some central methodological, hermeneutical, analytical, and strategic features in the displayed trends of theologisation for the sake of seeing where these trends succeed and where they seem to fail in their approaches and proposals. This critical assessment aims only to open the door for further, deeper, and broader endeavours towards evolving the Arabic-speaking theological tradition and moving forward with it in the future. Many issues and challenges which people who live in the Arab world face and strive with have not yet been tackled or expressed by the Arabic-speaking Christian theologians. So, perceiving where Arab-Eastern theological reasoning stands today will enable us to forecast to the best of our abilities where it should progress and what is yet to be dealt with and theologised about.

Regarding the process of selecting the theologians I opted for and not others, I used the following threefold criteria: first, I opted for theologians who speak the Arabic language as their sole, or sometimes dual, mother-tongue and who wrote the dominant majority of their texts in this language in the first place. Some of these authors have produced throughout the years theological writings in foreign languages (English, French, and German), or some of them had the privilege of having one or two of their texts translated into one of the primary academic foreign languages. I referred to these non-Arabic texts or their translations whenever I found this necessary for bringing clarity and breadth to the theological discourse of the relevant author. This notwithstanding, I deliberately targeted these authors' texts that are written in Arabic, in the hope that I can overcome the linguistic barrier and export these texts' content to the non-Arabic readers in my own presentations.

Second, I wanted to exclusively introduce Arabic-speaking Christian theologians who originally belong to, but also *still live in and are closely connected to*, the Arab world today. There are many Arab-Eastern theologians who live and work professionally today in the Western world or around the globe and who endeavour perpetually to produce writing on the Arab world and on the Christians therein. However, they do this in foreign languages and, one must say, *from without* the down-to-earth context of the real life and experiences of the Arab-Eastern Christians in the Middle East. Most of these authors may also be deprived of the ability to visit the Arab world and to maintain tight connections with it due to various reasons and circumstances. In this study, I wanted to introduce the readers to a *from-within*, insider-view knowledge of how the Arab-Eastern Christians think theologically and what kind of issues occupy the centre-stage of their theological reasoning as people who exist and think *inside* the Arab world, right at the heart of its living realities. What the Western readership misses is an insider view, and intrinsic perception, of the Christian theological thought in the Arab world as it is created and presented in the terms, and from the points of view, of the indigenous, Arabic-speaking Christians who have a first-hand experience and knowledge of the life-realities of that Christianity.

Third, and finally, I selected these theologians and no others due to the designated niches of thinking and theological reasoning they wrote about in their theological discourses. One can find today Arab-Eastern theologians producing all kinds of textual genres on all the conventional doctrinal, spiritual, biblical, and practical-theological subjects which any and every Christian theologian in other parts of the world writes about, and every Christian tradition throughout the history of Christianity has produced knowledge on. I avoided such theological samples because they do not necessarily convey any enlightening, educating knowledge on the specific, different subjects and issues that the Christians in the Arab world find themselves particularly occupied with and theologising about, primarily because they belong to and exist in that specific geographical zone on the planet. I wanted the readers to get acquainted with some of the central and unique questions and issues which the Arab-Eastern Christians construct their own different theological thought about. The authors I selected are certainly not the only theologians one can find in the present or the past of the Arab Middle East, but each one of them certainly represents a good example that matches this third angle of the selection criteria.

Before I delve into the chapters of the book, I must express my most profound gratitude and indebtedness to a legion of world-class scholars and very kind and generous supportive colleagues, friends, and acquaintances, from the Arab world and outside it, without whom the creating of this book's content would not have been possible. My very first appreciation and gratitude go indeed to the dear friend and intellectual mentor, the late professor Christoph Schwöbel, who on 7 October 2020, and in his capacity as one of the primary editors of *St. Andrews Encyclopedia of Theology*, emailed me an invitation to contribute an entry on Arabic Christianity. To him, I gladly and proudly dedicate this volume, as I remain not only always mindful of our theological interlocution during the years that preceded his sudden and sad departure, but also always deeply indebted to his invitation that encouraged me to embark on this adventurous project. I also thank the editorial team and board of *St. Andrews Encyclopedia* and their meticulous reviewing and working on the content of that small entry and then their generous invitation to me to read a paper on it at the European Academy of Religion sixth annual conference that took place at St. Andrews University, 19–22 June 2023. The discussions, comments, corrections, and suggestions I gathered from these editorial and conferential experiences sharpened my perspectives and stimulated further dimensions and enquiries on contemporary Arab Christian theology which would otherwise have been missing from this volume.

My most sincere appreciation and profound indebtedness go as well to all the colleagues, friends, and others who helped me gather the Arabic theological literatures I needed to read and use in this study throughout the past years. The list of names of those helpers is too long to be recalled fully here. To every single person who enabled me to get a book or any piece of Arabic writing composed by the theologians I introduce in this study, I express my profound gratitude and I gladly include them in the dedication I made at the beginning. To mention just a few names from among the many: Dr. Assaad Elias Kattan; Mr. Waseem Haddad; Dr. Sayf Shams al-Alusi; George Isac; Dr. Mouchir Basil Oaun; Rev. Dr. Mitri Raheb; Dr. Basem Samir El-Sharkawy; and Dr. Maria Qabbara. Finally, I would like to express my most sincere appreciation and gratitude to the editorial team of Regnum Books, Oxford for embracing my monograph and publishing it as one of their books. My specific appreciation goes to Dr. Paul Bendor-Samuel, the director of Regnum Books and the executive director of the Oxford Centre for Mission Studies, for expressing his sincere interest in my project and immediate acceptance of making it one of their publications. To him and his team I remain very grateful for the work they made to produce the text. I finally thank every Arabic-speaking theologian I introduce in this book for his or her dedicated work in the service of raising a genuine, brave, candid, and critical voice on behalf of the Arab-Eastern Christians and their life in the Arab world. If there is any epistemological value in this book it should be attributed to your own discourses and valuable intellectual and theological work. If, nevertheless, the book contains any weaknesses and flaws, they will be indeed my sole responsibility and my own failure in conveying your voices in the best manner possible.

1. Clearing the Conceptual Ground

Introduction: 'Arab Christianity'?

What does 'Arab Christian theology' stand for? What makes it different from other theological discourses? Is there even such a thing as 'Arab Christian theology' in the first place? Answering these questions in an objective and perceptive manner needs to start first with tackling the following preliminary enquiries: what is 'Arab Christianity'? Is there such a so-called reality in the first place, and if there is one, what does it designate? These fundamental enquiries are not just intellectually provocative. They also express a conceptual and philological puzzle of an oxymoronic nature. This is what, for instance, Kenneth Cragg once reflected when he stated

> When nouns serve as adjectives that may undergo some inconvenience – in the strict sense of that which does not seem 'to come well' with them. So, it is with 'Arab Christian.' One would more readily expect 'the Arab Muslims,' if looking for what 'Arab' is likely to describe.[1]

The question "what does 'Arab Christianity' stand for?" might even be more challenging to seek an answer to than the question "who are the Arabs?"[2] 'Who the Arab is is believed by scholars today to be a difficult question to answer or to develop a coherent and final response to.[3] Nevertheless, the intertwining of 'Arab' and 'Christian' seems to be more complicated, for it connotes versatile implications for people inside and outside the 'Arab Worlds' geographical territory. In the ensuing lines, I shall attempt at specifying what the phrase 'Arab

---

[1] Kenneth Cragg, *The Arab Christian: A History in the Middle East* (Louisville: Westminster/John Knox Press, 1991), p. 10.

[2] Such a question was raised by many orientalists and Westerners during the colonialist era, including T. E. Lawrence, or 'Lawrence of Arabia,' who starts his autobiographical narrative on his time in the Orient with the following statement: "A first difficulty of the Arab movement was to say who the Arabs were. Being a manufactured people, their name had been changing in a sense slowly year by year": T. E. Lawrence, *Seven Pillars of Wisdom* (Hertfordshire: Wordsworth, 1997), p. 5. Today's scholars do acknowledge the uncertainty of specifying the Arabs' identity, yet none of them deems the Arabs, like Lawrence, "manufactured people." For some studies on the Arabs in today's scholarship, see, for example, Peter Webb, *Imagining the Arabs: Arab Identity and the Rise of Islam* (Edinburgh: Edinburgh University Press, 2017); Robert Hoyland, *Arabia and the Arabs: From the Bronze Age to the Coming of Islam* (London: Routledge, 2001), and David Cook, "Syria and the Arabs," in *A Companion to Late Antiquity*, P. Rousseau and J. Raithel (eds.) (Chichester: Blackwell Publishers, 2009), pp. 467–478.

[3] See Theresia Hainthaler, *Christliche Araber vor dem Islam: Verbreitung und konfessionelle zugehörigkeit Eine Hinfürung* (Leuven & Paris & Dudley, MA: Peeters, 2007), p. 1: "Was Araber Sind, ist schwieriger zu beantworten" (ibid.). See also Jan Retsö, *The Arabs in Antiquity: Their History from the Assyrians to the Umayyads* (London & New York: Routledge, 2003).

Christianity' (and, *eo ipso*, Arab Christian theology) designates by trying to unpack what it *does not* stand for.

Arab Christianity as Ecclesial Community

The first thing 'Arab Christianity' does not signify in this study is an Arab Christian *Church*. There are Christian scholars from the Arab world who argued that one cannot at all speak about an Arab Christian Church in the history of the Levant and that 'Arab Christianity' does not exist except as a frank oxymoron. These scholars argue that the only explanation for such oxymoronic case is that the Christians in the Orient found, and still find, themselves obliged to *use* Arabic language for the sheer pragmatic need of survival in a majority-Muslim *Sitz im Leben* whose lingua franca is Arabic. This is what the Lebanese Protestant theologian George Sabra, for instance, argued ten years ago. In a short essay he published in 2014, Sabra cynically inquires: "Is it not important to ask ourselves why there never emerged an Arabic Christianity, an Arabic Christian liturgical tradition, analogues to a Syriac or Coptic or Armenian or Hellenistic or Latin tradition?"[4] Sabra personally answers his rhetorical question by insisting that the existence of Arab *Christians* before and after Islam, as well as the evident existence of Arab Christian literature and translations, do not constitute whatsoever any demonstration of the existence of an Arab *Christianity* or Arab Christian Church or liturgical inheritance.[5] Seemingly driven by a *habitus* of synonymising 'Arab' and 'Muslim' that is common among many Christians in the Orient, Sabra eventually affirms: "The fact that most Eastern churches today are Arabised in the sense that they use the Arabic language does not mean that they have adopted a culture shaped by Islam. Language may be an important component of cultural identity, but it is not necessarily the most important one."[6]

My study of Arab Christian theology does not want to claim that there is such a thing as an 'Arab Christian Church' in the sense of a specifiable, definable, and otherising ecclesiological or denominational confessional body. I principally agree that there is hardly ground for speaking about an Arab Christian *Church* in this particular sense. Yet, George Sabra and I must not ignore the fact that there are scholars today who are willing to contest this belief, at least from a historiological perspective. Theresia Hainthaler, for example, gleans from her geographical and historiological study of the Arab Christians that they did seem to have some kind of an ecclesial presence, as they lived surrounded by monks, martyrs, and bishops. Hainthaler goes as far as pointing out that "at least one patriarch of Arab origin can be specified," and when there is a prelate there is an

[4] George Sabra, "A Response to 'Christianity in a Culture Marked by Islam': Facts and Visions," in *Theological Review*, 35(2014), pp. 145–148, p. 147. My exposition and scrutiny of Sabra's thesis are borrowed from Najib George Awad, *After-Mission, Beyond Evangelicalism: The Indigenous 'Injīliyyūn' in the Arab-Muslim Context of Syria-Lebanon* (Leiden & Boston: Brill, 2021), pp. 147–149.

[5] Ibid., p. 147.

[6] Ibid., p. 147.

ecclesial body.[7] This as such does not definitively verify that there was something specifically defined and institutively called an 'Arab Christian Church.' Nevertheless, this is sufficiently plausible to make us hesitate before rushing into the conclusion that no Arab Christian Church did exist, and, thus, no Arab Christianity can be spoken of.

In his turn, Robert Hoyland traces the roots and responsibility of the evolution of Arabic texts during the sixth century A.D. and earlier by attributing this development to the "Christian missionaries who had been converting Arab tribes."[8] In his investigation of this Christian missionary work among the Arab tribes, Hoyland pauses at the building of ecclesial communities' which the Syriac Christian prelates were involved in during the fifth and sixth centuries. He confirms that "Syriac Christian church authorities were involved to an increasing degree with an emergent Arab Christianity." Hoyland offers the following as examples of such activities:

> In the early fifth century CE, Alexander, the bishop of Mabbugh (northeast of modern Aleppo), built a church at Rusafa dedicated to St. Sergius, to whom the Arab tribes of that region were much devoted, and both Jacob, bishop of Serug, and Severus, patriarch of Antioch, composed Syriac texts to celebrate this saint. This involvement also holds good for Christianity in Arabia. This, Philoxenus, bishop of Mabbugh, consecrated the first two bishops of Najrān in southeast Arabia in the early sixth century CE; the south Arabian martyr Elias had been a monk at the convent of Mar Abraham of Tella (east of Edessa) and had been ordained a priest by John, bishop of Tella.[9]

Neither Hoyland, Hainthaler, nor other scholars following this line of reasoning (nor myself) would take the many archaeological and historiological findings on such Syriac Christian missionaries' establishment of Christian communities among the Arabs, and for the Arabic-speaking communities, as evidence of the existence of a specific, rigidly defined denominational ecclesiological entity called 'the Arabic Church.' However, such denominational, sect-centred, and self-otherisingly identified perspectives apply to today's churchly divisions and existence in the Middle East, and the world all over, where Christian communities are rigidly and narrowly defined by means of their sharply delineated ecclesial and denominational identity. Such *Anschuung* must not be anachronistically applied to the existence of Christianity among the Arabs during late antiquity. Suffice it to realise, nevertheless, that one

---

[7] Hainthaler, *Christliche Araber vor dem Islam*, p. 146: "Zumindest ein Patriarch arabischer Herkunft läßt sich angeben."

[8] Robert Hoyland, "Epigraphy and the Linguistic Background to the Qur'ān," in *The Qur'ān in its Historical Context*, Gabriel Said Reynolds (ed.) (London & New York: Routledge, 2008), pp. 51–70, p. 57.

[9] Ibid., p. 59 (60ff). For similar attention to the Christian missionary churchly work among the Arabs and Arabic-speaking tribes during the fifth and sixth centuries A.D., see, for instance, H. Leitzmann and H. Hilgenfeld, *Das Leben des heiligen Symeon Stylites* (Leipzig: Hinrichs, 1908); I. Shahid, *The Martyrs of Najran* (Brussels: Soc. Des Bollandistes, 1971); J. S. Trimingham, *Christianity among the Arabs in Pre-Islamic Times* (London: Longman, 1979); and E. Key Fowden, *The Barbarian Plain: Saint Sergius between Rome and Iran* (Berkeley, CA: University of California Press, 1999).

can find enough historical and textual data to realise that such Christian communities that were established to serve the Christian faith among its followers from the Arab tribes, inside and outside Arabia, do represent the birth of an "emergent Arab Christianity," as Hoyland relates.

Be the above as it may, I totally beg to differ from George Sabra's conclusion that if there is no such Arab Christian Church, one cannot speak of an Arab Christianity at all. I find it surprising that the existence of writings, thought and even translations in Arabic are sufficient for him to call their authors 'Arab *Christians*,' but they are far from enough to call their Christianity Arabic *Christianity*. What is this 'Christianity' if not the thought, the traditions of writing, the mind, the knowledge, and the cultural-anthropological fingerprints that watermark the translations and the writings of these *Christians*? Only when we depart from treating Christianity as a single, absolute, onto-theological meta-narrative might we be warranted to decide, if at all, that the existence of human groups called 'Arab Christians' does not entail an existence of 'Arab *Christianity*.' There is enough scholarship in the field to demonstrate that these Arab Christians, who lived in the shadow of Islam from the Middle Byzantine/early Islamic era, did not just opt for speaking Arabic. They also Arabised their entire cultural, ecclesial, theological, and liturgical identity, and they did this voluntarily. There were not just Arab Christians, but there was also Arab Christianity in the Arab Muslim Orient.[10]

Arab Christianity as Christian Personnel

The second thing which 'Arab Christianity' does not narrowly or primarily designate, though it inclusively implies, is that it merely stands for 'Arab *Christians*.' This approach stems from a philosophical *Anschauung* of history, which reduces the biography of Christianity into a conglomeration of prominent individual personalities and treats them as representatives of the general character of their era. On such a perception of history, Ferdinand Christian Baur

[10] Awad, *After-Mission, Beyond Evangelicalism*, p. 148. For some studies on this, see, for example, Sidney H. Griffith, *The Beginnings of Christian Theology in Arabic: Muslim–Christian Encounter in the Early Islamic Period* (Aldershot: Ashgate/Variorum, 2002); S. H. Griffith, *Arabic Christianity in the Monasteries of Ninth-Century Palestine* (Aldershot and Bloomfield: Ashgate/Variorum, 1992); S. H. Griffith, *The Church in the Shadow of the Mosque: Christians and Muslims in the World of Islam* (Princeton, NJ: Princeton University Press, 2008); N. G. Awad, *Orthodoxy in Arabic Terms: A Study of Theodore Abu Qurrah's Theology in Its Islamic Context* (Berlin: De Gruyter, 2015); N. G. Awad, *Umayyad Christianity: John of Damascus as a Contextual Example of Identity Formation in Early Islam* (Piscataway: Gorgias Press, 2018); Riffat Ebied and Herman Teule (eds.), *Studies on the Christian Arabic Heritage* (Leuven: Peeters, 2004); Ora Limor and Guy Stroumsa (eds.), *Christians and Christianity in the Holy Land: From the Origin to the Latin Kingdom* (Turnhout: Brepols, 2006); Michael Gervers and Ramzi Bikhazi (eds.), *Conversion and Continuity* (Toronto: Pontifical Institute of Medieval Studies, 1990); Emmanouela Grypeo; Mark Swanson, and David Thomas (eds.) (Leiden: Brill, 2006); and David Thomas (ed.) *Syrian Christians and Islam* (Leiden: Brill, 2001).

once said: "... history becomes an aggregation of individualities, and where individuals should have become subordinate to the universal, to the historical progression conditioned by spirits' general course of development, what prevails is just that free play of individuals."[11]

This second sense is also not what this study aspires to in its dealings with Arab Christianity and its theology. This study does not aim at invoking the old German historicism of the eighteenth to nineteenth centuries; the approach of giant historical theologians and thinkers like, for instance, Johannes August W. Neander, who approached the study of history as a critical examination of privileged individuals and their lives, wherein "historical persons and events [circled around them] are given the 'full right of their individuality..." and where any fruitful historical understanding of theology is restricted to an "exact characterisation of individual spiritual tendencies (*Geistesrichtungen*), religious and theological, in various periods and according to their influences..."[12]

In Western scholarship, the monumental, multi-volume work of Irfan Shahid on the Arabs during the sixth century is a classic example of approaching Arabic Christianity as an expression of the Arab tribal and nomadic Christian communities, who either served as *foederati* for the Byzantines (e.g., the Ghassanids), or were Christian communities spreading in the Arab Peninsula and Sinai. According to Shahid, these Arab Christians were socially divided into 'A'rāb,' the nomadic tribes of wanderers, and ''Arab,' the city-settlers who lived an urban life in two historical cities in Sinai: Phārān and Raïthou.[13] For Shahid, these Arab Christians were mainly Monophysites and Nestorians in their theological affiliations. According to him, they were politically quite powerful *foederati* for the Byzantines and religiously "most zealous Christians." Their religious staunchness led Irfan Shahid to suggest that these Arab Christians were the primary evangelists who converted the Peninsula to Christianity. This was achieved, Shahid maintains, despite their missionary work's lack of any official ecclesial patronage.[14] Irfan also pays attention to the association of these Arab Christians with martyrdom and sainthood, due to their religious zeal and commitment to the Christian faith. He highlights in particular what he calls "the two Arab saints," namely, Cosmas and Damian, who were believed to have

---

[11] Ferdinand Christian Baur, *Church and Theology in the Nineteenth Century*, Peter C. Hodgson (ed.), Robert F. Brown and Peter Hodgson (trans.) (Eugene, OR: Cascade Books, 2018), p. 210 (209–211). Baur states this in his critical assessment of the approach to history developed by August Neander, one of Friedrich Schleiermacher's prominent disciples.

[12] J. August. W. Neander, *Antignostikus: Geist des Tertullians und Einleitung in dessen Schriften. Eine Monographie als Beitrag zur Geschichte der Glaubens- und Sittenlehre in den ersten Jahrhunderten* (Berlin: F. Dümmler, 1825), pp. iv–vi. On this approach to historical study, see also Peter C. Hodgson, *The Formation of Historical Theology: A Study of Ferdinand Christian Baur* (New York: Harper & Row, 1966) and Lord Acton, "Döllinger's Historical Work," in *English Historical Review*, 5(1890), pp. 700–744.

[13] Irfan Shahid, *Byzantium and the Arabs in the Sixth Century: Ecclesiastical History* (Washington, DC: Dumbarton Oaks Research Library and Collection, 1995), I/2, pp. 968–986.

[14] Ibid., p. 994.

hailed from the Arab Christians of Arabia and were martyred during the reign of Diocletian.[15] In addition to them, Shahid pauses at two other Arab Christian martyrs and saints that were highly venerated by the Ghassanids, St. Simeon the Younger and St. Julian.[16] Shahid's magnum opus draws a comprehensive picture of how these Arab Christian tribes and their central figures played a crucial role, not just at the forefront of the historical events that marked the presence of Byzantium in Greater Syria, Sinai, and the Arab Peninsula, but also in the evolution of the circumstances, conditions, and factors that led to the origination of Islam in Arabia and then its arrival to the Arab Christians in the *foederati* territories in the Middle East during the sixth century.

There are also Arab-Eastern scholars from the last century who similarly studied Christianity and its religious and cultural legacies via focusing on the Arab individuals or groups of affiliates after whom this Christianity was allegedly named, and on their roles and contributions. The Iraqi Christian scholar, Souhayl Qāshā, for instance, realises that such approach to Arab Christianity builds its hermeneutic of this Christianity on presenting the so-called 'Arab Christians' as isolated opponents of the surrounding Muslim context in which they existed and considered themselves as outsiders and 'others.' They are seen as those who belonged to an otherised, parallel, and sealed Christian *Sitz im Leben* and whose life circled around protecting this life-setting's best interest.[17] Qāshā not only understands Arab Christianity, but also Christianity as a whole, from the perspective of the particular personnel who belonged to it and represented its existence. So, the origin of Christianity in the first century A.D. is designated by the role and impact of the disciples of Christ and the first generation of apostles. Then, the expansion of Christianity is focused on because it demonstrates the work of the monks, hermits, and preachers.[18] So, for example, Christianity in Iraq becomes centralised on the narrative of the evangelical works of the apostles Addai and Mary, who spread the faith in Raha, Nisibin, Mosul, and the Mesopotamian territories.[19] For Qāshā, Christianity is totally reduced down to the Christians: its story is their biographical narrative; its legacy is their personal contributions; its history is their individual and communal repertoire. This Christianity is defined as, and shaped by, its Christian followers' biographies, and it is seen as the daughter that was born from the womb of the circumstances which the Arab Christian affiliates lived under and were victims of the circumstances of the Arabs who affiliate to it.[20] So much so that Qāshā even suggests that the Arab Christians had a religious belief, yet they were not truly Christianised (*lam yatamasḥanū*).[21]

---

[15] Ibid., pp. 963–965.

[16] Ibid., pp. 965–966.

[17] Souhayl Qāshā, *Ṣafaḥāt min Tārīkh al-Masīḥiyyīn al-'Arab Qabl al-Īslām* (Pages from the History of the Arab Christians before Islam), (Jounieh: al-Maktabah al-Buluṣiyyah, 2005), p. 9.

[18] Ibid., p. 11.

[19] Ibid., p. 12.

[20] Ibid., p. 26.

[21] Ibid., p. 288.

Before Souhayl Qāshā, and during the first two decades of the twentieth century, the Jesuit Chaldean Catholic orientalist Louis Cheikho (1859–1927) also talked about Arab Christianity by presenting it as a designation of a group of Arab intellectuals, scientists, statesmen, poets, and theologians, whose contributions left inerasable marks on the Middle Eastern scene, before and during Islam.[22] These Arab Christians, according to Cheikho's investigation, were three hundred scientists in total, distributed in terms of specialisation as follows: 215 medical doctors; 63 translators; 40 philosophers and logicians; 15 astronomers; 10 mathematicians; 7 astrologists; 5 alchemists; 4 pharmacists; 1 geographer; 1 genealogist, and 1 astrolabist.[23] The same focus on followers and personnel applies also to Cheikho's other discourse on the Arab Christian politicians, statesmen, and court scribes in Islam. Cheikho studies the roles and contributions of these Christian figures from early Islam up to the Mamlukids era and Andalusian rule. He counts overall 75 persons who served as ministers; 300 who served as scribes, and 31 others who were appointed in executive leading positions in the caliphal court.[24]

Today's Arab scholars who pause at recent Arab Christianity prioritise approaching this latter topic from the angle of studying the Arab *Christians* and their situation in the Middle East. Even when the intention is to shed light on the theological thought and cultural status of this Christianity, the point of departure and epicentre of this attention is the insufferable and existential human living conditions of the Arab Christians. So much so that the suffering and enduring hardship of these Christians become part and parcel (if not even the foundational context and prolegomenon) of the understanding of 'Arab Christianity' itself.[25] Some other scholars even apply a socio-anthropological enquiry (of Weberian-like features) that replaces 'Christianity' epistemologically and conceptually with 'Christians' and then asks: how does a particular group of people convert from a pagan into a monotheistic belief [i.e. Christianity], then from this latter into another monotheistic belief [i.e. Islam]?"[26] The nature and meaning of this Arab Christianity, accordingly, are to be determined via chasing after the roots of the 'native Arabs' (*'Arab aqḥāḥ*) and their conversion to Christian religion,

---

[22] See the introduction of Louis Cheikho, *'Ulamā' al-Naṣrāniyyah fī al-Islām, 622–1300* (The Scientist of Christianity in Islam, 622–1300), Kamīl Ḥushaymih (ed.) (Rome: Pontifical Oriental Institute/Jounieh: al-Maktabah al-Bulusiyyah, 1983), pp. 11; 17–18.
[23] Ibid., p. 21.
[24] See the introduction of Louis Cheikho, *Wuzarā' al-Naṣrāniyyah wa-Kuttābuhā fī al-Islām, 622–1517* (The Ministers of Christianity and its Scribes in Islam, 622–1517), Kamīl Ḥushaymih (ed.) (Rome: Pontifical Oriental Institute/Dhūq Mikhail: Arab Christian Heritage/Jounieh: al-Maktabah al-Buluṣiyyah, 1987), p. 26.
[25] Thus, for instance, Mosheer Basil Aoun, *Al-Fikr al-'Arabī al-Dīnī al-Masīḥī: Muqtaḍayāt al-Nuhūḍ wal-Tajdīd wal-Mu'āṣarah* (The Christian Arab Religious Thought: The Prerequisites of Resurgence and Renewal and Contemporaneity), (Beirut: Dār al-Ṭalī'ah, 2007), pp. 47–88.
[26] See, for instance, Salwā Balḥāj Ṣāliḥ-al'āyib, *Al-Masīḥiyyah al-'Arabiyyah wa-taṬawurātihā: Min Nash'atihā īlā al-Qarn al-Rābi' al-Hijrī/al-'āshir al-Milādī* (Arab Christianity and its Evolvements: From its Birth till the 4th/10th Century) (Beirut: Dār al-Ṭalī'ah, 1998), p. 6.

how they interacted with Christianity, and what the conditions were of these Arabs in their life-context with Islam.[27]

What is quite dangerous in this conceptual reduction of Arab Christianity to Arab Christian individuals or groups of people who affiliate to it is the attempt of some Arab Middle Eastern intellectuals and authors to implement this reductionism in politicising and ideologising Christianity. They pursue this by means of rooting it in a pan-Arabist ideology that traces the origin of Christianity back to the geographical territories of the Arab Peninsula or *Arabia*. This pan-Arabist thesis states that Christianity itself in its oldest form (not just its Arabic-speaking followers) is Arabic in origin. It first appeared in the Arab Peninsula, either in the areas of Najrān or ʿAssīr in al-Ḥijāz region, before it was exported to the tribes of the Greater Syria and the Fertile Crescent and then to the entire Roman Empire.[28] Such an Arabist sentiment, as I argued elsewhere, is the production of an ideology that dominated the political and ethno-sociological scene of the early twentieth-century Arab world, and it still finds foothold in the Arab intellectual arena today. Known by the name of 'Arabism' or 'pan-Arabism,' this ideology attracted a considerable portion of the Middle Eastern populations and energised their attempts at reviving the Arab antique consciousness that circles around reasserting the primacy of Arabic nationhood and civilisation.[29] This Arabist sentimentalism drives some Christians from the region to subconsciously and biasedly attempt to prove that the fountain of almost every cultural or religious heritage once appeared in the Near East, existed first among the Arabs, and sprang out of their homeland.[30]

In this attempt at reading the Arab Christians' background, as well as Christianity generally, 'Arab Christianity' becomes the name of those Christian individuals or groups of peoples whose origin is claimed to be the Arab Peninsula or *Arabia*. Such an ideologised understanding of 'Arab *Christians*' is "heavily

---

[27] Ibid., p. 7.

[28] Among the Arab authors who developed this allegation, two must be read in particular. See Kamāl Ṣalībī, *al-Baḥth 'an Yasū': Qirā'ah Jadīdah fī al-Anājīl* (The Search for Jesus: A New Reading in the Gospels) (Amman: Dār al-Shurūq, 1999) and Fāḍil al-Rabīʿī, *al-Masīḥ al-'Arabī: al-Naṣrāniyyah fī al-Jazīrah al-'Arabiyyah wa al-Ṣirā' al-Bīzanṭī al-Fārisī* (The Arab Christ: Christianity in Arabia and the Byzantine–Persian Conflict) (Beirut: Rīāḍ al-Rayyīs, 2009). I have deconstructed these two authors' theses and responded to their ideologised, pan-Arabist approach in Najib George Awad, "Is Christianity from Arabia? Examining Two Contemporary Arabic Proposals on Christianity in the Pre-Islamic Period," in *Orientalische Christen und Europa: Kulturbegegnung zwischen Interferenz, Partizipation und Antizipation*, Martin Tamcke (ed.) (Wiesbaden: Harrassowitz Verlag, 2012), pp. 33–56.

[29] Awad, "Is Christianity from Arabia?", pp. 51–54. See also C. E. Dawn, *From Ottomanism to Arabism. Essays om the Origin of Arab Nationalism* (Chicago & London: University of Illinois Press, 1973); A. Hourani, *Arabic Thought in the Liberal Age, 1798–1939* (Cambridge & New York: Cambridge University Press, 1983); and R. Khalidi, "Arab Nationalism: Historical Problems in the Literature," in *American Historical Review*, 96(5), 1991, pp. 1363–1373.

[30] Awad, "Is Christianity from Arabia?", p. 53. See also Philip K. Hitti, *A History of the Arabs from the Earliest Time to the Present* (New York & London: St. Martin's Press, 1970).

loaded with anachronistic, political and ideological, presumptions coloured by the contemporary, rather unpleasant condition of the Arab world."[31] In this study, 'Arab Christianity' is not treated as narrowly and one-sidedly connotative of the Arab affiliates to Christianity. Such a focus does not actually help when it is founded on politically and ideologically tailored pan-Arabist sentiments. More significantly still, such a focus, I believe, does not actually help when one aims at studying 'Arab Christianity' as something expressive, among other things, of *theology*. Historically and ethnically speaking, the first creators of Arab Christian theology during early Islam (the second/eighth century onwards), at least the most prominent ones we know about, were not actually native Arabs from Arabia (*ʿArab aqḥāḥ ʿāribah*). The most known prominent creators of Arab Christian *Kalām* (theology), like Theodore Abū Qurrah, Ḥabīb Khidmah Abū Rā'iṭah, ʿAmmār al-Baṣrī; Yaḥyā b. ʿAdī, Sāwīrūs b. al-Muqaffaʿ, al-Ṣāffī b. al-ʿAssāl, and others, hailed actually from non-Arab ethnic backgrounds (Syriac, Coptic, or Aramaic). In addition, those who produce Arab Christian theology in today's Arab world, where Christians exist still, are mostly also not native Arabians in ethnicity or not regionally from Arabia. So, from these historical and ethnological perspectives, reducing 'Arab Christianity' to merely the 'Arab Christians' is not epistemologically and hermeneutically appropriate.

Arab Christianity as an Expression of a Linguistic Entity

The third understanding of 'Arab Christians' which one can find in scholarship is the one that interprets this phrase from a purely linguistic perspective. Kenneth Cragg is famous in his association of the nomenclature "Arab Christian' with Arabic-language or Arabic-speaking choice. In his book *The Arab Christian*, Cragg develops a hypothesis on the linguistic connotations of Arab Christianity. For him, the linguistic connotations are the *crux* of speaking about Christianity by means of associating it with 'Arab-ness.' This association, he then adds, is constitutively definitive of the negative ramifications which the adjective 'Arab' causes to that genre of Christianity. Associating itself with the term 'Arab' traps the Christianity of the Middle East, according to Cragg, in "a strange paradox," because Arab-ness is substantially definitive and constitutive of 'Islam' and not of Christianity. So, "when Arabicization ensued throughout the [Middle East in the seventh century A.D.]," Cragg surmises,

> Arabic-speaking Christians were caught in a strange paradox, which has attended them ever since. The paradox passes from language to identity, from the medium of faith and culture to the psyche and the soul. The language that gives them identity has its supreme identity elsewhere.[32]

For Cragg, the 'elsewhere' stands for 'Islam' and the 'Qur'ān: the Christians found themselves holding a self-perception that problematically lies in, and is derived now from, a religious text other than their own. The religious text called 'Qur'ān,' furthermore, even accuses them of abrogating and forging their own holy scripture (the Gospels). "The unilateral relation of Arabic and the Qur'ān,"

---

[31] Awad, "Is Christianity from Arabia?", p. 54.
[32] Cragg, *The Arab Christian*, p. 31.

Cragg concludes, has become ever since "peculiarly the burden of Arab Christianity."[33] Cragg confesses that Arabic-speaking Christians existed six centuries earlier than the birth of Islam. Yet, he decides that these six centuries of Arab Christianity before Islam must not be counted when we approach Arab Christianity's case during the Muslim era. The reason Cragg gives for this decision is that Islam came in the seventh century to erase totally and put a definite end to the centuries that were antecedent to its existence. With Islam, the 'Arab Minds' (so Cragg says, without exactly telling us what this phrase stands for exactly) started to associate Arab-ness with the Qur'ān; the thing that made the non-Muslims who identified themselves with this Arab-ness suffered from a self-perception dilemma and existential conundrum. It is this paradoxical "Arab-ness inherent in the very nature of the Qur'ān and of Islamic origins that conditioned Arab Christianity," according to Cragg.[34]

Cragg's now seriously questionable hypothesis is not just full of historical flaws. It is also loaded with a number of seriously questionable pre-conceptions and presumptions. First of all, associating Arab-ness with Islam and the attempt at making the latter exclusively representative of the former only started in the history of Islam during the last decade of the seventh century and not before. Even when this happened, the Christians who belonged to, and lived in, the Muslim Caliphate did not deem it a problem or an identity-formation threat. They rather decided to re-write their very own theological traditions and to develop their particular cultural and intellectual thought in no other than the lingua franca of their homeland, Arabic. Had they felt that there was a dilemmatic, threatening impact on their identity because of the association of Arab-ness with Islam, they would have not opted for that choice in the manner and to the extent they did.[35] What Arab-ness was associated with, and became inherent in, during the early Muslim era was not primarily and essentially 'Islamic *culture* and *civilisation.*' Such cultural association was not deemed a threat to the Christians of the Muslim Caliphate, as extant historical and textual data inform us.

On the other hand, Cragg seems to be departing from a ready-made and pre-constructed imagination of the substantial cultural, sociological, and anthropological differences and contrasts between the Christians and the Muslims of that very same Middle Eastern context. It is as if the Christians of that context lived in sort of solitary, cocooned, and stark self-otherising stance that made them only tangentially, circumstantially, and pragmatically interact with and relate to the parallel and opposed 'Muslim *Sitz im Leben*' that is seemingly pre-constructed in Cragg's mind. Such a pre-constructed point of departure tenders, consequentially, a far from accurate perception of the contextual, socio-anthropological, and interreligious nature of the world of early Islam as we get to know it from the extant historical, textual, and non-textual data alike. Yes, "family and clan loyalty and the pattern of the feud, with their

33 Ibid., p. 32.

34 Ibid., p. 34.

35 On the contextual, historical, and theological aspects of such volitional Arabisation process, see Najib G. Awad, *Orthodoxy in Arabic Terms* and Awad, *Umyyad Christianity*.

claim on male prowess, were basic assumptions of life"[36] in the early Islamic context of the Arab Peninsula, and maybe afterwards as well. But, these very same assumptions were characteristic of the life of the Christian tribes and families and clans as well, as scholars recently started, more and more, to realise.

Speaking about Muslims and Christians as two *parallel* and *opposed* societal entities, on the basis of placing Christian faith and Islam as two religious phenomena standing against each other, turns Arabic speaking and linguistic Arab-ness into an inevitable source of tension, dilemmatic self-perception, and identity crisis. This is what Cragg conjures up and inductively presumes in his hypothesis, ending up conjuring a circular argument which stems from opposition and parallelism and ends, expectedly, with dilemma and paradox.

I believe that Cragg's approach is inappropriate to anatomise and probe the connotations and nature of the description 'Arab Christianity.' I do agree with him that the linguistic aspect is a substantial and significant element in understanding the term 'Arab' in this nomenclature. However, I disagree with him in reducing the meaning of this term to the linguistic aspect alone. I believe that 'Arab Christianity' designates *more than just* a certain association with a particular language, i.e., Arabic. It also includes elements that are more comprehensive and foundational, from the perspective of which the language itself must be approached and its role must be understood. I deduce such a conviction from the fact that the Christians and Muslims in the early Islamic era did not co-exist as two parallel, opposed, and totally otherised communities who pursued consistent attempts to confirm their alterity, not just on the religious and theological levels, but also on the human, cultural, and societal levels as well. For the Christians of that era, Arab-ness was not a cause of a dilemma or a paradox breeding an identity crisis. It was, rather, the means they linguistically used to re-invent themselves afresh and to renew their identity in what they deemed to be their very own *native* living context.

Arab Christianity as a Nomenclature of a Particular 'Tradition'

In this book, 'Arab Christianity,' and the theology named after it, is neither treated in terms of the religious followers who affiliated to it (Arab *Christians*), nor is it approached as a nomenclature of a specifiable ecclesial entity (an Arab Christian *Church*), nor, still, is it reduced to a mere expression of a linguistic association. It is, rather, used as connotative of a specific theological, intellectual, and cultural *tradition*. 'Tradition' is here used in the sense Hans-Georg Gadamer speaks about in terms of "historically effected consciousness" (*Wirkungsgeschichtliches Bewußtsein*).

In his monumental monograph *Wharheit und Methoden* (Truth and Method), Hans-Georg Gadamer presents 'tradition' as "an instrument for pursuing a new interpretation of self-identification and self-perception," not just of the textual,

---

[36] Cragg, *The Arab Christian*, p. 33.

conceptual content of a particular literary legacy.[37] Far from something from the past which we positively relate to from a distance, Gadamer presents tradition as something we belong to consciously and it affects us historically as a state of consciousness that we are part of. "Tradition," Gadamer states, is not "an object to be established like an experimental finding – as if Tradition was as alien … as an object of physics."[38] It is, rather, one of the elements of the process of understanding and of self-perception (*selber deutende*). 'Tradition' is a moment of conscious historical self-interpretation, which affects our relatedness to history. It makes us realise that "history does not belong to us; we belong to it."[39]

Be that as it may, studying or observing 'Arab Christianity' as 'tradition' for an Arab-Eastern Christian author, like me, implies a conscious awareness of Gadamer's confirmation that "we are always situated within traditions, and this is no objectifying process, i.e. we do not conceive of what Tradition says as something other, something alien." The tradition that 'Arab Christianity' names here is not something alien. It is always a constitutive component of the self and awareness of the Christians who relate to it. It is, as Gadamer says, "a model or exemplar, a kind of cognizance that our later historical judgment would hardly regard as a kind of knowledge but as the most ingenuous affinity with Tradition."[40] Here, the meaning of understanding itself, as Gadamer explains, "is to be thought of less as a subjective act than as participating in an event of Tradition."[41] 'Arab Christianity' does not, then, exist positively as something out there with a fixed ontological '*Dasein.*' Arab Christianity is, rather, an *event*: it *happens* when the knower participates hermeneutically in a particular theological and cultural consciousness (*Bewußtsein*) that is expressive of a particular tradition. Tradition here, Gadamer tells us, signifies "a hermeneutical condition."[42] This is why, Gadamer proceeds, "Tradition is not simply a permanent precondition; rather, we produce it ourselves inasmuch as we understand, participate in the evolution of Tradition and hence further determine it ourselves."[43] Speaking, thus, about 'Arab Christianity' as a tradition of a conscious historical effect one participates in is a choice that approaches 'Arab Christianity' and its theology alike as a state of belonging to a particular circle of understanding; to a particular hermeneutic circle to which certain understanding activity contextually belongs.[44] It connotes this state of awareness or consciousness that is affected by history; '*Wirkungsgeschichtliches Bewußtsein,*' as Gadamer calls it.[45]

---

[37] See also on Gadamer and tradition my elaboration on Gadamer's argument, which I borrow from in this section, in Najib G. Awad, *After-Mission, Beyond Evangelicalism*, pp. 205ff.

[38] Hans-Georg Gadamer, *Truth and Method*, Joel Weinsheimer and Donald G. Marshall (trans.) (London & New York: Continuum, 2004), p. xxx.

[39] Awad, *After-Mission, Beyond Evangelicalism*, pp. 276–278.

[40] Gadamer, *Truth and Method*, p. 283.

[41] Ibid., p. 291.

[42] Ibid., p. 291. "Belonging to a Tradition is a condition of hermeneutics."

[43] Ibid., p. 293.

[44] Ibid., p. 295.

[45] Ibid., p. 301.

This, however, does not mean that I present here a so-called 'Arab Christian tradition' as a figment of my personal, subjective, or private imagination or wishful thinking. This is far from being the case, since the understanding I borrow from Gadamer's thought does not treat 'tradition' as something we govern by means of our experience (whether in the sense of *Erfharung* or the one of *Erlebnes*). It is, rather, something that "expresses itself like a Thou," Gadamer intriguingly suggests. "A Thou," he explains, "is not an object; it relates itself to us." Tradition as 'Thou' in an 'I–Thou' relationship (the derivation of the 'I–thou' language game of Martin Buber is obvious here[46]), "is a genuine partner in dialogue, and we [as the 'I'] belong to it."[47] Tradition as a 'Thou' means relating to 'Arabic Christianity' as a tradition in such a manner that lets it "really say something to us";[48] something today's Arabic-speaking Christians may realise as being not against them or as challenging them. They, rather, receive this Thou-like tradition called 'Arab Christianity' as part and parcel of this Thou-like tradition, standing in full consciousness and with both feet, though not in a slavish (*hörig*) manner, within its stream. Tradition is that which says something to us, meets us as a question to which our attempt of understanding is an answer. It is a question that invites us to go beyond certain textual or verbal content. It invites us to understand 'Arab Christianity' as such as an answer to particular questions.[49] So much so that we can pretend to understand this theological-cultural tradition called 'Arab Christianity' if we succeed in perceiving the question to which this tradition was formed as an answer in the past and to which it is the answer in the present.[50]

Finally, talking about Arabic-speaking Christian theology as expressive of 'religious tradition' is inspired also by something Wilfred Cantwell Smith suggested almost six decades ago. Smith proposed that 'religious tradition' is the best notion to convey the dynamicity and historicity of religiosity that successfully preserves religious faiths' sense of process and change.[51] Studying a religious legacy in this sense means approaching it as a cumulative tradition, Smith explains, which includes the entirety of "all the objective data that constitute the historical deposit ... of the past religious life of the community in question."[52] Within the circle of approaching a particular religion or theology as a 'tradition,' Arabic-speaking Christianity as a theological tradition becomes the name of what '*this* theology' means to the Christian who considers it his or her

---

[46] Martin Buber, *I and Thou*, Walter Kaufmann (trans.) (New York: Simon and Schuster, 1970).

[47] Gadamer, *Truth and Method*, p. 352.

[48] Ibid., p. 353. "I must allow Tradition's claim to validity, not in the sense of simply acknowledging the past in its otherness, but in such a way that it has something to say to me" (ibid.).

[49] Ibid., p. 363.

[50] Ibid., p. 367. 'We understand only when we understand the question to which something is the answer ... For the text must be understood as an answer to a real question" (ibid.).

[51] Wilfred Cantwell Smith, *The Meaning and End of Religion* (New York: Macmillan, 1963).

[52] Ibid., p. 141.

'tradition,' as well as connoting what reality and selfhood mean to this Christian in the light of this theology and no other.[53] The notion of 'tradition' enables us to realise that theology is wholly historical in nature, and because it is historical, it is not, as Smith says, "a closed system," but rather a "changed and diversified" human and historical construct of those who participate in it.[54] Theology as a 'tradition,' in this sense of the notion, reflects what Wilfred Smith says to describe his notion of 'cumulative tradition.'

> The 'cumulative tradition,' as a concept, therefore, is not inflexible or final, either in content or in form. It is not given by the world, but is a human construct offered to order what is given. It is a device by which the human mind may rewardingly and without distortion introduce intelligibility into the vast influx of human history or any given part of it.[55]

In this study, and on the basis of the above understandings of Gadamar and Cantwell Smith, Arabic-speaking Christian theology is approached as historical 'traditions,' as this sense is interpreted by Diana Eck in her reading of Wilfred Cantwell Smith: "They are dynamic movements … [that] cannot be studied as if they were fixed entities that could easily be summarized and categorized, their so-called beliefs and practices catalogued and classified … [they] are not boxes of texts, commentaries and interpretations passed from hand to hand through the generations, but dynamic traditions, more like rivers, gushing, rolling, converging, branching out to water and transform new lands …"[56] In this sense, the connotations of the religious tradition called 'Arab Christianity' exceed the mere theological, doctrinal, liturgical, and spiritual realms of self-perception. They become, rather, designative of "a traditional way of life; a definition which implies history, lineage, culture, family rules and a sense of continuity," as Daniel Sahas once related.[57] Here, the religious background of certain communities, Sahas proceeds, "is neither a *thing*, nor *one* thing," but "people and the way they are known and can be identified ethnically, nationally, and traditionally."[58] Religion as tradition

> is observed and understood in terms of claims of history, tradition, ways, behavioral patterns of specific people. A people constitute a religion and religion is the totality of manifestation of a people's life, culture, conduct, tradition, and eschatological mission … religion [becomes] a wholistic ethnic identification … a civilizing force and a means of gauging culture.[59]

In the ensuing chapters, I endeavour to shed light on the theological reasoning of a tradition I call 'Arabic-Eastern Christianity.' I depart from studying this

---

[53] Ibid., p. 143.
[54] Ibid., pp. 145; 149.
[55] Ibid., p. 152.
[56] Diana L. Eck, "Dialogue and Method: Reconstructing the Study of Religion," in *A Magic Still Dwells: Comparative Religion in the Postmodern Age*, Kimberley C. Patton and Benjamin C. Ray (eds.) (Berkeley, Los Angeles & London: University of California Press, 2000), pp. 131–149, pp. 136–137.
[57] Daniel J. Sahas, *Byzantium and Islam: Collected Studies on Byzantine–Muslim Encounters* (Leiden & Boston: Brill, 2022), p. 6.
[58] Ibid., p. 7.
[59] Ibid., p. 8.

religious phenomenon, as Daniel Sahas advises us to do, "on [its] own terms," attempting thereby "to discover [its] essential dynamics and meaning for the faithful of a particular religious tradition."[60]

---

[60] Ibid., p. 50.

2. Arab Christian Tradition, Past and Present

Introduction

As the earlier chapter endeavoured to reveal, 'Arab Christianity' in this study is perceived as a historical, contextual phenomenon that is designative of a particular religious and intellectual Arab Christian *tradition(s)*. In this preliminary chapter, I endeavour to display a sketch of the milestones of the historical narrative of Arab Christianity in its homeland, the Middle East. The chapter does not attempt to be an exhaustive, comprehensive historiographical account on the biography of this Christianity. It just aims at highlighting major and central moments in this Christianity's history that reflect pivotal conditions and circumstances that influenced its existence and directly, or indirectly, inspired, shaped, and coloured its theological reasoning. The sketchy display starts with the earliest Arabic-speaking Christianity at the dawn of the Islamic empire in the seventh century, and it proceeds into major transformations and evolving stations during the post-tenth century, the Ottoman period, and the modern era.

The Birth of a Legacy

Chasing after the historical first moment, or 'big-bang,' of this tradition will drive us back in time into the second/eighth century, and will bring us into a direct encounter with the radical, transformative changes that led to the civilisational consummation of late antiquity in the heartland of the Middle Eastern region, Greater Syria. This forensic journey back to that late antique context requires readiness to travel beyond the territories of the recent, conventional treatment of Arab Christian theology as a Christian orthodoxy organically related to Greek-Byzantine heritage. We must go beyond such conventionality and head towards pondering seriously the substantial connection between this Arab Christian tradition of reasoning and the Middle Eastern Arab-Muslim context.[1] The arrival of Islam to the region from the Arab Peninsula, and its replacement of the previous Byzantine power therein, did not necessarily mark a crisis in the life of the Christians in that land. Quite the contrary. The establishment of a Muslim caliphate by the Umayyad dynasty and the transfer of its capital to Damascus "was initially beneficial to the Orthodox Christians of Syria and Palestine, at least in terms of providing them with an opportunity to

[1] I derive the ensuing lines of this section from the historical exposition in Najib G. Awad, "Arab Orthodox Christianity," in *Oxford Islamic Studies Online*, 2018, http://www.oxfordislamicstudies.com/article/opr/t343/e0265?hi=1&-pos=1#mat (consulted 8 February 2021).

maintain their elite status."[2] This opportunity was solidified by the Umayyads' success in bringing political stability and in creating reliable institutions of governance by embracing the administrative and political systems of the Byzantine empire and even maintaining Greek language as the language of bureaucracy. These things enabled the Christian Orthodox communities, who were Greek-speakers familiar with the old administrative system, to gain privileged official statuses and positions in the ruling machine of the newly created power.

The careful examiner of the Umayyad Caliphate era can, actually, fairly speak about two phases characteristic of the Umayyad rule's stance on people of non-Muslim background: the phase of the Sufiyanide family, and the one of the Marwanide family. During the first phase, the ruling Muslim family embraced the Hellenistic tradition and culture that permeated the occupied territories of Greater Syria and Egypt, and it maintained a continuity with the heritage of antiquity: Islam was not the marker of the end of late antiquity and its civilisational heritages, but the final and ultimate consummation and perfection of that past.[3] So much so that some scholars went as far as describing the Sufiyanide Umayyad Caliphate as "an Eastern Christian society under the rule of Muslims,"[4] or even deeming the early Umayyads "Byzantium after Byzantium."[5] Within this context, the Christian inhabitants of the new caliphal capital, Damascus, enjoyed special status, as their city became, beside Jerusalem, an Orthodox centre of influence and many Melkite Christian personnel occupied official positions that enabled them to have a considerable impact on the caliphal court's religious policy. It is not unlikely to speak in that context about the existence within the Christian communities of "a hereditary quasi-aristocracy ... that occupied prominent positions in the civil administration and church hierarchy."[6]

The situation of this first Umayyad ruling phase notwithstanding, the Christians of the Marwanide dynasty's rule in the ensuing decades witnessed the aggressive exertion of Arabisation, then Islamisation, policies by the Marwanide caliphs, starting from ʿAbd al-Malik b. Marwān (r. 685–705) and his son al-Walīd b. ʿAbd al-Malik onwards.[7] During this period, the Arabisation and ensuing Islamisation policies paved the way for the mounting of societal pressure over the non-Muslims and the non-Arabians, without causing necessarily a dangerous threat to the existence and life conditions of the Christians in the

---

[2] Samuel Noble and Alexander Treiger (eds.), *The Orthodox Church in the Arab World 700–1700: An Anthology of Sources* (DeKalb, IL: NIU Press, 2014), p. 16.

[3] Of the serious scholarly theses that set up a solid scholarly ground of the 'final consummation' idea, see, for instance, Aziz al-Azmeh, *The Emergence of Islam in Late Antiquity: Allah and His People* (Cambridge & New York: Cambridge University Press, 2014).

[4] Constantine A. Panchenko, *Orthodoxy and Islam in the Middle East: The Seventh to the Sixteenth Century*, Brittany Pheiffer Noble and Samuel Noble (trans.,), (Jordanville, NY: Holy Trinity Publications/Holy Trinity Seminary Press, 2021), p. 14.

[5] Ibid., p. 16.

[6] Ibid., p. 19.

[7] Noble and Treiger (eds.), *The Orthodox Church in the Arab World 700–1700*, p. 17.

Caliphate. Some attempts at exerting individual taxations over non-Muslim communities started to gradually surface. The processes of reforming the Arabic script, the carried-out canonisation of the Qur'ānic text, and the translation of the state's records and paperwork into Arabic language were considered by ensuing Muslim historiographers as endeavours to put an end to the monopoly of Christian scribes in the administrative structures. This was a pivotal change in the overall identity and nature of the Caliphate, though it did not influence much the status and governmental roles of the Christians, because these latter either knew Arabic already, or they learned the language and mastered its use.[8] After all, the majority of the Christians, including the Greek-speaking ones, in Greater Syria and the Holy Land were not Greek in origin, but "Hellenized Aramaeans, as well as Arabs in Transjordan and the Negev,"[9] who all were already familiar with the Arabic language, and many of them even spoke it in various capacities.

The ensuing decades that witnessed the birth of a new Muslim caliphate, whose capital had now moved to Baghdad, were characterised by noticeably positive and promising conditions for the Christians in the shadow of Islam. It might be the case that "from the beginning of the 'Abbasid Era,' church construction declined, the quality of mosaics decreased, and the language of inscriptions deteriorated."[10] This, however, is not to be necessarily interpreted as the beginning of the end of the Christians' role and influential presence in the shadow of Islam. By the midst of the second/eighth century, Arabic language was already the lingua franca of the region and the predominantly used language at all levels of societal, governmental, and public life, and the dominant majority of the Christian generations of that era were far more knowledgeable of, and familiar with, speaking Arabic than any other language. The Arabic-speaking Christians of the Fertile Crescent region (along with the Muslims and the Jews) played a major role in creating an indigenous, Arabic culture, especially during the Abbasid rule. The creation of this culture kicked off in the capital of the Caliphate, Baghdad, where the Christians contributed substantially and referentially to the innovation of an Arab culture due to their deep learnedness of the classical Greek heritage and their skilful transmission of it via teaching, translation, and textual composition. What enabled the Christians to be a substantial part of this culture-creation process is the fact that "Christians of all communities were able to maintain a significant degree of social prestige," as many of the Christians in Baghdad "were relatively well-off and were employed as 'secretaries to the government, attendants of kings, doctors to the nobility, sellers of perfume, and financiers.'"[11]

Why did the beginning of this creational movement occur in Baghdad? Because, first, Baghdad was not just the political capital of the Abbasid empire, but also a beaming cultural and intellectual epicentre, whose leading societal and political figures financially and personally supported translators, scholars, authors, and cultured figures, and they gravitated to the capital from all corners

---

[8] Panchenko, *Orthodoxy and Islam in the Middle East*, p. 21.

[9] Ibid., p. 26. See also N. J. Awad, *Umayyad Christianity*, pp. 73ff.

[10] Panchenko, *Orthodoxy and Islam in the Middle East*, p. 31.

[11] Ibid., p. 20.

of the Caliphate. Second, Baghdad was the ideal centre for this movement because these scholars, translators, and authors did not only use the Arabic language while they were in the capital. They were, rather, allowed, if not also encouraged, to use and exchange their own native and foreign languages and use them in their intellectual activities alongside Arabic.

It was in such a linguistically versatile, inclusivist, and free atmosphere that the Christians capitalised on the philological and etymological affinities between Arabic and Syriac and used common terminological roots from both Semitic languages in their translation projects from Greek into Arabic.[12] These Greek-into-Arabic translational enterprises encompassed a massive spectrum of Christian, Muslim, and Jewish authorship on every subject known in that era: "astronomy and alchemy and the rest of the occult sciences; the subjects of the quadrivium: arithmetic, geometry, astronomy, and theory of music; the entire field of Aristotelian philosophy throughout its history: metaphysics, ethics, physics, zoology, botany, and especially logic – the *Organon*; all the health sciences; medicine, pharmacology, and veterinary science and various other marginal genres of writings, such as Byzantine handbooks on military science (the *tactica*), popular collections of wisdom sayings, and even books on falconry."[13] The Arabic-speaking Christian scholars were highly skilled multilinguals who not only conveyed knowledge from Greek and Syriac into Arabic, but also innovatively improved the Arabic language itself by incorporating into it many technical terminologies imported from other languages. On this unique linguistic innovativeness and creativity, Samir Khalil Samir says that the Arabic-speaking Christian thinkers and authors "realized … that the accurate understanding of the wealth and contemporaneity of a language lies not primarily in this language's inclusion of a large number of synonyms, but in its flexible ability to express all the conceptual and notional truths that exists in other international cultures."[14]

Be the above as it may, and though the Arab *Christians* existed in this particular region much earlier than the first/seventh century, as scholars relate today, 'Arab Christian theological tradition' had its birth at the dawn of the arrival of Islam from the Arabian Peninsula up to the Fertile Crescent region, and ultimately in the shadows of the Muslim Abbasid era, starting from the second half of the second/eighth century and thereafter.[15] This fact indicates that

---

[12] Bāsim Samīr al-Sharqāwī (ed.) *Madkhal īlā 'Īlm at-Turāth al-'Arabī al-Masīḥī* (An Introduction to the Science of Arabic Christian Tradition) (Cairo: Franciscan Cultural Center [C.C.F.], 2017), pp. 11–12.

[13] Noble and Treiger, *The Orthodox Church in the Arab World 700–1700*, p. 20. See also Dimitri Gutas, *Greek Thought, Arabic Culture: The Graeco-Arabic Translation Movement in Baghdad and Early Abbasid Society 2nd-4th/8th-10th Centuries)* (London: Routledge, 1998), p. 1.

[14] Samir Khalil Samir, *Daūr al-Masīḥiyyīn al-Thaqāfī fī al-'Ālam al-'Arabī* (The Christians' Cultural Role in the Arab World) (Beirut: al-Mashriq Press, 2004), pp. 36–39.

[15] See also David Thomas, "Arab Christianity," in *The Blackwell Companion to Eastern Christianity*, Ken Perry (ed.) (Oxford, UK/Malden, USA: Blackwell Publishers, 2010), pp. 1–22.

the theological creativity of the Christians of the region did not cease with the rising and the arrival of the counter-religious power called 'Islam.' It, rather, intensified and flourished in its innovation. It succeeded in creating a particular theologico-cultural tradition that left its significant marks on Islam and the Arab-Muslim civilisation itself. Such influence portrayed inerasable impacts in domains beyond the mere religious and sheer theological spheres of reasoning into state administration, culture- and civilisation-creating, social-economic and artistic influences, and literary and linguistic (Arabic) creativity.[16] It was the Arabic-speaking Christians of the Abbasid era who realised that the Arabic language needed serious updating and philological expansion to contain and absorb the newly acquired knowledge from antiquity. They, thus, worked meticulously in their own writings towards preparing the Arabic language to adopt to the philological, expressional, and compositional techniques that were acquired from Greek, Syriac, and Persian languages.[17]

What, consequentially, birthed Arab Christian theology in this context was an evolvement that occurred within the religious and cultural thought of its surrounding Muslim *Sitz im Leben*. The Muslims started to acquire the intellectual and philosophical acquaintance with the Hellenic, philosophical, and scientific heritage (due to the translating work of the Christian and Jewish scholars from Greek, Syriac, and Hebrew into Arabic). That made the Muslim thinkers, armed with the mentioned philosophical tools of reasoning, scrutinise and interrogate Christianity (and to a lesser extent, Judaism) rationally and theologically alike.[18] That was simultaneously accompanied by a cross-pollinational attitude from the Arabic-speaking Christians toward Islam that was motivated and energised by the influence of the very same exposition to the Greek intellectual heritage. The Arab Christian tradition is the offspring that was bred by these Christian thinkers' cross-pollinational attempt at re-articulating Christian belief and worldview (*Weltanschuung*) by, so to speak, 'Islamising' (in the cultural and intellectual sense of the word) and 'Arabising' their cultural heritage and theological legacies to produce a new rational tradition that demonstrates the true and right religiosity of Christianity.[19]

One of the constitutive defining features of the Arab Christian tradition is that philosophico-logical and rational genre of theological thought called in Arabic '*Kalām*.' The Arabic-speaking Christian intellectuals of the first/seventh to third/ninth centuries co-created this theological genre with Muslim theologians in the heart of the Umayyad and Abbasid caliphates. Some of the main creating figures of this Christian tradition (in its Chalcedonian and non-Chalcedonian versions alike) whose literary creativities are extant today are: John of Damascus, who wrote on Islam in Chapter 100/101 of his book *De Haeresibus* and was motivated by explaining Christian doctrines in a Muslim context in his

---

[16] Awad, "Arab Orthodox Christianity."

[17] Samir, *Daūr al-Masīḥiyyīn al-Thaqāfī fī al-'Ālam al-'Arabī*, p. 40.

[18] Awad, "Arab Orthodox Christianity."

[19] Ibid. See also Sidney H. Griffith, *The Church in the Shadow of the Mosque*, pp. 45–74 and N. G. Awad, *Orthodoxy in Arabic Terms*, pp. 64–87.

trilogy *Pege Gnosius* (The Fount of Knowledge);[20] Theodore Abū Qurrah, the first Christian author we know to regularly produce texts in Arabic on Christian theology in dialogue with Islam, which are shaped clearly after philosophical-syllogistic, Aristotelian-Neoplatonic logic and argumentation (Muʿtazilite);[21] the Jacobite Ḥabib b. Khidmah Abū Rā'iṭah al-Takrītī;[22] and the Nestorian ʿAmmār al-Baṣrī.[23] These latter three figures in particular represent together "the first full generation of creative thinkers among the Arabic-speaking Christian writers."[24] Beside these three fathers of the Arab Christian tradition and its theology, one can also mention the pseudonymous author of a text called *Fī Tathlīth Allah al-Wāḥid* (On the Trinity of the One God), which is deemed the oldest known work of Christian theology written in Arabic to speak to Islam on the Trinity and Christology (c. 755 A.D.).[25] One can also mention the author of the text called

---

[20] See on John, N. G. Awad, *Umayyad Christianity*; Daniel J. Janosik, *John of Damascus: First Apologist to the Muslims* (Eugene, OR: Pickwick Publications, 2016); and Peter Schadler, *John of Damascus on Islam* (Leiden & Boston: Brill, 2018). I also directly touch upon John of Damascus's direct impact on Islamic thought via his rational and theological ideas and orientations in a forthcoming essay that will be published in an anthological companion on John of Damascus by Brill in 2025. The tentative title of the essay is "When Umayyad Christianity Spoke *for/with* Islam: Traces of John of Damascus's Interaction with His Muslim Intellectual Context."

[21] As I argue in my forthcoming monograph, whose tentative title is *Christian Mu'tazilism: Studying the Crosspollination between Christian and Muslim Kalām and Intellectualism during the Early Abbasid Era*. On Theodore Abū Qurrah himself, see N. G. Awad, *Orthodoxy in Arabic Terms*; S. H. Griffith, *The Controversial Theology of Theodore Abū Qurrah (C.A.D. 750–C. 820): A Methodological Comparative Study in Christian Arabic Literature*, PhD. Diss. (Washington: The Catholic University of America/Ann Arbor, Mich: University Microfilms, 1978); S. H. Griffith, *Theodore Abū Qurrah: The Intellectual Profile of an Arab Christian Writer of the First Abbasid Century* (Tel Aviv: Tel Aviv University Press, 1992); Bassam A. Nassif, "Religious Dialogue in the Eighth Century: Example from Theodore Abū Qurrah Treatise," in *Parole de L'Orient*, 30(2005), pp. 333–340; Georg Graf, *Die arabischen Schriften des Theodor Abu Qurra, Bishofs von Ḥarrān (Ca. 740–820)* (Paderborn: Ferdinand Schöningh, 1910).

[22] On him, see Sandra T. Keating, *Defending the "People of Truth" in the Early Islamic Period: The Christian Apologies of Abū Rā'iṭah* (Leiden & Boston: Brill, 2006); S. T. Keating, "Ḥabib Ibn Khidmah Abū Rā'iṭah al-Takrītī's 'the Refutation of the Melkites Concerning the Union [of the Divinity and Humanity in Christ] III,'" in *Christians at the Heart of Islamic Rule*, David Thomas (ed.) (Leiden: Brill, 2003), pp. 39–54.

[23] See on him, for instance, Mark I. Beaumont, "ʿAmmār al-Baṣrī's Apology for the Doctrine of the Trinity," in *Orientalia Christiana Analecta*, 218(1982), pp. 169–191; S. H. Griffith, "ʿAmmār al-Baṣrī's *Kitāb al-Burhān*: Christian *Kalām* in the First Abbasid Century," in *The Beginnings of Christian Theology in Arabic*, pp. 145–181; and Griffith, "The Concept of *al-Uqnūm* in ʿAmmār al-Baṣrī's apology for the Doctrine of the Trinity," in *Actes du premier congrès international d'ètudes arabes Chrètiennes*, Samir Khalil Samir (ed.), *Orientalia Christiana Analecta 218* (Rome: Pontificum Institutum Studiorum Orientalium, 1982), pp. 169–191.

[24] Griffith, *The Church in the Shadow of the Mosque*, pp. 61–62.

[25] On this text, see Margaret Dunlop Gibson (ed.), *An Arabic Version of the Acts of the Apostles and the Seven Catholic Epistles with a Treatise on the Triune Nature of God* (London: Cambridge University Press, 1899), pp. 74–107; Mark Swanson, "Some

Kitāb al-Burhān (The Book of Demonstration) by Eutychius of Alexandria.[26] One must not finish invoking a few major examples of many authors without pointing to the Christian, Arabic-speaking Jacobite of the fourth/tenth century, Yaḥyā b. ʿAdī. Being the disciple of the Aristotelian philosophers, the Christian Bishr b. Mattā and the Muslim Abū Naṣr al-Fārābī, this *mutakallim* became at one point the head of this philosophical school, beside being an avid polymath and theologian.[27]

The above are just a few names of the major creators of Arab-Eastern Christianity's theological and intellectual tradition. In their attempts at portraying Christian theology to Muslims, these Christians translated Christian thought from Greek and Syriac into Arabic, transmitting it, through their transcultural narratives and hermeneutics, beyond the boundaries of Hellenic-Byzantine culture, traditions, and identity into a late antique realm of identity-formation that is characterised by Arabic and Islamic cross-pollinational features, bearers, and webs of meaning.

The Beginning of Decline

The above was the major early birth of this tradition called 'Arab Christian theology.' Unfortunately, starting from the fourth/tenth century onwards, and in the light of the prevalence of Traditionalism over Rationalism (culminating in the Ḥanbalite and Ashʿarite victory over Muʿtazilism and *falsafa*), Arab Christianity's theological and socio-cultural tradition was seriously subdued by systematic suppression, marginalisation, and even intellectual enmity.[28] Partnership between Christians and Muslims started to become quite uneasy, as the Christian thinkers and the cultured, let alone the commoners alike, started to be tangibly deprived of the chance of a real "participation in a society where [they] might be made to feel they properly belonged."[29] The Christians were

---

Considerations for the Dating of *Fī Tathlīth Allah al-Wāḥid* (Sinai Ar. 154) and *al-Jāmiʿ fī Wujūh al-Imān* (London British Library Or. 4950)", in *Parole de L'Orient*, 18(1993), pp. 117–141.

[26] See, for example, Eutychius of Alexandria, *The Book of Demonstration*, W. Montgomery Watt (trans.) (Louvain: Peeters, 1960), vols. I–II.

[27] See on him, for instance, Gerhard Endress, *The Works of Yaḥyā Ibn 'Adī: An Analytical Inventory* (Wiesbaden: Reichert, 1977); Saḥbān Khlayfāt (ed.), *Maqālāt Yaḥyā b. 'Adī al-Falsafiyyah* (Yaḥyā b. ʿAdī's Philosophical Essays) (Amman: Jordanian University Press, 1988); Emilio Platt, *Yaḥyā b. 'Adī, Theologien Chrétien et Philosophé arabe* (Leuven: Department of Orientalistiek, 1983); and Augustin Périer (ed.), *Petits Traités Apologétiques Yaḥyā Ben 'Adī* (Paris: J. Gabalda Editeur/Paul Geuthiner Editeur, 1920).

[28] See my study in Arabic, Najib George Awad, "*al-Kalām al-Mu'tazilī bi-Ṣifatihi 'Ābiran lil-Adiyān: fī al-Baḥth Taṭālu'iyyan wa-Siyāqiyyan 'an Tawajjüh Mu'tazilī Masīḥī*" (Muʿtazilite *Kalām* as Cross-religious: In Search Crosspollinationally and Contextually for a Christian Muʿtazilite Orientation), in *Ostour Journal*, 20 (2024), pp.31-55.

[29] David Thomas, *Christian Doctrines in Islamic Theology* (Leiden & Boston: Brill, 2008), p. 3. See also N. G. Awad, "Al-Mujādalah in al-Mā'mūn's Court: When Could it

forced to live as *dhimmis* and no more as equals, and they were pushed "towards an identity that threatened to swamp their own."[30] All the non-Muslim belief systems and traditions, even those that were Arab among them, became valueless, detrimental, and even dangerous to the status and stability of the 'superior Islam.' Christian thought was paid attention to by the broader Muslim public merely occasionally and for sheer pragmatist and interrogational purposes that aimed at exposing its incoherence and demonstrating the superiority of Islam in comparison to it.[31]

To this, the Christians were forced to react by resorting to withdrawal and self-enclosure, hardly interested any more in developing or sustaining public theological, intellectual, or cultural enterprise and fully prioritising, instead, their personal and communal survival: Arab Christianity transformed into a mere expression of Arabic-speaking *Christians*. No wonder that the size of what used to be the predominant public majority started from the fifth/eleventh century to drop down rapidly and dramatically. Conversion to Islam became one of the most anticipated options to rescue oneself from hard living conditions.[32] In addition to the external pressurising and challenging conditions, the Christians also suffered from problematic situations they caused themselves by means of their own private skirmishes and rivalries. Hugh Kennedy correctly summarises the various internal factors behind the decline of Christianity in the Muslim world, and his diagnostic attestation is worth quoting at length:

> The decline of Christianity can be attributed to many causes. Among these were certainly the grinding burden of the poll tax, the fierce rivalries between Christian sects, often eager to appeal to the Muslim authorities for support against their hated opponents, and the tendency of ambitious figures in the Christian community to convert for career reasons. The Christian population, being largely unarmed and unmilitarized, also suffered disproportionately from the impoverishment and Bedouinization … in the 9th and 10th centuries.[33]

Interesting in Kennedy's diagnosis is his invitation for us to avoid reducing the multi-faceted factors behind the decline of Christianity to mere religious persecution, as well as his candid detection of the intra-Christian conflicts and clashes as one of the causes behind such decline.

Have Been Composed? Reflecting on Historicity vis-à-vis Socio-Cultural Data," in *Oriens Christianos*, 103(2020), pp. 144–169, pp. 149–151.

[30] Thomas, *Christian Doctrines in Islamic Theology*, p. 3; and Awad, "Al-Mujādalah in al-Mā'mūn's Court,", p. 149.

[31] Ibid., p. 150 and Thomas, *Christian Doctrines in Islamic Theology*, pp. 5–7.

[32] On the phenomenon of conversion and the hardship and other socio-political, economic, and domestic circumstances that delineated it, see, for example, Michael Gervers and Ramzi J. Bikhazi (eds.), *Conversion and Continuity*; A.C.S. Peacock (ed.), *Islamization: Comparative Perspectives from History* (Edinburgh: University of Edinburgh Press, 2017) and Nimrod Hurvitz, Christian C. Sahner, Uriel Simonson, and Luke Yarbrough (eds.), *Conversion to Islam in the Premodern Age: A Source Book* (Oakland, CA: University of California Press, 2020).

[33] Hugh Kennedy, "Islam," in *Interpreting Late Antiquity: Essays on the Postclassical World*, G. W. Bowersock; P. Brown, and O. Grabar (eds.) (Cambridge, USA/London, UK: Belknap Press/Harvard University Press, 2001), pp. 219–237, p. 229.

At any rate, this situation did not improve but worsened exponentially in the ensuing centuries, right from the Fatimid era to the Mamlukied era, down to the Crusaders period to the dawn of the Ottoman Empire, and down, eventually, to the end of the nineteenth century. One of the climaxes of this decline was experienced during the North African Fatimid Caliphate. When this new, Ismāʿīlī-Shiʿite power, for instance, swapped over Palestine, its armies devastated the monasteries and forced massive numbers of monks to escape as far north as Constantinople. Later on, one of the Fatimid, probably mentally unstable, caliphs, al-Ḥakīm (r. 996–1021), "unleashed unprecedented persecution of Christians (and Jews) in both Egypt and Palestine, destroying countless churches, including the Holy Sepulchre itself." The decline was intensified, consequentially, by the mass emigration of Christians due to such persecutions.[34] One can generally say, nevertheless, that the beginning of the numerical decline of the Christians from the eleventh to twelfth centuries onwards is expressive of depriving them of equal rights and freedom in the post-Fatimid Muslim rules, but it is not necessarily demonstrative of a mass-scale elimination or massacres on the basis of religious or doctrinal causes.

It is true, for instance, that during the Ayyubids' rule, the Copts in Egypt and the Christians in general lost their unique status and privileges, and their *dhimmitude* status became a restraining burden over their lives. Yet, these Christians were not subjected to a mass persecution or a communal suppression during that era. When Ṣalāḥuldīn al-Ayyūbī (1137–1193 A.D.) seized power in the twelfth century after the collapse of the Fatimids' rule, he re-imposed the *dhimmitude* system over the Christians in an attempt to remind them of their second-rank social and economic status compared to the Muslims. He even sacked many Christians from their positions in the service of the state, which forced many of these Christians, in their endeavour to maintain these positions and their privileges, to give up their Christian religious belief.[35] This notwithstanding, the ensuing decades revealed to the Ayyubids their pragmatic, inescapable need for the Christian intellectuals and skilful assets to administer and run the state and its affairs. This opened a margin for these Christians under the Ayyubid rule to be able to exist peacefully without their communities being exposed to any targeted collective atrocities or abuses.

What, more prominently and factually, worsened the life conditions of the Copts in Egypt and the Christians all over the Ayyubid kingdom in the thirteenth century was the perpetual Crusaders' attacks and raids against major cities under the Ayyubids' control. One can also add as another factor the Mamluks' invasions and raids. A raid, for instance, like the one made by Sultan Baybars against Antioch during the thirteenth century (1268) added further wounds to the Christian communities, as the Sultan and his troops attacked the city's population, destroyed monasteries in the city's vicinity, and forced the

[34] Noble and Treiger, *The Orthodox Church in the Arab World, 700–1700*, pp. 24–25.
[35] See Fr. Wadīʿ the Franciscan, *Dirāsah 'an al-Mu̇taman b. al-'Assāl wa-Kitābih "Majmū' Uṣūl ad-Dīn" wa-Taḥqīqih* (A Study on al-Mu̇taman b. al-ʿAssāl and a Critical Edition of his 'The Summa of Religious Foundations') (Cairo & Jerusalem: The Franciscan Friars Press, 1997), 31: 68–69.

patriarchal seat's removal from Antioch to Damascus.[36] Another example of similar pressurising incidents was the exposure of the Christians in the city of Damietta to pressure and their suffering from charges of treason from their Muslim co-inhabitants, who considered them a 'secret army' for the Crusaders.[37] What merits remembrance here is that "at the beginning of the era of the Crusades (1096–1271 A.D.), Christians still accounted for about half the population in Syria and Egypt."[38] This indicates that the Christians' hardship and challenging life circumstances did not lead to their extinction or disappearance from the scene, though it transformed radically their life priorities and statuses.

These multi-faceted and complex developments suggest that the sceptical and inimical stance towards the Eastern Christians did not originate from an intrinsic hostility which was naturally and generically symptomatic of the religious co-existence of the indigenous Christians and Muslims of the land. It was rather a reactionary stance caused by external circumstances and triggered by extrinsic, foreign sources accompanied by contextual and practical internal, Christian-to-Christian factors. The Christians' *dhimmi* status under the rule of Islam and their down-to-earth co-existence with Muslims do not necessarily demonstrate that their life conditions were marked by default with religious persecution and hostility from the Muslims.

Diving Down and Climbing Up the Abyss

One of the particularly crucial historical stages in the biographical history of Arab Christianity and its theology is the rising of the Ottoman Empire in 1453 A.D. The fall of Constantinople at the hands of Mehmet the Conqueror (*Muḥammad al-Fātiḥ*) shook the Arab Christianity tradition and its identifying imagination to the core. It irrevocably erased the effectiveness and prominent contributions of Arab Christianity in its homeland.[39] What remained of it were only those members of churches who continued speaking in Arabic, yet they hardly maintained any further influential interest in cultural, intellectual, or theological innovation and creativity. Creating intellectual and epistemological traditions was no longer a priority or requirement. Developing inclusive, cross-boundary, or trans-religious traditions was no longer even something to think of as a survival strategy. Christianity was reduced to the rapidly shrinking groups of Christian individuals or minor communities, who sealed themselves, now hermetically, in their particularist, confessionalist, and ethnic circles of self-perception (Greek, Syriac, Armenian, Copt, etc.).

The rather ironic and thought-provoking factor is that this negative situation counter-generated, consequentially, some positive and far from detrimental conditions for the Christians. By relegating Arab Christianity as a '*tradition*' (theological and cultural) to the margin and replacing it with a centralisation of

---

[36] Noble and Treiger, *The Orthodox Church in the Arab World, 700–1700*, pp. 31–32.
[37] Wadīʿ the Franciscan, *Dirāsah 'an al-Mu'taman b. al-'Assāl wa-Kitābih "Majmū' Uṣūl ad-Dīn" wa-Taḥqīqih*, 34–38: 71–72.
[38] Panchenko, *Orthodoxy and Islam in the Middle East*, p. 14.
[39] Awad, "Arab Orthodox Christianity."

the conditions of the Christian *populations*, the Ottoman ruling power stopped treating Christianity as a source of instability, disunity, and treason, and ceased considering it a religious threat to Islam. It started, instead, to loosen the tight hold around the Christians and to manifest considerable tolerance and empathy, even pragmatic appreciation, toward them. This security granted the Christians, eventually, survival and longevity to their communal presence. So much so that some historians today express their belief that these Christians lived "in prosperity and protection under the Ottoman authority."[40] Others have started to pause at certain Christian communities lived in the shadow of the Ottoman rule, like the Copts in Egypt, and to study their "involvement in Ottoman Egyptian bureaucracy and society … [in] military organization, trade, literary culture, [and the] judiciary."[41] On the other hand, the historian of Eastern Christianity, Heleen Murre-van den Berg, pauses also at the situation of the Christians of Iraq during the late Ottoman period, maintaining that the Ottomans were tolerant towards, and embracive of, the Christians of the Sultanate to such an extent that the former suffered from disturbances from other minority groups rather than from the Ottoman administration:

> Over the centuries the Ottoman administration was to prove relatively benign for its Christians and Jewish minorities. Christians in northern Mesopotamia suffered more from local disturbances (from the Kurds), or from the ongoing military campaigns directed at the neighboring Persians, than from discriminatory measures as such.[42]

The Christians of Iraq, Murre-van den Berg proceeds, benefited substantially from the Ottoman stability; so much so that, as she relates, "northern Iraq's minorities constituted a considerable part of the local population. Current estimates are that about one third consisted of Christians of the Church of the East and the Syrian Orthodox Church, Jews, as well as groups of Armenians and Yazidis."[43] The peak of the considerable positive ramifications that stemmed from the Ottomans' tolerance of, and benign attitude towards, the Christian minorities, according to Murre-van den Berg, was the birth of a new Christian

---

[40] Thus, Vrasidas Karalis, 'Greek Christianity after 1453," in *The Blackwell Companion to Eastern Christianity*, pp. 156–185, p. 156. See also S. H. Moffett, *A History of Christianity in Asia, Vol. 2: 1500 to 1900* (Maryknoll, NY: Orbis Books, 2005); Asterios Argyriou, "Christianity in the First Ottoman Era (1516–1650)," in *Christianity: A History in the Middle East*, Habib Badr, et. al. (eds.) (Beirut: Middle East Council of Churches, 2001), pp. 605–630; Vincenzo Poggi, S. J., "Christians in the Second Ottoman Era (17th Century)," also in *Christianity: A History in the Middle East*, pp. 655–674; and Bruce Masters, *Christians and Jews in the Ottoman Arab World: The Roots of Sectarianism* (Cambridge & New York: Cambridge University Press, 2001).

[41] Febe Armanios, *Coptic Christianity in Ottoman Egypt* (Oxford and New York: Oxford University Press, 2011), p. 9.

[42] Heleen Murre-van den Berg, "Chaldaeans and Assyrians: The Church of the East in the Ottoman Period," in *The Christian Heritage of Iraq: Collected Papers from the Christianity of Iraq I-V Seminar Days*, Erica C. D. Hunter (ed.) (Piscataway, NJ: Gorgias Press, 2009), pp. 146–164, p. 146.

[43] Ibid., p. 147. See also D. Khoury, *State and Provincial Society in the Ottoman Empire: Mosul, 1540–1834* (Cambridge: Cambridge University Press, 1997).

ecclesial denomination during that period, instead of the elimination of any of the already existing Christian communities:

> The most important development of the early Ottoman period is the emergence of the Chaldaean Church, which over time has become as large or perhaps slightly larger than that part of the Church of the East which did not unite with Rome.[44]

Overall, Murre-van den Berg's display tenders the conclusion that "during Ottoman rule, the Church of the East displayed a remarkable vitality, despite the wholesale destruction of the early fifteenth century and the fact that this period, although relatively peaceful, was not an easy time in which to live."[45]

At any rate, one can generally surmise here that, as long as the Christians busied themselves with mere survival concerns and ordinary life affairs, and as long as they pledged, and maintained, loyalty towards the Sultanate's authorities and paid their designated taxes, they were rewarded with relative autonomy with regard to ecclesial involvement in educational, domestic, and familial matters.[46] Some of the personnel from these Christian communities even enjoyed certain privileges and prerogatives in the Ottoman context. Moreover, "in the Ottoman world, where *dhimmīs* frequently visited Muslim legal courts to resolve their social and economic disputes, non-Muslim religious leaders became increasingly trusted with exercising moral authority over their communities."[47] On the specific nature of the marginal status the Christians lived under in the Ottoman context, Jane Hathaway says the following noteworthy comments:

> 'marginal' in this context does not necessarily connote oppression or even subordination. Although members of some of these [Christian] groups were certainly disadvantaged and even wretched, others, notably prominent non-Muslim [figures], occupied privileged positions of influence; their minority status arguably helped them to attain such heights … although they belonged to communities that were officially denied the full rights of the Ottoman sultan's free male Sunni subjects, they operated close to the very power center that defined and upheld these rights.[48]

It was in the Ottoman context of the nineteenth century that these Christian and other non-Muslim groups were administered after the *millet* system that aimed at exerting uniform policy to treat these minorities all over the empire.[49]

The internal situation of the Christian communities during the Ottoman rule is primarily characterised (due to the confessionalising ramifications of the exerted *millet* system) by regression into divided denominations reflective of

---

[44] Murre-van den Berg, "Chaldaeans and Assyrians: The Church of the East in the Ottoman Period," p. 155. See also H. Murre-van den Berg, "The Patriarchs of the Church of the East from the Fifteenth to the Eighteenth Centuries," in *Higoye: Journal of Syriac Studies*, 2:2 (1999b) http://syrcom.cua.edu/Hugoye/index.html [accessed 25.2.2021].

[45] Murre-van den Berg, "Chaldaeans and Assyrians: The Church of the East in the Ottoman Period," p. 161.

[46] Awad, 'Arab Orthodox Christianity."

[47] Armanios, *Coptic Christianity in Ottoman Egypt*, p. 10.

[48] Jane Hathaway and Karl K. Barbir, *The Arab Lands under Ottoman Rule, 1516–1800* (London & New York: Routledge, 2013), p. 188.

[49] Ibid., p. 191.

diverse localised, ethnic languages, liturgical traditions, and nationality-shaped confessions. This central feature of Christianity under Ottoman rule is a manifestation of a "high degree of mobility and geographical dispersion" of communities that occasionally shared common territorial presence and lived within its borders as rivals.[50] The existence of different denominations and confessions (centred around nationality and ethnicity in their self-perceptions) in the same territory meant that they were not intimate with each other, nor were their clerical leaders truly close to their living contexts and populations. Instead, these prelates exercised their clerical authority from monasteries, and they did this in a personal rather than territorial manner. A case in point is the region of Antioch and the title of 'See of Antioch' which, since that period, was co-shared by "the Melkite, Syriac Orthodox and Maronite Churches."[51]

These ecclesial communal entities' divisiveness and rivalry seem to have occupied them more than their presence under an Islamic reign. Back when Sultan Selim I launched military campaigns between 1512 and 1520 to conquer Mesopotamia, Syria, and Egypt and to place them under the Ottoman Sultanate flag, the Christians of these territories did not experience subordination to Islamic rule as a new precedent, but rather as a habitual situation they were familiar with since the arrival of Islam to the area centuries earlier. A couple of centuries afterward, nevertheless, these Christians no longer comprised the majority of the population, as they were when the Arabian Muslims first conquered their territories in the seventh century, or even when Salim I embarked on his conquests, when the Ottomans found themselves conquering the Levant, wherein the Christians were a minority and were dispersed into fragmented ecclesial communities.[52]

During the eighteenth to nineteenth centuries, what worsened the above situation of the Middle Eastern Christians, in addition to their coping with the Ottoman rule's religious and communal restrictions, was primarily the arrival of the Catholic, and then the Protestant, missionaries (something that these two Christian Western traditions had actually endeavoured to achieve since the sixteenth century). This *ad extra* dramatic factor led to the Latin Churches' interference in a battle-like confrontation of what was pre-conceptually alleged (never verified) "'abuses' and 'errors' of the Eastern Christians, leading to a certain 'latinisation,' while striving to bring the lost sheep back into the fold of Catholicism."[53] This intrusion generated major historical and lasting changes and developments.

> The Eastern Churches then underwent further fragmentation … all the Eastern Churches split into two opposing parties, either accepting or rejecting the union with Rome … the Arabic-speaking 'Greeks' of the Patriarchate of Antioch

---

[50] Aurélien Girard, Cesare Santus, and Karène Sanchez-Summerer, "Introduction: A New History of Middle Eastern Christians," in *Middle Eastern and European Christianity, 16th–20th Century: Connected Histories*, Bernard Heyberger, A Girard, C. Santus, V. Kontouma and K. S Summerer (eds.), M. Robitaille-Ibbett (trans.) (Edinburgh: Edinburgh University Press, 2023), pp. 10–48, p. 11.

[51] Ibid., p. 12.

[52] Ibid., p. 12.

[53] Ibid., p. 12.

> (Melkites) experienced a serious schism in 1724, with the establishment of two rival hierarchies throughout the Middle East. In the Church of the East, the Catholics, who took the name of 'Chaldeans', broke off definitively in 1830 ... the first approaches of the Syriac Church to Rome also date to that century ... the installation of a Catholic Patriarch of 'Cilicia' in Lebanon in 1740 consecrated the birth of an Armenian Catholic Church. Finally, in 1895, the small Coptic Catholic Church also obtained the establishment of its own patriarchate in Cairo.[54]

In the contemporary time, the previously described conditions enabled the Arab Christians to survive in the predominantly Muslim context of the Middle East. One of the crucial, even problematic, aspects that characterised the Arabic-speaking Eastern Christians' life in the Orient in the modern era is related to the claim that these Christians need protection as a *dhimi* minority by European 'Christian' powers. The roots of this 'protection' policy dig deeply in the history of the relation of Eastern Christians to what they had deemed, since the sixteenth century, 'the Christian lands' of Europe. A noticeable number of Eastern Christians endeavoured throughout the ensuing centuries to visit the European shores and even to try to settle as immigrants on them, justifying this move by means of introducing themselves as "victims of Islamic tyranny."[55] This resorting to Europe originated an early protectionist attitude towards these Christians who existed in the shadow of the Ottoman Empire. Afterwards, during the nineteenth and the twentieth centuries, protecting the Christian minorities in the Orient took a frank diplomatic and ideological curve, as the intervention of the European countries in the territories of the Ottoman Empire during the nineteenth century, and the newly created post-Ottoman Arabic countries during the twentieth century, became more explicit and intensive. The weight of this intervention became heavier when the Eastern Christians were exposed to perpetual anti-Christian accusations of treason and became the victims of hate-mongering stances over various Ottoman and post-Ottoman cities and countries.[56] The Arab-Eastern Christians started now to "effectively turn their attention more to Athens, Rome, Paris, London and Moscow, rather than to the centers of Muslim culture and scholarship."[57]

---

[54] Ibid., p. 13.

[55] Heyberger, *Middle Eastern and European Christianity, 16th–20th Century*, p. 142.

[56] Ibid., p. 143. For instance, in the nineteenth century, this led to the development of a humanitarian agenda for Mount Lebanon, Damascus, Anatolia, and Crete following the massacres and atrocities the Christians witnessed there between 1860 and 1897. See, on this, for example, Anastassios Anastassiadis (ed.), *Visionages fragiles: les relations interconfessionnelles dans le Sud-Est européen et la Méditerranée orientale 1854–1923: Contraints Locales et enjèux internationaux* (Athens: Ecole francaise d'Athèns, 2013) and Bruce Masters, *Christians and Jews in the Ottoman Arab World: The Roots of Sectarianism* (Cambridge & New York: Cambridge University Press, 2001).

[57] Sidney H. Griffith, "Between the Cross and the Crescent: Co-Existence, Clash of Theologies and Interreligious Dialogue," in *Towards a Culture of Co-Existence in Pluralistic Societies: The Middle East and India*, D. W. Winkler (ed.) (Piscataway, NJ: Gorgias Press, 2020), pp. 9–42, p. 21 (pp. 21–22). See also in the same volume, Herman Teule, "Middle Eastern Christians in the Ottoman Empire and its Relationship with the West: The Case of the East-Syrians in the Diyarbakir Region between the 16th and the Early 18th Century," pp. 43–58.

During the nineteenth and early twentieth centuries, the European powers' pressure made the Ottoman Sultan sign capitulation memorandums (*'ahdname*) that warranted these foreign powers the right to protect the Christians who lived within the Ottoman Empire's borders.[58] Among the European powers, the French (in their mandatories in Syria and Lebanon) were the largest beneficiaries and utilisers of the protection policy. They adopted this policy in the Middle East in the hope that, in return for protection, the Catholics in specific, and the Christians in general, in the Orient "would support French expansion in the Mediterranean ... the emancipation of Eastern Christians was thought of in the context of the French ... growth of influence in the Middle East."[59] Far from being purely political and imperialist in nature, the French exploitation of this situation was equally religious and proselytising in orientation. The French took advantage of the circumstances to spread Roman Catholicism, not among Ottoman Muslims, but chiefly among Orthodox Christians working as agents for them in Syria. This led to the reconciliation of a large number of these Syrians with the Vatican and their conversion to 'Syrian Catholics.'[60]

To the misfortune of the Arabic-speaking Eastern Christians, this protectionism policy is not only constitutive of the history and identity of the European colonial powers in the modern time. It inescapably became part and parcel of the history and perceived identity of Arabic-speaking Christians of that predominantly non-Christian region.[61] This caused these Christians all sorts of troubles and hardships in their relations within their broader, Arab-Muslim living context. It made them consistent victims of all kinds of distrust and disloyalty accusations and discourses. This inerasable stigma seems to linger deep beneath the surface of the religious and intellectual reasoning that are symptomatic of the Arabic-speaking Christians' theological thought and discourses. In almost every theological discourse composed by an Arabic-speaking Eastern Christian, the examiner senses behind the language, writing style, and content a tendency to tender justificatory, advocative, and even apologetic pleading for the Arabic-speaking Eastern Christians before a pre-imagined and presupposed judgemental jury made of the Muslim and Arab readers.

---

[58] Heyberger, *Middle Eastern and European Christianity*, p. 148.

[59] Ibid., p. 151. The same policy was also applied in Armenia and Persia, where France was declared by the Armenians and the Chaldeans as "protector of the Catholics throughout the world" (ibid., p. 152).

[60] Hathaway, *The Arab Lands under Ottoman Rule, 1516–1800*, p. 197. Hathaway points out that "a virtual colony of Syrian Catholics formed even in Egypt, where they were instrumental in commerce between their native Syria and the mediterranean ports of Alexandria, Damietta and Rosetta" (ibid., p. 197). See also Johannes Pahlitzsch, *Graeci und Suriani im Palästina der Kreuzfahrerzeit* (Berlin: Dunker und Humboldt Verlag, 2001) and K. Ciggar and H. Teule (eds.), *East and West in the Crusader States III* (Leuven: Uitgeverij Peeters, 2003).

[61] Heyberger, *Middle Eastern and European Christianity*, p. 153.

Surviving Today

The Arab *Christians* still exist in that region today, though their demographic size has witnessed substantial diminishment. They survived many challenging circumstances during the previous centuries. But they also similarly persisted into the postcolonial and post-imperial era of independence and the establishment of the Arab states, even more recently beyond the 'Arab Spring' phase that wreaked havoc on the Arab world during the second decade of the twenty-first century. If you ask these Arab Christians about their life in the Arabic-speaking world, the majority of them would relate that their main life-challenge is far from primarily theological, ecclesial, or even religious in nature. It is, rather, more existential, beyond intellectual and cultural concerns related to convictions. The ultimate question they face is, will Christianity *per se* survive and still exist amidst the turbulence of the twenty-first-century's Arab, Islamic, Middle East?[62] In the ensuing chapters of this monograph, I unpack how such a Shakespearean 'to-be-or-not-to-be' concern leaves its marks on the mind of the Arabic-speaking Christians who endeavour to develop Arab Christian theological discourses today and how it shapes the orientations and concentrations of these theological voices.

In light of the abovementioned historical context, one can say that Arab-Eastern Christianity and its theological *tradition* was not as lucky as the Arabic-speaking *Christians*, and it did not manage to survive as the latter did. Early Arab-Eastern Christian tradition was relegated to the dark margins and was buried in the history books and on the dusty shelves of the libraries of the remaining monasteries and patriarchal houses in some Arab countries. Having realised this, some Christian intellectuals and scholars in the Middle East tried to launch a revivalism campaign to resurrect the historical Arab-Eastern Christian tradition and bring it to the attention of the contemporary public in the Middle East. This revivalism attempt took place in two separate historical periods. The first period started after the collapse of the Ottoman Empire and lasted till the midst of the twentieth century, 1948 specifically, when the Arab world was drifting into the radical, life-changing ramifications of the establishment of the State of Israel and the ensuing Arab–Israeli conflict. On the other hand, the second period started during the nineties of the twentieth century, and it continues today, as new generations of Christians from the region began to acquire academic postgraduate education on the history of Eastern Christianity from Christian–Muslim perspectives, and as study centres and research institutes on Arab-Eastern Christianity were established at various universities in countries like Lebanon, Egypt, Iraq, Jordan, Palestine, and Israel.

The reviving movement these scholars pursued to renew the attention to ancient Arab Christian tradition and its theology circled mainly around searching for ancient manuscripts written by the Arabic-speaking Christian intellectuals and authors who lived mainly during the early Islamic era, but also in the following centuries. These extant texts were unearthed, and critical editions and commentaries on them were developed, before these editions were made available to the Arab-Muslim readership and to the international scholarly world.

---

[62] Awad, "Arab Orthodox Christianity."

Of these main Christian scholars, the public of the Arab world remembers and recognises figures like Louis Cheikho, Constantine Bāchā, Boṭrous al-Bustānī, Ībrāhīm and Nāṣīf al-Yāzigī, Alphonce Mingānā, ʿĪsā al-Maʿlūf, Joseph Nasrallah, ʿʿĀdel Theodore Khoury, George Qanawātī, and Samīr Khalīl Samīr.

In its turn, Western academic scholarship, starting from the nineteenth century, has produced an entire, still unceasingly expanding, library on this ancient Eastern Christianity in its Arabic and non-Arabic branches. What remains seriously understudied is the situation of these Arabic-speaking Christians in their *ad intra*, realistic (not imagined or preconceived), contextual, and down-to-earth realities. When it comes to perceiving the real situation of the Christians in the Arab world and constructing a realistic picture about their life therein, the stunning array of ecclesial diversity and plurality, and the interreligious intermingling which these Christians practise with Muslims in their daily life contexts (let alone the multi-denominational and multicultural life their *Sitz im Leben* displays) can sometimes be a serious concealment, rather than disclosure, of the real situation that motivates, and even determines, their theological imagination and reasoning.[63] The external façade of a rich history of plurality that is portrayed via the denominational versatility hides behind it an internal, parallel history of suffering, uncertainty, fear, pressure, difficulties, death and perpetual strife for survival as a minority in a non-Christian majority world, starting at least from the second half of the twentieth century up till this moment.

The Arab-Eastern Christians of today recognise this parallel history as a no less, if no more, stunning, still-progressing process of existence in the region, and they try to reflect on it explicitly and implicitly in their religious and theological discourses. They embrace seriously, though not necessarily vengefully, the fact that this is the other, grim, side of their historical existence's story in the area. David Kerr is perceptive in acknowledging that such a parallel existential state of beingness overburdens the Christians and their diversity alike with theological disagreements between the churches. This includes the question of the *dhimmi* statuses the Muslims imposed on the non- Muslim citizens, with the drastic ramifications of the Crusaders' invasion of the region in the name of Christ, and the many other past rules and situations that perpetuated, rather than demolished, the Christians' difficult conditions for centuries.[64] In the Christian theological orientations and focuses of the Near East or the Arab world, as we will see in the ensuing chapters, one not only hears the echoes of the past history of survival through difficulties. One also encounters the features of the Arab Christians' theological assessments of and stances on the difficulties they encounter in today's world.

---

[63] See my extensive analysis of the Christians' situation in today's Middle East in Najib G. Awad, *And Freedom Became a Public Square*, pp. 59–67. The ensuing lines above are borrowed from this monograph.

[64] David A. Kerr, "A Western Christian Appreciation of the Eastern Christianity," in *Who Are the Christians in the Middle East?* Betty Jane Bailey and J. Martin Bailey (eds.) (Grand Rapids, USA/Cambridge, UK: W. B. Eerdmans, 2003), pp. 3–11, p. 5.

The Christians of the Arab world are no longer treated as *dhimmis* today, and the majority of their Muslim compatriots no longer consider them remnants, or allies, of those 'Templars' who came from Europe to 'repossess the Holy City, Jerusalem' with a crucifix ornamenting their shields and military attire. However, the Arab-Eastern Christians do still reason about their religious faith and life as those who live under critical and difficult situations relating to their number and influence. In today's scholarship, the researchers of World Christianity and its intercultural, global relationships tend to emphatically point to the transformation of Christianity in modernity from a dominantly European and North American religious phenomenon (and these powers' colonising tool, sometimes) into a worldwide, genuine, and cultural, ethnically, and geographically versatile community.[65] They even go further in affirming that this transformation reveals a crucial geographical shift of Christianity's centre from Europe and the north-western half of the globe into its south-eastern half, as well as to the rapidly escalating spread of Christian belief through Africa, Latin America, Middle Asia, and the Far East.[66] Nevertheless, and contrary to Africa, Asia, and Latin America, one can hardly notice a radical, evident growth of the Christian community in a Muslim majority-area like the Arab world. Despite the renewal and revival movements one can witness in the autochthonous Near Eastern churches, like the Coptic Church in Egypt, and the evangelising activities of the Arabic-speaking fundamental and charismatic Protestant churches, like the ones of Syria, Lebanon, Jordan, and Palestine, the Christians' numbers in this part of the world have drastically decreased during the twentieth century due to the high emigration rate of the region's Christians. The scale of the Christians' decline is indelibly high on the demographic, sociological and cultural scales, as a quick look at the radical decrease in the percentage of Christians in the region's countries during the past forty years clearly shows.

In his anatomisation of the Arab-Eastern Christians' situation in today's Arab world, the Lebanese author Jerome Shahin enumerates a collection of factors that challenge the Arab-Eastern Christians. He calls the first challenge the "demographic hemorrhage" (*al-īstinzāf al-dīmūghrāfī*), and he relates that it is one of the most threatening questions facing the future of these Christians. He pauses at these voices which warn of the impending extinction, decay, or emigration that wait for these Christians if they remain in their homeland, and he also points to those who started to call the Middle Eastern Christianity "the sinking Atlantis" (*aṭlanṭā al-ghāriqa*). Shahin personally maintains that, regardless of the accuracy or exaggeration of these pessimistic views, there is no doubt that the number of the Christians in the Arab Middle East is declining

[65] See, for instance, Noel Davies and Martin Conway, *World Christianity in the Twentieth Century* (London: SCM Press, 2008).

[66] Philip Jenkins, *The Next Christendom: The Coming of Global Christianity*, rev. ed. (Oxford & New York: Oxford University Press, 2007) and Kwame Bediako, *Christianity in Africa* (Edinburgh: Edinburgh University Press/ Maryknoll: Orbis Books, 1995).

exponentially, and this demographic regression is bred by various factors and different circumstances.[67]

The second challenging factor Shahin focuses on is political Islam. This trend of Islam, Shahin relates, is a common threat to all Christians without exception, because it aims at establishing an 'Islamic State' that is prone to treat Christians as second-class citizens. Shahin believes that the principle of 'Islam is religion and worldliness' (*al-Īslām dīn wa-dunyā*) can generate circumstances antagonistic to human rights and equality. This will manifest strongly in an Islamist State that imposes Muslim *Sharia* over all aspects of societal living and will sectarianise the state (*al-dawla al-ṭā'ifiyya*) and will *dhimmitudise* the non-Muslims in society.[68]

The third challenge the Arab-Eastern Christians primarily face today, according to Shahin, is churchly schisms and divisions. Ecclesial schisms, Shahin notices, are also detectable in the worldly church outside the Arab world. Yet, according to him, churchly divisions in the Middle East are the cause of more dire and negative ramifications, because the Christians in that region are already a minority and spread too thin over a rather too large number of diverse denominations. Such diversity is not always a sign of healthy plurality and diversity, but a symptom of fragility, vulnerability, tension, conflicts, and rivalry among a very small group of people who are already degenerated and weakened by their numerical reality.[69]

The fourth challenge Shahin points to is what he calls "Western meddling" (*al-tadakhkhul al-gharbī*). Far from merely deeming it a fraternal and friendly contact with Middle Eastern Christianity, Shahin construes the Western role in the life of the Eastern Christians throughout history as nothing but a manifestation of interference and intrusion. The Eastern Christians, according to him, did not at all benefit from such interference under the name of 'protection' (*ḥimāya*). They were, rather, the primary victims of this protectionism's consequences. In the modern era, the West's relation to Eastern Christianity, Shahin believes, has an even worse impact on the latter. Since the West is less religious and more secular today, it is more sceptical and hostile towards Islam, and its connections to the Arab world are purely pragmatic, utilitarian, and exploitative.[70]

Some of Jerome Shahin's diagnoses and assessments of the situation are arguable and prone to critical evaluation. Yet, one cannot disagree with his overall, fourfold description of the Arab-Eastern Christians' challenges and situation in today's Arab world. Suffice to end this brief survey by relating that, underneath the external facade of variety, colourful interaction and interreligious co-existence, which fascinate the foreign tourists and visitors to the Arab Near East, lurks a parallel, more sophisticated, and less idealist, history. In this history,

---

[67] Jerome Shahin, *al-Masīḥiyyūn al-'Arab: al-Taḥaddiyāt al-Rāhina wa-Khayārāt al-Maṣīr* (The Arab Christians: The Contemporary Challenges and the Choices of Destiny) (Beirut: an-Nūr Orthodox Press, 2008), pp. 129–132.

[68] Ibid., pp. 132–133.

[69] Ibid., p. 134.

[70] Ibid., pp. 135–137.

the Christians purported to survive and maintain their rich, variable particularities despite their historical reduction into single monolithic, homogenous *millet*, and notwithstanding the public historical identification of the Christians with the often distrusted and hated European powers because they both shared the same religious faith. Unless one apprehends in depth these challenges and their role in the formation of the Arab-Eastern Christians' story in the Arab world, it is hardly possible to detect in the external view of the Christian–Muslim coexistence in the region the details of the complexity of this coexistence. More significantly and essentially still, without perceiving this underlying history, one will not be able to dive far enough into the depths of the theological reasoning and discourses of the Christians on this part of the globe.

3. Arab Christian Theological Tradition in Western Scholarship

Introduction

One of the challenges that face the developing of a genuine, from-within reading and understanding of a particular religious or historical tradition lies in the epistemological cartography that is practised in the modern academy. This epistemological game played by Euro-American scholarship aims at eulogizing authors from this Western background and they bestow upon them declared referentiality and decision-making prerogatives regarding theory-production. In this epistemology, one can trace the marks of an intellectual totalitarianism, which scholars sometimes assume in their attempts at defining all the modes of knowledge and evaluating and charting them in relation to one another. This totalitarianism manifests itself in the readiness of scholars to exclude and re-configure a large swathe of historical data in order to make them fit into a preconceived narrative.[1]

In this chapter, I shall touch upon some Western scholarly approaches to the Arabic-speaking Christian tradition and demonstrate that their reading and interpretation of the historical context of these Christians' interreligious co-existence with Islam, as well as this scholarship's reading of the intellectual and theological values and worth of these Christians, both stem from a premeditated application of the mentioned epistemological strategy. This strategy manifests in manipulating and selectively dealing with historical data in a manner congenial with a preconceived narrative about how the Christians and the Muslims lived in the early Islamic period in the Arab-Eastern context. After unravelling some of the known referential voices on this Arab-Eastern interreligious co-existence and case study in Western scholarship, I shall propose a different, more genuinely intrinsic and *ad intra* reading of the Christian and Muslim co-existence and intellectual interreligious correlation in the Arab-Eastern *Sitz im Leben.*

The Western scholarship's serious and purposeful relation to and interest in Eastern Christianity in general and in Arabic Christian traditions in particular witnessed a climax in the nineteenth century, when this interest established its scholarly identity within the frameworks of the orientalist and missiological trends of reasoning that characterised the Western intellectuals' interest in (or curiosity about!) the non-Western territories of the globe. While one can note today innumerable studies written by Western scholars (or scholars based in the West, for that matter) on these two Christian traditions, the Eastern and the Arab alike, one hardly finds a reliable comprehensive, analytical, and critical study written on how these Western scholarly enterprises approached and read these

---

[1] Joseph E. B. Lumbard, "Decolonizing Qur'ānic Studies," in *Religions*, 176(13), 2022, pp. 1–14, pp. 3–5.

traditions methodologically. How did they interpret them? What are the presumptions and preconceptions that generated and shaped their stances on Eastern-Arab Christianity? In other words, while we have enough hermeneutics related to the components and themes of this subject in Western scholarship, we yet lack hermeneutics on the hermeneutics; attempts at de-caking the cake, so to speak.

In 2014, Samuel Noble and Alexander Treiger co-edited English translations of a collection of extant Arabic Christian texts from the early Islamic era. In the introduction to their volume, Noble and Treiger pause at the assessment and appreciation of Arabic-Eastern Christianity in modern Western scholarship, and they diagnose a situation like the one I shed light on here. They point out that, among the contemporary scholars of Christian traditions in the Western academic context, there is a general presumption that today's Middle East is actually void of Christian presence, and the Christianity that once existed in it has not flourished elsewhere, "leaving its original heartland devoid of an indigenous Christian presence," so that "the very notion of Arab Christianity appears to many to be a contradiction in terms."[2] Noble and Treiger maintain that, even among Western scholars who are familiar with the existence of this Christianity, one rarely finds any mention of one single author or text from this Arabic Christian heritage. None of these authors' names or their intellectual textual productions, they confirm, are noticed "in the standard histories of Christianity available to the Western reader, and the existing translations of such texts are not easily accessible to the nonspecialist."[3] Among the authors Noble and Treiger invoke, there is Jaroslav Pelikan and his five-volume text *The Christian Tradition*, where one merely finds "scattered references to one or two Arabic-writing Christian theologians."[4] They also bring to our attention John McGuckin and his monographs, *The Orthodox Church* of 2008, and the two-volume *Encyclopedia of Eastern Orthodox Christianity* of 2011. According to them, in both books McGuckin makes the reader conclude that the Arabic Christian communities in historical Eastern cities/patriarchal seats, like Antioch, Alexandria, and Jerusalem, declined drastically and disastrously, so that "there is hardly any need to comment on these communities' subsequent fate."[5] While McGuckin incorporates into his *Encyclopedia* entries on Orthodoxy in Latvia and Lithuania, one finds no article on Orthodoxy in Lebanon, for instance. Added to this, "there is not a single entry in the entire encyclopedia on any Arabic-writing Christian theologian."[6]

[2] Noble and Treiger, *The Orthodox Church in the Arab World 700–1700*, p. 4.
[3] Ibid., p. 4.
[4] Ibid., p. 4. See also Jaroslav Pelikan, *The Christian Tradition: A History of the Development of Doctrine* (Chicago, IL: University of Chicago Press, 1975–1991).
[5] Ibid., p. 5. See John A. McGuckin, *The Orthodox Church: An Introduction to its History, Doctrine and Spiritual Culture* (Oxford, UK/Malden, USA: Blackwell Publishing, 2008 and J. A. McGuckin (ed.), *The Encyclopedia of Eastern Orthodox Christianity* (Oxford, UK/Malden, USA: Blackwell Publishing, 2011).
[6] Ibid., p. 5. The two authors notice, nevertheless, that the recent years witnessed some change in this orientation, as some Western scholars started to include some chapters on the 'Arabic Tradition,' like Kenneth Parry, *The Blackwell Companion to Eastern*

I do concur with Noble's and Treiger's general review of the stance of Western scholarship on Arab-Eastern Christianity. Nevertheless, my reading of the strategies of Western scholarship's hermeneutics of Middle Eastern and Arabic Christian traditions alike would dig deeper and investigate more closely the variants within the framework of the Western stance on this Christianity. This forensic examination of the trends of this stance invites me to propose a dual orientalist approach in this scholarship: the first is degrading and trivialising in appraisal, while the second is targeting and essentialising in nature.

The Degrading Orientalist Appraisal

The first approach to the Arab-Eastern Christian tradition is mostly detectable in the legacies of missionaries and orientalists, whose stance on this Christianity invokes a reduction of Arab-Eastern Christian tradition down to the *individuals and groups* which these Westerners encountered and interacted with when they visited the Middle East during the nineteenth and early twentieth centuries. These individuals and groups of Arab-Eastern Christians are often, 'exoticised,' in the sense of 'exotic' which Hilary Kilpatrick specifies as "what appears foreign, strange and incomprehensible to the casual observer."[7] The travelogues of many European orientalists on their visits to the Orient are loaded with all sorts of degrading, trivialising, and inferiorising descriptions and stances on the Christians of the Middle East. To say the least, such travelogues convey depreciating, categorising, and labelling sentiments and expressions reflective of the cultural and intellectual superiority of these orientalist travellers towards a Christianity they deemed totally subordinate to the Western one.

On these orientalist travelogues, the Egyptian scholar Anouar Abdel-Malek once wrote an important essay, published originally in French in 1963 under the title 'L'Orientalisme en Crise' and then in an Arabic translation in 1983 under the title "*al-Istishrāq fī Azmah*" (Orientalism is in Crisis). In this essay, Abdel-Malek displays a plethora of reports and sentimental reactions which the European orientalist travellers to the Middle East jotted down in their travel handbooks. One of the subjects contained in these reports is the conditions and situations of the Christian communities in the Middle East. According to Abdel-Malek, most of these orientalists were not at all impressed with the Christians they encountered in that region. They satirically relate that these Christians are miserably fragmented and torn apart by sectarianism and confessionalism, and they seem to be unable to live without conflicts, divisiveness, and enmity among each other. Some of these travellers express their utter frustration at their failure in distinguishing and perceiving the exact foundations and differences that draw

---

Christianity (Malden USA/Oxford, UK: Blackwell Publishing, 2007); Augustine Casiday (ed.), *The Orthodox Christian World* (London: Routledge, 2012); Margaret M. Mitchell and Frances M. Young (eds.), *The Cambridge History of Christianity* (Cambridge & New York: Cambridge University Press, 2006); and Wolfgang Hage, *Das orientalische Christentum* (Stuttgart: Verlag W. Kohlhammer, 2007).

[7] Hilary Kilpatrick, "'Exotic' Christianity as a Translation Problem," in *Orientalismo. Exotismo y Traducción*, Gonzalo F. Parrilla and Manuel C. F. García (eds.) (Cuenca: de Castilla-La Mancha, 2000), pp. 217–228, p. 218.

the dividing lines between the numerous Christian denominations. This is conveyed in a statement Abdel-Malek cites from a travel booklet of two French orientalists, who cynically, almost sarcastically, express their frustration and deprecation of the Middle Eastern Christians in the following words:

> What a diversity! What dauntingly meticulous discrepancies! How can one find clarity in the midst of these tiny dogmatic curves and maneuvers and diverse rituals. Dear Lord, I have met numerous kinds of patriarchs, bishops, and religious clerics. So many various rituals as colorful as a rainbow. At one moment, I thought that I held the grip of this puzzling diversity. Yet, today I no longer have such a confidence. I am afraid that if I started counting the sects and confessions, I will end up inventing a new heresy.[8]

As bewildering and worth demeaning for these orientalist travellers were the various linguistic traditions the Christians followed in conducting their churchly rituals. The travellers' frustration and deprecation manifested itself, for instance, in the caricatured depictions and descriptions they jotted down in their diaries about the diverse Eastern Christian churches' celebrations in the city of Jerusalem. The travellers express their utter irritation at hearing some of the ritual hymns and liturgies conducted in Greek, others conducted in Arabic, and yet others in Coptic languages. Then, the travellers articulated their satirical disdain of this diversity by relating that most of the times such multilingual ritual celebrations ended up with a fight between the worshippers from different denominations, which would require the interference of the British mandate police forces.[9]

Another example of such degrading and trivialising tendencies can be found in the works of the Scottish-American missionary and Arabist, Duncan Black Macdonald.[10] Upon delving into Macdonald's extant archive, one can detect his sensitivity and positivity towards Islam and his non-discriminative appraisal of the Muslims and their historical and contemporary legacies. What is puzzling, nevertheless, is the almost impossibility of finding in his writings on the Middle East (whether in his travelogue or in his intellectual studies) any mention of the Eastern-Arabic Christian tradition or even of its Christian affiliates. There is no noteworthy comment, remark, or opinion on this Christianity and its followers, whether in relation to missionary work or in relation to the history of the Orient. Macdonald never even refers to, or reports on, his personal interaction with the Copts or other followers of local Christianity during his visit to the Middle East. One can only spot one rare occasion where, in a private letter he wrote to one of his students, Macdonald alludes merely to the Arab Christians in a conspicuously depreciative manner. He recommends his student to learn the Arabic language

---

[8] Anouar Abdel-Malek, "*al-Istishrāq fī Azmah*" (Orientalism in Crisis), Ḥasan Qubaysī (trans.) in *Al-Fikr al-'Arabī Journal*, 33(5), 1983, pp. 70–93, p. 74.

[9] Ibid., p. 75.

[10] I borrow the following ideas on this from Najib G. Awad, *After-Mission, Beyond Evangelicalism*, pp. 35–41 and Najib G. Awad, "'Understanding the Other from Within': The Muslim Near East in the Eyes of Duncan Black Macdonald," in *The Muslim World*, 106(3), 2016, pp. 523–538.

from the Muslims and to "avoid the Christian Arabic."[11] Elsewhere, Macdonald alludes in passing to the Christian Copts without naming them, as he calls them the "non-Muslims" or the "minorities" in Egypt.[12]

Duncan Black Macdonald is not alone in his negligence and indifference among the Western missionaries. Other American Protestant missionaries in the Middle East were even more wearily confused by the Eastern and Arab Christianity traditions and their followers. They tended, thus, either to belittle these Christians' existence and to treat them as a non-considerable model of primitive, backward Christianity. Or, they totally trivialised and degraded these Christians and their traditions by deeming them dead churches, merely "Christian in name, Christian in form, well typified by the mummified human body taken out of the tombs."[13] The stance of the American missionary in Syria-Lebanon, Henry Harris Jessup, for instance, on the Arab-Eastern Christianity and its followers and representatives, is a case in point. In the memoirs of his service years there, Jessup attacks the local Christian clerics in bluntly aggressive terms. He describes them by saying: "As donkeys have a worldwide reputation for stupidity, it is eminently proper to set the Syrian priests next in order, for, with rare exceptions, they are marvels in ignorance … and they are not only ignorant, but many of them are very vicious men." Jessup then proceeds by stating that "school children in America know more of arithmetic and geography and Bible history than almost any Greek [that is Roman Orthodox] priest in Syria; for they are chosen generally, not from among the graduates of schools, but from among the lowest of the people."[14]

A similar indifference and deprecation toward Eastern-Arab Christianity traditions and their followers, and the same reductionist reading of the history and present of the Middle East as exclusively the story of Islam, surface also in the attitude of orientalist scholars from outside the missionary circles. A good example of this is the famous scholar Ignaz Goldziher. Generally, Goldziher held a relatively positive stance on Islam and he attempted to conjure a rational justification of its far from rigidly fixed nature. For him, Islamic intellect was progressive, dynamic, and evolutionary to such an extent that it manifests as a continuous conflict between Sunnitism and consistent, innovative attempts at

---

[11] Awad, *After-Mission, Beyond Evangelicalism*, p. 35; Awad, "'Understanding the Other from Within,'" p. 537. See also Jermain Bodine, "The Legacy of Duncan Black Macdonald," in *Occasional Bulletin of Missionary Research*, 4(4), 1980, pp. 162–164, p. 163.

[12] Awad, *After-Mission, Beyond Evangelicalism*, p. 35. See also Duncan B. Macdonald, "The New Egyptian Constitution," in *International Review of Missions*, 1921, pp. 305–320.

[13] So one of the missionaries called Andrew Watson wrote in his reports. See Heather J. Sharkey, *American Evangelicals in Egypt: Missionaries Encounters in an Age of Empire* (Princeton, NJ: Princeton University Press, 2008), p. 19. See also Mitri Raheb, "Shifting Identities: The History of Christianity in the Modern Middle East," in *Shifting Identities: Changes in the Social, Political and Religious Structures in the Middle East*, Mitri Raheb (ed.) (Bethlehem: Diyar Publisher, 2016), pp. 9–39, p. 18.

[14] Henry H. Jessup, *Syrian Home-Life*, Isaac Riley (ed.) (New York: Dodd & Mead Publishers, 1874), pp. 136–137.

expanding the parameters, and even exceeding the boundaries, of the Sunnite rigidity.[15] This positive belief in the dynamicity and innovation of Islamic thought, however, is starkly contrasted with Goldziher's crudely negative and depreciative appraisal of Arab-Eastern Christianity.

In his translation of Goldziher's diary, Raphael Patai relates that indifference and deprecation are symptomatic of Goldziher's attitude toward religious groups other than Islam in the Middle East. Patai relates that Goldziher's diary on his trip to the Arab Middle East during 1890s

> makes it clear that Jews, Christian Arabs, and foreign Christians were only tangential to his interest. His main, almost exclusive, concern was with the Muslim Arabs, and it was they who the youthful scholar [Goldziher] observed with insatiable appetite and inexhaustible energy, and from whom he tried to absorb everything he could learn.[16]

At one point in his diary, Goldziher states: "I must confess that I am unable to like the Christian Arabs."[17] Goldziher explains this sentiment by revealing his weariness of these Christians' attempts at adopting European languages and education and assimilating the Western cultural-religious mentality. He believed that they zealously endeavoured to pursue this assimilation to an extent that Goldziher deemed degrading of their original Arabic-Muslim roots and background. Soaked with disdain, he accuses them of doing this in a fanatic manner, as if plotting "to kill a natural product [namely the original Muslim heritage of the Orient] which … surely had the right to exist."[18]

Goldziher's stance on Arabic-Oriental Christianity is not private or exceptional in the European, particularly German, scholarly field of Arabist and Islamist studies that characterised the beginning of the area of reasoning called 'Orientalism' in the universities. The pioneer of the establishment of a scientific area of study called 'Orientalism' in Germany, Johan Jacob Reiske, for instance, believed that the Christian Arabic literature one finds in the historical heritages of the Arab-Muslim world "cannot cope with that of the Muslims."[19] Within the

---

[15] Ignaz Goldziher, *Vorlesungen über den Islam* (Heidelberg: Carl Winter Universitätsbuchhandlung, 1910), pp. 285ff. Goldziher's approach stands against that of Alfred von Kremer, who believed, on the contrary, that innovation had merely prevailed in Islamic history for a very short time, before it vanished from the scene and emptied the space for rigidity and stasis: Alfred von Kremer, *Culturegeschichte des Orients: Unter den Chalifen* (Wien: Wilhelm Braumüller, 1875).

[16] Raphael Pattai, "Introduction: 'The Great Goldziher,' a Psychological Portrait," in *Ignaz Goldziher and His Oriental Diary: A Translation and Psychological Portrait*, Raphael Pattai (trans. & ed.) (Detroit, MI: Wayne State University Press, 1987), p. 67.

[17] Ibid., p. 110.

[18] Ibid., pp. 35–36.

[19] Johann Fück, *Die arabischen Studien in Europa bis in den Anfang des 20. Jahrhunderts* (Leipzig: Otto Harrassowitz, 1955), p. 123. See also on Eastern Christianity in German Academic Orientalist studies the valuable study of Carsten-Michael Walbiner, "Christian Arabic Studies in Germany during the Last 150 Years: A Short Survey," in *Proceedings of the Arabic and Islamic Sections of the 35th International Congress of Asian and North African Studies (ICANAS), II*, A. Fodor (ed.) (Budapest: Eotvos Lorand University/Csoma de Koros Soceity, 1999), pp. 239–247.

framework of this demeaning appraisal, Carsten Walbiner realises that, in early German Orientalism, "while Syrian studies had a permanent platform in the *Zeitschrift der Deutschen Morgenländischen Gesellschaft* (*ZDMG*) during the first four decades of its existence, and [it] occupied a considerable space, not a single contribution was made in the same period on the Christian Arabic Literature."[20] The degrading appraisal of the Arabic Christian heritage left the Christian side of Arabic history and culture completely neglected. For the staunch academic orientalists who worked in universities, "Christian Arabic literature was of no, or only minor, interest."[21] So much so, Walbiner maintains, that "the Arabic literary productions from among the ancient Christians [were] still hidden in the corners of forgetfulness, and many scholars [did] not know them at all." This is something that clearly demonstrates "the widespread disinterest of German Orientalists in the Christian Arabs and their heritage."[22] Be that as it may, Goldziher's deprecation of Arabic-Eastern Christianity and his total concentration on Islam alone is symptomatic of the overall European and German orientalist views of that form of Christianity: "In this period, German Orientalism could be identified with studies on Islam … the Christian Orient is dealt with as [merely and narrowly] 'special sub-discipline' of Semitistic and Islamic Sciences … [for this peripheral discipline was considered] of secondary importance in comparison with the study of the Islamic world."[23] As if this Christianity is not actually part and parcel of, or inherent in, the Islamic world, but an alien entity which fatefully happened to exist in it due to unfortunate historical coincidences.[24]

These are just a few examples of this orientalist deprecation and trivialising stance on Eastern-Arab Christianity traditions. One can also dig for traces of similar attitudes in the writings of others from that trend of Western scholarship, like Emil Nöldeke and Louis Massignon, just to mention two important figures. Overall, the core tendency of this orientalist intellectual orientation is to undermine completely, or even totally discredit, any value or significance in the so-called Eastern and Arab Christian legacy. The Middle East is exclusively and exhaustively Islam and the Muslims alone. Tracing any theological, intellectual,

---

[20] Walbiner, "Christian Arabic Studies in Germany during the Last 150 Years: A Short Survey," p. 240. This essay's thesis was re-articulated later on in German in Carsten-Michael Walbiner, "Die Entwicklung der Christlich-Arabischen Studien in Deutschland: Ein Kurzer Überblick," in *The Journal of Eastern Christian Studies*, 58(3–4), 2006, pp. 253–263.

[21] Walbiner, "Christian Arabic Studies in Germany during the Last 150 Years: A Short Survey," p. 241.

[22] Ibid., p. 242.

[23] Ibid., p. 243.

[24] Walbiner intriguingly concludes with these thought-provoking and eye-opening words: "All in all, these sporadic dealings with Christian Arabic literature were far away from being sufficient enough to establish these studies steadily at German universities … Christian Arabic studies are almost absolutely neglected at German universities … more characteristic for the recent situation is the fact that at the German Orientalists' Conference in Leipzig (1995) only one lecture was dedicated to Christian Arabic Studies" (ibid., p. 244). See also C. Walbiner.

or cultural creativity in this region means exploring Islam's religious and civilisational heritages only. For this approach, Arab Christian theology is a non-existent thing. Sidney H. Griffith eloquently speaks about this stance when he says: "It is almost as if in the Western imagination the religious discourse and the intellectual concerns of Middle Eastern Christians were frozen in time, in the form they had at the time when the Islamic hegemony came over them in the seventh century."[25] Probably, this deprecation in today's Western scholarship is echoing the ancient Latin Christians' stance on the Christians of the Orient, who were used to be construed "as schismatic or even heretical and so as people who left the church centuries ago."[26]

The Targeting and Essentialising Orientalist Trend

The second orientalist approach to the Arabic Christianity tradition is one that is more seriously scholarly and investigative than the first approach, and it focuses particularly on the theological and religious dimensions of this tradition. Most of the Western scholars who study Arab Christian theology and its origin and early years tend to focus on its apologetic polemic and claimed defensive nature, and to deem the Christians' contribution to the Arabic theological genre of rational religious discourse known as '*Kalām*' as these Christians' primary, if not singular, instrument for survival and identity- and legacy-protection against, or in sharply dividing parallelism with, Islam. In this scholarship, knowing Christian Arab *Kalām* is pragmatically useful in the service of the contemporary attempt to understand the genesis and development of early Islamic theology and how the Christians survived its threat.

The interest in this Arab Christian *Kalām* for perceiving the evolution process of Muslim thought started in modern Western scholarship with the pioneering work of a Catholic priest from Munich, Georg Graf (1878–1955), who prepared the first collective German translation of the then-known manuscripts of Arab Christian *Kalām* and published them in a multi-volume publication titled *Geschichte de christliche arabischen Literatur* (1947). Earlier than this publication, Graf also produced studies and German translations of the *Kalām* of Theodore Abū Qurrah, like his *Die arabischen Schriften des Theodor Abu Qurra, Bishoffs von Ḥarrān (ca. 740–820)* (1910) and *Das Theodore Abu Kurra Traktat über den Shüfer und die wahre Religion* (1913). In addition to Graf, one cannot here forget the significant revivalism attempts of the originally Iraqi Assyrian scholar Alphonse Mingana (1878–1937), whose scholarly contributions to the field took place mainly during his living and working years in the United Kingdom (Birmingham and Manchester). To Mingana, scholars today appreciatively attribute the critical editions of major Christian–Muslim apologies (though his work provoked criticism among experts), one of which was the text of ʿAlī b. Rabbān aṭ-Ṭabarī's refutation of Christianity, and another text was of the debate between the Abbasid Caliph al-Mahdī and the Nestorian Patriarch Timothy I. Famous today among scholars is what is called 'Mingana Collection

[25] Griffith, *The Church in the Shadow of the Mosque*, p. 2.
[26] Ibid., p. 3.

of Manuscripts,' which he collected and catalogued at Selly Oak College, Birmingham.[27]

After Graf and Mingana, and by the help of their pioneering works, the interest in Arab Christian *Kalām*, and its extant literature in the archives and libraries of ancient monasteries and churches of Palestine, Israel, Egypt, Syria, north-eastern Iraq, and the Syriac towns in south-eastern Turkey, have grown exponentially in Western academia. In recent Arab Christian *Kalām* scholarship in the West, the scholarly work and productions of authors like Heinrich G.W. Goussen, Joshua Blau, Shlomo Pines, Spencer J. Trimingham, Alfred Guillaume, Michel Hayek, Paul Khoury, Hava Lazarus-Yafeh, Harry Wolfson, Fuat Sezgin, Emilio Platti, Sidney H. Griffith, David Thomas, Mark Swanson, Samir Khalil Samir, and Gerhard Endress, just to mention the major few, are studied by all the students and scholars of Arab Christian *Kalām* around the world.

Principally, the abovementioned Western scholarly interest, predominantly and locationally, tends to focus on the strict theological and interreligious content of this tradition. It avoids as much as possible marrying its research and investigation with old or contemporary political or ideological preconceptions and worldviews, which one can usually coincide with in the history of Western thought towards the non-Western worlds. This principal ethical rule acknowledged and appreciated, one cannot but sometimes detect some preconceived tendency lingering beneath the surface of disciplined scientific neutrality. Such a tendency is reminiscent of what one witnesses in the politicised and ideologised versions of orientalism. When such a tendency becomes extreme in its traces, the scholarship on Arab Christian theology resembles a premeditated obsession with a 'clash of civilisations/nations' mentality and worldview. On the other hand, in its moderate and controlled, less tailored form, this tendency manifests itself in a mere binary, Christianity-versus-Islam reading of the nature, purpose, and content of the Arab Christian theological discourses from the Late Antiquity/early Muslim era.[28] This seems to be the prevalent situation all over so many publications one finds today on the Christians' life and existence in the Muslim-majority context of the Orient. Scholars do not seem to be articulating a conclusion they gleaned at the end of their objective investigation of the historical narrative of the Christian–Muslim relations in the long history of the MENA (Middle East and Northern Africa) region. They seem, instead, to be inductively departing in their research from a taken-for-granted presumption that

[27] Read a biographical exposition of Mingana's legacy in Samir Khalil Samir, *Alphonse Mingana 1878–1837 and His Contribution to Early Christian-Muslim Studies* (Birmingham: Selly Oak Colleges, 1990).

[28] See a criticism of these two views of Eastern Christianity in Western scholarship in Bernard Heyberger, "Eastern Christians, Islam and the West: A Connected History," in *International Journal of Middle Eastern Studies*, 42(2010), pp. 475–478; Paul S. Rowe, "The Middle Eastern Christian as Agent," in *International Journal of Middle Eastern Studies*, 42(2010), pp. 472–474; and G. Michael Wickens, "Western Scholarship on the Middle East," in *Comparative Civilizations Review*, 13(13/6), 1985, pp. 62–72.

> [this history] offers little hope in terms of peaceful and harmonious coexistence ... there can be little doubt that the two faiths hardened in their dogmatic positions, leading to a mutual exclusion. The conflicts of those days continue to cast their shadow over Christians of the East and their Muslim counterparts.[29]

Let me state at this point that one would be over-idealistic and intellectually naïve if he or she presumed an ideal, absolute, and unchanging state of '*Convivencia*' as definitive of the Christian–Muslim life and history in that region. There are certainly direly dark moments in the historical narrative of their co-existence that are evident of a polarisation and binarism that are far from depicting a peaceful and harmonious case in point. However, my problem with such a binary-centred view like the above is that most of the scholars in the field seem to premeditatedly presume it, inductively, or eisegetically, depart from it, and then construct onto it their own ensuing analysis and conclusions, instead of reaching deductively such a conclusion at the end of their investigating process.

This is how, for instance, Kenneth Cragg approaches Arab Christianity in his *The Arab Christians*. Driven by a binary view of this Christianity's place *over against* Islam, Cragg does not focus on this Christian tradition's theological or intellectual contributions to the creation of the world of Islam. He remains totally remote from even pondering the possibility of deeming this Christian tradition a part-and-parcel constituent of the world of Islam. He, rather, considers it a religious and theological otherising *identity*, against which Islam stands. He reads the story of this Christianity with Islam as a biography of hardcore self-alteration within a challenging non-Christian life-setting, wherein Arab Christianity has to labour and survive.[30] All Arab Christianity's historical narrative, Cragg opines, becomes a dramatic, almost tragic, chronicle of conflictual encounter that placed this Christianity under the yoke of "the stresses of destiny and vocation in co-existence with Islam – stresses in which issues of faith and worship have perpetually tangled with questions of land and people, of place and belonging."[31] And when Arab Christianity's theological, intellectual, and cultural contributions to the "growing sophistication of the Muslim mind" are paused at, these contributions are interpreted as made by those who are treated as a tolerated minority (*dhimmi*), politically subjugated, and communally

---

[29] Mike Kuhn, "Conquest and Christian–Muslim Relations during the Islam Era (Seventh to Eleventh Centuries)," in *Surviving Jewel: The Enduring Story of Christianity in the Middle East*, Mitri Raheb and Mark A. Lamport (eds.) (Eugene, OR: Cascade Books, 2022), pp. 19–35, pp. 33–34. In his essay, the author departs from a definite preconception of the interaction between Islam and Christianity in the early period that essentialises polemics and enmity and aims at extracting moments of clash and tension from within the history of their co-existence in order to prove what the author has already departed conceptually from. The same attitude is also reflected to a certain extent in the title, which the editors of the anthology that contains Kuhn's text opted for: 'Surviving Jewel.' As if the Christians in the Arab Middle East did nothing throughout their history with Islam except surviving and seeking enclosure and self-protectionism.

[30] Kenneth Cragg, *The Arab Christian*, p. 10.

[31] Ibid., p. 11.

downgraded under Islam.[32] Intellectual innovation, including the theological kind, becomes first and foremost a defensive tool and pragmatic, protectionist necessity to guard the Christians and save them from disruptive Muslim policies. This is reflective of the "deep dilemmas both of faith and psyche," Cragg claims, which Arab Christianity drowned in because of its co-existence with Islam. Theologisation, Cragg says, is an apologetic or pure protectionist strategy that ultimately aims at enabling Arab Christianity "to reckon with the abiding instinct of Islam to conscious superiority and dominance."[33]

A preconception of Muslim–Christian co-existence as expressive of a polarising and binary situation was also suggested by the famous historian of *Kalām*, Josef van Ess. In an essay he wrote in 1975 on the beginning of theological practice in the history of Islam, van Ess argues that during the Umayyad and the early Abbasid eras, the Christians and Muslims shared "a common stock of ideas" and "common treasury of arguments" that were simply available for everyone in society.[34] Van Ess gleans from this that one need not, therefore, "appeal for a Christian 'influence'" that led to the Muslims' learning from Christianity how to create theological reasoning. Van Ess's suggestion of the Christians' and Muslims' co-usage and co-implementation of a commonly available stock of ideas and theological arguments gives the reader an impression that he is endorsing an open, cross-boundary, and symbiotic context of co-existence enjoyed, and even co-generated, by the Christians and the Muslims in the *Sitz im Leben* of the Umayyad and early Abbasid worlds. Far, actually, from such a conclusion, directly after stating his mentioned propositions, van Ess states almost the opposing view and a sharply contrasting depiction of the Christian–Muslim co-existence conditions of that era. The picture he conjures suggests that, far from being a mutually open, symbiotic, and real interaction, the Muslims found themselves living in the midst of a Christian majority. Instead of interacting openly as two co-existing entities, both religious groups kept contact between each other conspicuously weak and tangential. The Muslims, van Ess admits, "needed the Christians, and [they] sometimes held them in high esteem ... but [they] did not ask for their advice in theological questions."[35] One here might think that even if, for the sake of argument, one conceded that no personal advice was sought by Muslims from Christians (although we do know that the Muslim caliphs and princes had Christian advisors serving in their courts), what can one say about textual consultation and textual exposition? If there was a common stock of ideas and arguments available to all to use and implement, then the Muslims must have been familiar with the sources of these ideas and arguments and able to consult them in such a manner that suggests an interaction and mutual relatedness between the Christians and Muslims, on religious and other matters alike, that is certainly more than just 'weak' or almost

---

[32] Ibid., p. 11.

[33] Ibid., p. 280.

[34] Josef van Ess, "The Beginnings of Islamic Theology," in *The Cultural Context of Medieval Learning*, J. E. Murdoch and E. D. Sylla (eds.) (Dordrecht: Springer, 1975), pp. 87–111.

[35] Ibid., p. 100.

none. To make his depiction even more surreal, van Ess invokes a contemporary example of a Christian–Muslim co-existence to support his 'no-interaction,' 'tangential existence' depiction. What van Ess suggests merits citation at full length:

> We may perhaps compare the situation to what can be experienced even nowadays in a 'Levantine' city like Beirut. Different communities live together, they deal with each other, they do business with each other, they do the administration and – today – even politics together, but they *never* talk to each other about their religion and consequently they are to an astonishing degree ignorant of what their neighbors believe ... there is also distance and an unmistakable amount of mutual contempt. Had there been religious contacts, there would have been controversy; but there is not one text pointing in this direction.[36]

For someone who comes from this 'Levantine' world, and who lived in the contemporary Beirut for eight years of his life, van Ess's depiction of the city and the situation therein is jaw-dropping, to say the least. Ess forgets, it seems, that these Christians and Muslims who live in Beirut not only do business, administration, and politics together. They also share and co-use the very same intellectual literature and sources, use the very same public platforms, and get exposed to the very same discourses and trends of reasoning, be they religious or not. If they do not talk about religion (saying that they 'never' do so is a surprising exaggeration), this does not mean they are 'ignorant' about each other's beliefs. Talking and verbal exchange are not always sufficient demonstrations of knowledge, let alone accurate knowledge. Sometimes, excessive, un-calculated talking is demonstrative of nothing other than ignorance, in fact. On the other hand, van Ess presumes affirmatively that if any religious contact takes place between the Christians and Muslims in that part of the world, it is certainly going to be in the form of 'controversy.' Why should this be always the case? Why only 'controversy' as the expression of religious, or even non-religious, contact between the Christians and the Muslims of the Levant? Van Ess never explains. The only plausible explanation for van Ess's hypothesis I can suggest is that he, like almost all the classical Western scholars of the history of the Middle East, originates from an eisegetically pre-meditated conception of the Christian–Muslim co-existence in the Orient. "This hypothesis claims that, ever since their presence together in the Middle East's *Sitz im Leben*, the Christians and the Muslims lived as two separate, binarily positioned, enclosed communities, trying to survive in parallel to each other, if not in totally protectionist, self-otherising polarisation with the other. If life circumstances force them to attend to some essential life requirement together, they then interact and intermingle. Otherwise, they just try to deal with their co-existence in the most vigilant, prudent, and pre-emptive manner possible.

In his monumental monograph on Arab Christian theology, Sidney H. Griffith notices the 'Christianity-opposite-Islam' framework which inspires the scholars' tendency to emphasise the defensive, protectionist, and survival-obsessed orientations of Arab Christianity in the land of Islam. These scholars, Griffith relates, were not primarily "much concerned with the history of the development

---

[36] Ibid., p. 100.

and expression of Christian culture and learning in Arabic." They were, rather, interested in "the perilous demographic state" and the decline of the Christians under Islam, as well as "the multiple hardships endured by Jews, Christians and other 'people of the Book' in their experience of life in the special status ... that has recently been designated by the neologism, *Dhimmitude*."[37] Against this concern, Griffith proposes an equal attention to "the story of the religious, cultural and intellectual achievements of the Arabophone Christians."[38] Rather than just viewing Islam as a challenge or a threat, Griffith proposes for consideration that Islam provided the life of the Middle Eastern Christians with the circumstances that "fostered the articulation of a new cultural expression of Christian doctrine, this time in Arabic, and it provided the cultural framework within which the several Christian denominations of the Orient ultimately came to define their mature ecclesial identities."[39]

When it comes to the Arabic theology which the Christian intellectuals (*mutakallims*) developed within that co-existing context with Islam, Griffith seems to be following the scholarship orientation at large in his deeming of that theology a defensive and apologetic response to Islam that is now seen as primarily a 'challenge,' and that eventually led to the creation of a state of '*clash* of theologies' between the Christians and the Muslims.[40] Griffith is so profoundly able and versed a scholar as to realise that the Christian–Muslim interrelations throughout history neither exemplified a state of '*Convivencia*' (which he deems "more legendary than real"[41]), nor does it amount to "a clash of civilizations" state of interrelatedness, like the one that was popularly proliferated by Samuel P. Huntington in the twentieth century.[42] This notwithstanding, Griffith believes that these two religious groups ended up inevitably addressing their private challenges in a state of over-against-ness that manifested as striving "to articulate their confessional identities vis-à-vis one

---

[37] Griffith, *The Church in the Shadow of the Mosque*, p. 1. See for instance, Andrea Pacini, *Christian Communities in the Arab Middle East: The Challenge of the Future* (Oxford: Clarendon Press, 1998) and the populist writings of Bat Ye'or, *The Decline of Eastern Christianity under Islam* (Madison, NJ: Fairleigh Dickinson University Press, 1996) and Bat Ye'or, *Islam and Dhimmitude: Where Civilizations Collide* (Madison, NJ: Fairleigh Dickinson University Press, 2002).

[38] Griffith, *The Church in the Shadow of the Mosque*, p. 2.

[39] Ibid., p. 4.

[40] Griffith, "Between the Cross and the Crescent: Co-Existence, Clash of Theologies and Interreligious Dialogue," pp. 23ff. On this phrase, see also Emilio Platti, "Islam et Occident: *Choc de theologies*?" in *Mélanges*, 24(2000), pp. 347–379.

[41] Ibid., p. 16, nt. 19. See also S. Griffith, *The Church in the Shadow of the Mosque*, pp. 154–155.

[42] Griffith, "Between the Cross and the Crescent: Co-Existence, Clash of Theologies and Interreligious Dialogue," p. 23. On the contrary, Griffith states that "within the World of Islam ... Christians and Muslims participated together in the creation of the classical Islamic civilization. It became a heterogenous, multicultural, cosmopolitan and interreligious commonwealth especially in its heyday in Baghdad and environs from the mid-eighth century to the mid-therteenth [sic] century, which is many ways continued well into the twentieth century in spite of the hardening of the interreligious discourse from the later thirteenth century onward" (ibid., p. 23).

another *ever more sharply*."[43] "Christian thinkers," he says, "who lived among the Muslims were already doing theology with the *challenges* of Islam uppermost in their minds."[44] Christian theology (*Kalām*) is now composed in the language of Islam (Arabic) in order for Christianity to protect itself and make a counter-resisting case for the Christian religion and truth before the antagonistic Muslim offenders. Theology became a medium of clash-centred interaction, developed to serve the Christian scholars' task of fighting back against the most formidable adversaries of the Christian creed, the Muslims.[45] Theology was the Christian theologians' and leaders' reactionary attempts at incubating the Christians from the dangerous enculturation into the world of Islam, as well as the main instrument of their rebuke of those Christians who opted for concealing what in their faith displeased the Muslims and manifested instead an attitude of dissimulation.[46]

Christian Arab theology, then, was conjured up for a twofold purpose: 1) To react apologetically to the challenge of the adversarial religious context that threatened the sheer existence of Christian faith; and 2) To rebuke and expose the dissimulators and weak compromisers among the Christians who, instead of othering themselves from the Muslims and maintaining a dividing line of binary alterity between Christianity and Islam, assimilated to the Muslim culture and surrendered to enculturation by the Muslim world.[47] After all, Arab Christian theology becomes a resource, a historical record, on the development of Muslim theological thought on one side, and on the survival-strife and resisting counter-attack of Christian thought on the other. Both were generated from a *clash* of theologies characteristic, if not definitive, of the relationships between Muslims and Christians in early Islam.[48] One must mention here that Griffith principally concedes that, apart from theology and on the level of communal societal co-existence, the Jews, Christians, and Muslims manifested in their life together "the underlying sibling relationship and history of commonality between the three communities of faith."[49] However, when it comes to intellectual and religious reasoning, Griffith still stands with the confrontation-centred and essentialising orientalist reading, as he still speaks about the Christian theology of the early Islamic era as a conflictual, defensive, and protection-centred strategic side in a 'clash of theologies' or a survival-focused wrestling battle. "The *defense* of the Christian faith against Islam," as Griffith once emphasised, was "the *principal* theological concern" of the polemical texts of *Kalām* in Arabic.[50] The religious and intellectual pressure of Islam over Christian thought,

---

[43] Ibid., p. 23.
[44] Griffith, *The Church in the Shadow of the Mosque*, p. 45. Italics are mine.
[45] Ibid., p. 57.
[46] Ibid., p. 58. These Christian theologians described this dissimulating attitude as hypocrisy (*nifāq*).
[47] Ibid., pp. 59ff.
[48] Ibid., p. 157.
[49] Ibid., p. 5.
[50] S. H. Griffith, "'Malkites,' 'Jacobites' and the Christological Controversies in Arabic in the Third/Ninth-Century Syria," in *Syrian Christians under Islam: The First Thousand Years*, David Thomas (ed.) (Leiden & Boston: Brill, 2001), pp. 9–55, p. 10.

he suggests, has even driven the Arabic-speaking theologians to pragmatically and deliberately obscure the deep theological disagreements between the three main Christian communities in the land of Islam – the Melkites, Jacobites, and Nestorians – trying thereby to create one united defensive front against the common, non-Christian, adversary.[51]

In his turn, David Thomas initially pauses at, and appraises positively, the religiously and culturally pluralist features of the Islamic world, highlighting the high degree of tolerance which the non-Muslims enjoyed in their life among Muslims. This notwithstanding, when it comes to anatomising the theological heritage of the Arabic-speaking Christians and the nature and purpose of such theological activity, Thomas also reads it from binary, protectionist, polarising, and starkly otherising 'Christianity-versus-Islam' and 'clash of theologies' perspectives. He maintains that, though tolerated and undaunted by their *dhimmi* status, the Christian theologians were not allowed to forget the superiority of Islamic faith over Christianity or to feel at ease before the opposing Muslim theologians. On the contrary, they were perpetually "put on the defensive and, rather than initiate discussion, [they are] forced to respond to questions about the legitimacy of [their] beliefs." So much so, Thomas proceeds, that the theological encounter with Muslims always bore "the features of an interrogation in which the Christian is required to account for and justify the points on which he differs from Islam."[52] While their intellectual sophistication in relation to other living and societal aspects were admired and practically valued, the Christians' belief and theological reasoning were not just suspected, but "even despised," Thomas states.[53] This offensive attitude, Thomas concludes, forced the Christians – out of obligation and urgency, not from free choice and cross-pollinational creativity – to conjure discourses of a theological nature to fight back and protect their religious existence from the attacks and hatred of the other, 'superior' belief. And, if achieving this survival priority entails speaking to Muslims by means of their own language and from within their own rationale, this was non-negotiable; a pragmatic option pursued by borrowing Muslim techniques and concepts to develop a weapon that could fire back at Islam from within. Such a strategy, obviously, does not leave any space for potential cross-pollination, reciprocal assimilation, or co-creativity, as Thomas seems to be postulating. After all, the Muslims, according to Thomas, showed no demonstrative sign that they were "persuaded by anything the Christians wrote about their faith." On the contrary, the Muslims "rather sustained series of refutations of all that the Christians attempted to prove."[54]

See also S. H. Griffith, "From Aramaic to Arabic: The Languages of the Monasteries of Palestine in the Byzantine and Early Islamic Periods," in *Dumbarton Oaks Papers*, 51(1997), pp. 11–31.

[51] Griffith, "'Malkites,' 'Jacobites' and the Christological Controversies in Arabic in the Third/Ninth-Century Syria," p. 54. See also G. Troupeau, "Le livre de l'unanimité de la foi de ʿAlī ibn Dāwud al-Arfādī," in *Melto*, 5(1969), pp. 197–219.

[52] David Thomas, "Introduction," in *Christians at the Heart of Islamic Rule*, pp. vii–xiii, pp. vii–viii.

[53] Ibid., p. viii.

[54] Ibid., pp. viii; ix–x.

Be that as it may, Thomas proposes that the Christian *mutakallims* wrote theology as thinkers and authors who "were aware of being outside and [who] tried a little too hard to attain acceptance while taking advantage of Muslim forbearance." They did this, Thomas proceeds, "as those who

> Bear the marks of a social group that knows toleration could tip over into ostracism and persecution ... [thus] they encountered misunderstanding and rejection of their beliefs ... [and] in many small ways they were regularly made to see that their place in Muslim society does not confirm them as integral to it. There was always some distance and uncertainty.[55]

On the level of societal interaction, and within the daily life of co-existence, Thomas is willing to acknowledge a relative amount of influence, even confluence, and exchange between the Muslims and the Christians. He does not even mind stating that these two groups lived side by side as people who "followed similar routines and occasioned only marginal interest in matters of divergent faith and religious observance."[56] When, that is, 'Arab Christianity' is taken to designate the Arab *Christians* as individuals and groups, the integration symbiosis and co-affiliation conditions of existing are embraced and even emphasised.[57] On the contrary, when the attention is shifted toward Arab Christian tradition and theology, the reading of the Christian–Muslim relational dynamic is different, almost starkly opposing. When it comes to theology, the mood is more akin to treating the theological interactions as manifestations of "confrontational exchanges,"[58] implemented in the service of conflict-winning purposes triggered by the polarising pressures Islam exerted on the Christian faith. It is deemed to be the case that the Christians got involved in theological affairs as those who evidently viewed themselves on the defensive and withstanding front, as if they saw themselves as those who were already defeated and over-powered.[59] So, while the Christians' and Muslims' cultural and intellectual attainments on the daily life and societal levels "led them to a measure of collaboration and sharing," the theological and dogmatic stances of Christianity and Islam produced a sort of sustainable and consistent "hostility and confrontation."[60] Eventually, according to Thomas, the persons' and communities' collaborations and sharing were overshadowed by the hostility and divisive antagonism of the theologies. The former "sadly diminished to vanishing point," while the latter, theology-bred, enmity "persisted and grew with menacing rigor," Thomas stipulates.[61]

Known also in this field of study is Richard Bulliet's thesis on Islam's relation to the other non-Muslim groups and communities that inhabited the regions that

---

[55] Ibid., p. x.
[56] David Thomas, "Introduction," in *Christian–Muslim Relations: Bibliographical History; Volume 1 (600–900)*, D. Thomas, B. Roggema, J. P. Monferrer Sala, J. Pahlitzsch, M. Swanson, H. Tuele, and J. Tolan (eds.) (Leiden & Boston: Brill, 2009), pp. 1–19, p. 5.
[57] Ibid., pp. 5–6.
[58] Ibid., p. 7.
[59] Ibid., p. 11.
[60] Ibid., p. 18.
[61] Ibid., p. 19.

Islam had occupied since the beginning of the first/seventh century. Bulliet develops a thesis on the creation and development of an Islamic society, state, and religion in the Middle East. He establishes this thesis on a preconceived causal relationship between the Muslims' exertion of a grand-scale religious comparison, on one side, and the creating and expanding of what became "the Muslim societal history and society," on another.[62] The Muslims realised, Bulliet argues, that their minority status would not enable them to dominate and make their religious belief prevail over the larger populations who followed rival religions. This is why the Muslim rulers imposed, by all means imaginable, including "governmental pressures and mob violence,"[63] a conversion process, at least, Bulliet states, "to a point at which internal threats to the dominance of the Islamic religion became inconceivable."[64] The outcome of this conversion policy ended up being a deliberate and strategic "mass religious or ideological conversion," implemented as a policy of domination for the sake of generating a single, monolithic, and homogenous social existence whose core nature was intolerable of plurality, diversity, and multi-religiosity.

Bulliet concedes evident and inescapable variations between the rates of conversion one can glean from the extant data on the different territories of the Islamic Caliphate. He also recognises the diverse processes by which the conversion policy was applied due to the particular circumstances of every location.[65] However, Bulliet confirms, the conversion policy Islam perpetrated over the other, rival religious groups was nothing but a manifestation of a mass-ideological attack against every non-Muslim for the sake of transforming every human, social existence into an Islamic one alone. Islam achieved its superiority by means of this strategy through achieving conversion by means of "persecution, differential taxation based upon religion, and direct or indirect financial rewards for converts."[66] Within this hermeneutic framework, Bulliet understands conversion not as an act of relinquishing a certain belief and adopting another (something he calls 'religious conversion'). For him, it is primarily a non-theological, social practice of moving "from one religiously defined social community into another."[67] This reading suggests that what we have during early Islam is a to-be-or-not-to-be clash between religious groups over social identities, each representing a religious community striving either to dominate others (the Muslims) or to protect itself from homogenisation attempts perpetrated against them by the Other (the non-Muslims). In such a social

---

[62] Richard W. Bulliet, *Conversion to Islam in the Medieval Period: An Essay in Quantitative History* (Cambridge, USA/London, UK: Harvard University Press, 1979), p. 1. Before exerting this conversion policy, Bulliet suggests, the Muslim conquerors of Persia and Byzantium brought with them to the new scene "something far more primitive and undeveloped, a mere germ of later developments" (ibid.).

[63] As it is suggested in a vein similar to Bulliet's in Nehemia Levtzion, "Conversion to Islam in Syria and Palestine and the Survival of Christian Communities," in *Conversion and Continuity*, pp. 289–311, pp. 197–299.

[64] Bulliet, *Conversion to Islam in the Medieval Period*, pp. 2; 4.

[65] Ibid., pp. 7ff.

[66] Ibid., p. 31.

[67] Ibid., p. 33.

conversion context, according to Bulliet, "a convert might appear as a religious malcontent before conversion, and very likely as a zealot or spiritual athlete after conversion,"[68] for he or she joined the circle of the predominant perpetrator of the mass ideologisation policy: Islam in this case.

Richard Bulliet's thesis was seriously criticised, and his quantitative, name-changing-based methodology of assessing the conversion scale during early Islam have been already deconstructed and contested.[69] Yet, his determining preconception of polarisation and binarism was not, in fact, questioned. The relevance of his thesis to this study is that we find here another intriguing example of a Western scholar departing in his attending to the extant textual and historical data on the early Islamic era from a preconceived idea that divides the *Sitz im Leben* of the Middle East during that era into religiously, socially, and culturally polarised, binary, and dialectically competing communities. One of them is dominant and prevalent politically and militarily over the remaining communities. So, it implements this power in the service of imposing its own religious, societal, and cultural *Weltanschuung* and making it the sole ruling and controlling source of identification. The Muslims, as the powerful side, exert their own values and worldviews by means of imposing a mass-conversion ideology over the Christians and others, threatening thereby their own belief and existence alike. It is the very same clash-centred, polarising, and binary Islam-versus-Christianity preconception played out one more time here.

Some scholars recently took the mass-conversion thesis beyond Bulliet's depiction of a setting wherein the ruling, politically powerful Muslims tried to impose their religious belief and create their own society by means of forcefully, even violently, converting the Christians and followers of other faiths to Islam. This was taken further by talking about this conversion strategy as the cause of a considerable martyrdom-rate among the Christians themselves due to their exposure to a radical religious violence which accompanied the making of the early Muslim world.

This was the thesis which Christian Sahner entertained us with in his 2018 book, *Christian Martyrs under Islam*. In his book, Sahner departs from a confession that the limited body of sources extant in our hands on the early Muslim world leaves us with "a slander base of evidence" on how this world was created.[70] Sahner also states his belief that conversion to Islam was not conducted always "by the sword," and it should not be read as an expression of a consistent, systematic Muslim persecution of Christians.[71] The Christians, he related, were "allowed to live as they wished" as long as they paid the poll tax (*jiziya*) and succumbed to the public law. The relations between Muslims and Christians

---

[68] Ibid., p. 35.

[69] See Thomas A. Carlson, "Contours of Conversion: The Geography of Islamization in Syria, 600–1500," in *Journal of the American Oriental Society*, 135(4), 2015, pp. 791–816. Carlson's direct and targeted response to Bulliet's methodology is explicitly stated on pages 813–814.

[70] Christian C. Sahner, *Christian Martyrs Under Islam: Religious Violence and the Making of the Muslim World* (Princeton & Oxford: Princeton University Press, 2018), p. 4.

[71] Ibid., p. 5.

knew even, as Sahner confesses, a peaceful co-existence and the two communities acted with each other as "members of a shared, increasingly integrated society."[72]

It seems that the above positive note on the Christian–Muslim relations during early Islam is just one of the means Sahner uses in the introduction of his monograph to simply demonstrate his knowledge of the different available views in recent scholarship on that era and its context. The remaining chapters of the book develop a different, opposite reading. Sahner's extended elaborations rather illustrate an early Islamic setting that is almost predominantly centred around episodes of violent Christian persecution and martyrdom. His thesis, as he himself relates, militates against "what Arabs today call *'ayish mushtarak*, or a 'common way of life,' not against a backdrop of constant hostility."[73] For Sahner, what the extant sources report on the Christian martyrdom stories is more likely to be the true case during early Islam, since such violence is what one usually "expects to find when Christians existed under non-Christian powers in the premodern middle East."[74] The history of Christianity in this part of the world, for Sahner, narrates nothing but the story of Christians exposed to violence, death, and persecution from the prevailing Muslim-majority.

Sahner endeavours, then, to prove that the history of Christian–Muslim co-existence is merely a story of a Christian identity-formation "grounded in memories of bloodshed, antagonism toward Islam and hostility to Christians, who switched sides."[75] Sahner builds his claim on the data he finds in the extant hagiographical sources, which he decides to treat as reliable and authentic *historical* recordings. These data, Sahner stipulates, offer reliable evidence of the Christians' and Muslims' existence in a clash-centred and inimical context. The Christian–Muslim scene of early Islam fuelled nothing but reciprocal violence. In this context, the Christians, Sahner relates, advocated a 'no compromise' stance on the surrounding Muslim society and culture, and they violently abused those Christians who converted to Islam:

> The real enemy in many [Christian] sources is not the 'outside outsiders' – that is, the Muslim persecutors. Rather, it is the 'inside outsiders' – that is, the bad Christians who convert to Islam and refuse to go back. The bad Christians who ingratiate themselves with Muslims at court, the bad Christians who refuse to protect the apostasy of their family and friends, and the bad Christians who show too great an interest in the culture of their Muslim neighbors.[76]

Not just the Christians treated the Muslims as 'outsiders' and advocated a "resistance or anti-assimilationist view"[77] (as Sahner says) against their Muslim context. The Muslims also explicitly expressed their rejecting and highly suspicious attitude towards the Christians and their existence in the Caliphate, according to Sahner:

---

[72] Ibid., p. 6.
[73] Ibid., p. 6.
[74] Ibid., p. 5.
[75] Ibid., p. 7.
[76] Ibid., p. 213.
[77] Ibid., p.214.

> Christians were increasingly regarded as a fifth column in Abbasid society, as a source of potential treason that had to be checked and suppressed … Christians were often portrayed as potential back-stabbers of their Muslim neighbors.[78]

Within this inimical self-otherising and antagonistic Christian–Muslim existence, martyrdom became, Sahner concludes, the instrument which the Christians of the Middle East relied on "to configure a sense of community."[79] Sahner even goes so far as claiming that martyrdom is still today the Christian identity-formation's and community-creation's primary means to survive the conditions of existing in the present Muslim-majority Middle East. In a fashion reminiscent of van Ess's naiveté about Beirut, which I pointed to earlier, Sahner ends his book with the following interesting words that merit citation at length:

> Anyone who walks the streets of Beirut today will know that the city is filled with memorials to different martyrs. They are found in practically every neighborhood, whether Christian, Sunnī, Shīʿī or Druze. The Martyrs, most of whom died during the Lebanese civil war of 1975 to 1990, are men and women who perished trying to protect their communities' interests, as well as their particular notion of political and religious truth … In a city of deep internal divisions … martyrs play an essential role in reinforcing grievances of the past. These, in turn, shore up the identity of communities in the present, guaranteeing that no one forgets the bloodshed that created them.[80]

Such an almost caricatured depiction of today's city in the Middle East is not really different from the sentimentalised and almost fantasy-like description of the cities of the Middle East which orientalist travellers, missionaries, and scholars divulged in their writings on the visits they made to the region between the end of the nineteenth and the early twentieth centuries. A careful reader of Christian hagiographical texts from the late antique and early Muslim eras will not, I believe, fail to realise the huge conceptual and practical differences between how the Lebanese use the term 'martyrs' today and how this term was used, and what it described, in the early Islamic era. The Lebanese civil war, as so many Lebanese would inform Sahner, was not a religious war rooted in any clash of faiths over conversion and apostasy, or even over assimilation and resistance pertaining to culture or to beliefs. It would be simplistic to reduce the contemporary language-game into a philological perception from the past. On the other hand, searching for the constructed, pre-tailored imagination of the Christian–Muslim coexistence of Sahner's thesis in a contemporary Middle Eastern city like Beirut is, to say the least, epistemologically unreliable and historically anachronistic. The Middle East is not in a state of *stasis* but in a consistent process of flux. Treating it as a static case in point serves Sahner's attempt at validating his preconceived, eisegetical, orientalist imagination of the Christians' situation in the Muslim world. However, this strategy does not offer

---

[78] Ibid., p. 244. Sahner backs his view up here with ideas borrowed from Jean Maurice Fiey, *Chrétiens syriaques saus les Abbasides surtout à Baghdad (749–1258)* (Louvin: Secrétariat du Corpus SCO, 1980) and Robert Hoyland, *In God's Path: The Arab Conquests and the Creation of an Islamic Empire* (New York & Oxford: Oxford University Press, 2015).

[79] Sahner, *Christian Martyrs Under Islam*, p. 251.

[80] Ibid., p. 251.

an objectively authentic reading of the multi-faceted, multi-layered, and highly changeable Christian–Muslim scene in that region. Finally, what one might experience as the Christian–Muslim context of Beirut should not be stereotypically overgeneralised as demonstrative of the Christian–Muslim life in other cities and parts of the Middle East and the Arab-Muslim world, whether the one of today or the one of early Islam. One must not fall into this trap and get "tempted to imagine that something similar [to Beirut] happened in the medieval period," as Sahner suggests.[81]

Sahner plays the very same game of placing the Middle East in a Procrustean framework also in relation to Syria and the co-existence between the Muslims and the Christians there. In a travelogue-like book he published in 2014 on a visit he made to Syria and on his experience of interacting with people in the antique 'Bab Tomah' neighbourhood in the historical heart of the city, Sahner does his best to prove what seems to be a ready-made conviction which he came to the country carrying in his luggage; namely, that Syria is an ideal example of the prevalence of sectarianism and its belligerent manifestation in the stances of the Syrian Christians and Muslims towards each other. He recalls conversations with Christian and Muslim individuals he either house-shared or intermingled with during his stay in that neighbourhood, focusing in particular on what clearly seems to be selected and maybe re-shaped statements which some of these individuals said. Sahner determinatively detects in these statements unquestionable evidence of "the banal logic of sectarianism in Syria," as well as demonstrations that "it was a sectarianism born of resentment: resentment [from the Muslims] toward the minority as the achiever, as the outlier or dubious foreign loyalties, as the dissenter who rejected the culture of the mainstream." It seems clearly to be the case that the few conversations he had with some individuals were sweepingly morphed into referential representatives of the country's entire society and its diverse communities. The opinion of one Muslim he talked to in Damascus drove Sahner to construct an absolute conclusion about the whole Muslim population in Syria and to determine that there is in this country a sectarianism "born of a certain view of society: a view that said Syria would be better off without its weak parts, left as a monolith impervious to internal division."[82] Sahner does not express any readiness to consider that such a voice might just be one among many other Muslim ones that might be different and that might reflect, rather, a more pluralist point of view. He simply takes such statements as exemplary identifications of the stance of the entire Muslim community of Syria towards minorities. I must say that, if my mother, maternal aunt, maternal uncles, and maternal grandparents, who lived all their childhood and youth in 'Bab Tomah', in their family house near Ananya's Church on the Straight Road, heard Sahner's conclusion, they would have been weary and puzzled, if not appalled, because all the stories I gathered from them on their life with Muslims are totally different (I am not going to even start narrating my childhood and youth stories).

---

[81] Ibid., p. 251.

[82] Christian C. Sahner, *Among the Ruins: Syria Past and Present* (Oxford & New York: Oxford University Press, 2014), p. 73 (pp. 39–76).

Further into his book, Sahner narrates an incident related to the Syrian revolution that began in 2011. He relates that he and other colleagues met, in spring 2013, Syrian opposition activists to discuss the ongoing crisis in Syria. Sahner does not care to hide at all his serious annoyance from one of the Syrian ladies who were in that gathering, when this lady rejected his colleague's claim that there is sectarianism in the country and insisted that the Syrian revolution and opposition includes Syrians from all sects and religious backgrounds.[83] To Sahner's mind, as he bluntly states, the Syrian lady's view was categorically wrong. Believing that he owns the correct view (which he probably built on his pre-tailored and fabricated conclusions from his earlier trip to Syria), Sahner states: "how could someone so deeply involved in the war not see it – the constant retribution by Salafi sheikhs against 'godless' Alawis? The influx of Shiʿi soldiers from places like Lebanon, Iraq, and Iran? The careful targeting of religious sites by both sides in order to fan the flames of war? If these did not count as the signposts of sectarianism, I wasn't sure what did."[84] Sahner does not care to pause at the fact that the examples he invoked do not speak about a Christian–Muslim sectarian faction, but about a Sunnite-Shi'ite political and power-gaining competition that took a very dangerous and bloody twist on Syrian soil. Such a clash influenced the revolution and deformed it (something about which I have written extensive journal articles in Arabic over the past years), but it was not its root and it was not the outcome of sectarianism that ignited the revolution in Syria. The opposition lady was right in stating that the revolution and the opposition against the regime in Syria came from all sects, religions, and factions. I know this because I personally am a Syrian Christian who stood with the revolution and supported it (though I was publicly against the militarisation and Islamisation attempts that ended up aborting the public revolution). The point is that one must not construct an essentialising, collectivist, and hegemonic judgement on a complex context like Syria and its revolution, or its society as well, upon particular, individual views and stances, because the scene is much more complicated than such essentialisation and oversimplification. But, if one approaches from a conviction that the history of that region is characterised solely by binarism, polarisation, divisiveness, and sectarian hatred, one would fall easily into the personal trap of tailoring the context and the situation to fit into an predetermined pattern.

In Sahner's books, we encounter another example of an essentialised imagination and orientalised, binary preconception of the Middle East as a context. The co-existing and interreligious characteristics of life therein are often axiomatically believed to be characteristic of antagonism, binarism, polarisation, radical dialectic otherising, and even lethal violence. It is such a premeditated, eisegetical prejudice which stems from a belief that communal identity-formation in that part of the world is always *binary* and *reactive* and "an assertion of difference in presence to a moment of political stress or cultural uncertainty."[85]

---

[83] Ibid., p. 95 (pp. 95–97).

[84] Ibid., p. 96.

[85] This conviction about the Near East is proliferated in all the essays of an anthology published a few years ago. I cite here from the introduction to this anthology, page xvi.

Such a presumption is totally one-sided. It hinders the realisation of an equally constitutive fact in the history of interreligious identity-formation processes in the Middle East. The religious communities there also evolved their identities in a *symbiotic*, *proactive* manner that demonstrates similarities by means of interrelating with the others. The picture was not always mutilated by polarisation (political or religious) and clashes of self-otherising over-against-ness, as the conventional, essentialising, orientalisation tendency in Western scholarship decided sometimes to conjecture.

Before ending the thread of examples I unfolded in this chapter, I must also point out that one can detect the very same clash-centred and binary reading of the Arab-Eastern Christians' life in the context of Islam in the discourses of scholars who originated from the Middle East and the Arab world, but conducted their professional scholarly career in the Western/European academic field of Oriental Studies. Suffice here to mention one prominent example of these Arab scholars: the famous Egyptian scholar of early Arab-Eastern Christianity in the world of late antique Islam, Fr. Samīr Khalīl Samīr. In an essay he wrote in 2001 on Arab-Eastern Christianity and its history with Islam, Samīr approaches from a philosophical conviction that "the other is always a threat to me."[86] He constructs on this presumption an overview of the Christians' stance on Islam and their life in its shadow during the past fourteen centuries. This is how Samīr describes this interreligious co-existence:

> For almost 14 centuries, Islam represents the grandest challenge against the Eastern Christians; both on the level of daily-life (politically, socially, and ecclesiologically), and on the level of thought and intellect (culturally, dogmatically, and religiously). This re-invokes deeply the discussion over their particular identity. Islam is *as such* 'othering' in all the senses of the word.[87]

Notice here the stark self-otherising language and the emphasis on binarism to such an extent that it presumes that enmity and confrontation are substantially inherent to the existence of the "Christian society in the East" (*al-mujtamaʿ al-Masīḥī fī al-sharq*). This is what Samīr describes as a persistent, endless, confrontational situation that forces this Christian 'society' to "salvage its identity" against diverse 'otherings,' of which the most starkly polarising and antagonistic to Christianity is "the Muslim world with all that it represents, as well as its cultural posture, the Arabic culture."[88] Samīr's voice here mirrors quite clearly the voices I discussed in the Western academic approaches to Arab-Eastern Christianity. It is a from-within version of the very same discourse and orientation.

When, in Western scholarship, one detects the aforementioned insistence on reading the theological and non-theological interactions between Arabic-

---

See Philip Wood (ed.), *History and Identity in the Late Antique Near East* (Oxford & New York: Oxford University Press, 2013).

[86] Samīr Khalīl Samīr, "Lāhūt al-Sharq al-Adna al-Ḥadīth fī al-Ṣilah bayn al-Hawiyyah wal-Ghayriyyah" (The Theology of the Modern Near East. On the Connection between Identity and Othering), *al-Mashriq*, 75(1), 2001, pp. 25–56, p. 55.

[87] Ibid., pp. 28–29.

[88] Ibid., p. 51.

speaking Christian *Kalām* and culture and the Muslim ones as emphatically a 'clash of theologies' and defensive, protectionist societal and cultural operations against the categorically oppositional and permanently binary religion of Islam, one gleans that, in this scholarship, Christian–Muslim relations in the Arab-Muslim world represent religious binarism between two groups who happened to exist in the same habitat, yet decided to exist as two opposite and separate islands within it. One gets the impression that, for these scholars, the Arabic-speaking Christians' *dhimmitude* status was not a contextual, circumstantial situation, but a fateful destiny or even a personal choice. It seems that the hermeneutics of these Christians' theological legacy is predominantly and preconceptually pursued to the eisegetical end of imaging these Christians' theology as self-determined resistance to, and self-alienation from, symbiotic relationality and integration into the Muslim *Sitz im Leben*. As if these Christians are considered to almost be voluntarily reconciled with their *dhimmi* status and clinging to it because they decided to reject any possible cross-pollination or affiliation with those others whom, it is believed, they deemed a categorical, permanent threat to their own faith.

Such a clash-centred, segregationist binarism may not actually be the outcome or the deduced conclusion of the Western (or Westernised) scholars' reading of Arab Christian theological texts of the early Islamic era. It might, rather, be the induced, premediated, and ideologically pre-determined starting point that colours these scholars' reading of texts and determines their conclusions and assessments; before, that is, the hermeneutic and exegetical process even begins. There is in the broader Western scholarly field of reasoning on the Middle East, on the Christians in the Orient, and on the interreligious Middle Eastern context in general an overarching preconception of the Christian–Muslim interaction as "an oppositional clash between two totally antagonistic, separate entities who try to survive [*from* each other, not just alongside each other] by reciprocally excluding and banishing each other."[89] There is also an overwhelmingly prevalent presumption that all the intellectual and theological interactions between the Christians and the Muslims are monolithically demonstrative of apologetics and polemics and almost life-or-death debates over faith. I do find a valuable perception in what Clare E. Wilde said once in her study of the Christian–Muslim interlocutions during early Islam. Wilde is quite accurate in realising that

> Muslim familiarity with Christian and Jewish arguments need not always be set in a controversial environment. For, particularly in the early centuries of Islam,

[89] I have deconstructed this presumption in detail elsewhere. See Najib G. Awad, "Is 'Post-Christendom' a Relevant Hermeneutical Framework to the Situation of the Christians in Greater Syria? Towards a Critical Appraisal," in *Post-Christendom Studies*, 1(2016), pp. 31–76, pp. 39–49; and N. G. Awad, "Interfaith Relations and Middle East Christianity: Beyond Dialogue, Toward Interrelationality," in *Surviving Jewel*, pp. 215–231.

Muslims were encouraged to ask the Jews and Christians for help in filling in the details of the stories of the biblical prophets to whom the Qur'ān alludes.[90]

The abovementioned essentialisation tendency might actually originate from the scholarly leaning towards reducing the historical, cultural, and intellectual intermingling between the Christians and the Muslims in early Islam down to some polemical and antagonistic theological data related to one single dimension among many others; namely, the monolithic, codified, textual one. Once, Uwe Vagelpohl warned about the reductionist, essentialising, text-centred tendency in the contemporary scholarly study of the Greek–Arabic translation movement during early Islam. Vagelpohl related that the studying of Greek and Islamic sciences and philosophy had been often pursued as an investigation of isolated texts belonging to two parallel traditions standing against each other. Vagelpohl warns that such an "isolating perspective" not only presumes that "ideas expressed in a specific linguistic and cultural context retain their meaning unchanged from the moment of their creation and throughout their transfer into different languages." This reductionist essentialisation of the interaction between texts also underestimates "the possibility of a diffusion and mutual inspiration of cultures in the Near East, be they Christian and Islamic or Greek and Arabic."[91]

Uwe Vagelpohl's warning regarding the translation movement applies to the studying of the Christian–Muslim *Kalām* and interreligious theological reasoning during early Islam. One must not essentialise this interaction by reducing it into mere textual attestations and then treat these texts as merely polemical weapons used in the service of self-protectionism and survival. One must not reduce the multi-faceted, multi-layered, and sophisticated co-existence and cross-pollinating history of the Christians and Muslims to a study of textual defence–offence discourses "in isolation from its political and intellectual context,"[92] wherein various valuable forms and incidences of reciprocal social, cultural, and intellectual modification and assimilation of ideas can be detected. Instead of a 'clash of theologies' or even 'one track of influence: from Christianity to Islam' perspectives,[93] there is a need for forging a new approach that notices equally and ponders seriously the moments of reciprocity and cross-pollination between Arabic-speaking Christians and Muslims. Such an option needs to be seriously considered not only on the social, cultural, and ordinary-life levels, but on the level of theological interaction as well. The attention to cross-pollination has started to gain momentum in scholarship over the past few years. Scholars started to re-read the theological and intellectual interactions between Christian and Muslim theologians of the early Islamic era and to pay,

---

[90] Clare E. Wilde, "*Lingua Sacra*? Some Reflections on Christian Discussions of *Faḍā'il al-Suryāniyya* and *I'jāz al-Qur'ān*," in *Eastern Crossroads: Essays on Medieval Christian Legacy*, Juan Pedor Monferrer-Sala (ed.) (Piscataway, NJ: Gorgias Press, 2007), pp. 61–82, p. 80.

[91] Uwe Vagelpohl, *Aristotle's Rhetoric In the East: The Syriac and Arabic Translation and Commentary Tradition* (Leiden & Boston: Brill, 2008), p. 2.

[92] Ibid., pp. 1–2.

[93] Such an approach that emphasises that Islam derived all its theological reasoning methods from Christianity was stressed by scholars like Harry Wolfson, Henry Sweetman, Shlomo Pines, Robert Hoyland, and others.

this time, more piercing attention to the cross-pollinating state of existence which these theological interlocutions were generated from and which they themselves originated. Within this reading framework, it is now believed that what explains the situation are not hermeneutic notions like 'influence,' 'defence,' 'polemic,' 'resistance,' 'survival,' or even 'binarism' and 'dialectic.' What does this hermeneutically well is, rather, the key notion of 'diffusion.' This notion invites us to realise symbiotic, correlational, and inter-connected trends of co-existing and co-reasoning between various theologians from different traditions, without hierarchical or superiority-centred orientations or pre-conditions.[94]

Arabic-Eastern Christianity in Today's Western Imagination

In 2011, Lura Robson from Portland State University produced an excellent paper on how Christianity in the Arab world is conceived in the Western academic and public imagination today. Robson accurately notices the relegation of the topic of Christians in the Arab world to the far margin of interest and investigation in the West, not just in the Western scholarship and imagination of that part of the world during the nineteenth century, but also until this very present era. If Arab-Eastern Christianity is ever paid attention to, Robson relates, such attention remains confined to the historians of religion and their research on the ecclesiastical history restrictively at the divinity schools or the theological seminaries. And, if one spots public attention to the Arab-Eastern Christians in the Middle East, such attention would be journalistic in nature, and it would draw a caricatured, dramatised image of them as "victims of their Muslim overlords, in need of rescue by the West."[95]

Highly valuable and worth pondering in Robson's essay is the conglomeration of reasons she believes lie behind the negligence of Arab-Eastern Christianity in today's Western academic sphere. These reasons are summarised in the points below:[96]

1. The Arab-Eastern Christians' experience is overlooked because Western historians seem to be hesitant to use the 'religious comparison' strategy to analyse the situation of the minority groups in the Middle East. They seem to be afraid that such a comparative analysis would simply mirror the Western prejudiced view of that region "as a hotbed of primitive religious feelings" or unintentionally "fuel a minority local perspective that views religion as the basis for all identity."[97]
2. Middle Eastern historians are forced by ideas-creating and decision-making centres in the West to produce analyses that circle around nationalist and regional focuses, and not religious ones. This eventually originates historical studies that

[94] See James E. Montgomery, "Islamic Crosspollination," in *Islamic Crosspollinations: Interactions in the Medieval Middle East*, Anna Aksoy, James E. Montgomery, and Peter E. Pormann (eds.) (Exeter: Gibb Memorial Trust, 2007), pp. 148–193.
[95] Laura Robson, "Recent Perspectives on Christianity in the Modern Arab World," in *History Compass*, 9/4(2011), pp. 312–325, p. 312.
[96] Ibid., pp. 313–315.
[97] Ibid., p. 313. See also Sami Zubaida, "Islam and Secularization," in *Asian Journal of Social Science*, 33/3(2005), pp. 438–448.

"do not acknowledge the existence of Christian communities as distinct groups within the nation."[98]

3. The lingering prevalence of the stereotypical imagination of a permanent "hostility between Christian and Muslim minorities and an oppressive monolithic Muslim majority" prevent any motivation towards revising such a clichéd belief by re-reading the histories of the Arab Christian communities.[99]

4. There is a controversial, presumptive belief that the Arab-Eastern Christians had close alliances with Western imperialism. Therefore, they just echo and replicate in their existence, views, and discourses the Christianity of their 'patrons and protectors.' This also detrimentally "contributed to the dearth of scholarship on the Arab Christian experience."[100] As if it is believed that studying Arab Christianity would add no new knowledge or a different understanding to what the West already knows of Christianity. It would be just encountering a replica, let alone a poorly mimicked imitation, of what the West is the original *archē* of.

5. Arab-Eastern Christianity has been, and still is, treated as just "an outpost of Western imperial interests than an authentically Middle Eastern entity worthy of close study."[101] According to Robson, the antagonistic stance on Islam in the West has certainly enhanced the lack of willingness to pay attention to Middle Eastern Christian experience.

6. There is a reductionist, almost ideologised, imagination which has stigmatised Western scholarship's study of Arab Christianity since the nineteenth century. As I showed in the previous sections, the modern Arab Christians, like their ancestors, are "conditioned primarily by a long pre-modern experience of religious resistance to Islam."[102]

Laura Robson plausibly suggests that the above listed factors are the main reasons behind the continuous relegation of Arab-Eastern Christianity to the far margin of scholarly and academic interests in the West. Those who work in the academic world in Western countries would find considerable truisms also in her realisation that:

> Even in the context of global Christian studies ... Arab Christians have been largely ignored. The field focuses primarily on Christian communities spawned by Western Protestant and Catholic mission efforts ... [this approach's] underlying assumption is that Christianity has Western roots. The histories of the various Arab Christian communities, who are mainly not converts and who profess an indigenous, non-Western form of Christianity, do not fit easily within this paradigm ... [Added to this factor,] there is the broad assumption [also permeating global Christian studies]

[98] Robson, "Recent Perspectives on Christianity in the Modern Arab World," p. 313. See also Usama Makdisi, *Artillery of Heaven: American Missionaries and the Failed Conversion of the Middle East* (Ithaca: Cornell University Press, 2008).

[99] Robson, "Recent Perspectives on Christianity in the Modern Arab World," p. 314. See also Robert M. Haddad, *Syrian Christians in Muslim Society: An Interpretation* (Princeton, NJ: Princeton University Press, 1970) and R. B. Betts, *Christians in the Arab East: A Political Study* (Athens: Lycabettus Press, 1975).

[100] Robson, "Recent Perspectives on Christianity in the Modern Arab World," p. 314.

[101] Ibid., p. 314.

[102] Ibid., p. 314.

> that Islam is a – perhaps the – primary unifying factor justifying the area of study of the Middle East … the Middle East is [imagined as] a reasonably homogenous Muslim region that can usefully be placed in opposition to a predominantly Christian West.[103]

Being an Arab-Eastern Christian scholar who has been living in the Western world and working in the academic sphere on both sides of the Atlantic Ocean for the past quarter of a century, I do find many valid and accurate observations in Laura Robson's analysis. I also agree with her perception of a change in orientations and approaches toward this Christianity, the birth and growth of which one can spot upon the horizon of scholarly studies in Western academia. There has recently started a tendency among scholars to take more seriously than ever before the fact that the Arab-Eastern Christian communities are not exactly coherent and homogenous, and they are actually perpetually impacted by their homeland's ever-changing conditions. They are also not living in isolation from their Muslim compatriots in a cantonising-like state of protectionism. On the contrary, as Robson eloquently states, "Arab Christians have forged their communal identities and practices through constant and active engagement with their local, regional and national communities – an important re-integration of Arab Christian narratives into the broader history of the region, and a reminder of the heterogeneity of the Arab Christian historical experience."[104]

During the past two decades, the Byzantinist and John of Damascus scholar Daniel Sahas has also developed a perceptive reading of the Christian–Muslim co-existing dynamic during the early Islamic era. He demonstrated in various writings that the Christians of Syria-Palestine did not at all consider themselves crypto-Byzantines struggling to survive in their fateful existence in the land of Islam. Far from being the case: these Christians, Sahas argues, believed in their belonging and affiliation to the Arab-Islamic context of the newly rising Muslim empire. Sahas goes as far as highlighting the central Christian figure of John of Damascus and his family as an exemplary representation of this Christian integration into the Arab-Muslim world.[105] Sahas even suggests that around this central Christian figure and his legacy a *circle* of "ideological and reform-minded Christian movement" was formed during the Umayyad and the Abbasid eras. This circle contained those exponents of John's strong affiliation to the Arab-Muslim world of Syria-Palestine and his belief in the integrative and symbiotic connection between Christianity and Islam in that region. This circle of Christians refused to consider itself an alien and estranged group who belonged secretly to the Byzantine world and were obliged to carve for

---

[103] Ibid., p. 315.

[104] Ibid., p. 317.

[105] See Daniel J. Sahas, *John of Damascus on Islam. The 'Heresy of the Ishmaelites'* (Leiden: Brill, 1972) and D. J. Sahas, *Byzantium and Islam: Collected Studies on Byzantine–Muslim Encounters* (Leiden & Boston: Brill, 2022), pp. 291–381. I have also discussed at length and demonstrated John of Damascus's deep rootedness and total affiliation to the Arab-Muslim life-setting and contextual character of the Umayyad world in Syria-Palestine during the sixth and seventh centuries A.D. See N. G. Awad, *Umayyad Christianity: John of Damascus as a Contextual Example of Identity Formation in Early Islam* (Piscataway, NJ: Gorgias Press, 2018).

themselves a sheltering abode in the world of Islam. This circle refused to "function with a cultural, linguistic and ideological vacuum," and operated, instead, self-consciously and self-assuredly as genuine members in the Arab-Muslim society of Syria-Palestine.[106] The methodology this Syro-Palestinian circle implemented towards Islam was one of inclusiveness and cross-pollination, which, Sahas emphasises, was a methodology demonstrative of "distinction not only from that of the Western but even from that of the Constantinopolitan Christendom."[107] What we have in John of Damascus and this Syro-Palestinian circle is an example of a Christianity that was "deeply rooted in the Syriac-Arab culture" of early Islam, and the members of this circle "exerted a sense of pride in [this] Syriac-Arab culture" and were feeling at home even within the Arab environment.[108]

What Robson and Sahas are inviting Western scholarship to pause at is the necessity of re-assessing and re-reading the Western narrative of the Christian–Muslim interrelations in the Arab-Eastern context, whether in the past or the present. It is an invitation to realise that the story of interreligious connections and co-existence in the Eastern world must not be read through the lens of the Latin-European history of Christian–Muslim relations. The story of the Christian–Muslim co-existence in the East centres around heterogeneity, integration, and active engagement more than the Western-Latin one. This is not just evident in the past, as Daniel Sahas ably demonstrates. It is also quite manifest in the present. Contemporary Arab-Eastern Christian scholars and theologians are a lively example of this heterogeneity, integration, and active engagement in the life of Arab-Eastern Christianity. The examples of theologians I shall be discussing in the ensuing parts of this study clearly demonstrate the depth and full-scale rootedness of contemporary Arab-Eastern theologians in their indigenous Arab-Muslim *Sitz im Leben* in the world. Their theological trends of reasoning, as I will demonstrate later, echo loudly their proclamation of the authentic Arab and Middle Eastern nature of their historical experience, religious discourses, and theological *Weltanschauung*. The dominant majority of the theological examples I will present will categorically defy the Western journalistic-like depiction of Middle Eastern Christianity as existing "in an irreversible state of decline" and clinical state of oppression and jeopardy. The theologians I shall introduce reject this caricatured construction, and they deconstruct in various manners the "longstanding narrative of Arab Christian victimhood and marginalization"[109] in their particular theological and intellectual discourses. Each one of them conjures a theologically coloured discourse to demonstrate that the Arab-Eastern Christian communities they belong to are "vibrant communities committed to active and creative participation in regional, national and local politics."[110]

---

[106] Sahas, *Byzantium and Islam*, pp. 331, 337.
[107] Ibid., p. 349.
[108] Ibid., pp. 350–351.
[109] Robson, "Recent Perspectives on Christianity in the Modern Arab World," p. 318.
[110] Ibid., p. 318.

Concluding Remarks

The above analysis invites us to pause at the possibility of finding some Western scholarly readings of the Christian–Muslim Middle Eastern context that approach it as reflective of one religious community suffering by another and striving to survive, maintain its existence and faith, and fight for its religious validity against consistent intellectual, verbal, societal, religious, even physical, violence and oppression. This might be reminiscent of Homi Bhabha's speech about the discursive reading of other cultures and individuals on the basis of an essentialised, pre-fabricated, "authorized version of otherness."[111] But, in my view, it might also conversely reflect an implicit, intrinsic tendency to legitimise authorised versions of one's own *self*. In other words, we might be having in these discourses a reading of an imagined, rather than real, 'Other' in the service of confirming a Western, interreligious self-perception shaped after the conventional stance on Islam that one finds in the history of the interactions and altercations between Islam and the Christian Latin, European world.

Such a preconceived background and discoursing strategy, I reckon, must be contested, and its applicability to the context of Arab-Eastern Christianity must be seriously questioned. Some scholars today have already started to pursue such an interrogative scrutiny of this alleged presumption and to argue that:

> Early Islamic society stands out clearly in … its pluralism and open-mindedness to an extent rarely found in later Islam and totally absent from the medieval European scene. Muslim [but also Christian] authors were always fascinated with religious issues, and even under the evolving Sunni [and creedal orthodoxies] their curiosity in this field was unabated. They asked questions, searched for available written material, compared verses from the Quran with verses in the Bible, or words in Hebrew with words in Arabic, and held sessions in which members of various sects and religions took part and analyzed rationally, in an intellectual atmosphere, different tenets of belief … these discussions were very different from later, court enforced disputations in medieval Europe … [and they] are mentioned in detail in Muslim, Christian, and Jewish sources.[112]

In 2012, Andrew Sharp wrote a valuable monograph on the stances of the Christian Orthodox tradition on Islam throughout history and in today's world. At the conclusion of his study, Sharp makes the following declaration, which is worth pondering:

> Orthodox Christians have far too long listened to those who would turn historical relations between their ancestors and Muslims into a caricature of hatred, competition, and intolerance. In order to come to terms with who they are in the present, they must rediscover a more accurate and positive view of the relationship between Orthodox Christianity and Islam, so as to counter the fixation on the

---

[111] Homi K. Bhabha, *The Location of Culture* (London: Routledge, 1994), p. 88.

[112] Hava Lazarus-Yafeh, "Preface," in *The Majlis: Interreligious Encounters in Medieval Islam*, H. Lazarus-Yafeh, M. R. Cohen, S. Somekh, and S. H. Griffith (eds.) (Wiesbaden: Harrassowitz, 1999), pp. 7–12, p. 8.

negative aspects of that relationship espoused by many over the past couple of centuries.[113]

Sharp, then, proceeds to postulate that the history of Christianity in the shadow of Islam reveals to us that "the further Christians were from Constantinople, the more positive their attitude toward Islam and relations with Muslims, that being particularly the case among Arab, Coptic, and Syrian Christians within the Empire and under Muslim rule."[114] This is what the intellectual, theological, philosophical, and cultural interaction between the Christians and the Muslims in the Middle East also demonstrates and emphasises. The passion of the Arabic-speaking Christians and Muslims alike for knowledge and theological learnedness drove them to make their intellectual interests and educational attempts travel across the dividing confessional borders. These theologians' influence and borrowing *habitus* exceeded one-sidedness and were reciprocally experienced. Reading Arab Christian theology from the perspective of cross-pollination enables us to perceive that this theology was historically inter-contextual and trans-contextual in nature. It is designative not of a historical scene of binarism, enmity, polarisation, and obsession with self-otherising, but one that "encompasses wider cultural connections" beyond narrow and segregationist dynamics of reception and rejection.[115] Early Islamic era's Arab Christian theology, as well as Muslim theology, for that matter, manifest before us a genuine, cross-pollinating context of ideas- transmission that is pursued via regularised, back-and-forth penetration.[116] Theology here is not a manifestation of 'culturation,' 'enculturation,' or 'counter-culturation.' It is expressive of a 'transculturation' process that is evenly co-created and elicited by the theologians of both religions.[117]

It is this cross-pollinating methodological approach to Arabic-speaking theology, in its Christian and Muslim versions alike, that is needed in contemporary scholarship to deconstruct any potentially essentialising notions and preconceptions of theology and theological identity-forming traditions. It invites scholars to travel beyond what has been construed as statically established theological, intellectual, and religious dividing boundaries between Muslim and Arab Christian *Kalām* traditions.

---

[113] Andrew Sharp, *Orthodox Christians and Islam in the Postmodern Age* (Leiden & Boston: Brill, 2012), p. 235.

[114] Ibid., p. 236.

[115] Ibid., p. 138 and Ruth HaCohen, "Intercontextual Musical Currents and Performative Traditions in Twentieth-Century Palestine/Israel and Germany," in *Comparative Studies in the Humanities*, pp. 15–39, pp. 15–16. See also Jose Medina, *Speaking from Elsewhere: A New Contextualist Perspective on Meaning, Identity and Discursive Agency* (Albany, NY: State University of New York Press, 2006).

[116] Montgomery, "Islamic Crosspollination," p. 163.

[117] Ibid., pp. 164–165. See also on transculturation, Mary Louis Pratt, *Imperial Eyes: Travel Writing and Transculturation*, 2nd. ed. (New York & London: Routledge, 2008).

4. Arab-Eastern Christian Theology, Past and Present

Introduction

The Arabic-speaking theological tradition of Eastern Christianity in the past (during early Islam) is different from the Arabic-speaking theological discourses this Christianity produced in the present (contemporary Arab world). One, therefore, must speak about them as two distinctive theological trends within the historical biography of this Christianity. One can even go as far as saying that, except for some relative rate of connectedness, the Arabic-speaking theology of the past and that of the present are considerably different and hardly related. The theological tradition might linger, for certain circumstantial purposes, within the memory of contemporary Eastern Christians. It hardly, nevertheless, plays a constitutive or evident role in shaping the mind of these Christians or grounding the theological discourses they develop.

In the ensuing pages, I shall discuss Arabic-speaking Eastern theology as two distinguished phenomena. One goes back to the early Islamic centuries (first/seven to eighth/fourteenth centuries), while the other represents some main theological voices one can find in the present context of Eastern Christianity in the Arab world (twentieth to twenty-first centuries).

Arabic-Speaking Eastern Theology in the Past

The theological tradition of this early Islamic era is essentially associated with, if not totally defined as, an intellectual genre of theological reasoning called 'the science of *Kalām*.' '*Kalām*' was the nomenclature of a particular rational, theological, systematic discourse that was cross-boundary, cross-pollinating, and interreligious in nature. One can validly and straightforwardly encounter in that context Christian, Muslim, and Jewish, or even freethinking (atheist-like), *Kalām* discourses exchanged and corrected during that era. *Kalām*, in that sense, was not a religious discourse, but a trans-religious and trans-cultural one. It was not an intellectual property or trademark of one community, belief, sect, or school. Yet, one can still speak about different *Kalām* discourses that touch upon theological subjects from the perspectives and distinctive doctrinal and scriptural perceptions that are characteristic of each belief system. Sometimes, the theologisation activity called *Kalām* was developed to highlight the belief components that make one religion different from others: a theological, rational demonstration (*Kalām*) to articulate what makes the Christian faith other than Islam, Judaism, Manicheism, Buddhism, etc. Alternatively, it was developed to demonstrate that a certain faith's truth and value are equal to those of other beliefs, or even exceed them and rise rationally above them: Christian faith and its doctrinal components (e.g. Trinity, Christology, Crucifixion, Incarnation, soteriology etc.) are equally rational and logically plausible, if not more rational or the most rational, compared to those of other beliefs.

Etymologically speaking, *Kalām* in Arabic means 'speech,' 'talk,' or 'words'; and *Mutakallim* means 'one who makes the speech,' 'one who gives the talk,' or 'one who utters the words.' Thus, the opposite of *takallama* (talked) in Arabic is *sakata* (remained silent).[1] This term seems to have been in use long before the words *Kalām* and *mutakallimūn* became technical names of a particular genre of reasoning and knowledge. The Muslim scholar Saʿd al-Dīn Masʿūd al-Taftazānī (d. 1390 A.D.) suggests, for example, that the term '*Kalām*' was used in threefold manner in the early time of Islam: 1) to designate any discussion of separate issues; 2) to refer to God's speech (*Kalām Allah*); and 3) as an expression of talking about or discussing religious matters in a logical and philosophical manner to impress opponents.[2] The contemporary Egyptian scholar Muhammad Abdel-Haleem seems to be sceptical about *al-Taftazānī*'s exposition, and he deems it anachronistic in nature, as it post-dates "the [historical] appearance of '*'Ilm al-Kalām*' as an established science in the second/eighth century." He seems also to be unsatisfied with that explanation in Western scholarship that searches for a non-Islamic origin of the concept of '*Kalām*' that is borrowed from Syriac or Greek, like '*dialexis*' and '*logos*.'[3]

In his turn, the Jewish scholar Shlomo Pines relates that the terms '*Kalām*' and '*Mutakallimūn*' were used in their earliest history to express persuasion and debate within political frameworks. As an example of this use, he invokes an incident from the second/eighth century on the eve of the birth of the Abbasid rule, when the chief of the Abbasid insurrection against the Umayyads, Abū Muslim, sent convoys to proliferate religious and political propaganda among the inhabitants of the city of Merv about him and his army. These convoys were described as '*Mutakallimūn*.'[4] Pines seems to be backing up his understanding of the origin of the use and connotations of '*Kalām*' by something said by the Muslim philosopher, Abū Naṣr Muḥammad al-Fārābī (872–951 A.D.), who relates that '*Kalām*' is associated with the task of "supporting and triumphing for" (*al-nuṣrah*).[5] '*Kalām*' names the speech that supports a certain belief, whether this belief is rational or not, al-Fārābī suggests. For, some *mutakallims*, he states, defend the convictions of the sects (*ārā' al-milal*) by demonstrating that such convictions must not be examined by opinions or scrutiny, or even human reasons (*laysa sabīluhā an tumtaḥan bil-ārā' wa al-ruwiyyah wal-'uqūl al-insiyyah*).[6] Overall, al-Fārābī seems to strictly associate *Kalām* with

[1] See Muhammad Abdel-Haleem, "Early *Kalām*," in *The Routledge History of Islamic Philosophy*, Oliver Leaman and Sayyid H. Nasr (eds.) (Abingdon: Routledge, 1995), pp. 71–88, p. 71.

[2] Ibid., p. 72.

[3] Ibid., p. 72. See also on this Michael Cook, "The Origins of *Kalām*," in *Bulletin of the School of Oriental and African Studies*, 43(1980), pp. 32–43, pp. 42–43.

[4] Shlomo Pines, "A Note on an Early Meaning of the Term *Mutakallim*," in *Israel Oriental Studies*, 1(1971), pp. 224–240.

[5] See Abū Naṣr al-Fārābī, *Iḥṣā' al-'Ulūm* (Enumerating the Sciences) (Beirut: *al-Īnmā'* Nationalist Center, 1991), p. 39.

[6] Ibid., p. 41.

defensiveness and support of a certain cause and granting it triumph over other causes.

It is possible that Shlomo Pines alludes to the same perception when he associates the earliest use of '*Kalām*' and '*Mutakallims*' with the practice of propagating and defending the Abbasid version of Islam on the political, social, and institutional levels of that era. This might also be what inspires Alexander Treiger in his chasing after the origins of *Kalām*. He seems to have also read Pines and al-Fārābī, and he is following suit in emphasising the apologetic, defensive, or triumphalist orientations and considering them definitive of the early versions of the meaning of *Kalām*. '*Kallama*,' the verb in Arabic, means, according to him, to talk with *opponents* (not interlocutors) by asking questions and reducing their positions to meaningless alternatives.[7]

Classical in Western scholarship is Harry Wolfson's thesis on the origin and meaning of *Kalām* as a theological phenomenon. Instead of tracing the earliest usages of the Arabic terms and their etymological connotations, Wolfson focuses on the use of the term '*Kalām*' when a specified science of theological reasoning called '*'Ilm al-Kalām*' was created in the Abbasid context of the second/eighth to third/ninth centuries. Wolfson concedes the basic meaning of '*Kalām*' as 'words' and 'speech.' He, then, instantly moves into arguing that the entire science of *Kalām* is a Muslim derivation or importation from Christian theology, especially in the latter's rational versions that were shaped after Greek philosophy. So, '*Kalām*' became the translated Arabic term of the Greek philosophers' use of the technical term '*Logos*' to speak about 'word,' 'reason,' and 'argument.' This trafficking of '*Kalām*' from being descriptive of a 'manner of speech' or 'strategic activity' into the name of any special branch of learning that involves logical (Neo-Platonic and Aristotelian) rationalisation turned those who practise it (the *mutakallims*) into the masters or exponents of a specific, rational, logical, and demonstrative branch of learning.[8] This makes '*Kalām*' that genre of reasoning that aims at: 1) developing a unified system of belief out of the various texts of the religious books and dogma; and 2) to face and respond to what was deemed a 'heretical' interpretation of faith. Wolfson's understanding seems to echo something the Muslim historiographer ʿAbdulraḥmān Ibn Khaldūn (1332–1406 A.D.), once related when he opined that '*Kalām*' is the discussion of these articles of faith (*al-'aqā'id al-Imāniyyah*) that are constitutive of the content of theological reasoning.[9]

Wolfson is not the first to suggest Christian (philosophical) roots to '*Kalām*' in early Islam. Christian H. Becker already argued for this at the beginning of the last century.[10] Similarly, Josef van Ess confirmed the extra-Islamic origin of

---

[7] See Alexander Treiger, "Origins of *Kalām*," in *The Oxford Handbook of Islamic Theology*, Sabine Schmidtke (ed.) (Oxford: Oxford University Press, 2014), in: https://www.oxfordhandbooks.com/view/10.1093/oxfordhb/9780199696703.001.0001/oxfordhb-9780199696703-e-001 [accessed 4.8.2021].

[8] Harry A. Wolfson, *The Philosophy of the Kalām* (Cambridge, Mass. & London, UK: Harvard University Press, 1976), p. 1.

[9] Ibid., p. 4.

[10] Christian H. Becker, "Christliche Polemikund islamische Dogmenbildung," in *Zeitschrift für Asseriologie und verwandle Gebiete*, 26(1912), pp. 175–195.

this theological genre in his 1977 publication.[11] Van Ess seems also to be reading '*Kalām*' as a genre of theological defensive and *nuṣrah*-centred discourse. He uses this presumption as an evidential indicator of the Christian origins of '*Kalām*.' Michael Cook notices that van Ess finds Arab *Kalām* reminiscent of a "long tradition of Christian writings instructing the faithful in how to argue their cause."[12] In an ensuing essay, van Ess also argues that the Greek model of dialectic argument (*dialexa*), which he believes to be attested in the Christian patristic theology, is similarly the root of *Kalām*.[13] In his study of van Ess's mentioned essay and proposal, Michael Cook seems to be suspicious about Greek-speaking Christianity's influence on Muslim *Kalām*, or on *Kalām* during the Abbasid era. Cook questions this hypothesis by arguing that the early Muslims of that era were more intellectually in touch with Syriac than Greek Christianity. Thus, for him, Syriac, rather than the Greek, is more plausibly "the immediate source of Muslim borrowing."[14] If such borrowing from Syriac tradition took place, Cook opines, it was "most likely to have taken place in Syria."[15] Though Cook does not cast away the borrowing option per se, he sheds serious doubts on our ability to find definitive evidence to absolutely confirm it. He seems, rather, willing to concede that *Kalām* in early Islam was also a unique and underived genre that had its own, built-in originality. Cook expresses this in the following words:

> I subscribe to the view that the raw materials of [Islamic] culture are for the most part old and familiar, and that it is in the *reshaping* of these materials that the distinctiveness and interest of the phenomenon [of *Kalām*] resides.[16]

It is my belief that the question of 'from where did Islam borrow, or was inspired by, *Kalām*?' needs not at all to be the central enquiry. This question hides behind it a presumption that Christianity and Islam were two religions standing in parallel to each other, in a binary tangential positioning as two separate yet not necessarily antagonistic sides. This view is not quite an accurate reading of all the dimensions of the real *Sitz im Leben* of that era. It is my belief that the relation between Christianity and Islam at that period was not a one-way trajectory, nor was it shaped after a 'dependence-influence' equation. The context was far more complex, cross-pollinating, cross-boundary, and correlational in nature. It was one that was shaped after a cross-religious, two-way track of communion and co-existence. Neither did the Christians slavishly borrow *Kalām* from the Muslims, nor were the Muslims inspired by *Kalām* by a direct, dictating influence from the Christians. Both theologians from the two religious campaigns reciprocated what they equally learned and similarly

---

[11] Josef van Ess, *Anfänge muslimischer Theologie: Zwei Antiqadaritische Traktate aus dem ersten Jahrhundert der Higra* (Wiesbaden: Feranz Steiner Verlag, 1977).
[12] Ibid., pp. 16ff; 22; 24; 36; 104. See also Cook, "The Origins of *Kalām*," p. 33.
[13] Van Ess, "Disputationspraxis in der islamischen Theologi. Eine vorläufege Skizze," in *Keleine Schriften by Josef van Ess*, Hinrich Biesterfeldt (ed.) (Leiden & Boston: Brill, 2018), vol. 2, pt. V, pp. 911–947.
[14] Cook, "The Origins of *Kalām*," p. 34.
[15] Ibid., p. 40.
[16] Ibid., p. 43.

adopted from Greek philosophy and late antiquity's intellectual and cultural heritage. *Kalām* is not the byproduct of influence and borrowing *habitus* practised by one faith in its interaction with another faith. *Kalām* is the outcome of an intellectual cross-pollination between two theological traditions who both were re-born and baptised by the very same intellectual water of Greek philosophical reasoning.

The above initially demonstrates that the question of the origin of *Kalām* and 'who derived it from whom, or from what?' is still unsettled. The point I try to make here is that more important, than the enquiry into origin and source in relation to Arab-Eastern Christianity is the reason that led the Christians to develop such a theological discourse and no other during that period. Sidney Griffith attends to this enquiry in his *The Church in the Shadow of the Mosque*. He suggests that the Arab-Eastern Christians of that Islamic era found themselves living within a new political, social, and cultural milieu. Therefore, the Christians developed a theology in Arabic, wherein they "articulated their Christian doctrines in parallel, almost in tandem, with the evolving patterns of Islamic religious thought in the same period."[17] According to Griffith, these Christians wanted to demonstrate the rational calibre and logical tenability of Christian faith in religious idioms and language games that are now inherent to the lingua franca of their *Sitz im Leben*: Arabic and primarily Arabic. The reliability and plausibility of the Christian *Kalām* discourse are no more decidedly based on a criterion derived from *ad intra* Christian dogmatic and scriptural foundations. The Christians needed now to develop a *Kalām*-like theology, the plausibility, authenticity, and meaningfulness of which is measured by the *ad extra* criterion of rational verifiability that is applied to the *Kalām*-like theology of the Muslim (and Jewish) *mutakallims*. This is why Christian Arabic-speaking theology in its earliest forms, whether doctrinal or scriptural, philosophical or spiritual, was frankly and predominantly "dialogical in form and literary structure."[18] It is always a theology that is crudely a talk (*kalām*) on 'God-talk' with an '*other*,' with the *different* other.

This is why the extant *Kalām* texts depict either 1) Christian theologians standing before Muslim nobilities (caliphs or princes) and theologians in the court of the Muslim ruler (*majlis)*; 2) theological explanations of Christian doctrines written after a 'questions-and-answers' model of interlocution; 3) theology written and developed via letters exchanged either between a Christian theologian and Muslim one, or between two Christians, one seeking the wisdom and theological knowledge of the other to respond to enquiries the seeker is challenged with by a Muslim; or 4) samples of theological defensive explanations of Christian doctrines composed in a systematic and philosophical manner (*maymar/mayāmir*) to discuss all issues raised between the Christians and the Muslims over common items of belief (e.g. God, divine attributes, religious texts, free will, prophethood, reason, etc.).[19] In all these forms of Christian Arab *Kalām*, the intentions of the Christian writers, Griffith concludes,

[17] Griffith, *The Church in the Shadow of the Mosque*, p. 75.

[18] Ibid., p. 76.

[19] Ibid., pp. 77–92.

"were to commend the credibility of the Christian [doctrines] in the very idiom of the Islamic religious discourse of their day." This meant, Griffith proceeds, that the theology that was originally articulated in Greek or Syriac "came to be translated and transposed into the Arabic discourse of the intellectual world of Islam, in a design and vocabulary very different from that of the patristic era and largely unfamiliar to Christians outside of the Islamic world."[20] It is certainly the case that such an Arabisation of Christian theological legacy had (and maybe still has) direly challenging and inerasably transforming consequences that deserve our scrutiny to see whether what took place in the Arab Christian theologisation enterprise was a case of enculturation, acculturation, or deculturation, and what could be the potential ramifications of these on this Christianity.[21]

The careful anatomisation of the Arab Christian *Kalām* demonstrates that this theological tradition manifests the following central characteristics and components:

1 – *Reason-centred Demonstration*: The Christian Arabic texts of *Kalām*, as well as the Muslim and Jewish ones, tell us that theology during early Islam circled around questions related to epistemological foundations: what is the foundation of the belief in the truthfulness and plausibility of the religious message?[22] The Arab, Christian, Muslim, and Jewish *Kalām* responds to this enquiry by methodologically relying on a philosophical, deductive reasoning, wherein reason (*'aql*) not only verifies the truth of faith and its textual message, it also *examines* and exposes it to logical and rational scrutiny.[23] The centralisation of '*'aql*' (reason) in *Kalām* is grounded in the following conviction: the purpose of developing a logically argued theology is not to end up with a consensual argument on one single belief (*ijmā'*). It is, rather, to disclose that the pondered theological subject can be interpreted, studied, and analysed by sheer cognitive perception, and that the logical argument used to explain it is rationally solid and plausible.

The Melkite *mutakallim* of the second/eighth- to third/ninth-century Abbasid era, Theodore Abū Qurrah (750–832 A.D.), is an ideal Christian case in point of rationalist *Kalām* in that intellectual context. He is an Arab Christian theologian who predominantly follows an 'arguing from reason' method.[24] For example, Abū Qurrah's *Mayar fī Wujūd al-Khāliq wal-Dīn al-Qawīm* (Discourse on the Existence of the Creator and the Right Religion) reveals his belief that determining the truth of any religious belief cannot be achieved except by means of "an external reliable criterion of investigation from without the religion *per*

---

[20] Ibid., p. 96.

[21] Something I touched upon in my study of Theodore Abū Qurrah's *Kalām*: Najib G. Awad, *Orthodoxy in Arabic Terms*, pp. 411–429.

[22] As I argued in Najib George Awad, "'Min al-'Aql wa-laysa min al-Kutub': Scriptural Evidence, Rational Verification and Theodore Abū Qurrah's Apologetic Epistemology," in *Exegetical Crossroads: Understanding Scripture in Judaism, Christianity and Islam in the Pre-Modern Orient*, George Tamer, Regina Grundmann, Asaad Elias Kattan, and Karl Pinggéra (eds.) (Berlin & Boston: De. Gruyter, 2017), pp. 95–118, p. 116.

[23] Ibid., p. 117.

[24] Ibid., pp. 107–108.

se."[25] This criterion, for Theodore, is nothing other than the sheer power of rational verification.

2 – *Proof-texting Strategy*: In addition to centralising reason (*'aql*), Arab-Eastern Christian *Kalām* also relied on textual attestation and implemented its constructing theological arguments and demonstrations. In today's scholarship on Christian *Kalām*, there is a debate over the biblical texts which the Christian theologians used in their *Kalām* in Arabic. Scholars wonder if the Christian *mutakallims* relied on an Arabic version of the Bible they had available and if it was commonly used among Christians of that time. Or did they rather read the available Greek and Syriac versions of the New Testament and the Hebrew text of the Old Testament and then offer their own personal, Arabic translation of every verse or pericope they employed in their *Kalām*? Among today's scholars, it is the Lebanese Baptist Hikmat Kachouh who argues that there were Gospels written in the Arabic language circulated and regularly used by the Christians even before the seventh century and the dawn of Islam. Kachouh proposes that enough evidence indicates that "the second half of the eighth century [must not be seen] as the starting point in the history of the Arabic Gospel text, but a time in which the Arabic text has gone through various revisions of more primitive exemplars."[26] These primitive exemplars, Kachouh proposes, go back in time at least to the sixth century, and they represent translations from Syriac to Arabic made by Christian congregations in south Arabia, perhaps in Najrān.[27]

Against Kachouh's thesis, Sidney Griffith argues that such an early Arabic Gospels version hypothesis is heavily "based on a series of ever more tenuous extrapolations." Griffith then states that "wishful thinking for written literary production, as opposed to a handful of inscriptions or probable notes as *aides de memoire* ... is no second basis for postulating an earlier, written currency of either Arabic poetry or the Gospels in Arabic."[28] Against the first/sixth century hypothesis, Griffith argues that no plausible evidence for an existence of an Arabic version of the Bible can be found beyond the late second/seventh to early third/eighth centuries. Griffith is willing to concede the possibility of the existence of *portions* of the Bible in Arabic in Arabia as early as the beginning of the second/seventh century.[29] Griffith also acknowledges the existence of oral and some written Arabic translations of biblical excerpts from the Gospels and Psalms in liturgical data from the late first/sixth to early second/seventh centuries. However, he insists that such data was produced in the monasteries of Palestine, not in Najrān of the Arabia.[30] These Arabic translational attempts

---

[25] Ibid., p. 109. See also Theodore Abū Qurrah, *Mayar fī Wujūd al-Khāliq wal-Dīn al-Qawīm* (Maymar on the Existence of the Creator and the Right Religion), Ignace Dick (ed.) (Jounieh: Librairie St. Paul/Rome: The Papal Oriental Institute, 1982), ch. 8, pts. 2–3, 6–8, 20–21 (pp. 211–214).

[26] Hikmat Kachouh, *The Arabic Versions of the Gospels: The Manuscripts and their Families* (Berlin & New York: De Gruyter, 2012), vol. 1, p. 333.

[27] Ibid., vol. 1, pp. 368–370.

[28] Griffith, *The Bible in Arabic: The Scriptures of the 'People of the Book' in the Language of Islam* (Princeton, NJ: Princeton University Press, 2015), p. 51.

[29] Ibid., p. 52.

[30] Ibid., p. 3.

could have spread in the form of liturgical data and reached the Arabs who lived on Arabia's periphery. Yet such transmission was purely oral and not textual.[31] This possibility conceded, Griffith proceeds, the problem remains that "aside from extrapolations scholars have made from much later material ... no conclusive documentary or clear textual evidence of a pre-Islamic written Bible in Arabic translation has yet to come to light."[32]

More important than the question of the existence and date of origin of an Arabic Bible is how the religious text was used in the service of the theological reasoning in Arab-Eastern Christian *Kalām*? It does not require much effort from the researcher to realise, upon reading the extant Arab *Kalām* texts from early Islam, that the Christian and Muslim theologians alike consistently included religious scriptural attestations in their polemical and apologetic stocks. Starting from at least the late second/seventh century, these theologians used biblical and Qur'ānic verses and suras to defend their theological claims and interpretations.[33] The realisation of this fact drove contemporary scholars to consider the 'proof-texting' strategy the default characteristic of theological reasoning in the Arabic-speaking context of the early Islamic centuries. Of this strategy, David Thomas says that it was used "as illustration of a supporting example of points which have already been established on other grounds [i.e. the ground of reason]."[34] What these theologians did, Thomas explains, was follow a pragmatic strategy: they snatched from the religious texts of their opponents "verses which would

---

[31] Ibid., p. 15.

[32] Ibid., pp. 41–42.

[33] I borrow my exposition here from Najib G. Awad, "'Min al-ʿAql wa-laysa min al-Kutub,'" pp. 96ff. For some other literatures on this subject, see, for instance, Sidney Griffith, "The Qur'ān in Arab Christian Texts: The Development of an Apologetical Argument; Abū Qurrah in the Mağlis of al-Ma'mūn," in *Parole de l'Orient*, 24 (1999): pp. 203–233; David Cook "New Testament Citations in the Ḥadīth Literature and the Question of Early Gospel Translations into Arabic," in *The Encounter of Eastern Christianity with Early Islam*, Emmanouela Grypeou, Mark Swanson and David Thomas (eds.) (Leiden: Brill, 2006), pp. 185–224; Barbara Roggema, "A Christian Reading of the Qur'ān: the Legend of Sergius-Baḥīrā and its Use of Qur'ān and Sīra," in *Syrian Christians under Islam, the First Thousand Years*, David Thomas (ed.) (Leiden: Brill, 2001), pp. 57–74; Mark Ivor Beaumont, "Early Christian Interpretation of the Qur'ān," in *Transformation*, 22 (2005): pp. 195–203; Martin Accad, "The Gospels in the Muslim Discourse of the Ninth to the Fourteenth Centuries: An Exegetical Inventorial table (Part I)," in *Islam and Christian–Muslim Relations*, 14 (2003): pp. 67–91; M. I. Beaumont, "Muslim Readings of John's Gospel in the 'Abbasid Period," in *Islam and Christian–Muslim Relations*, 19 (2008), pp. 179–197; Juan Pedro Monferrer-Sala, "An Arabic-Muslim Quotation of a Biblical Text: Ibn Kathīr's al-Bidāya wa-l-Nihāya and the Construction of the Ark of the Covenant," in *Studies on the Christian Heritage: In Honour of Father Prof. Dr. Samir Khalil Samir, S.I. at the Occasion of His Sixty-Fifth Birthday*, Rifaat Ebied and Herman Teule (eds.) (Leuven: Peeters, 2004), pp. 263–278; and Griffith, *The Bible in Arabic*, pp. 175–203.

[34] David Thomas, "The Bible in Early Muslim Anti-Christian Polemic," in *Islam and Christian–Muslim Relations*, 7(1996), pp. 29–38, p. 29.

support their own case" and would serve in defending their faith via nullifying the belief of the other.[35]

In his turn, Mark I. Beaumont concurs with Thomas's reading, adding that the Christian theologians opted for this 'proof-texting' method because they hoped that it would basically demonstrate the unworthiness of the Qur'ānic text to the title 'divine revelation' and the lesser authentic prophethood of Muhammad as attested to in the Qurʿān, as well as the textual attestation's support of the basic elements of Christian faith.[36] The 'proof-texting' strategy, then, represents before us a method of theological reasoning that exhibits the textual attestation (whether one's own text or the text of the opponent) in the service of both defending one's own theological discourse and exposing the fallacy of the discourse of the interlocutor. Mark Swanson describes this method as an evident case of 'exploitative imitation,' wherein the theologian implements the texts by any means possible without paying "any particular attention to the original context of [this text's] phrases."[37] Be that as it may, Swanson stipulates that 'proof-texting' "does indeed play a major role in the Arabic Christian apologetic literature, especially in popular texts that … answered readers of the truth by Christian faith and the certainty of its vindication in fair debate."[38]

In this case, one can fairly say that Arab-Eastern Christian theology in its earliest form was as biblically oriented as rationally founded and text-based as reason-centred. It is plausible that the Gospels of the New Testament, more than any other biblical texts, occupied the centre of the theologians' attention and controversies. This was grounded in the fact that the Gospels contained the basic theological teachings about Jesus Christ and the deity He used to call 'Abba.' Because, that is, they are the sources of the most challenging doctrines in Christian faith for the Muslim mind: the Trinity, Christology, Incarnation, and Crucifixion.[39]

3 – *Doctrinal Focus.* The Arab-Eastern theology in its earliest form (*Kalām*) was heavily soaked in the doctrinal content of Christian thought. The radical discrepancies between Christian and Muslim monotheistic beliefs lay primarily in the doctrinal components of the Christian theological understanding of the deity of the Christian religion and the identity of the founder and the core subject of this religious belief: the doctrine of the Triune God and the doctrine of Christ (Christology) and its two main connected discourses, the doctrine of the Incarnation and soteriology. The Christian theologians found themselves confronted with solid intellectual criticisms and theologico-philosophical

---

[35] Ibid., p. 30. See also Awad, "'Min al-ʿAql wa-laysa min al-Kutub,'" p. 97 and Sabine Schmidtke, "The Muslim Reception of Biblical Materials: Ibn Qutayba and His *A'lām al-Nubuwwa*," in *Islam and Christian–Muslim Relations*, 22(2011), pp. 249–274.

[36] M. Beaumont, "Early Christian Interpretation of the Qur'ān," pp. 195–203.

[37] Mark Swanson, "Beyond Proof-texting: Approaches to the Qur'ān in Some Early Arabic Christian Apologies," in *The Muslim World*, 88(1998), pp. 297–319, pp. 316–317.

[38] Ibid., p. 303.

[39] See Martin Accad, "The Ultimate Proof-Text: The Interpretation of John 20.17 in Muslim–Christian Dialogue (Second/Eighth–Eighth/Fourteenth Centuries)," in *Christians at the Heart of the Islamic Rule*, pp. 199–214.

challenges from Islam against these doctrinal constituents. They decided to respond to the challenge, and to counter-act the criticism, with even more affirmative, solid, and unbeatable ones. "Instead of either compromising some Christian [doctrinal teachings] for the sake of survival and security, or sacrificing their own life and being commemorated as heroes by attacking Islam, these *mutakallims* endeavoured in their intellectual [doctrinally focused] projects to establish an 'Arab Orthodox' or 'Arab Christian [doctrinal] identity' in the world of Islam by interacting with Islam [on a frank doctrinal level], and not despite Islam's existence."[40]

Within this context, the doctrines of the Trinity and Christology gained far more attention and enjoyed much higher prominence than other Christian doctrines. They were discussed and re-articulated beyond the boundaries of mere Christian–Christian, purely and narrowly confessional, and intrinsic reasoning. Theology on God and Jesus Christ is now developed as an instrument for defending one's own religious identity and distinction, not just mere theological choices or sectarian representative discourses. The Muslims, as Mark Swanson relates, "while acknowledging al-Masīḥ, 'Īsā b. Maryam (Jesus the Son of Mary) as a great prophet and apostle sent by God, called a central cluster of Christian convictions into question, namely that Jesus is the incarnate Son of God who died the death of crucifixion 'for our sake and for our salvation.'"[41] For Muslims, as the contemporary Muslim scholar Seyyed Hossain Nasr once said, "the non-crucifixion of Jesus is the one irreducible fact separating Christianity from Islam."[42] On the other hand, the incarnation of God in a human form was never conceived by the Qur'ān or Islamic thought. "The Christians would sooner or later have to defend their conviction that Jesus Christ was the eternal Son of God who had become human to rescue humanity from the results of sin through his death on the cross."[43] Responding to these challenges by means of just reciting the classical Christological Orthodox explanations and pedagogies that the Christians entertained in past centuries was no more efficient and was not pleasant to the ears of the Muslims. The Muslims were not truly interested in the technical nuances of the Christological hermeneutics of the incarnation, salvation, and two natures which the Melkites, Jacobites, and Nestorians debated within the narrow circles of Christian controversies. They wanted, rather, the Christians to demonstrate the plausibility of Christology based on the common monistic, philosophically based, common thought in the early Muslim context, as well as in light of the Qur'ānic attestation of Jesus, the Son of Mary. It is, thus,

---

[40] Awad, *Orthodoxy in Arabic Terms*, p. 67.

[41] Mark N. Swanson, "Apologetics, Catechesis and the Question of Audience in 'On the Triune Nature of God' (Sinai Arabic 154) and Three Treatises of Theodore Abū Qurrah," in *Christians and Muslim in Dialogue in the Islamic Orient of the Middle Ages*, Martin Tamcke (ed.) (Beirut: Oriental Institute, 2007), pp. 113–134, p. 113.

[42] Seyyed H. Nasr, *Islamic Life and Thought* (London & New York: Routledge, 1981), p. 210 and Mark I. Beaumont, *Christology in Dialogue with Muslims: A Critical Analysis of Christian Presentations of Christ for Muslims from the Ninth and Twentieth Centuries* (Eugene, OR: Wipf & Stock, 2005), p. 10.

[43] Beaumont, *Christology in Dialogue with Muslims*, p. 12.

correctly noticed that "the Islamic context radically changed the way Christology had to be discussed."[44]

The same applies to the role the Doctrine of the Trinity played in early Arab-Eastern theology. The Muslims often heard the Christians emphatically stating that Christianity is a monotheist faith. Yet, they were not quite persuaded that what the Christians articulated in their religious teaching on God and His Word and Spirit (*kalimatah wa ruḥah*) was truly expressive of the Qur'ānic monotheistic teaching on God and His Word and Spirit. What the Christians needed to explain and theologically verify was not the discourse on God's Word and Spirit per se, nor even necessarily on God's eternal metaphysical attributes (e.g. One, eternal, infinite, transcendent, omnipresent, omniscience, etc.). What they needed, rather, to demonstrate rationally and scripturally was the philosophico-metaphysical discourse about God's relational and personal nature, in God's self and in relation to history and creation alike. The Muslims had problems with "what they identify as the contradiction within the [Christian theology of the divine] Godhead between persons [i.e. '*hypostases*' in Greek, or '*qnumi*' in Syriac] who are both distinct from one another, yet also equal and identical [as one essence]."[45] In other words, how can the one be three and the three be one without logical contradiction with, and a threat to, monism?

Again, and as in the case of Christology, the Muslims were not interested in the various Christian–Christian technical interpretations of the three-in-one Being of God that the Christian theologians exchanged within the closed circles of ecclesial reasoning. They wanted, rather, to see if the Christians could truly offer a plausible and logically tenable explanation and verification for their Trinitarian hermeneutic of God's oneness *from within* the rational and theological framework of Islamic thought itself. Among the Muslims in early Islam, a highly heated controversy was taking place over God's attributes and their relation to divine oneness. There was a burgeoning discussion among Muslims over whether it was theologically tenable to believe that God has numerous attributes, or whether one must only recognise one Attribute in God that resonates with the divine's absolute monadic essence. For the Muslim mind, "any attribute (*ṣifah*) applied to an entity being described implies the existence of a noun, which in turn indicates … 'a kind of entitative reality' within the subject described."[46] Be that as it may, speaking of 'Father, Son, and Spirit' meant that there are three attributes that are indicative of three nouns; thus, three entities and never one. The Arab-Eastern Christian theologians of that era found themselves obliged to rearticulate the Doctrine of the Trinity's content within the framework of this Islamic discussion over God's oneness and its relation to the

---

[44] Ibid., p. 64.

[45] D. Thomas (ed. and trans.), *Anti-Christian Polemic in Early Islam: Abū 'Īsā al-Warrāq*'s *'Against the Trinity'* (Cambridge & New York: Cambridge University Press, 1992), p. 31.

[46] Thomas W. Ricks, *Early Arabic Christian Contributions to Trinitarian Theology* (Minneapolis: Fortress Press, 2013), p. 11. See also Richard M Frank, *Beings and Their Attributes: The Teaching of the Basrian School of the Mu'tazila in the Classical Period* (Albany: State University of New York Press, 1978), pp. 10–13.

divine 'names' (*asmā'*), which were even ninety-nine names in Islam, and not just three.

Arabic-Speaking Eastern Theology in the Present

It will not be remote from the truth to state that contemporary Arabic-speaking Eastern theology is considerably different in constituents and components from the ancient Arabic-speaking Eastern theological reasoning. The contemporary theological discourses are still rooted in scriptural attestation and reasoning. But they are far from relying on a proof-texting strategy of reasoning. If anything, contemporary Arab-Eastern theologians, even the Protestants among them, are more noticeably sceptical and interrogative, instead of exhibiting any proof-texting tendency. They counter-act this method because they seem to be uncomfortable with how this approach to religious scripture is used in the service of negative and challenging 'false-theology' discourses. This is what, for instance, the theological discourses that touch upon the issues of liberation, contextuality, the land, and women's role in the church invite us to conclude (see the ensuing chapter).

On the other hand, the dominant majority of the contemporary theological discourses available today, at least the ones I shed light on in this volume, do not seem to be occupied with any concern about re-constructing modern theological reasoning on the doctrinal and dogmatic components of Christian belief. The theologians of the Arab world seem to be consciously concentrating on other theologising aspects they deem more central, demanding, challenging, and needed in their living context. And, if on one occasion we find books written in Arabic on doctrines and dogmatic teaching, their contents tend not to be divulging anything original or uniquely expressive of a specific Christian reasoning which one does not coincide with or read about in other parts of the Christian world.

Finally, while contemporary Arab-Eastern theologies are grounded in cognitive and critical reasoning, they are not necessarily immersed in an apologetic, polemical, or demonstrative project that is based on an acknowledged rootedness in philosophical rationality. In this sense, the recent Arab-Eastern theologians are not *mutakallims* or spokesmen of *Kalām*, like their theological ancestors during early Islam.

There is probably one central characteristic that is still common between Arabic-speaking Eastern theology of the early Islamic era and the Christian, religiously oriented texts one can find in the Arab-Eastern context of today. I have already demonstrated in another publication that the Arabic-speaking Christian rational theology (*Kalām*):

> Was not just a purely and singularly apologetic or polemic instrument in the sole service of religious self-otherizing and self-superiorization. *Kalām* was also, if not mainly, one of the manifestations and evidences of the states of rootedness,

affiliation, and identification by means of one, common, trans-religious cultural and intellectual identity that became characteristic of the early Abbasid milieu.[47]

In the same vein, one can realise a similar tendency in the theologising attempts of some of the Arab-Eastern theologians of today. These theological endeavours are not purely 'God-talk' or fully and crudely '*theo*-logical' in content and focus. They are, rather, perennially religious, attentively socio-cultural, and inescapably politicised in implications and outcomes. The reason behind this is that the Christian Arabic-speaking, Eastern intellectuals today, like their ancestors of yesterday, use theological reasoning and discourse as manifest instruments of their genuine rootedness, affiliation, and identification with the very same cultural and intellectual identity, or self-perception processes, that are symptomatic of the contemporary, predominantly Arab, and Muslim-majority *Sitz im Leben*. Through the issues and the challenges that they touch upon and try to theologise or religiously interpret, today's Arab-Eastern theologians implement theological reasoning as a common identity-forming instrument that aims at presenting the Christians before the Muslims as compatriots from the very same life-setting (not from a parallel, adjacent one), who also strive towards shaping a common, particularly Arab-Eastern, cultural and intellectual character. Theologisation is, therefore, employed in the service of a more foundational and prior task beyond theological reasoning itself: "An element of common operation toward cultural and societal self-identification that is interwoven with these [theologians'] rationalization [or de-rationalization, for that matter] of religious belief."[48]

Apart from the above-described common feature, contemporary Arabic-speaking Eastern theological discourse remains totally different from the first, ancient Arab-Eastern theological legacy of *Kalām*. One can even validly opine, I reckon, that the recent Arab-Eastern textual genre is not truly '*theo*-logy'; not exactly 'God-talk'; not necessarily '*vernünftigen Theologie*,' '*Gottesgedenken*,' or '*Wissenschaft von Gott*' (to borrow conceptual terms from Wolfhart Pannenberg's etymological deposit[49]). It is, rather, a socio-political, cultural, and interreligious discourse constructed in semi-theological and biblical language and terms and by means of a general religious rationale. It tries to touch upon deeply existential, anthropocentric, and contextual issues from the perspective of some religious preconceptions and traditional Christian convictions that are not necessarily related to God, faith, the Gospel, or to any doctrinal heritage. Instead, they are more frankly rooted in the Christian individual's personal religiosity that lies in relatedness to, and perception of, the relevance of Christian belief to their own contextual and subjective (individual or communal) life conditions. What counts and enjoys priority is not a re-thinking and re-interpreting of the Christian doctrines and biblical message to the broader Arab-

[47] Najib George Awad, "*Creatio ex Philosophia*: *Kalām* as Cultural Evolution and Identity-Formation Means in the Early Abbasid Era," in *The Muslim World Journal*, 4(109), pp. 510–534, p. 534.

[48] Ibid., p. 534.

[49] See Wolfhart Pannenberg, *Theology and the Philosophy of Science*, Francis McDonagh (trans.) (Philadelphia: Westminster/John Knox Press, 1976).

Eastern context. It is, rather, the re-shaping and the re-articulating of today's Arab-Eastern challenges and life conditions in a manner that can demonstrate that the Christian religious discourse (crudely and generally speaking) is relevant and valuable to the attempt at responding to the needs and requirements of a *Sitz im Leben*, which is no more prevalently Christian, but rather non-Christian (and to some Eastern Christians, anti-Christian) in nature and identity. In the ensuing chapter, I shall be displaying various models of contemporary Arabic-Eastern theological reasoning that will demonstrate this theological tradition's particularity and its differences from the ancient, *Kalām*-like theological heritage of ancient Arab-Eastern Christianity.

5. Main Contemporary Trends of Arab-Eastern Theologies

Introduction

In this chapter, I introduce to the reader some major trends of theological discourse which one can find available in today's Arab-Eastern Christian context. As the reader will realise, we do have sporadic models of theological reasoning shaped after predominantly socio-political, cultural, existential, and generally religious concerns and challenges. The trends I discuss are by no means exhaustive of all the theological voices and writings one might coincide with in the Arabic-speaking intellectual and public Christian scene today. One must also never forget that in the context of the Arab world, there are also theology-like discourses and literature that are Muslim in authorship, and they express approaches to doctrines of religious faith from contextual and cultural perspectives that are similar to those of their Christian partners in that region. The subject of this study, anyhow, is Arab-Eastern *Christian* theology only, and it therefore focuses on selected trends of contemporary theological reasoning that are detectable on the Arab-Eastern Christian scene.

Before delving into the particular focus of the ensuing pages, I must here point out that if one surveyed the Christian theological context and historical biography of the Arab-Eastern Christians during the twentieth and twenty-first centuries, to say the least, one would find many books and papers written by Arabic-speaking theologians on all kind of doctrinal, scriptural, dogmatic, ecclesiological, and systematic constructive subjects and themes from the Christian faith. One would find texts interpreting Christian creedal theological doctrines, exegetical and commentary-like studies of the biblical books and verses, theological hermeneutics of subjects related to human existence and being-ness from theological perspectives, as well as spiritual and homiletical publications written from pastoral and personal perspectives. Yet, reading these texts would reveal to the researcher that their authors did not aspire at producing theological reasoning and hermeneutics that are, by any means imaginable, contextually, culturally, or situationally shaped and constructed. The content of these books might simply be an Arabisation of theological voices and discourses on Christian doctrines, Scripture and spiritual life that have been already created, developed, and produced in the Western (mostly European and American) world and published in other, foreign, languages. Or, it might also be a re-echoing of mainline theological views and interpretations which one can find proliferating and voiced in any other Christian theological writings around the Western Christian theological world.

In an essay he published in the famous Arabic Catholic journal *al-Mashriq*, the renowned Egyptian scholar of Arabic Christian traditions in late antiquity, Fr. Samīr Khalīl Samīr, offers a historiological narrative on the impact of

Western/European Christian theology on the theological thinking of the Christians in the Arab Middle East. Samīr argues that, during the modern era, the Arab-Eastern Christians broke with the Arabic tradition of late antiquity, Christian and Muslim alike, due to what they deemed to be "an era of decadence" (*'aṣr al-inḥiṭāṭ*) that had spanned the region for the previous four centuries. Instead of rooting their theological mind in the Arabic Christian thought of late antiquity, the Arab-Eastern Christians of modernity turned towards the West and embraced the Western (Catholic and Protestant) Christian theological traditions.[1] Samīr associates the culmination of this embrace of Western theology with the establishment of Catholic and Protestant churches in the Orthodox ecclesial context of the Middle East, which eventually influenced in depth the Christian Orthodox thought of the local churches and their members, and it led to their 'Westernisation' or 'occidentalisation' (*al-farnaja*). This meant losing any touch with the indigenous, historical Arab Christian theological thought, Samīr confirms.[2] The Arab-Eastern Christians started to use this theological adoption and inculturation in re-constructing a new Christian identity derived from the West. So much so, that we can find in the region, according to Samīr, "Western Catholic (and later on, Western Protestant) theological thought, penetrating slowly into the Oriental churches, including the Orthodox ones, like the Coptic Church, who lost since time immemorial its links with the previous [Arab Christian tradition]."[3] Later on, Samīr proceeds, the contemporary Arab Christian theologians endeavoured to reconcile the Catholic and Protestant Western theological discourses with the Eastern patristic traditions, especially the Greek and Byzantine ones.[4]

Fr. Samīr's historical exposition manifests in its full ramifications in the theological texts I mentioned above. This demonstrates why such texts do not present any theological content that would introduce us to any theological trends of thought that are *uniquely* or *exclusively* Arabic, Oriental, or Middle Eastern Christian in nature. What this study tries to introduce to the non-Arab and non-Eastern readers are theological voices that consciously and ambitiously try to produce a theological voice that is deeply and frankly rooted in the unique and particular contextual situation and enquiries of the Arab-Eastern Christian communities and which aspires to be an echo of these Christians' very own indigenous voice.

On the other hand, looking at the present Arab-Eastern theological scene would demonstrate that some Arab-Eastern Christian voices preferred to produce an indigenous, contextually rooted theological reasoning in the region in the form of 'statements,' 'documents,' or 'manifestos,' instead of singular books, papers, or a coherent, comprehensive, thesis-centred project. As an example, one can point here to three of the most recent statements/manifestos/ documents

---

[1] Samīr Khalīl Samīr, "Lāhūt al-Sharq al-Adna al-Ḥadīth fī al-Ṣilah bayn al-Hawiyyah wal-Ghayriyyah" (The Theology of the Modern Near East: On the Connection between Identity and Othering), p. 34.

[2] Ibid., p. 35.

[3] Ibid., p. 36.

[4] Ibid., p. 36.

produced by Christian groups in the region.[5] The first is called the 'Kairos Palestine' document. It was composed in 2009 by an ecumenical group of Christian Palestinians. The statement was titled: "A Moment of Truth: A Word of Faith, Hope and Love from the Heart of Palestinian Suffering." It formulated a contextualised theological reading of the region from the perspectives of suffering.[6] The second document, a manifesto-like text, was produced in 2014 by a group of Middle Eastern Christian academics and young scholars. The issued statement was titled "From the Nile to the Euphrates: A Statement on Christian Responsibility and Citizenship Law." It addressed the future of the Christians in the Middle East, calling for improving and amending the legal system in such a manner that would grant all the citizens in the region, from all backgrounds, equal management of human resources, education, and the labour market, and to evenly gain protection for their dignity, equality, and spirituality.[7] The third example of such a theological, group-like initiative is a document issued in 2021 by a group of Christian lay and clerical personnel from Lebanon, Jordan, and Palestine. The statement was titled "We Choose Life in Abundance – Christians in the Middle East: For a Renewal of Theological, Social and Political Choices." The text aspired at presenting a contextualised reading of the situation in the Middle East from geo-political, ecclesial-religious, and strategic-futural perspectives, endeavouring to offer readings on subjects like human rights, freedoms, justice, citizenship rights, and diversity.[8]

This study does not pause at such statements/manifesto-like initiatives, despite their value and expressiveness of essential concerns and challenges occupying the people in the Middle East. The study does not do this because none of these documents presents a truly coherent, fully- fledged, or constructively factual *theology* discourse or hermeneutics. They, rather, seem to be primarily and ultimately gaining their Christian theological character and identity from the personal, private, Christian, ecclesial, and theological backgrounds and the representational statuses of their composers. The core content and theses of the documents as such could have easily been also written by non-Christian, theologically oriented authors from the same region, and the founding theological and biblical presumptions, preconceptions, points of departure, and frame-working rationales could all have been generated by Christian theologians from other parts of the world. In other words, such documents can introduce us to generic and general theological voices deeply rooted in contextualisation. But they will not truly demonstrate coherently particular, specific, or unique *Arab-Eastern* fully-fledged and focused *theologies*, which one can pause at as exclusively expressive of theological reasoning and theology-creation in that specific part of the world. One must say that the content of these statements is mostly developed to address the general,

---

[5] I benefit here from the useful summary of these three documents' background and content in Viola Raheb, "Middle Eastern Theologies," in *Emerging Theologies from the Global South*, Mitri Raheb and Mark A. Lamport (eds.) (Eugene, OR: Cascade Books, 2023), pp. 259–272.

[6] Ibid., p. 264.

[7] Ibid., p. 265.

[8] Ibid., p. 266.

broader public in an over-simplifying, even sometimes populist, language full of generally promoted, wished-for and even exchanged cliches. The concern about such a popularity makes the authors compromise, most of the time, the theological depth, the critical rigour, of one's own self, the intellectual and hermeneutical seriousness, and the analytical thoroughness that are needed to develop an authentic theological voice.

Coming to terms with, and getting some knowledge of, the particular trends of theological reasoning that enable us to learn something unique about the Arab-Eastern Christian reality is achieved by looking, rather, at some trends of theological discourse written by Arab-Eastern theologians during the past few decades. I mean, specifically, those discourses that were developed to address directly contextual and existential questions which the Arab Middle Eastern Christians confront, and to offer interpretations of them from within the depth of their conditionality and situatedness. Be that as it may, what I try to do in the ensuing sections is expose before the reader what I believe to be a few basic and primary representative models of theological discourse that can offer a fair, coherent, and reliable presentation of the main trends of reasoning and the primary determining intellectual presumptions and contextual motifs that motivate the Arab-Eastern Christians to think theologically and to write theology in the way they do. The theological trends I shall discuss were all developed between the last quarter of the twentieth century and today. This study does not aim at developing a historiological anatomy or to chase genealogically after the evolution of the Arab-Eastern Christians' theological reasoning during the modern era. This is only an expository study that aims at highlighting what one could witness as theological trends of thought on the Arab-Eastern scene in recent times.

Two last notes before we proceed: the theologians this monograph covers all speak the Arabic language and hail from an Arabic cultural background. Yet some of them produced their theological texts in foreign languages and not in Arabic. Their theology is more appropriately called 'Arab-Eastern,' rather than 'Arabic' or 'Arabic-speaking' in this case. On the other hand, it is quite interesting that the scholar does not find in the present theological discourse any fully fledged, specific theological reasoning on the subject of the immigration of Christians to the West, which is one of the most direly challenging threats the Arabic-speaking Christian communities realistically suffer from in their contemporary history. The issue of immigration might be sometimes alluded to here and in the literature of the Arabic-speaking theologians. However, we do not have yet a specified, coherent, and self-existing 'Theology of Immigration' from the Arab-Eastern context's perspective.

Liberationist Arab-Eastern Theology

One of the main contemporary theological discourses that the Arab-Eastern Christians started to develop during the last quarter of the twentieth century is an Arab, Middle Eastern version of the theology of liberation. At that very specific time, this genre of theological reasoning had also evolved and gained momentum in Latin America and then the United States. It was a Palestinian-Anglican theologian, who did his academic training in California and San Francisco, USA, who first brought the liberationist theology genre with him back to Palestine upon his return from his study journey in the States. It was him who decided to launch the first attempt at creating an Arab-Palestinian version of liberation theology, and this is why his theological contribution is the one I am going to pause at to introduce one of the recognisable trends of theologisation in the Arab-Eastern context of today.

The person I am talking about here is the Anglican Palestinian theologian and clergyman Naim Stefan Ateek. Ateek appeared on the theologico-intellectual scene of the Arab Middle East in 1989, when Orbis Books published in English his monumental, pioneering Arab liberationist theology monograph, *Justice and Only Justice*. Ateek's theological reasoning is a paramount illustration of the fact that theology in the Arab-Eastern context is not pure 'God-talk,' but a discourse on the human socio-political conditions by means of religious terms and affiliations. Ateek sets up his theologising project within the core, defining crisis of the Palestinian '*Existenz*' and 'self-awareness' (in the Gadamarian sense of *Selbstbewußtsein*). The Israeli–Palestinian conflict is not just a circumstantial, external conflict that radically wreaked havoc on the Palestinians' life conditions. It is also a profound, essential crisis that shapes the very foundations of how the inhabitants of the historical Palestine – Christians, Muslims, and Jews alike – relate to, and constitute, their self-awareness. This fundamental presumption drives Ateek to ground his theological reasoning in the framework of the intertwining of politics and religion and of historical and personal perceptions that create boundaries between the people in the Middle East. Such a segregationist situation, Ateek proposes, brings to attention the need for a theologised discourse on the reconciliation between justice and love. Without such a reconciliation, he maintains, the rift will not be healed, and the Christian, Muslim, and Jewish peoples will not get together again.

When it comes to the question of 'why yet another book on the Palestinian–Israeli conflict after all the scores that already exist about it?,' Ateek's response is that *Justice and Only Justice* was written to offer the yet lacking approach to this conflict from biblical and theological perspectives that are developed by someone who is personally experiencing the subject of the theological reasoning practically in his own real life, and who is capable of reflecting on it to people who are "from all professions and walks of life," not scholars or professional theologians.[9]

In this orientation, one detects the liberationist features of Ateek's approach and perceives the driving preconception behind his decision to write *theology*, and not a political or general intellectual discourse. He is driven by means of his pre-conviction that liberation comes from within, from the spiritually rooted experience that makes people read their political experiences of injustice and oppression through the lenses of their personal belief and religious tradition. After all, in his discourse, Ateek aspires at speaking *with*, if not also *on behalf*

[9] Naim S. Ateek, *Justice and Only Justice: A Palestinian Theology of Liberation* (Maryknoll, NY: Orbis Books, 1989), p. 1.

of, the Muslims and the Jews, not just *about* the Christians and *to* them alone.[10] What seems to be equally motivating Ateek's development of an Arab *theological* voice and none other on this dauntingly political and historical crisis is his belief that one witnesses either "a dangerous *religious* abuse of the conflict" by means of either "stagnant" religious discourses, or religious views that are "imported from abroad";[11] that is, from a foreign and alien vantage point; from without the true *Sitz im Leben* of the matter.

Relying on such imported religious-like discourses, Ateek argues, prevented the emergence of "indigenous theologians" from the Palestinian churches.[12] Be that as it may, theologising on the Palestinian crisis is not, for Ateek, just a presentation of a liberationist hermeneutics of the Palestinian–Israeli conflict. It is equally, if not primarily, a liberationist emancipation of the Christian Palestinian churches from their intellectual stagnation by means of liberating the religious reasoning itself, as well as on the basis of a liberating religious cognition. Ultimately, Ateek's version of Arab-Eastern theology is a liberationist interpretation offered to the people of that region, including the Jews: "I trust … that [the Jewish readers] can recognize a human spirit trying to reach them, talking about the real possibilities of peace and appealing for the realization of justice for all the peoples of Israel-Palestine."[13]

The outcome of Ateek's above-described rationale is a theology-like discourse "firmly based on the Bible," as he claims. It endeavours to offer a discourse "meaningful to Palestinian Christians" that "stems from biblical roots," although it simultaneously "struggles with certain ways in which the Bible itself has been misunderstood, misinterpreted and misused by many people."[14] What would stand as a liberation of the Bible from such misunderstanding, misuse, and misinterpretation in the case of the Palestinian context? Ateek answers in the following manner:

> This theology … emphasizes the liberating aspects of the Word of God – that has been there in the Bible all along but that, unfortunately, has been neglected – and it helps us to focus on it. It brings the Word of God to us in our daily lives, attuning our ears to what God is saying to us today and to what God wants to do through us in this world that God loves and to which God has sent Christ. A theology of liberation is a way of speaking [biblically] to a particular situation, especially where oppression, suffering and injustice have long reigned.[15]

In these programmatic elucidations, Ateek imagines before us an Arab-Eastern theologisation enterprise that is not shying away from attending to a political crisis by means of tools from outside the political, intellectual, and conceptual tool-kit itself. The contextual aspect of such a liberationist theology, which differentiates it from other models of liberation theology in other parts of the world, is that it manifests a genuine Arab-Eastern cultural conviction that all

[10] Ibid., p. 2.
[11] Ibid., p. 3. Italics are mine.
[12] Ibid., p. 3.
[13] Ibid., p. 3.
[14] Ibid., p. 6.
[15] Ibid., p. 6.

human conditions are birthed from the womb of religiosity and are seeded in the soil of frank religious worldviews (something that is staunchly emphasised and stated by the Muslims and the Jews of the region). Thus, any healing imagined from a crisis which the humans of that region are tormented by is unachievable without addressing the crisis, diagnosing it, and prescribing its cure from within, and by the help of, the religious imagination and the religious texts. This is why in this Arab-Eastern theological model, 'liberationist' is synonymous with 'biblical,' and 'political' is understood as 'religious.'

Ateek proposes that the cornerstone of an Arab-Eastern liberationist theology like the one he constructs consists of two central subjects. The first subject is 'justice': "Palestinians everywhere have been talking about the injustice done to them – to young and old, educated and uneducated, rich and poor, male and female, religious and secular, Muslim and Christians – all talk about the problem of justice."[16] Any Arabic-speaking Eastern theologisation, Ateek affirms, must inescapably reflect on justice to be a communicative and relatable theology to the people of that religion in general, and of Palestine in particular.

On the other hand, the second constitutive issue that such an Arab-Eastern liberationist theology must address is 'the Bible' per se. In Ateek's project, the Bible is not just the main medium for conjuring up a theological discourse to address particular problems. The Bible as such is 'a problem,' a 'challenge,' which any theologising attempt in this particular context must address, must deal with frankly, must confront openly. Little have I found liberationist theological texts deeming the Bible in itself as part of a problem . In other international liberationist theological discourses, the Bible is more dominantly treated as one element of the solution, if not the primary source of such a solution. One might find liberationist theologians unpacking and unravelling the problematic, even evil, ramifications of certain exegetical readings and hermeneutic approaches to the books of the Scripture. Yet, hardly, I reckon, can one encounter a theologian of liberation holding the Bible per se, not its interpretation, accountable for a crisis. In his Arab-Eastern liberationist theology, Naim Ateek seems to be doing so, or at least pointing to situations where the Bible is deemed by people to be a challenge or a problem that needs tackling.

In what sense is the Bible a challenge to the Arab-Eastern, Palestinian context? According to Ateek, "if some parts of it are applied literally to [the Palestinians'] situation today, the Bible appears to offer to the Palestinians slavery rather than freedom, injustice rather than justice, and death to their national and political life."[17] For instance, the Bible contains the term 'Israel' all over the texts of the Old and the New Testaments, and it associates this term with statements on God's blessing. Before the establishment of the State of Israel, Ateek elaborates, the Arab-Palestinian Christians had no problem whatsoever with this term. They did not associate 'Israel' with "any existing state on the face of the globe," nor did they deem it a nomenclature signifying the ancient kingdom of Israel, though that history was familiar to them. 'Israel' meant, rather, "a religious community of devout worshippers of Ancient Israel's God –

---

[16] Ibid., pp. 74–75.
[17] Ibid., p. 75.

the one true God in the belief of present-day Jews, Christians and Muslims."[18] However, the nomenclature 'Israel,' which connoted the 'spiritual people of God,' started to designate something crudely and frankly political and military after the establishment of the State of Israel. This drove many Palestinian and Arab Christians to withdraw and express serious unease, bitterness, and hesitation, whenever in the churchly worship they found liturgical orders of worship inviting them to read, recite, or pray in unison certain biblical texts that contained the term 'Israel': "The name conjures up today a picture of a small, middle-Europe type state, with bickering political parties, like all such states, with a rigid … foreign policy with respect to its neighbors."[19] What we end up dealing with here is a situation where the followers of the belief of this religious book (the Bible) fall into a state of suspicion and weariness from content in the Scripture. They develop such a scepticism towards the religious book which, for them, is supposed to be a source of hope, salvation, divine love, peace, and justice, and not a reminder and confirmer of what represents in their life the ultimate cases of injustice. The Bible, in this case, nurtures and kindles the fire, instead of extinguishing it. In the Arab-Eastern liberationist theology which Ateek proposes, the central methodological and theological questions are:

> How can the Bible, which has apparently become a part of the problem in the Arab–Israeli conflict, become a part of its solution? How can the Bible, which has been used to bring a curse to the national aspirations of a whole people, again offer them a blessing? How can the Bible, through which many have been led to salvation, be itself saved and redeemed?[20]

Ateek believes that what makes the transformation of the Palestinians and the Arab Christians' stance on the Bible a very challenging task is the fact that, since the Bible is the Christians' access to the Christ-like understanding of God, whatever attributes one ascribes to the Bible become, consciously or unconsciously, attributive of God per se. So, the God of the Bible, who is believed usually to be the God who saves and liberates, becomes for the Palestinians (but also for the Arab-Eastern) a "partial and discriminating" deity.[21] While the existence of God in itself is not a matter of doubt or primary enquiry for the majority of these Christians, the *nature* and *character* of this God are the source of a serious scepticism and ambiguity, if not distrust: "What is God really like? What is God's relation to the new State of Israel? Is God partial only to the Jews? Is this a God of justice and peace?"[22]

This scepticism towards the Bible and the suspicion about God's being generates, eventually, distrust, even disbelief, in the value, nature, and role of the church, especially as Arab-Eastern churches stand helpless and impotent before such questions and the situation itself. Many clergies tried in their own ways to redeem the church and advocate for the Bible and its God by suggesting various methods for interpreting and reading Scripture (e.g. spiritualising it, approaching

[18] Ibid., p. 76.
[19] Ibid., p. 76.
[20] Ibid., p. 77.
[21] Ibid., p. 77.
[22] Ibid., p. 78.

its texts critically and scientifically, or allegorising them). None of these attempts succeeded, because while they found ways to approach the literal content, they did not truly answer "whether, or not, the text is the word of *God* ... and whether it reflects the nature, will, and purpose of *God* ... [and whether] what is being read is an authentic insight from God about who God is. Is it an authentic insight from God about persons or relationships or about human nature and history?"[23]

The attentive reading of Ateek's theological project in *Justice and Only Justice* makes the scholar dare to postulate that what we have here is not essentially liberationist 'God-talk' or conventional liberationist *theo*-logy, despite the thesis's overwhelming embeddedness in theological vocabulary and rootedness in biblical rationale. It seems that we have here an Arab-Eastern theologisation on, or a theologised call for, liberation *from* particular ambiguity and suspicion related to God and 'God-talk'; the genesis moment of which occurs nowhere else than when the Christians in Palestine or the Arab-Eastern read the Bible and encounter its God. This seems not like a theology calling for liberation by means of a God-talk or by the help of the Bible. It is, rather, a call for liberation *from* a God-talk that is derived from a particular connectedness to the Bible: liberation from theology by means of de-theologising certain challenging theology.

The liberationist de-theologising project manifests itself in one of Ateek's essential postulations. He attentively explains that counter-acting potential biblical and theological prejudices must not be pursued by making the Bible serve a reactionary attempt at creating a counter-theology to "support subjective Palestinian claims and prejudices."[24] The alternative approach, which Ateek proposes to avoid this trap, lies in a call for pursuing a crudely Christo-centric reading and to Christologically relate to the Bible and its God. Whatever Jesus Christ discloses about God in the story of his life, ministry, death, and resurrection *is* the ultimate meaning and access for knowing who is the God of the Bible, what is His will and what He supports or condemns. "Jesus the Christ," Ateek states, "thus becomes – in Himself and in His teaching – the true hermeneutic, the key to the understanding of the Bible, and beyond the Bible to the understanding of the action of God throughout history."[25] For Ateek, focusing on Christ will enable the Arab and Palestinian Christians to liberate themselves from the scepticism toward God and the weariness from the wordings of the Bible. Christ will become the eye-glasses they use to read the Bible in its two Testaments. By means of this Christocentric hermeneutic, Ateek opines, "the Bible ... can be retained in its entirety, while its contents would be judged by

---

[23] Ibid., p. 79. Ateek continues elaborating on this by asking: "To put it bluntly, is it basically [a collection] of statements from humans put into the mouth of God, that has become confused as an authentic and valid message from God to people? ... what is eternally true in the Bible and what is conditioned? What is lasting and what is temporal?" (ibid.).

[24] Ibid., p. 79. Such a trap, Ateek concedes, "puts us in a quandary: Is all knowledge of God subjective? Does it not become an arbitrary matter of judgment depending on the prejudices of the individual?" (ibid., p. 82).

[25] Ibid., p. 80.

this hermeneutic and scrutinized by the mind of Christ."[26] For Ateek, such a reading alone is the best key for liberating the Christians' interpretation and reading of the Bible. It offers them a theological reasoning that is "grounded in the knowledge and love of God as revealed in the life, death, and resurrection of Jesus Christ."[27]

Ateek's main proposal is that, through frank and unreserved Christologisation, the texts can bring about hermeneutical liberation. Only then "biblical texts and contemporary events or crises become an occasion for hearing and communicating the Word of God today."[28] This Christological liberating hermeneutic, according to Ateek, enables us to realise that, regardless of terminology and literal content, the Bible contains three central themes about God's nature and will. First, God is by nature just. He is the God of justice. Second, God conveyed to His creation warnings about the absence of justice through his prophets and messengers. And third, God is the God of hope. In Him and His salvation lie the fulfilment of justice and its prevalence over injustice.[29] Upon this understanding of the nature of God, Ateek concludes, liberationist Palestinian theology would re-interpret all other aspects related to the Palestinian–Israeli conflict, like Zionism, the land, and whether this land is Palestine's or Israel's. We must theologically proceed from the God of Jesus Christ towards the meaning of these aspects, not the other way around.

Twenty-eight years after *Justice and Only Justice*, Naim Ateek produced another monograph on Palestinian liberation theology, titled *A Palestinian Theology of Liberation*. In this volume, Ateek endeavours to travel with his earlier theological project from the circle of personal-experiential perception, which grounded the thesis of his 1989 book, into a more programmatic and systematically constructed circle of reasoning. This time, he does not primarily argue for the need for liberation by offering an experiential justification for such a necessity. Instead, he tries to frame his liberationist theologisation attempt within a constructed, self-definable genre of theological reasoning called a 'Palestinian Theology of Liberation.' He argues that this nomenclature defines a particular discourse with a historical narrative that, this time, exceeds the Palestinian–Israeli conflict alone and travels back in history, long before today's Palestinians found themselves striving with life, faith, the Bible, and even God, after the establishment of the State of Israel. Nonetheless, Ateek still concedes that the creation of a specific theological discourse called 'Palestinian Liberation Theology' occurred in the twentieth century, not earlier, and it was shaped as a response to, or as an outcome of, the ramifications, consequences, and multi-faceted implications that originated from four major historical factors: the

[26] Ibid., p. 80.
[27] Ibid., p. 81.
[28] Ibid., p. 82. Ateek continues saying, "we do not need to force a text to legitimate our own ideology or prejudices; we are free to open ourselves to hearing what God in Christ has to say to us through that text today" (ibid.).
[29] Ibid., pp. 86–92.

Holocaust, the war of 1967, the rising of religious Zionism, and the first Palestinian uprising (*Intifāḍah*).[30]

This conceded, Ateek now chases after the historical roots that lie behind associating such liberationist thinking on these four contemporary factors with the exclusive history of the Palestinian *Christians* and no other community. This is not just a socio-political liberationist theologising on today's situation. Palestinian theology of liberation is the culmination, and even consummation, of the long historical narrative of the Christians in the Middle East, which stretches back in history to the theological controversies of the patristic antiquity, to the coming of Islam to the Fertile Crescent in the seventh century, to the Middle Ages and the arrival of the Protestant missionaries and, finally, to the arrival of the Zionists and the State of Israel.[31] The entire historical trajectory, Ateek stipulates, is a single, multi-chapter novel, strictly of the Christians of Palestine, their struggle with the challenges of profound existential and religious natures, and their strife to find in the theological basket of their religious belief the tools for liberating themselves. This history is now presented as the intellectual and hermeneutical manger or womb of the present attempt at constructing a definable, particular theology of liberation *for*, *from*, *about*, and *in* Palestine.

According to Ateek, the components and constitutive elements of this Palestinian theology of liberation are as follows: this theology is developed within a narrowly specified context; namely, "the Palestinian context and situation in life."[32] It tries to find answers to the question of 'where are you, God, and how do you relate to our life's conflict?'; as this enquiry is asked by the people who belong historically, existentially, contextually, and religiously to the historical land called 'Palestine.' Second, this theology, Ateek states, is fundamentally one that does not primarily answer this enquiry theoretically or cognitively, but rather, through praxis. It does this as it seeks "the [actual] liberation of our people from oppression … and from the unjust and illegal occupation of Palestinian land, [as well as] the liberation of Israeli Jews from the sin of oppressing … the objective is to liberate both the oppressed and the oppressor."[33] Third, Ateek continues, this is a bottom-up, from-below theology. It does not start from the academic and scholarly hermeneutic and exegetical efforts of specialised biblical scholars. It, rather, starts from the grassroots *reading* of the Bible in the circles of the Church. It is a theology that is not developed from the biblical scholars' armchairs, but from the biblical reflections of the local ecclesial communities "through the eyes of faith."[34] Fourth, it is an inclusivist and ecumenical theology. It rejects discriminating people in the name of confessionalism and denominationalism. Fifth, it is interfaith theology that approaches non-Christians from the perspective of the belief that "God is the creator of all, and God's love and care embraces all."[35] Sixth, it is a human-based

---

[30] Naim S. Ateek, *A Palestinian Theology of Liberation: The Bible, Justice and the Palestinian–Israeli Conflict* (Maryknoll, NY: Orbis Books, 2017), pp. 31–40.

[31] Ibid., pp. 15–24.

[32] Ibid., p. 139.

[33] Ibid., p. 139.

[34] Ibid., p. 140.

[35] Ibid., p. 140.

theology that aims at championing human dignity and being by focusing on the human conditions of oppression and injustice. Seventh, since it is a theological confrontation of oppression and injustice by means of the belief in the God of Jesus Christ, this theology liberates from violence by means of peace. It is a nonviolence, if not anti-violence, theology. Eighth, in the midst of the dauntingly oppressive and unjust context of Palestine, a theology that is inclusivist, interfaith, ecumenical, humanitarian, and anti-violent becomes an incarnation of a genuine prophetic theology. It is prophetic because it "courageously speaks truth to power."[36] Last but never least, this theology of liberation is crudely Christological in nature, where "Jesus Christ is both the model and paradigm of faith, and where Christ is the guide and the hermeneutic that can help us discern the authentic word of God."[37]

It is on the basis of these constituents that a theology of liberation, according to Ateek, would liberate the Palestinians (and the Arab Christians, for that matter) from reading the Scripture in ways that "depict God as being violent," or exerting on the texts an eisegetical interpretation of biblical texts that "reflect a tribal and exclusive understanding of God."[38] Ateek goes as far as proposing that such theology liberates the Christians from calling the Bible 'the Word of God' unreservedly and arbitrarily. It invites them, instead, to judge and assess when and how they can call the Bible the 'Word of God' upon the criterion of Jesus Christ: "Jesus Christ must be the determining hermeneutic."[39] In a logic reminiscent of Martin Luther's Christocentric 'canon-within-canon' perspective, Attek invites the Arab-Palestinian Christians not to rush into saying 'this is the Word of the Lord' after reading any biblical text in the church, when the read text reflects a theology that is not reflective of, or determined by, Christ's hermeneutic criteria:[40]

> Before reading the text, pastors, priests, and ministers should ask themselves, does this reading reflect the mind and love of God as shown to us in Jesus Christ? It is uncomfortable to hear the congregation say 'thanks be to God' after a reading that is, to say the least, unedifying. Clergy need to have the courage to omit those verses that are not in line with the spirit of Christ and the New Testament.[41]

This means that the theology of liberation Ateek develops calls sometimes for liberation from the Bible, not just by means of the Bible's message or on the basis of its textual attestations, as if it is a call for liberating the Palestinian Christians from the Bible by means of Jesus Christ. I do theologically find validity in liberating the Christians from Biblicism and instructing them, as Karl Barth already taught many decades ago, that the Word of God is first and foremost Jesus Christ, and not a written text. In the Arab-Eastern context, where Christians live in the heartland of the Muslim faith that absolutises and sanctifies God's words as manifested and divulged only and absolutely in the Qur'ān, it is

[36] Ibid., p. 140.
[37] Ibid., p. 141.
[38] Ibid., p. 141.
[39] Ibid., p. 141.
[40] Ibid., p. 141.
[41] Ibid., p. 142.

theologically useful, and necessary, I reckon, to remind Christians that they are theologically 'the people of the Person,' not 'the people of the Book,' like the Muslims are, and like the Qur'ān itself calls the followers of ʿIsā b. Maryam (e.g. Q 3: 64, 113, 199; 5:15, 19, 68; 29: 46).

Having conceded the above, how can Christians be liberated from the Bible by means of Christ, if the Bible itself is their only access to anything related to Christ or which attests to Him? Even the idea that Jesus Christ is the hermeneutic determinant is based on, and derived from, the reading and interpreting of the Bible itself. Had it not been for the written word, we would have not have been able to encounter the incarnate Word and to perceive that the latter is the criterion for the former. On the other hand, Ateek permits the Christians to "omit those verses that are not in line with the spirit of Christ and the New Testament."[42] But who and how do we ascertain what is 'the spirit of Christ and the New Testament,' and what would be the accurate and authentic content of this spirit? Ateek does not answer this question. If the danger lies in a certain reading of particular texts that foster a dangerous theology, is not the call for dispensing with these texts and highlighting others itself based on the very same textual attestation? Yes, Christ is the determining hermeneutic of the Bible. But Christ as a 'hermeneutic' is as such the outcome of a pre-determined hermeneutic of what stands as an exegesis of the Bible and what does not. Who determines the accurate theological meaning of Christ's hermeneutical referentiality, and on what basis do we determine that the reader (or the texts' selector) is applying Christ as a hermeneutic criterion in an accurately hermeneutic, Christ-like manner?

Putting the abovementioned methodological discussion aside, Naim Ateek's theology is a valuable example of how Arab-Eastern Christians endeavour to construct their own version of liberation theology. It is a theological discourse that aims at relating the Christians of that region to their broader, non-Christian co-inhabitants. It pursues this not in a defensive or protectionist manner, but in a self-corrective and self-critical one. It calls the Arab-Eastern Christians to liberate themselves ultimately from challenging and damaging approaches, readings, and interpretations of the Christian textual sources of belief (the Bible). It inspires them to do this by making Jesus Christ's message the new criterion, the new hermeneutical key, that invites them to re-read the Bible on the basis of love of God and love of neighbour. "Our view of God," Ateek affirms, "informs our view of our neighbor. If our God is a God of love and mercy, then we must relate to our neighbor in such a way."[43]

Another interest in developing theological discourse from a liberationist perspective in the Arab-Eastern context is echoed in Egypt. The main figure one can pause at to discern his attempt at constructing an Arab-Eastern liberationist theology in this Arab country is the Jesuit theologian William Sidhum. Father Sidhum is known in Egypt for his influential work in the social service domain. His attention to the praxical, socio-political, and cultural aspects of the Christian Gospel and theological tradition is publicly recognised and appreciated. More

---

[42] Ibid., p. 142.

[43] Ibid., p. 147.

importantly, he is one of the recognised Christian Egyptian theologians who believe in an interreligious and cross-religious liberationist call, wherein the Christians and the Muslims work together toward creating and pursuing a common liberationist religious discourse in the service of their shared *Sitz im Leben*. Theology for him seems to be not an instrument for the Christians' liberation *from* the conditions of living with the different other. It is, instead, a means for liberation *together with* the other from common dehumanising conditions.

Such a fundamental presumption drove Fr. Sidhum to edit in 2005 an anthology on a potential *Arab* (not just Egyptian Christian. In this, he is different from Attek's narrow liberationist *Palestinian Christian* project) liberationist theology that is not one-sidedly Christian, but Christian–Muslim. In this anthology, Sidhum invited a selected group of prominent Egyptian Christian and Muslim researchers and scholars to conjure up together such an Arab liberationist voice. The authors gathered in a workshop titled "Liberation Theology: Problems and Views," which was held in King Maryūṭ, Egypt on 5 May 2003.[44] In the ensuing lines, I highlight some of the core claims and conceptions that were divulged by some major Christian voices from the gathering scholars (this is a study on the *Christian* Arab theology in particular, not the Muslim one too), and I try to present a constructive description of such a version of theological reasoning.

In his prelude to the anthology, Fr. Sidhum explains that the call for creating a liberationist voice that is inspired by the Latin American liberationist experience comes at a crucial and highly complicated time, in the Arab region in particular and the Middle East in general. This part of the world, Sidhum stipulated, is not totally exposed and denuded after the fall of the 'fig leaf' (*Waraqat al-Tīn*), which the Arab Christians and Muslims alike tried to conceal by their feebleness, sickness, and vulnerability. In this region, Sidhum proceeds, all the conventional political and ideological slogans and discourses that were proliferated during the past decades have totally collapsed: the Nationalist, the Pan-Arabist, the Liberal, the Leftist, and lately the Islamist as well. Now, the time is ripe for creating a new voice to take the region beyond the boundaries of this total-failure situation.[45] According to Sidhum, it is from the Latin American liberationist theology and nothing else that the Arabs can learn how to develop their own theological perception of liberation. From the Latin American experience, he proposes, the Arabs can derive a liberationist theological discourse that is hermeneutically and methodologically based on the following fourfold critera: 1) experience (*praxis*) precedes theory; 2) change starts from below, from the public praxis, and it proceeds peacefully; 3) defending the

[44] The papers were later on published as the following anthology: William Sidhum, S.J. (ed.), *Lāhūt al-Taḥrīr: Rū'iyah 'Arabiyyah Islāmiyyah Masīḥiyyah* (Liberation Theology: An Arab, Muslim–Christian View) (Cairo: A. R.S.E/C.R.E.M.E.D., 2005) (in Arabic). All the English translations from the Arabic text are mine. I express my gratitude to Dr. Candice Lukasik, the anthropologist of religion and the expert in Coptic Christianity for providing me with a list of names of contemporary Egyptian Christian theologians from all denominations, including the name of Fr. William Sidhum.

[45] Ibid., p. 7.

individual's integrity comes before defending the institution; and 4) existence conceptually precedes being.[46]

In her paper for the workshop, Magī ʿAbdulmasīḥ offers a practical theological application of the fourfold methodological criteria which Fr. Sidhum proposed for developing an Arab liberationist theology. ʿAbdulmasīḥ argues that, from the Latin American liberationist experience, we learn the lesson of questioning all the classical theological, from-above answers which religious beliefs impose authoritatively on human individuals and human existence, demanding total compliance with them. All such from-above, far from praxical, answers, ʿAbdulmasīḥ says, "are 'meaningless, if not also dead … [they] are irrelevant and useless."[47] What theology does to liberate, ʿAbdulmasīḥ suggests, is invite us to re-read our religiosity, *habitus*, *modus operandi*, but ultimately our entire history. If we want to meet Christ again, we must not only seek such an encounter with Him in the biblical stories of the Gospels. We should also be able to find a way to meet Christ in the situation and point of view of the unjustly treated and their suffering from worldly evil.[48] What theology is about is not metaphysical, transcendent speculations on God, Creation, and spirituality. It is basically reflective of, and rooted deeply in, the different human, from-below experiences that are stained with injustice, oppression, evil, suffering, depravity, and poverty.[49]

Such an upside-down twisting of the theological construct not only changes our perception of reality. It also transforms our reading of the Gospels in the Bible. The liberationist, from-below reasoning, ʿAbdulmasīḥ proposes, makes us approach the Bible and interpret it from a perspective that is frankly forensic and anatomising in nature: 1) It invites us to critically approach the texts and to investigate them historically. 2) It makes us interrogate the authors' intentions and writing strategies. 3) It, finally, makes us anatomise the ideological presumptions of the readers and users of the biblical texts. "The meaning of the religious text," ʿAbdulmasīḥ affirms, "cannot be elucidated or gleaned only from a literal reading of the text. This is such a most destructive *habitus*. God's word or will do not exist in words or sentences in the religious writs."[50]

In his paper to the workshop, Samīr Murquṣ follows suit and similarly focuses on the applicability of William Sidhum's fourfold methodological criteria for pursuing a liberationist theologisation attempt. Murquṣ's point of departure is his belief that liberationist theology must not be addressed as a political project. According to him, it is rather "a cultural-spiritual project in the first place … that relies on the spiritual-cultural formation and construction styles of the human individual and community."[51] Murquṣ goes as far as considering the liberationist

---

[46] Sidhum, "Ishkāliyāt al-Maṣāḍir al-Falsafiyyah li-Lāhūt al-Taḥrīr" (The Problems of the Philosophical Sources of Liberation Theology), in *Lāhūt al-Taḥrīr*, pp. 17–21.

[47] Magī ʿAbdulmasīḥ, "Lāhūt al-Taḥrīr: As'ilah Mutajaddidah" (Liberation Theology: Renewed Inquiries), in *Lāhūt al-Taḥrīr*, pp. 29–36, p. 31.

[48] Ibid., p. 32.

[49] Ibid., p. 32.

[50] Ibid., pp. 33–34.

[51] Samīr Murquṣ, "Tajribat Lāhūt al-Taḥrīr" (The Experience of Liberation Theology), in *Lāhūt al-Taḥrīr*, pp. 99–125, p. 101.

discourse as not a theology (Murquṣ is not a theologian by profession, but a social and political scholar) in the first place. It is, rather, a historical, public, and sociological discourse first and foremost, in Murquṣ's opinion. Principally, Murquṣ realises that liberationist theology grants central place to the purely theological concept of '*imago Dei.*' Yet he focuses on the praxical and historically embedded operational implications of this notion, rather than on its religious, theological, or ontological connotations. For him, perceiving the nature, components, and epistemological coherence of this theological project lies not in interpreting its conceptual, doctrinal, biblical, and metaphysical claims and preconceptions. It, rather, lies in tracing the liberating ramifications of such a project by unearthing them in the social and historical context of the evolving life of those who created this theology and who implemented it alike.[52]

By means of the above logic, Murquṣ proposes that a potential Arab liberationist theology cannot be imagined merely on the basis of a new reading of religious scripture and new approaching dimensions toward religious doctrinal tradition. It must primarily be built on a discernment and apprehension of the particular social, political, and economic circumstances and components of the particular historical context of the Arab people.[53] It is indeed the case that the needed byproduct of such discernment is not a pure political or economic discourse or agenda. After all, such discourses, if they were created, will not model a "liberationist *theology*," as Murquṣ seems to perceive. As we saw, Murquṣ starts by acknowledging that liberation theology is a 'cultural-spiritual' phenomenon. This conceded, Murquṣ's methodological point here relates that any from-below theologisation for the sake of liberation (similar to the Latin American approach) must ground the spiritual-cultural plant in the soil of the economic, social, and political suffering of the living people. It must do so, if it wants to become a liberating voice for *them* and not in the abstract, and if it wants to address *their* suffering and not suffering as an abstract idea. In other words, theological liberation must be *historical* liberation. In addition, for such a theology to be biblical, it must be one that "interprets the religious texts in the service of the goodwill of the human individuals and communities and the future."[54]

The above attempts at developing liberationist Arab-Eastern theological voices are probably the only serious examples one can find in the geographical context of the Middle East. They depict a serious attempt at conjuring up a theology to address down-to-earth existential challenges in the heartland of Eastern Christianity. Naim Ateek's model can be deemed a *microcosmic* liberationist attention that focuses on Palestine and the crisis in the lives of the Palestinian people in particular. Yet his project can be applied to the broader Arabic-speaking communities, Christian and Muslim alike. On the other hand, William Sidhum seems to be holding a more ambitious dream of developing a *macrocosmic* liberationist voice that, from the beginning, is developed not by the

[52] Ibid., pp. 102ff.
[53] Ibid., p. 112.
[54] Ibid., p. 125.

Egyptians and for the Egyptians alone, but for the Arabs, and one that is conjured up not by the Christians alone, but by the Christians and the Muslims together.

The latter model of liberation theology gives the impression of a more attentive concern about systematising and methodologising the liberationist project and building it on cognitively and epistemologically solid and clearly defined foundations. On the other hand, the former liberationist project of Ateek seems less interested in the systematic and methodological aspects, and far more concerned about the final product and the ultimate content of the imagined liberationist process: the liberating and salvaging of the Palestinian people from their struggle with the existence of Israel and the challenging implications and ramifications of such an existence on how the Palestinian Christians relate to their own biblical tradition. Overall, it is important in the future to pay attention to these two attempts at creating Arab-Eastern liberationist theologies. Unfortunately, this attempt, as I can relate, has not yet been adopted and taken further ahead by other Arab-Eastern theologians, nor has it been studied and scholarly assessed by any Arab-Eastern thinkers. This remains, I reckon, a serious shortcoming that is yet to be attended to on the Arab-Eastern intellectual scene.

Contextualised Arab-Eastern Theology

The second model of Arab-Eastern theology one can find in today's Middle East is substantially contextual or contextualised in nature and approach. This model is fully occupied with the question of locational, cultural, and contextual particularisation and self-individuation. It attempts to demonstrate that a nomenclature like 'Arab Christians' is not oxymoronic, though those Christians who are named after it in the Middle East find themselves easily targeted by the Jews and the Muslims who co-exist with them in that part of the world.

One of the Arab Christian theologians who, throughout the past couple of decades, has produced intensive literature on such contextualised theological reasoning is the Palestinian-Lutheran theologian Mitri Raheb. Raheb's intellectual production centres heavily on the Palestinian cause and the Palestinian–Israeli conflict, just like Naim Ateek. Nevertheless, he personally avoids calling his theological project 'liberationist theology,' preferring to call it 'Palestinian contextual theology' instead. Over the past almost three decades, Raheb has published a considerable number of monographs and editorials wherein he, sometimes monotonously and redundantly, just re-utters the very same ideas perpetually, without any further noteworthy elaboration or deeper digging into what he has already proposed and argued for in his previous or other texts. Be that as it may, in the ensuing sections, I shall not visit every single text Raheb composed. I will only pause at some key texts that, in my reckoning, help us to coherently discuss the main components of his own version of contextualised theology.

The conceptual beginning of Mitri Raheb's contextualised theology discourse lies in his preconception of who is the Christian in the particular geographical context of his personal community in his homeland: who is the *Palestinian* Christian. On this, Raheb says the following:

> The Palestinian Christians see themselves as the descendants of these first Jewish and non-Jewish Christians, who were able to survive a turbulent history of 2000 years. Christianity was not imported to Palestine. In fact, it is the only *'product'* that was successfully exported from Palestine to the whole world. In a sense, Christianity is a *'Palestinian Trademark.'*[55]

As excessively hyperbolic and supremacist as this statement may sound to non-Palestinian ears, its inner conceptual logic underpins the foundations of Mitri Raheb's attempt at developing a contextualised discourse in semi-theological terms that are centred on the Palestinian geo-political experience and serve its preconditions, expectations, and purposes. Here, Palestinian Christianity is not one particular Christianity among equal, though distinguished, others. It is, rather, *the* one, if not almost the only, true, authentic, and genuine Christianity which ever existed. Christianity is the Palestinians' 'trademark,' Raheb says. As if the early followers of Jesus Christ started on the trajectory associated with their Master by virtue, and on the basis, of their geographical location (although the followers of Jesus were called 'Christians' for the first time in Antioch, not in Palestine). They spread their faith through the known world on the basis of their Palestinianism and as merchants selling the 'product' that was manufactured in Palestine (as Mercedes Benz, for example, is a trademark of Germany). This rationale invites us to pause at the nature, logic, and purpose of the contextualisation game that Raheb plays in his various publications' religious discourses. The ensuing lines would unravel this game's components in a broad, systematic manner.

What are the things that make Christianity a Palestinian 'trademark' instead of any other Christianity? According to Raheb, this exclusive superiority is earthed, first, in the fact that Jesus of Nazareth was 'a Palestinian' (Jesus identified in terms of geographical context, in a logic reminiscent of the political ideologies of 'Pan-Arabism,' the dogma of 'the Arab world,' and 'Syrian-Nationalism,' the dogma of 'Greater Syria,' that are known in twentieth-century political thought in the Levant). This, second, lies in the fact that "the Gospel of Jesus Christ was contrary to faiths based on laws, always eager to relate to one's own culture and context."[56] Third, Palestine's referentiality and superiority are rooted in the fact that, though religiously a minority, the Palestinian Christians are part and parcel of an extended and historically prominent civilisational and cultural *Sitz im Leben*: the Arab civilisation. The Palestinian Christians are part of the Arab Christians, who "were among the first Christians."[57] Fourth, the Palestinian Christians are, in Raheb's view, *the* bridge between the Arab Christians and the worldwide Christian churches. The Palestinian Christians, therefore, and despite their occasional suffering from both sides and betrayal by them, "often functioned as transcenders of boundaries and as bridge builders."[58]

---

[55] Mitri Raheb, "Sailing Through Troubled Waters: Palestinian Christians in the Holy Land," in *Dialogue: A Journal of Theology*, 41(2), 2002, pp. 97–102, p. 98. Italics are mine. Raheb uses the same title as the name for his book, M. Raheb, *Sailing Through Troubled Waters: Christianity in the Middle East* (Bethlehem: Diyar Publisher, 2013).

[56] Ibid., p. 98.

[57] Ibid., p. 99.

[58] Ibid., p. 100.

They perform this role, Raheb alleges, despite the difficult challenge of resisting "all the different groups who try to pirate this ship and to lead it to their own ends."[59] All of what this supreme source and absolute representative of Christianity face, as he states, "are but attempts to instrumentalize the fate of the Palestinian Christian community to their own political ends."[60]

The story of the producers of Christianity (the Palestinians), according to Raheb's Palestinisation scheme, is essentialised into a narrative of conspiratorial hermeneutic strategy perpetrated by all the non-Palestinians (especially the European Christians and Zionists and whoever stands under the rubric of what Raheb calls "'the follower of the 'Empire'"[61]) against Palestine and its people. Recreating a Palestino-centric, contextualised theological (genuinely 'Christian,' in Raheb's logic) discourse means withstanding the European and Western biblical exegesis and hermeneutics and replacing them with a new theological reasoning, wherein the land called 'Palestine' and its native people (Muslims, Christians, and Palestinian Jews, according to Raheb) become the central, criterial, and defining hermeneutical keys, not just to the interpretation of the Bible, but also to the perception and fulfilment of the meaning of divine salvation as attested to in the Scriptures.[62]

In the framework of this proposed geo-centric contextualisation, Raheb turns the Land and the People into constitutive components of the Gospel's core message of salvation, not just narratively and historically, but even theologically. He deems the Land and the People not just items or components in the biblical Gospels, but as additional 'gospels': the fifth and the sixth gospels, in specific. As the 'Fifth Gospel,' 'the land' delineates before us the geo-political standing of Palestine. Without it, Raheb claims, "we cannot understand the meaning or importance of liberation and salvation," for "the theme of liberation from occupation becomes such a central theme throughout history and plays such a central role in the Bible."[63] On the other hand, the people of this criterial, referential land, the Palestinians, "constitute something like a Sixth Gospel."[64] These people per se are the cornerstone Gospel-element of the Scripture. The Palestinians are "an important continuum from the Biblical times until today," and they "are but the outcome of all these dynamic history and geo-political developments. Their understanding of the context is important in understanding the Biblical text."[65] By implication, all other non-Palestinians, the Christians included, become the otherised foreigners. They become part of the contra-

---

[59] Ibid., p. 100.

[60] Ibid., p. 101.

[61] On the idea of 'Empire' and its implementation in Mitri Raheb's theological project, see M. Raheb, *Faith in the Face of Empire: The Bible Through Palestinian Eyes* (Maryknoll, NY: Orbis Books, 2014), pp. 55–66.

[62] M. Raheb, "Toward a New Hermeneutics of Liberation: A Palestinian Christian Perspective," in *The Biblical Text in the Context of Occupation: Towards a New Hermeneutics of Liberation*, Mitri Raheb (ed.) (Bethlehem: Diyar Publishers, 2012), pp. 11–28.

[63] Ibid., p. 15.

[64] Ibid., p. 16.

[65] Ibid., p. 17.

Gospel or the pseudo-Gospel groups whose entire relation to Christianity is summarised in historical attempts to conspire against the people of the land of Palestine. The Palestinian Christians are attacked by the Christian Europeans, and the native Palestinian Jews are subdued by the Zionist and Ashkenazi Jews, while, the Palestinian Muslims are ignored because they are not part of a Judeo-Christian culture.[66]

What we have here is a contextualised (inescapably discriminative and exclusivist) theologisation that endeavours to create a new 'Gospel-like' message that is centred on Palestine, not necessarily on God; a 'Gospel-like' view, whose Messiah or 'Suffering Servant' is the Palestinian people as such, not (any more) Jesus Christ, or Jesus Christ is included in this messianic scheme in so far as He *is* Palestinian and even only *because* He was Palestinian. The Bible, and its Gospel message for that matter, cannot, then, be read or understood unless it is read as the voice and reality of Palestine and of the Palestinians, always and only: "Reading the Bible with Palestinian eyes," Raheb orates, "makes one feel as if the Bible was written now and for such times like these."[67] Not every or any 'now,' but the 'now' of Palestine. Not every and any human time, but the time of the Palestinians and them alone, since Christianity in its entirety is their 'trademark.' Any other reading of the Bible, therefore, is not genuinely Christian, but expressive of the conspiracy of the inimical 'empire' against the true Christian Gospel of Palestine and its indigenous people.

For Raheb, the empire's conspiracy goes way back in history to the time of Paul the Apostle and his non-Palestinian voice's attempt to suppress the land, when he made Jesus Christ the epicentre of the Gospel biblical message. Against Paul's Christo-centric 'conspiracy,' Raheb proposes a 'terra-centric,' a 'Palestino-centric,' scriptural message and hermeneutics. The conspiratorial misreading of the Bible was not only perpetrated in the West, but also committed by those native people who converted to Western churches.[68] What is needed to revive the terra-centric theological reasoning against its enemies is a theology that is pursued in total dependence on geo-political analyses conducted by Palestinians, and on the basis of the Gospels of Palestine and the Palestinians. Any other theology is "in fact fundamentalist," Raheb stipulates.[69] This is how Raheb articulates this Palestino-centric theological call:

> It is time to develop a hermeneutics that takes our longstanding rootedness in this land seriously; a theology where biblical history is seen as part of our people's history, where our spiritual forefathers are also our ancestral forefathers … once this is done, the fulfillment of the biblical promises and the fulfilment of our national aspirations are two sides of the same coin and not contradictory at all … the divine rights and the human rights become reconciled again. It is time to read the entire Bible, the entire history of Palestine and all six Gospels together.[70]

[66] Ibid., p. 18.
[67] Ibid., pp. 18–19.
[68] Ibid., p. 24.
[69] Ibid., p. 26.
[70] Ibid., p. 27.

So, where is the core subject of theology (as God-talk), namely God, within the picture? The beginning of the answer is in Mitri Raheb's above cited saying: "The divine rights and the human rights become reconciled again." The climax of this reconciliation, as Raheb proposes elsewhere, manifests in the fact that "in the face of an omnipotent empire the occupied have no one to turn to but God. When people are overwhelmed by the power of empire and drowning in the feeling that other states or peoples can help them defeat the empire, there is no option about where to seek help ... God alone remains."[71] Here, 'God' and religious belief in God alike become instruments in the sole service of the people's geo-political conditions and expectations. Why? Because, for Raheb, theology is in the service of the land and its people (the fifth and sixth gospels); in the service of the right original owners of Christian religion, the Palestinians, and "religion [is] the default response to the geo-politics of [Palestine]."[72] 'God' per se becoming "a factor in geo-politics" instead of the geo-political is discerned as a factor within the framework of God's incarnational, revelational, salvific history: From *Heilsgeschichte* into *Landsgeschichte*. If the case is not so, Raheb argues, theology changes nothing on the ground and is merely a matter of psychology. Be that as it may, 'God-talk' for Raheb means the discourse on how God changed the geo-politics of the empire when "God identified Himself with this land [i.e. Palestine]."[73] "God came to Palestine to change the dynamics of the geo-political reality, and [God] succeeded ... This country needed God badly to transform the battlefield into holy land."[74] The beginning of this was in Jesus, who was believed by the Christians of the land to be the Messiah. Yet now, Raheb opines, the idea of divine intervention (which is traditionally associated with Jesus) is replaced with the direct intervention of the faithful ones: "It was now those who believed in Christ who had to step into this world to engage and to bring change to the empire."[75]

From this geo-centric theology and soteriology, Raheb takes his thesis to its ultimate logical end when he divulges his stance on *who* is to read the Bible referentially and authentically, and not just on *how* one ought to read the Bible and interpret it. For Raheb, it is not just Christianity that is a Palestinian trademark. The Bible itself, in its Old and New Testaments equally, is a Palestinian by-product. Thus, only the Palestinian people of the land can actually read it and understand it as it should be read and understood. "The Gospels," he states, "are closely connected to a certain Land ... one cannot understand the Gospels if they are disconnected from their original context, which is Palestine."[76] One not only fails to understand the Bible without knowing the geography, the geo-politics, and the history of Palestine. More crucially, one would not be able to read the Bible coherently and comprehensively without listening to the Bible "*with the ears* of the people of the Land."[77] Now, who owns

---

[71] M. Raheb, *Faith in the Face of Empire*, p. 85.
[72] Ibid., p. 45.
[73] Ibid., p. 89.
[74] Ibid., p. 91.
[75] Ibid., p. 96.
[76] Ibid., p. 97.
[77] Ibid., p. 97.

such ears? The people of the land, the Palestinians. Thus, understanding in the discourse Raheb postulates hinges not merely upon 'knowing,' but primarily upon '*belonging*': it is not enough to know the Palestinian context and people, so to speak. One should pre-conditionally also acquire the Palestinian 'ears' and be a Palestinian oneself (Raheb speaks about 'listening *with the ears* of Palestinians). This seems to be the logic that underpins Raheb's statement that "the Bible is a Middle Eastern book. It is a product of that region with all of its complexities."[78]

To be fair to his overall project, Raheb elaborates to a certain extent beyond the above displayed Palestino-centric, otherising self-identification boundaries in his various and numerous writings. Another major element in his contextualisation attempt is his stance on the relation between religion and politics in the Middle Eastern region. In the specific context of the Middle East, Raheb believes, religion and politics can never be separated. Thus, he suggests that some of the constitutive enquiries in such a contextualised theology discourse must be: "What positive contribution can the religions make to just, peaceful, and a new Middle East?"[79] Raheb's sincere and frank belief in the positive, let alone referential, role religion can play is the foundational point of departure in his development of a contextualised theological discourse on the Arab-Palestinian setting in the Middle East in general.

Raheb believes that, in such a context moulded by religion, faith and politics cannot be segregated, yet they must also not be blended either. Demarcating boundaries must, rather, always be maintained between them in the midst of, and not despite, their co-existence and intertwining. They must speak to the context as two sides of one and the same coin that focuses ultimately, if not solely, on the goodwill of the human being.[80] One of the consequences of the intermeshing of religion with politics, as Raheb seems to be suggesting, is the turning of the Palestinian–Israeli conflict into a struggle between two opposed religious identities with disproportionate power and religious influence. This resulted from the Israelis baptising politics with religious, dogmatic water and their use of this mixture in exerting on the Palestinians a military occupation that denied them their religious and cultural particularities, not just their political rights.[81]

According, then, to Mitri Raheb, the Middle Eastern secularists' claim that most of the problems in that region are connected to religion is not quite accurate.[82] Raheb concedes that religion is often part of the problem rather than of the solution in that region. He even confesses that there is "too much religion" in the Middle Eastern context. Yet Raheb argues that the existence of too much

[78] Ibid., p. 1.
[79] M. Raheb, "Educational Co-Operation among Christians, Muslims and Jews in the Middle East," in *British Journal of Religious Education*, 18(1), 2014, pp. 59–62.
[80] M. Raheb, *I Am a Palestinian Christian*, Ruth C. L. Gritsch (trans.) (Minneapolis: Fortress Press, 1995), p. 43. See also N. G. Awad, *And Freedom Became a Public Square: Political, Sociological and Religious Overviews on the Arab Christians and the Arabic Spring* (Berlin & Vienna: LIT Verlag, 2012), pp. 125–127.
[81] Raheb, "Mission in the Context of Fragmentation", in *International Review of Mission*, LXXXVI/343, 1997, pp. 393–398, pp. 394–395.
[82] Raheb, *The Faith in the Face of Empire*, p. 91.

politics might, actually, be the main factor that leads religion into trouble. In his view, "the politics of the superpowers in the last two centuries and the failure of international favoring bodies in creating a just peace have pushed people to religion."[83] Here, religion is not the source of failure and crisis. It is, rather, expressive of their existence, and it mirrors their extent and true sources.

In his attempt at suggesting an agenda for a contextualised theological contribution to the twenty-first-century's Palestinian context, Raheb elaborates on the implications of such a theological contribution to the life of the Arab world, wherein religion and politics intertwine and correlate in such a complex manner.[84] Mitri principally argues that in such a religiously moulded and politically loaded context, faith and politics cannot be separated at all, even when the thinker tries to develop a centralised theological reasoning. Anticipating the possible misreading of his stated belief, Raheb does not stop at marrying politics and faith, or divulging a justificatory explanation of such a marriage in the Arab-Palestinian context. He, further, emphasises in a similar explanatory manner that no conflation or total identification of politics with faith is to be concluded from his claim. The demarcating boundaries between the end of politics and the beginning of faith are to be strictly maintained at the same time. These two sides of the equation are supposed to enrich each other's perspectives and serve together in speaking to the concerned context as two faces of one and the same coin; namely, the goodwill of the Palestinian and Arab human beings. Neither politics nor faith, then, must use the other as a tool for achieving its own ultimate goals or turn the other into an instrument in the service of its discourse and agenda's domination in societal and civil life. Raheb's qualified claim, which one meets in the many texts he has produced throughout the years, is not irrelevant to the recent Palestinian and Arab scenes alike. It is a fact that in the Palestinian–Israeli and the Arab world's internal conflicts alike, politics is never out of the picture but almost always part and parcel of the problem. At the same time, the Palestinian and Arab world's contexts, in their Christian, Muslim, and Jewish societal segments, are inherently religious in nature and religiosity has never left the public sphere or been thrown to its margins. Be that as it may, Raheb's contextualised theological reasoning is perceptively accurate in its presumption that religion is an inescapable contributor to the solution of any conflict in the region, and its role is essential in any change and reformation attempt. From this angle, one can say that the Christians are expected to make a contextualised theological contribution, not only toward peace and justice in the region, as Mitri Raheb correctly maintains, but also toward the establishment of new states and civil societies that are shaped after plurality, democracy, the rule of law, human rights, freedom, and coexistence.

Overall, Raheb's contextualised theology-like reasoning wants to offer us a sincere reflection on the particular life-setting of the Christian Palestinians and Arabs in the Middle East by means of drawing the attention of the world to the historical, religious, anthropological, and cultural superior individuation of the

[83] Ibid., p. 92.

[84] I do borrow my display of Raheb's view in this whole paragraph from my previous analysis in N. G. Awad, *And Freedom Became a Public Square*, p. 126.

geography where the story of Jesus Christ took place and the story of the messiah-like Palestinians is still running its course in the heart of dire and unimaginable turbulence and life challenges. If there is anything unique about the theological reasoning that stems from this context, Raheb suggests, this distinction lies primarily, if not solely, in the above-mentioned preconception of the land and its people.

It is my belief that, within the framework of conjuring an Arabic-speaking theology-like discourse, another voice similar to Mitri Raheb's in its context-focused and socio-political orientations and perspectives comes from the Protestant community of Egypt. It is the voice of the churchman and theologian Andrea Zaki Stephanous. In his approach, Zaki tries to extend the boundaries of provincialism into regionality, yet he follows Raheb's geo-centric contextualised perspective to a certain extent. The difference worth pondering between the two is that, while Raheb focuses in his contextualisation attempt on the socio-political components of the specific setting of Palestine, Zaki seems to be aspiring at extending the contextual boundaries beyond locality and tackling the socio-cultural scene of the Arabic-speaking region in its totality. This, nevertheless, does not make Zaki deviate from the particularist context of Egypt and the dynamics of living and co-existing in the Muslim-majority Egyptian and Arab settings alike. In the ensuing sections, I briefly unpack the main consistencies of Andrea Zaki's contextualised, pan-Arabist (over-against Raheb's 'pan-Palestinianist') theological reasoning. I do this by touching upon claims and propositional analyses Zaki divulges through various texts he has produced during the past years.

In the same vein as Raheb, Zaki concedes that religion is a dominant factor in the social, political, and cultural contexts of the Arab world. Religion in that region, he says, controls "the personality and defines the identity" of the populations. He further stresses that religion in that geography frames the individuals' forms of political participation.[85] In a slight departure from Mitri Raheb's rather positive and embracing appraisal of the impact of religion on politics, Zaki displays his scepticism, if not serious reservations, about the role of religion on the political scene. Zaki does not deny the importance of the rootedness in religious backgrounds in the Middle Eastern context. He notes, however, that "reducing all forms of identity down to the religious ones led to the restriction of pluralism, created mono-allegiance, and it encouraged the tendency of hiding behind religion."[86] His concern about such interference stems from his observation of the growth and proliferation of 'political Islam' specifically and its pervasive seeping into all life's aspects, to such an extent that led to the suppression, or displacement, of nationalist, supra-religious identities and affiliations. 'Political Islam' becomes a manifestation of excluding non-

---

[85] Andrea Zaki, "al-Thaqāfah wal-Hauwiyyah" (Culture and Identity), in *Naḥwa Lāhūt 'Arabī Mu'āṣir* (Toward a Contemporary Arab Theology) (in Arabic), Andrea Zaki (ed.) (Cairo: al-Thaqafah Press, 2007), pp. 487–531, p. 489.

[86] Ibid., p. 508. I have made my own English translation of Zaki's Arabic texts.

Muslims from public spheres and judging their affiliation upon the criterion of a specified religious belief (i.e., Islam).[87]

Against this, Zaki calls for replacing religiosity as the primary identity-formation constituent with 'Nationalism,' more specifically with 'Arabism.' He deems the latter more inclusive a criterion for the non-Muslim (Christian) Arabs to form, assess, and verify their identity with, especially that the Christians, according to him, live with a 'minority mentality' (*'aql al-aqalliyyah*) in Egypt and the Arab world, and they tend to be torn apart by the paradox of religious-versus-nationalist identity.[88] Zaki personally calls for "a new understanding of Arabism that exceeds mono-religiosity and is capable of including various religions, and of dealing with the historical phases that precede the entrance of Islam to the political thought of the diverse communities of the Middle East."[89] This new understanding, Zaki alleges, centres around the notions of 'Nationalism' and 'Patriotism,' which withstand political Islam's association of identity and affiliation with religious belonging on one hand, and the association of the state with the Islamic *Ummah* alone on the other.[90] Here, Zaki proposes that Arabism travels beyond two problematic alternatives: either embracing religion as, per se, an identity and citizenship, which would generate an Islamic State that excludes the non-Muslims from authority, or, embracing anti-religious nationalism and making it the essence of the state's formation, which leads to the creation of a secular state that segregates religion from politics.[91] What worries Zaki seriously is the common attempt among many Arab Muslim scholars, in the past and the present, to marry 'Arabism' with 'Islam' and almost define the former by virtue of the latter. 'Arab' and 'Muslim' are seen as two sides of one and the same coin; or two instruments in the service of one and the same struggle of the Arab world with the colonial West.[92]

Zaki wants to develop, instead, a new understanding of an Arab identity, which he (rather nebulously) calls 'dynamic Arabism.' This Arabism's dynamicity lies, first, in its multi-faceted and pluralist history that exceeds the boundaries of the history of Islam alone to encompass other Middle Eastern religions and cultures.[93] This dynamicity, second, pays attention to cultural particularity. These two characteristics, Zaki suggests, make dynamic Arabism the needed cultural criterion which alone can help all the Arabs, the Christians mainly, to form dynamic identities; in-process identities journeying through a trajectory of continuous construction.[94] Such an understanding of identity from the perspective of the so-called 'dynamic Arabism,' Zaki argues, must become the foundation of the Christians' theological reasoning. It alone, he proposes,

---

[87] Ibid., pp. 489–491.

[88] As he alleges in Andrea Zaki, "Al-Daūr al-Tajdīdī lil-Masīḥiyyīn al-'Arab" (The Renewing Role of the Arab Christians), in *al-Ma'ārij Journal*, 24(173), 2014, pp. 78–84, pp. 80–81.

[89] Zaki, "al-Thaqāfah wal-Hauwiyyah" (Culture and Identity), p. 491.

[90] Ibid., p. 493.

[91] Ibid., pp. 496–498ff.

[92] Ibid., p. 498.

[93] Ibid., p. 499.

[94] Ibid., pp. 502–503.

enables the Christians to conjure up a "theology of the minority" that is fostering of citizenship and co-existence rather than passive resistance or violent sectarianism. Again, we have here another contextualised theological voice that, just like Raheb's, calls for a theology based on, preconditioned by, and responsive to the geo-politics of the living Christian and non-Christian communities in that specific *Sitz im Leben.*

One of the main challenges that prevents the Christians from pursuing such a dynamic identity-based theology yet, according to Zaki, is the Christians' occupation with overcoming their life's turbulences by means of a "minority mentality" (he criticises 'minority' here despite his call for conjuring a 'theology of the minority' earlier!) that drives them to cling superstitiously to a longing for Jesus Christ's second eschatological (millennial) coming, which they derive from a literalist reading of the Bible. Zaki argues that such an apocalyptic, Biblicist longing for futural and eschatological, far from realistic historical or praxical, salvation from a minority status and exclusion, has ramifications that are far beyond theological and doctrinal in nature. It is, rather, a religious view with direly influential consequences that are pertinent to politics, society, and culture.[95] Just like politicised religiosity (i.e., political Islam), such apocalypticism traps the Christians theologically in a self-perception drowned in a divisive, destructive, and backlashing identification mentality. The Christians would also fall into a state of protectionism when they surrender to their minority status and they would hermetically seal themselves behind a religious, sectarian identity.

Such a tendency, Zaki says, "generates dual thought, and it impacts the credibility of nationalist affiliation."[96] For Zaki, the apocalyptic, Biblicist approach is inaccurate theology, because it haunts the Christians with a metaphysical, heavenly homeland that estranges them from the earthly, historical affiliation to their living location and alienates their self-perception from the potential inclusiveness of the dynamic Arab identity.[97] Driven by their minority status, the Christians, Zaki suggests, drown themselves in a whirlpool of "dreams-visions" (*aḥlām-rū'a*) that lie in a total reliance on a supernatural, divine interference and support. Such a dream-visional state of mind, Zaki surmises, represents a religious view with factual political, social, and cultural designations. It represents a state of escapism from the pressurising and challenging reality toward an ideal, imaginable, futural world embedded in the afterlife and not in the historical world per se.[98]

Against this orientation, Zaki proposes that the Arab Christians need an Arabic theology capable of contributing to the development of a concept of 'citizenship' and to the fostering of democracy. The theology that speaks only about heavenly intervention and passive longing for the *eschaton* and the afterlife

---

[95] Ibid., p. 507.
[96] Ibid., p. 508.
[97] Ibid., pp. 511–512ff.
[98] Zaki, "Al-Daūr al-Tajdīdī lil-Masīḥiyyīn al-ʿArab" (The Renewing Role of the Arab Christians), p. 80.

is against citizenship, Zaki opines.[99] True theology is one that stems from the belief that "faith is a call for activating the future in our present time."[100] Jesus's eschatological message of the Kingdom of God was a liberation for the land (again the land, like Raheb) from empirical colonialism. It personifies an achievement of a victory that was not just spiritual, but also political and economic (reminiscent of Raheb's 'geo-politics').[101] The Arab contextual theology that is inspired by Jesus's messianic history, Zaki opines, is one that must simultaneously adhere to a theological reference and commit to a cultural context.[102] From this particular perspective, developing theology means immediately constructing a culture that is expressive of an Arabic dynamic identity. Theology here *is* culture, and it is the source, or the womb, of culture's formation. Moreover, theology here is a new theologised *political* worldview or a *politicised* theology of context that is erected on the following fourfold foundation: 1) The general principal of "loyalty" (*walā'*) that exceeds narrow, unilateral affiliation. 2) A pluralist exegesis of the religious text that takes into consideration the human dimensions of the composition and understanding of the textual content of religiosity. 3) An acknowledgement of the notion of 'cohesion' (*al-tamāsuk*) as the basis of a co-existence that manifests itself in equality and justice. 4) A formation of a theologised political worldview on an attention to the constitutive role of 'institutionalisation' that exceeds the mere individualist and privative roles and intentions.[103]

What is the theological reference Andrea Zaki proposes as the foundation of his contextualised, culturalised, and politicised theological proposal? Zaki proposes the 'Social Gospel' hermeneutics of the historical Jesus's life and ministry as such a foundation. He argues against the classical evangelical separation between evangelism, on one hand, and social service, on the other. In contrast, Zaki follows the theological trend which believes that '*evangelion*' and '*diachonia*' are intertwined and correlated. Their interconnectedness exceeds Platonic dualism and any linear, hierarchical relatedness, wherein evangelism precedes *diachonia* and overrides it. Instead, "evangelism and social service are equally required, and none of them is prior to the other."[104]

Zaki believes that this Social Gospel-centred theology would amend the Christian Church's role in Egyptian society. Both the Orthodox and the Protestant Copts, he relates, used to historically focus on evangelising the Egyptian, predominantly Muslim, society, instead of conducting activities in the service of the social needs of this context.[105] The Christians followed thereby the

---

[99] Zaki, "al-Thaqāfah wal-Hauwiyyah" (Culture and Identity), pp. 514–515.

[100] Ibid., p. 519.

[101] Ibid., p. 519.

[102] Ibid., p. 522.

[103] Zaki, "Al-Daūr al-Tajdīdī lil-Masīḥiyyīn al-'Arab" (The Renewing Role of the Arab Christians), pp. 83–84.

[104] Andrea Zaki, *al-Massīḥ wal-Naqd al-Tārīkhī: Qiṣṣat al-Ṣirā' bayn al-Kirāzah wal-Taghiyyīr al-Ijtimā'ī* (Christ and Historical Criticism: The Story of the Struggle between Evangelism and Social Change) (in Arabic) (Cairo: al-Thaqafah Press, 2002), pp. 80–81.

[105] Ibid., p. 90.

conventional understanding of the 'Gospel' as a call for eternal life, not as a call for earthly change. The social work was deemed a non-biblical cause. Against this, Zaki follows the voice that calls for paying attention to the social and praxical dimensions of the Gospel's attestations of Jesus's historical healing ministry, wherein Jesus actively attended to people's needs without preaching to them with words.[106] "If we looked at what Jesus did," Zaki states, "we see that He wants to help society to examine its ethical life and to take moral issues into consideration, so that this will drive them to exert justice and to be righteous and adherent to the public good, instead of seeking personal ambition, power and influence."[107] Be that as it may, the needed contextualised theology, according to Zaki, is one that is based on "an accurate Biblical understanding of Jesus's life and ministry," and one that makes the latter "our preconception and entrance toward social change."[108]

In a book he published in 2021, Andrea Zaki expanded his theological discourse on implementing Jesus's Social Gospel in pursuing a contextualised societal change. He resumed touching upon the question of whether God's salvific call lies in commissioning the Christians to launch a changing ministry in the historical world, or in orienting them toward passively longing for the eschatological fulfilment of the heavenly Kingdom of God. This time, however, he tackles this enquiry from the perspectives of the Church's connection to society in the Egyptian context, on one side, and of the call for developing a theological take on co-existence, on the other.

Zaki argues that the past centuries in general, and the last five decades in particular, confronted the Christians (Orthodox, Catholics, and Protestants alike) in Egypt with various existential and socio-political crises that generated tension, and sometimes fractures, in their relations to society. Historically, Zaki relates, the Christians in Egypt centred their relation to society around the primary, and almost solo, task of proclaiming the Word of God and evangelism (*i'lān kalimat Allah [wa] al-kirāzah*).[109] This prioritisation was pursued at the expense of the Church's presence and role in the social context of the country. The Church, eventually, paid that price for the following factors: 1) The Church strived to survive in a rapidly Islamised broader society. 2) The Church was driven toward evangelism by particularist, narrow theological view. 3) The Church understood the Gospel eschatologically as centred in eternal afterlife, instead of praxically as centred in historical social change.[110] Recently, and in the aftermath of the Arab Spring, Zaki proceeds, the challenges for the churches escalated and became more dire than before, forcing the Christians to question their connectedness to society and role in it. The Christians were one of the public segments that were exposed to systemic marginalisation from the post-Arab-

---

[106] Ibid., p. 92.
[107] Ibid., p. 95.
[108] Ibid., p. 99.
[109] Andrea Zaki, *Min Lāhūt al-Shafāfiyah ila Lāhūt al-'Ayish al-Mushtarak: al-Kanīsah wal-Mas'ūliyyah al-Mujtama'iyyah* (From the Theology of Transparency into Theology of Co-existence: the Church and Societal Responsibility) (Cairo: Dār al-Thaqāfah, 2021), p. 20.
[110] Ibid., p. 20.

Spring Islamised public sphere and authority in Egypt.[111] Though the Christians participated in the Arab Spring revolution in Egypt, their consequent, deliberate marginalisation caused a total relapse in the Christians' relation to society and made them disbelieve in their role of pursuing social change. It forced many of them to retreat into hiding inside the walls of the churches.[112] Nevertheless, the past decade also witnessed the return of the Christians to the public sphere to participate in the ousting of the Muslim Brotherhood's regime in the revolution of 30 June 2013.

This fluctuating connectedness to society, Zaki concludes, invites the Christians to ponder the possibility of establishing a steady and consistent presence and role in society upon a constructive theology about the notion of 'co-existence.' On the meaning and goals of co-existence, Zaki states the following:

> The context of co-existence designates learning the method of common life with another person or another group who believe in different convictions or lives in a different manner, and the goals of co-existence include accepting the other, the ability to interact with him, as well as maintaining an accurate and positive relation with the different other, whether an individual or a group.[113]

This means, Zaki explains, that one must exist side-by-side with the other on all levels of existence, including the social, the religious, the sectarian, the confessional, the linguistic, the nationalist, and the regional alike. Therefore, 'co-existence' is not just a relevant notion for the context of ideological conflicts. It is also suitable and plausible in relation to the context of general social affairs. Theologically speaking, the Egyptian Church can participate, Zaki proposes, in conjuring up an understanding of 'citizenship' that exceeds the political realm of reasoning and encompasses also the other aspects of human co-existance, like the social, cultural, and economic. This is how the Gospel notion of 'justice' backs up the civil notion of 'equality' in the Egyptian context, and it makes the religious imagination therein contribute to the co-existence state of being called 'civil society.'[114] It is this contribution of the theological notion of 'justice' that necessitates the Church's directing of its theological imagination towards the society it exists, and co-exists, in. There is "a consistent dialectic relation connecting the Church's theological message to the Church's social role and its interest in the public affair."[115] Towards this contextualised perspective, the Egyptian Church must direct its theology.

What validates and warrants such directedness, according to Zaki, is the fact that, beside pluralism, the idea of co-existence is inherently constitutive of the theological worldview of the Bible. In both its Testaments, the Bible beams with examples that demonstrate the substantial relation between 'plurality' and 'co-existence' in the structural textile of God's Creation and Salvation history

[111] Ibid., pp. 57ff.
[112] Ibid., p. 58.
[113] Ibid., p. 109.
[114] Ibid., p. 110.
[115] Ibid., p. 111.

alike.[116] Be that as it may, Zaki believes that the Egyptian Church should develop a theological discourse on co-existence that is based on the biblical theologies of Creation and Redemption. God's creating the human in His image, Zaki suggests, is a theological message declaring that God wants His Creatures to enjoy their full individual and social rights.[117] So, by developing a theology on pluralist co-existence, the Church in Egypt contributes to the restoration of the '*imago Dei*' in the human life of the Egyptians; the one, that is, that the humans were deprived of due to injustice and inequality.[118] On the other hand, Jesus Christ's ministry did not aim at dissolving all people, notions, and cultures into one, homogenous whole. Jesus, rather, proclaimed the Kingdom of Heaven for all people in the depth of their diversity, offering them the same values of equality, truth, and justice.[119]

A co-existence theology in the Egyptian context, Zaki concludes, must declare the divine purpose that is attested to in the Bible; namely, granting human life the values of "dignity, equality, responsibility" (*al-karāmah, al-musāwāt, al-mas'ūliyyah*).[120] Within this biblicalised theology framework, Zaki postulates, there is no genuine co-existence without maintaining religious dignity and freedom. Advocating for human rights by means of protecting religious freedom, Zaki opines, does not at all contradict or deviate from Jesus's redemptive sacrifice on the Cross. It is theologically approved and commanded to ground co-existence in the act of defending the other's rights of religious belief and of practising this belief freely without one personally holding the same belief or affiliating with it.[121] Theology of co-existence, in conclusion, is the contextualised theological voice that is suitable to the Egyptian and Arab contexts, in Zaki's opinion, because it is the one that enables the local Egyptian Church "to work as a religious institution with a commitment toward human rights and the dignity of all human beings."[122]

Land-Based Arab-Eastern Theology

Touching upon 'the land' idea and God's promise of a land to His Israel (Abraham and his descendants) is a subject the investigator can detect in other trends of Arab-Eastern theological reasoning in today's context. For example, in their various theological writings, both Naim Ateek in liberationist, and Mitri Raheb in contextual, theology trends (which we visited earlier) touch upon the issue of the land and the divine promise associated with it. Both speak about the central status the land of Palestine occupies in the Israeli–Palestinian historical conflict, and they highlight its theological implications for the life of the people in their homeland, Palestine. This conceded, neither Ateek nor Raheb present the

[116] Ibid., pp. 113ff.
[117] Ibid., p. 115.
[118] Ibid., p. 115.
[119] Ibid., p. 116.
[120] Ibid., p. 117.
[121] Ibid., p. 128.
[122] Ibid., p. 130.

idea of 'the land' as a benchmark in their theological reasoning. The idea is, rather, presented as one serious item within a broader, more foundational, cognitive framework and methodological overview.

In the contemporary Arab-Eastern theological context, nevertheless, there are other Arabic-speaking theologians whose contributions have surfaced during the twenty-first century, who treat the idea of 'the land' and the divine promise related to it in the Bible as a more central, hermeneutic, and basic framing concept in their theologisation. The authors of such a land-based theological understanding may not have produced full-fledged, systematised theological discourses like the ones of Ateek, Raheb, and others we have already encountered or will be encountering later. So, one needs to pause merely at single texts written by different Christian writers; texts that are basically composed by church ministers or clerics with primary pastoral and spiritual concerns, rather than staunchly academic and scholarly ones. Thus, one might encounter in these expositions pastoral and homiletical perspectival tones, rather than scholarly or systematically theological ones. The authors of these texts, finally, lived, or still live, in the heart of the Arab Middle East, in Palestine, Syria, Jordan, and Lebanon, where Christians have first-hand experience of the Israeli–Palestinian conflict over the land, and where the concern about the land of historical Palestine digs deeply into the Arab-Eastern Christians' imagination and belief-perception. In the ensuing paragraphs, I shall introduce to the reader two examples of these Arab-Eastern theological voices that focus on the land. The first is the voice of the Syrian Evangelical theologian Riad Kassis, and the second is the voice of the Palestinian Lutheran theologian Munthir Isaac.

Let me start first with Riad Kassis, since his writing was produced earlier. In 2007, Kassis, the Syrian Protestant pastor and Old Testament scholar, contributed a chapter-long theological explanation of the meaning of covenant in Protestant theology and this meaning's impact on the Middle Eastern context. This chapter was written in the Arabic language, and it appeared in an anthology on Arabic theology that was published in that year.[123] In this chapter, the author conceptually connects the notion of 'covenant' to the Old Testament's promise of the land of Palestine that God bequeathed to His Israel. He deems the land's promise the foundational backbone and theological framework of the understanding of the divine–human covenant, relating that "the hermeneutical school [the author follows] for understanding the subject of covenant is directly influenced by the subject of the land of Palestine and its cause."[124]

---

[123] Riad Kassis, "Mafhūm al-ʿAhd fī al-Fikr al-Injīlī wa-Ta'thīrih fī Wāqiʿ al-Sharq al-Awsaṭ: Dirāsah Tārīkhiyyah, Kitābiyyah, Lāhūtiyyah wa-Akhlāqiyyah" (The Concept of Covenant in Protestant Thought and its Impact on the Middle East's Reality: A Historical, Biblical, Theological and Ethical Study), in *Naḥwa Lāhūt ʿArab ʿMuʿāṣir* (Toward a Contemporary Arabic Theology), Andrea Zaki (ed.) (Cairo: Al-Thaqāfah Press, 2007), pp. 39–94. The author echoes in this chapter the same conclusions he delineated in a publication on the idea of the land in the Bible which he published back in 1990. See Riad Kassis, *al-Arḍ fī al-Kitāb al-Muqaddas* (The Land in the Bible) (Damascus: Alif Bā' al-Adeeb, 1990).

[124] Kassis, "Mafhūm al-ʿAhd fī al-Fikr al-Injīlī wa-Ta'thīrih fī Wāqiʿ al-Sharq al-Awsaṭ: Dirāsah Tārīkhiyyah, Kitābiyyah, Lāhūtiyyah wa-Akhlāqiyyah," p. 64.

Kassis suggests that 'the land' theme is a central issue in the entire Old Testament and its overall understanding. In all the promises God made to Abraham, Isaac, and Jacob, He pledges to bequeath a land to them and to their descendants. This pledge, Kassis relates, reveals that the land is a gift from God (*al-arḍ hiya ʿaṭiyyat Allah*), and it is even a conditional gift, which God graced Israel with, not upon merit, but upon love and charity. So, if Israel did not use this gift, and did not live on the land, according to God's will, God would take His gift back. This is what the Old Testament suggests, according to Kassis, when it relates that God delayed Israel's entrance to the land due to its disobedience and He also forbade Moses from entering the land because of his sins.[125] This is why in the Protestant tradition, like the one hailing from John Calvin, Kassis maintains, there is an association of the land-promise with allegiance to the covenantal agreement between God and the human. As God commits Himself fully to the covenant, the human agent must also commit him or herself equally to its demands and expectations, otherwise the promises related to the covenant are no more binding to God. On the other hand, the land in the Old Testament is not merely designative of God's conditional gift, but also indicative of comfort and safety: "Owning the land by Israel is not the main purpose, but enjoying comfort and safety" (*laysa imtilāk Īsrā'īl lil-arḍ huwa al-ghāyah al-raī'siyyah, bal at-tamattuʿ bil-rāḥah wal-amān fīhā*).[126] Yet, comfort and safety were not fulfilled, as the Old Testament states, for Israel was captured and taken into exile from the land, and the eschatological hope of fulfilling this promise was relegated to the future.

From the land and its promise in the Old Testament, Kassis moves into the New Testament's attestations. There, he notices the 'surprising' (*al-mustaghrab)*, almost total silence about both the covenant and the land in these Scriptures. He relates that the land is mentioned only once in the Gospels, specifically when Jesus says in his sermon on the mountain, "blessed are the humbles, for they inherit 'the land'" (Matt. 5:5). Kassis notices here that the verse is derived from a similar verse in Psalms 11:37. However, he points out that Jesus seems to have revised the verse by giving it a general, inclusivist, and cross-national perspective. Instead of 'land' (*arḍ*) in the narrow sense of a specific piece of earth, Jesus spoke about 'the land' (*al-arḍ*) in the global sense of the entire earth. Also, instead of speaking about the people of Israel alone, Jesus turned the verse into a statement inclusive of "all the he and she believers in Him who inherit the Kingdom of God" (*kull al-mū'minīn wal-mu'mināt bihi al-ladhīn yarithūn malakūt Allah*).[127] Kassis points to the Kingdom of God as the core-meaning of 'land,' instead of Palestine the particular geographical territory, upon his belief that the notion of 'land' in the Bible is ultimately *theological* and not geographical in nature. The meaning of this notion lies in the reality of the divine (*theo*-logy), not in the reality of human existence. "'The land' as 'the Kingdom of God,'" he relates, is "broader and more comprehensive than a piece

---

[125] Ibid., pp. 64–65.
[126] Ibid., p. 65.
[127] Ibid., p. 66.

of earth in a particular geographical location" (*malakūt Allah al-ladhī huwa awsaʿ wa-ashmal bikathīr min arḍ mā fī buqʿah jughrāfiyyah muʿayyanah*).[128]

One must point out here that Kassis does not want to create a dichotomic rift between the Bible's two Testaments in terms of how each speaks about the land. He does not, that is, intend to suggest that, while the Old Testament offers a materialist meaning of the land, the New Testament delineates a spiritual one. Far from alluding to a hierarchical discrimination in the textual attestation, Kassis affirms the following:

> We cannot place the Old Testament in the materialism corner and the New Testament in the spiritualism opposite one. Both contain materialist and spiritualist aspects equally. [What we should realize, instead] is a continuity regarding the issues of the covenant and the land between the two testaments. This continuity must be perceived, as we have pointed out, equally in terms of the covenant's persistence and the extension and broadening of the notion of 'the land' alike.[129]

'The land' now is theologically re-exegeted to stand for God's universal, inclusivist promise to all those who believe in Him among the humans of "a new material land inhabited with righteousness" (*bi-arḍ mādiyyah jadīdah yaskun fīhā al-birr*).[130] Be that as it may, the owning of the land of Palestine by today's State of Israel, Kassis argues, defies the core theological message of the Bible. "The immigration of the ethnic Jewish people to the land of Palestine during the past century is not grounded in the fulfillment of the Old Testament's promises, and it has no theological value or connotation," says Kassis.[131] He then proceeds in affirming that there is no theological indication in the New Testament whatsoever of a geographical, material piece of land in Palestine that is Jewish in identity.[132] Therefore, Kassis stipulates,

> Narrowing the Biblical content down to the discussion about the land of Palestine, and then using the former as a justifier for the occupation of the land, is an interpretation of the Holy Scripture in the service of a contemporary political issue the Bible is not related to. It is more convenient to solve the [political] conflict on peaceful bases and by means of negotiations grounded in the resolutions of the international society ... not on the basis of an Old Testamental verse from here or a pericope from there implemented in supporting the Zionist allegations.[133]

Kassis brings his theological re-interpretation of the land to a conclusion by calling the Christians of the Middle East to extend the mere distinction between the theological and spiritual perceptions of 'the land' in the Bible and its broader framework of reasoning that lies in God's graceful covenant with His Israel and the world believers, on one side, and the political, geographical notion of 'land' that underpins the Israeli–Palestinian conflict over Palestine, on the other. He

---

[128] Ibid., p. 66.

[129] Ibid., pp. 66–67.

[130] Ibid., p. 67.

[131] Ibid., p. 70.

[132] Ibid., p. 71. Kassis cites this claim from Christopher J. H. Wright, *An Eye for An Eye: The Place of Old Testament Ethics Today* (Downers Grove, IL: InterVarsity Press, 1983), p. 92 (pp. 88–102).

[133] Kassis, "Mafhūm al-ʿAhd fī al-Fikr al-Injīlī wa-Taʾthīrih fī Wāqiʿ al-Sharq al-Awsaṭ: Dirāsah Tārīkhiyyah, Kitābiyyah, Lāhūtiyyah wa-Akhlāqiyyah," p. 71.

invites them to travel beyond this distinction into discerning equally a differentiation between Judaism as a sublime, monotheistic faith founded in the Hebrew Scripture, on one hand, and "the Zionist movement as an ideological, colonialist and racist phenomenon, which uses the religious element in the service of mobilising its followers after its own political agenda," on the other.[134] The idea of 'the land' in the Bible, Kassis stresses, must be always approached within the framework of theology and spirituality, and should never be geographised or politicised.

A more recent example of a land-based theology text which one can find in Arabic-language bookshops is a volume written in Arabic by the Palestinian Lutheran pastor and theologian Munthir Isaac. In 2021, Isaac published an open-access book titled *Arḍ al-Mi'ād: Qirā'ah lāhūtiyyah Ḍimn as-Siyāq al-Filasṭīnī* (The Promised Land: A Theological Reading within Palestinian Context). In this text, Isaac looks at the biblical Old and New Testaments' attestations that speak about the land and about God's promise to Abraham and his descendants that Palestine would be the promised homeland for them. The twelve chapters of Isaac's book are fully immersed in a reading strategy which the author applies to the Bible in its two Testaments, attempting thereby to offer an alternative, mostly homiletical, bibliocentric discourse over-against the politico-centric and ideologised colonial reading of Zionist, mostly Western, Christianity. He speaks about what he describes "a *Christian* reading of the Old Testament's prophesies" (*qirā'ah Masīḥiyyah li-nubūwāt al-'ahd al-qadīm*).[135] This clearly suggests that the counter-readings that grant the land to the Jews alone on the basis of the biblical promise are 'non-Christian.' This non-Christian reading of the land in non-Palestinian, Western theology, according to Isaac, exploits the Bible in the service of the Israeli discourse that Palestine is for the Jews alone.[136] Consequentially, the Bible becomes a serious problem for the Palestinian Christians. For Isaac, this problematic text, however, is the very same text that offers the solution to the land crisis. Upon this conviction, he decides to counter in his book the Biblicist reading of the idea of the land that is developed by Christian and Jewish Zionism and to replace it with an equally Bible-centred counter-reading. This time, Issac, differently from Kassis, treats the notion of 'the land' as a frankly geographical and political concept, and he endeavours to inject into it theological perspectives and connotations that are antagonistic to the theological implications injected into it by Zionist hermeneutics.

Fundamental to Isaac's alternative bibliocentric theology of the land is his re-interpretation of the promise God made about the land in the Old Testament. He argues that the intrinsic connectedness between the land and the promise God made declares clearly that the land is the property of God alone and only: "The Holy Scripture is crystal clear about the notion of the land. For, it confirms that earth – the entire earth – is the sole property of God the Creator" (*mulk lil-Allah*

---

[134] Ibid., p. 72.
[135] Munthir Isaac, *Arḍ al-Mi'ād: Qirā'ah lāhūtiyyah Ḍimn as-Siyāq al-Filasṭīnī* (The Promised Land: A Theological Reading within Palestinian Context) (Bethlehem: Bethlehem Bible College, 2021), pp. 113–126.
[136] Ibid., pp. 8–9.

al-khāliq).[137] Thus, the promised land cannot be the property of any specific human nation; thus, not the property of Israel (*lam tamlik Isrā'īl fī al-Kitāb al-Muqaddas arḍ al-mī'ād*).[138] So, Palestine is not a land to be owned by any nation. All the nations that inhabited this territory throughout history, including the Jews (whose historical presence in Palestine is never denied or undermined by Isaac), were merely stewards, caretakers of the land, never its owners. On the other hand, the land's stewardship status has never been naturally granted as a prerogative or a merit to any of the inhabitants of the land. It has always been a responsibility that is warranted only on the basis of two prerequisites. The first is holiness (*al-qadāsah*): holiness is the precondition of the residence in the land (*fal-qadāsah maṭlab lil-suknā fil-arḍ*).[139] The second precondition is obedience (*aṭ-ṭā'ah*) to God and His command of justice (*'adl*): justice is the prerequisite of the fulfilment of the promise of allowing the people to inhabit the land (*al-'adl huwa sharṭ li-taḥqīq al-wa'd*).[140]

The book's ensuing chapters try to offer a comprehensive, biblio-homiletical explanation of the meaning of a 'promised land' in the Scripture. They pursue this by means of developing a re-interpretation (re-reading, rather than re-exegeting) of the land that presents it as an expression of a universal extension of territoriality which exceeds the particular geography of Palestine. The land stands for the entire Creation, for God owns all the earth, not just Palestine, though God's global sovereignty starts in the concrete geography of the land called Palestine. Isaac additionally offers a re-reading of the idea of 'people' per se from the same universalising, or globalising, perspective. Israel is God's people, but not exclusively. Israel is the first communal representative of God, but it is just an exemplary and symbolic starting-model: God's people, Israel (Isaac never denies this status for the Jews), are supposed to be only the prototype or the role model for other nations on their lands (*kān 'lā sha'b Isrā'īl an yakūna mithālan aw namūdhajan lil-shu'ūb al-ukhrā fī arḍinā*).[141] Yet, according to Isaac, Israel failed in playing this role-modelling, representational duty because it did not apply justice in the land. It lost, thus, its holiness and betrayed its disobedience.[142] The land is, therefore, subordinated to the more primary and foundational factor of faith in God (*al-īmān yasmū 'alā al-arḍ*).[143]

In today's Creation, Isaac concludes, all earth's nations are included within the biblical 'Israel,' who is called today 'God's Church' (*al-umam juz' min Isrā'īl al-kitābiyyah al-yaūm, wa-huwa mā-nusammih al-'ān bil-kanīsah*).[144] Be that as it may, as God is for all, the land too must be for all. It is for all who are called, and who obediently respond to, God's demand of stewardship. This is not a privilege or a prerogative for one nation. It is a responsibility we are all called

[137] Ibid., p. 17.
[138] Ibid., p. 19.
[139] Ibid., p. 20.
[140] Ibid., p. 22.
[141] Ibid., p. 62.
[142] Ibid., p. 63.
[143] Ibid., pp. 65–66.
[144] Ibid., p. 95.

to take care of sincerely and justly. "The Christian understanding of [the idea of] 'people of God,'" Isaac states, "is that God is the God of all, and he does not discriminate in His love and treatment between one people and another, or between one race and another."[145]

Isaac's main conclusion from the previous bibliocentric reading strategy is that the promised land is the land of the Palestinians. For the Palestinians, he states, it is "their land and the land of their ancestors. So, their rootedness in the land as Palestinians is deeply rooted in all the preceding nations. [Thus,] the matter is not just an abstract academic investigation, but a life-or-death and existential cause."[146] Isaac does not clearly or explicitly disclose whom he includes under the rubric or nomenclature of 'Palestinians,' and whether, for instance, the Muslims and the Jews, who also inhabit the land, are included or not. The ensuing pages of the last chapter of his book drop some hints that seriously invite us to postulate that he particularly means to speak about the Christians of Palestine as these 'Palestinians.' He turns all the discourse he constructed on the land, its promise, and the people of the promise into a discourse representative particularly of the Christians, and he speaks from that point up till the end of the book on the land for the Christian Palestinians. He establishes this Christian-centric understanding of the Palestinian land on a Christocentric perspective of the biblical attestation as such: Jesus Christ is the epicentre, the hermeneutic core of the interpreting of the Bible's message on the land and its promise. And, since the Christians are the Christ-like representatives in the land, then the spinal cord of the theology of the land seems to end up becoming the Christian Palestinian existence. Isaac does not end with this insinuation. He goes as far as claiming that if the land of Palestine is mainly an attestation of God and His promises to Creation, then it is the "fifth gospel" (*al-īnjīl al-khāmis*) beside the four scriptural Gospels, while the people who lived in Palestine throughout history are the 'sixth gospel' (*al-īnjīl as-sādis* – we already saw Mitri Raheb using these terms before), since their testimony is inherent to the testimony of the land.[147]

In the discourses of Riad Kassis and Munthir Isaac on the land and its theology, we do have two interesting examples of a theological concern that is characteristically genuine in the context of today's Arab Middle East. We have here Christian theologians trying to make sense of, rather, quite challenging biblical attestations and ideas, whose ramifications leave drastic and damaging traces on the life of the Arab-Eastern populations in that region. These two theologians try painstakingly to offer coherent and persuasive explanations of the content of the Christian book of faith to the non-Christians, mainly the Muslims, relating to their homeland. This audience, that is, which always looked suspiciously to the Christians of the region and questioned their allegiance to the

[145] Ibid., p. 97.
[146] Ibid., p. 174.
[147] Ibid., pp. 176–177. Isaac did not invent these terms himself. He, rather, borrowed them, as he states, from Mitri Raheb, "Shaping Communities in Times of Crisis: Narratives of Land, Peoples and Identities," unpublished conference paper in the International Center of Bethlehem, November 2005.

indigenous inhabitants of the land, especially the Arab Palestinians in the midst of their radical deprivation of a sustainable living state and comfortable and safe existence in the land of Palestine. Their theological discourses, thus, come conspicuously baptised with the water of extra-theological challenges and concerns. Their methodological strategies of interpretation and theologisation, therefore, come inevitably and inescapably with defensive and reactionary tones and arguments. Hard it is by nature for such a theology *on* the land (a land that is torn apart with more than three quarters of a century of conflict), rather than a theology *from* the land, to be written in scholarly neutrality and a phlegmatic academic mind.

Protectionist and Self-Enclosed Arab-Eastern Theology

The previous three trends of theological reasoning aspire at engaging the socio-political and contextual life conditions that take the Christians beyond the boundaries of their communal, ecclesial, or social circles of existence. There is, nevertheless, a fourth trend of theological reasoning which, to the contrary, invites the Christians to perceive an estrangement and alienation from the surrounding, predominantly non-Christian, environment and *Sitz im Leben*. It calls them to seek survival by means of either acting as a *dhimmi* community seeking protectionism, or clinging to a self-enclosed, self-otherising identity. One can find traces of such theological reasoning among the Christians in Egypt, Lebanon, and Iraq. In the ensuing paragraphs, I shall try to offer a brief sketch of such voices.

Maybe the best examples of such an orientation are today found in the Egyptian context. In Egypt lives the largest Christian community in the Arabic-speaking region. The Christians in Egypt are estimated to form a community of 10 to 12 million citizens out of Egypt's Muslim-majority population of 100 million citizens. Egypt has historically been always highly, even radically, over-religious in its Christian, Muslim, and Christian–Muslim historical, socio-cultural narratives. Religiosity and religious affiliation are inherently constitutive of the Egyptian public's self-perception and self-identification. This is applicable to the Egyptian staunchly religious, secular, and non-religious members alike. This is because religiosity is treated as 'identity' and as a fundamental component in the identity-formation process, which people cling to in their construction of their social, anthropological, cultural, and political self-awareness.[148] When religious identity is threatened in one way or another due to the numerical characteristics of the different communities in Egyptian society, where the country is overwhelmingly a Muslim-majority context, the weaker and smaller community tends to shrink back into a self-protectionist, insular, and

---

[148] Among the various texts on the Copts in Egypt, see, for instance, Nelly van Doorn-Harder (ed.), *Copts in Context: Negotiating Identity, Tradition and Modernity* (Columbia, SC: University of South Carolina Press, 2017); S. S. Hasan, *Christians Versus Muslims in Modern Egypt: The Century-Long Struggle for Coptic Equality* (Oxford & New York: Oxford University Press, 2003); and Wolfram Reiss, *Erneuerung in der Koptisch-Orthodoxen Kirche* (Muenster: LIT Verlag, 1998).

isolationist circle of existence, not just to guarantee physical survival and extended existence in its homeland, but more urgently to protect its own identity. One of the means of preserving religious identity is secluding oneself from the surrounding society, clinging stiffly to one's own spiritual and religious legacy, traditions, and belief system because they are deemed the constituents of one's own identity. The Coptic Christians in Egypt, in their various ecclesial denominations, seem to cling to this self-otherising, seclusionist spirituality sometimes. On this tendency in recent Egyptian history, the Coptic Orthodox Egyptian theologian and historian Febe Armanios comments in the following manner:

> Over the past three decades, bloody confrontations with Islamist radicals have made Copts acutely apprehensive about their political status, and in response, they have turned to the church, particularly to martyrdom tales, for solace. Clerical leaders have assuaged the laity's concerns by widely promoting these stories of suffering, fortitude, and eternal salvation.[149]

"Within a restrictive political and legal context," Armanios proceeds, "religious life emerged as the primary arena for the articulation of a Coptic voice," and it became "not only how believers engaged with their milieu, but also how they *drew boundaries* between themselves and other communities."[150] Such a segregationalist, binary-centred *habitus* is, in these situations, resorted to as the most secure means for instilling uniformity in religious existence. Spirituality and homiletical discourses are now used to convey "a specific Coptic identity… and [to distinguish] a pure Coptic morality from the perceived vices of other communities."[151] To be faithful to one's own religious identifying affiliation means to make your interaction with the surrounding 'hostile society' as minimal and pragmatic as possible. Such a situation, Febe Armanios concludes, "offers many colorful examples of the changing relationship between piety, ritual, and religious expression among Egypt's Copts."[152]

In the heart of this *Sitz im Leben*, and on the basis of this form of '*Selbstbewußtsein*', Coptic Christianity is consistently reminded of, and confronted by, its numerical minority status and communal vulnerability. This drives some pockets of theological innovation within this community to develop a religious awareness and imagination, wherein theological reasoning is not primarily, or ever, concerned about 'engagement,' 'interrelation,' and 'outwardness.' Rather, theological reasoning is pursued essentially for maintaining an essentialised sense of identity: it is a theology-like reasoning. The key preconceptions in it are expressive of 'protectionism,' 'conservation,' 'inwardness,' 'self-enclosure,' 'self-dhimmitudisation,' 'apologetics,' and 'self-otherising.' In Egyptian Christianity, we still witness discourses against 'heresies' to protect 'the Orthodox faith of the Ancestor Fathers.' We can find discourses quite sceptical of any theological attempt at contextualising Christianity, liberating it, or inviting it to openly engage in addressing the

[149] F. Armanios, *Coptic Christianity in Ottoman Egypt*, p. 147.
[150] Ibid., p. 148. Italics are mine.
[151] Ibid., p. 149.
[152] Ibid., p. 153.

contemporary conditions and challenges in the Arab, non-Christian, world 'out there' in the world outside the Church; the world wherein, if the Christians got involved, they would jeopardise their faith and expose it to heresies and enemies, and lose their ability to protect their existence and survive the overwhelming and devouring threats of the surrounding alien life-setting. Many scholars have paused at such a mindset and noticed the Coptic Christians' concentration in their theological reasoning on four areas of reasoning. First and foremost, dogmatic orthodoxy (patristic and strictly Chalcedonian versus non-Chalcedonian Christological controversies). Second, pastoral-ecclesial and ministerial theology. Third, polemic-apologetic theology to debate with radical Islam. And fourth, mystic-monastic spiritualised theology. The belief is that such fourfold theologisation is the means required to protect (Coptic) Christianity, to reserve its core faith, to maintain its identity in a foreign, antagonistic religious atmosphere, and to grant it tolerance and '*dhimmi*-like' protection from the ruling, religiously and socially stronger, other.

One of the seminal theological figures from contemporary Coptic Christianity whose writings mirror such a theological trend is the monastic theologian Matta al-Miskin (Matthew the Humble) (1919–2006). Father Matta is known as the pioneering and most influential figure in reviving Coptic monasticism during the seventies of the last century. When one looks at Fr. Matta's theological discourse throughout his various writings, one cannot but pause at his clarity about the ultimate and only 'specialty' (*Ikhtiṣāṣ*) of Christianity in human existence: "Building the kingdom of God." This means for him that the Christians must not be involved in the worldly affairs or socio-political matters of life, for such involvement would alienate them from Christ's salvation and drown them in the surrounding anti-Kingdom context:

> Any attempt to combine God's kingdom, as the ultimate goal of Christianity's specialty, with other goals – like demanding special rights for the Church to participate in Rule or in administering the State's policy or to request particular rights to possess something from the glories of this world, or attempting to grant the Church some influence or sovereignty – such an attempt means departing away from the ultimate target of the Christian specialty, namely the kingdom of God.[153]

Fr. Matta goes even further in rejecting any service in society the Christians may make out of ethical social motivations. Serving the poor and *diachonia* in society are made by the Christians not as part of their affiliation to worldly human life, but as expressions of the belief in Jesus Christ alone. Thus, he affirms, "they have no interpretations save within the boundaries of theology alone."[154] Christianity is not even called to tender social service to the world: there is no such thing like 'Social Gospel,' for "the Church does not serve the society. It, rather, serves faith. It serves the Messiah in the persons of those

[153] Matta al-Miskīn, *al-Kanīsah wal-Daūlah: al-Ṭā'fiyyah wal-Ta'aṣṣub* (The Church and the State: Confessionalism and Radicalism) (Naṭrūn Valley: St. Fr. Maqqār Monastery Press, 1969/2009), p. 16. The citations and others are my own translation from Arabic.

[154] Ibid., p. 20.

naked, wretched, and homeless."[155] The Church's mission is not to serve the society. The Church, rather, needs to be liberated from becoming hostage to the notions of social service.[156]

As Christianity is not called for social service, it is also urged to degrade and refuse any involvement in temporal power and sovereignty. The Christians must not resort to kings and rulers to consolidate and enhance their own influence and power. The more temporal, worldly power they gain, the less spiritually and *theo*-logically strong they remain.[157] "God cannot be glorified by the sovereignty of Caesar."[158] Yet, Matta then warns, refusing worldly sovereignty must not drive us to forget the biblical teaching, which orders the Christians to abide with the rulers' right to be succumbed to, to be glorified, and to be granted allegiance.[159]

Does the above retreating tendency mean that the Christians must totally alienate themselves from every single form of existence? Father Matta seems to be maintaining an exception in his theological rationale: the belonging to a homeland. Belonging to God's heavenly homeland, he suggests, does not annul, or conflict with, the affiliation to the earthly homeland, and belonging to the latter does not clash with belonging to the former.[160] The fallacy lies in conflating the two homelands into each other, or using one of them as an instrument for the other: "The service of the earthly homeland does not restrain the service of the heavenly homeland. Therefore, the person's combination of the required characteristics for the former and joining them to the ones of the latter shows humanity in its highest attributes how can it serve God, praised be His name."[161]

On the basis of the above distinction between Christianity's ultimate specialty, on one hand, and its existence in society, on the other, Matta develops a theological view on citizenship. He conjures up the specific notion of 'the Christian citizen.' In her life in the world, the Christian is part and parcel of the temporal sovereignty vis-a-vis her vocation in society. According to Matta, this citizen is free from the Church's control and patronage regarding worldly, societal, and stately affairs that are related to this Christian's role in society. Be that as it may, the Church servants or theologians, as free citizens, must abide by their vocation's responsibilities and jurisdictions. They must never interfere, dictate, or even speak about anything except Church affairs, and must pursue that speech within the circle of Christianity's specialty (the Kingdom of God and doctrines alone).[162] In this case, there is no place for a theological or churchly discourse that touches upon the human condition; the social, economic, cultural, political, or existential aspects of human existence. For, touching upon these matters means that the theologian or the Church servant compromises the Gospel message, the Orthodox faith, the doctrinal tradition of the heavenly sovereignty of God, for the sake of the worldly realm of existence. Such an attempt is pseudo-

[155] Ibid., p. 20.
[156] Ibid., p. 21.
[157] Ibid., p. 29.
[158] Ibid., p. 31.
[159] Ibid., pp. 32–33.
[160] Ibid., p. 35.
[161] Ibid., p. 38.
[162] Ibid., p. 41.

theology, if not pseudo-Christianity. Yes, Fr. Matta confirms, the Christian citizen must fulfil his duties toward the society and the State, and he or she must stand against corruption and the corrupting of the homeland. He or she must do that, however, as someone accountable before his or her conscience and before history, not as one who is responding to a theological or spiritual call. The role of theology is to protect the Gospel message of the heavenly kingdom *from* the contaminative meddling with the affairs of the worldly realm, as well as to separate belief from social life; the 'true Gospel' from the 'social Gospel.'

The most intriguing theological conclusion Fr. Matta develops out of this understanding of theology is his understanding of oppression and injustice. Earlier, we saw a liberationist Arab theologian (Naim Ateek) and a contextual Arab one (Mitri Raheb) both calling for developing theology as an instrument in the activism against oppression and injustice. There, theology is the tool for withstanding injustice and oppression. On the contrary, in this protectionist, self-enclosed theology of Matta the Humble, we have a totally different understanding of the role and purpose of theology. Theological reasoning, according to Matta, is not an instrument of resistance and confrontation. It is, rather, an instrument of compliance and embrace. Fighting persecution (*Iḍṭihād*) is not the role of the Christians or their theological reasoning. Understanding, instead, Fr, Matta confirms, that "in the Christian approach, persecution is a necessary truth, and it is, in fact, semi-definite, for who can blame God for it?" is what theology *must* be developed to serve. Theology is the instrument that enables us to concede injustice and oppression. It helps us to spiritualise them and comply with their existence. If we are weak and vulnerable; if we are a minority and jeopardised; if we are not free and secure, this is all part of our destiny in life. To be Christians, who are called to fulfil their witness and pass the temptation,[163] theology invites the Christians to succumb to difficult situations. It establishes such a call upon the belief that the future brings over God's hope and salvation. Theology's role, Fr. Matta states, is to convey to the Christian the following message:

> Accept persecution, and I also say 'accept it'; accept it with all your heart, accept it unjustified, accept it undebated, accept it in gratitude as Christ's commandment. Then, you will witness the occurrence of the grand miracle. For, you will instantly, and in your depths, realize that you are not an oppressed person, and that it is a matter of scales and percentages, and that you are in better condition than many others who are similar to you in talents and in everything.[164]

Furthermore, Matta seems to be suggesting that theology also enables us to discern the true, genuine persecution that is spoken about in the Gospel from other seeming and figurative persecutions that are not truly religious or faith-based.[165] Theology is what invites us to realise that personal, private, and circumstantial atrocities are not the authentic form of oppression the Bible speaks about. The real persecution is the one which the Christian faces due to his or her commitment to faith and Orthodox doctrine. Such persecution is not evil. It is a

163 Ibid., pp. 47–49.
164 Ibid., pp. 52–53.
165 Ibid., pp. 55–56.

necessity, Matta says. For clinging to faith and doctrine is "a guarantee for the straightness of the human soul, its healthiness, the steadfastness of its struggle and the accuracy of its reasoning."[166] Theology, thus, makes the Christians spiritually and religiously embrace their *dhimmitude* and survive by means of it. Theology is a discourse for accepting and pursuing spiritualised self-*dhimmitudisation.*

This relatedness to theological reasoning from the perspective of a contextual experience of, and from a concern about, persecution seems to be characteristic of the existential and co-existential experiences of some Christians in their life in the *Sitz im Leben* of the Arab Orient. Such an experience of persecution echoes every now and then in the voices of these Christian groups in Lebanon, Iraq, and Syria. Yet, this voice is heard in its loudest theological discursiveness on the Egyptian scene from groups inside the Coptic Christian community. Fr. Matta's discourse takes this persecution seriously into consideration, and it deems it a central factor in the life of the Copts in Egypt. It drives him to argue that "... religious revival [loses] its bearings once it [allows] itself to become involved in communal and political problems," and that "the clergy was to serve as a model of virtue for others, to help them through prayer and persuade them to repent – and not to cater to their material interests or defend their political rights."[167] This stance is generated from a particular sense of life under a consistent, historically perpetual, state of persecution, which eventually makes some Christians relate to the Church and treat it as 'a battleground.' On this battlefield, they confront persecution by means of practising as a community their own religious rituals (e.g. sacraments, biblical reading, prayers, evangelical reflections, etc.). Such enactment strengthens every individual Copt by realising that she and millions of other Copts have the power to gather in the Church and focus on their faith, despite their inability to enjoy a dominant presence in the broader society.[168]

It is not far from truth, according to some Coptic groups, that such a theological call for withdrawal and self-enclosure is the result "not only of personal experiences of discrimination, but also of a discourse of withheld rights and unfulfilled promises ... that left a deep impact on the Church and community and inescapably shaped people's worldview and political consciousness, whether they were personally subjected to difficulties or not."[169] Some Copts even went as far in their reading of the persecution-situation as deeming every form of political, societal, or economic pressure as an expression of a frank *religious* discrimination targeting the Christians by the broader non-Christian society.[170] This eventually left the Christian Copts in Egypt drowning in "the

[166] Ibid., p. 59.

[167] S. S. Hasan, *Christians Versus Muslims in Modern Egypt*, p. 94. See also Matta al-Miskīn, *Maqālāt Bayn al-Siyāsah wal-Dīn* (Essays between Politics and Religion) (al-Natrun: Dār Majallāt Marqus, 1977).

[168] Hasan, *Christians Versus Muslims in Modern Egypt*, pp. 209ff.

[169] Sebastian Elsässer, "The Copts in the January Revolution of 2011," in *Copts in Context: Negotiating Identity, Tradition and Modernity*, Nelly van Doorn-Harder (ed.) (Columbia, SC: University of South Carolina Press, 2017), pp. 21–33, p. 22.

[170] See, for example, the case of the Copts who lived in miserable life conditions not suitable for human beings in the 'Zabbalin' (the garbage collectors) neighbourhood in

dilemma of how best to manage the alternate pressures of isolation and assimilation."[171] The call for isolation becomes, according to a recent study on the Copts, an expression of the intertwining of 'territorial identity' and 'religious identity' in relation to Egyptian Christianity. This situation is rooted in the conviction that "Christians in Egypt are confronted with various manifestations of marginalisation and with a historiography that suggests a process of retreat from national to church spaces during the twentieth century, which has resulted in withdrawal and isolation."[172]

In such a specific context, it is not unexpected or unlikely to witness the development of a theological voice which calls the Christians to focus on the heavenly kingdom in order to liberate them mentally, spiritually, and psychologically from the darkness and insufferable state of 'the earthly realm of existence.' This retreat-centred theological voice, as it is argued, needs not be deemed a call for *permanent* disconnection and withdrawal, but rather as a temporary one wherein the Copts can refresh and renew their religious identity and heritage and re-empower themselves.[173] This conceded, one cannot but sense that in such a theological voice there is a presumption that the Church as a particular, self-otherised space exists in *parallel* to the national or public space, and not as a part of it. The call for a self-enclosed, spatial, and perceptual relatedness to the broader Egyptian context in such a theology, even if it was not ultimately isolationist in purpose, cannot but prove the fact that "Coptic spaces can be described as parallel spaces,"[174] rather than inherent ones. And, if such disengagement and self-enclosure in the theological voice "was not entirely voluntary," but rather reflective of "a general national trend that squeezed the public sphere from all but elite voices"[175]on the Egyptian scene, this means that the Christian voice we have here is an ideal manifestation of a *reactionary* and totally *defensive* theology.

Culture-Centred Arab-Eastern Theology

This trend of theological thinking not only endeavours to develop a discourse to respond to, or deal with, the Arab-Eastern context. More fundamentally, it seeks to construct a theological discourse *from*, or a representation of, the Arab cultural tradition and context. 'Arabism' is here assessed and examined as a potential framework and foundation for developing an Arab Christian religious thinking that travels beyond the boundaries of religious sources and derives from the secular, humanist, and non-religious (not necessarily anti-religious) ones. The

Cairo in Mariz Tadros, "The Undesirables of Egypt: A Story of Persecution and Defiance," in *Copts in Context*, pp. 34–51.

[171] On this dilemma in the history of the Coptic Orthodox Christian community in Egypt and how it was addressed by the Copts, see Elizabeth Monier, "Spatial Practices of 'Retreat' Among Egyptian Christians: Isolating or Empowering?", in *The International Journal of Levant Studies*, 2(2020), pp. 5–28, p. 6.

[172] Ibid., p. 7.

[173] Ibid., p. 8.

[174] Ibid., p. 9.

[175] Ibid., p. 10.

two examples I could find on such a theological voice come both from Lebanon, and they similarly centralise the question: is it possible for Arabism in its religious Christian and Muslim manifestations to become the intellectual source of a secularised, modernist, and humanist Christian theological voice? The two authors I found as exemplifying this discourse preconceive two different answers to the above-stated enquiry. The first and earlier voice is of the Maronite Lebanese theologian Michel al-Ḥāyik. This voice develops Christian reasoning on the basis of a strongly pessimistic answer to this question. On the other hand, the second, more recent, voice is that of the Greek Catholic Lebanese theologian and philosopher Mouchir Baseel Aoun. This voice echoes a pragmatic, less pessimistic, though cautious, stance. In the ensuing paragraphs, I briefly shed light on the voice of this theological trend as it is expressed in the discourses of the two above-mentioned theologians.

In his reflection on the potentials of developing a humanist theology from within Arabism, Fr. Michel Ḥāyik clearly expresses his own distrust in such a possibility. He argues that Arabism cannot be the source of any possible intellectual, humanist, and modernist discourse, be it theological or purely non-religious alike. This is the case because Arabism, according to Ḥāyik, represents "a constructive deficiency and defect that infects the Arab self at the depth of its core."[176] What hinders Arabism from becoming a source for developing an inclusive modernist, humanist theology, Ḥāyik states, is the fact that Arabism is exclusively and totally paired with, if not defined by, Islam alone. It is attached organically to Islam, and it is Islam's byproduct. Neither the populist nor the Christian secularist theories in the region succeeded in divorcing Arabism from Islam and expanding the boundaries of the former beyond the latter, Ḥāyik emphasises. Be that as it may, Ḥāyik concludes, one cannot find an Arabic embracing and accommodation of the secularist, modernist perceptions of the universe, existence, the human being, and history from which the Arab Christians' theological thought is shaped. The reason behind this impossibility is that Arabism cannot exceed the boundaries of the Islamic perception of the universe, existence, human beingness, and historicity. "Arabism embraced Islamic monism and made it its exclusivist view of homeland and tradition," Ḥāyik argues. The meant that, for the Arabs, as there is one God only in heaven, there is only one perception of reality (the Muslim one) on earth.[177]

---

[176] Mouchir Aoun, "al-Fikr al-ʿArabī al-Dīnī al-Massīḥī al-Muʿāṣir fī Taṣaūurihi lil-ʿUrūbah al-Mustaqbaliyyah" (The Contemporary Arab Religious Christian Thought in its Conception of the Futural Arabism), in *al-'Urūbah wal-Qarn al-Wāḥid wal-'Ishrīn* (Arabism and the 21st Century), Muḥammad Ḥilmī ʿAbdulwāḥid (ed.) (Beirut: Arab Scientific Publishers, 2009), pp. 257–293, p. 276. See also Ḥāyik's various texts and newspapers articles, like M. Ḥāyik, *al-Masīḥ wa-Lubnān wa-Filasṭīn* (Christ, Lebanon and Palestine) (Beirut: al-Karmah Press, no date); Ḥāyik, "al-ʿUrūbah Mushkilat al-ʿArab" (Arabism is the Arab's Problem), in *al-Nahar Newspaper*, 5 November 1979; Ḥāyik, "Kal-Masīḥ Kunnā Rahā'inan lil-Ummam Ḥatta al-Aqrabīn" (Like Christ, We Were the Nation's Hostages, even the Close Ones), in *al-Nahar Newspaper*, 22 April 2000.

[177] Aoun, "al-Fikr al-ʿArabī al-Dīnī al-Massīḥī al-Muʿāṣir fī Taṣaūurihi lil-ʿUrūbah al-Mustaqbaliyyah," p. 277.

In such a closed, exclusivist Arabism, the non-Muslim Arab and her theological and intellectual bearers are the rejected, the secluded, strange other, and pluralism is a threat to the cultural cohesion represented by Arabism.[178] Ḥāyik does not react to this situation by condemning Islam or rejecting the integration between cultures and religions (in this, he is a moderate secularist calling for a mild secular thought, like Mouchir Aoun, as will appear below). He, nevertheless, pauses seriously at the danger that religiosity and monism can cause when it undermines plurality, religiously and culturally alike. Unfortunately, Ḥāyik stipulates, associating Arabism with the monistic dogmatic thought of a single religious faith (Islam) transformed Arabism into an exclusivist and otherising anti-pluralist phenomenon, preventing non-Islamic thought (Christian theology) from contributing further to the attempts at curing the exclusivist condition of Arabism.[179] There is no salvation to Arabism, Ḥāyik suggests, except by allowing its non-Muslim voices (the Christians) to heal it from its profound schizophrenia and narcissism by calling Arabism to retrieve its plurality and open itself up to the non-Arab, worldly, modernist, and non-religious voices.[180]

In the very recent Arab world's intellectual atmosphere, Ḥāyik's thesis is overshadowed and almost sidelined, for the attention is directed towards a more timely and fresh thesis, similar to his, on the Lebanese scene. In the contemporary intellectual context of Arab-Eastern Christianity in Lebanon, the recent prominent proponent of this secularised Arab theological voice is the Greek Catholic theologian and philosopher Mouchir Baseel Aoun. In my conversation with Aoun about his project, Aoun related to me that he preferred to call his theological project 'mild secularised theology' (*Lāhūt 'Almānī Mu'tadil/Laṭīf*). By this, Aoun wants to make it clear that his project does not promote a radical, exclusive version of secularism that rejects religion or pushes away the other faith in the Eastern context, Islam. He calls, instead, for a *theological* discourse that certainly includes religiosity and embraces and recognises positively the faith of the Muslims in the Arab region. The secularity of this theology lies, thus, not in any '*anti*-like' stance. It is a secularity which teaches that, in the Arab multi-religious context (as Aoun shared with me), no possible co-existence can be imagined without re-reading religious self-perception not just from religious but also non-religious texts. Aoun's secularised theology relies heavily on pluralist and modernist (in the sense of *Aufklärung*) views that centralise human rights and modernity's socio-cultural and ethical values. In the ensuing lines, I briefly display a systematic anatomy of Aoun's 'mild secular theology' discourse.

Aoun departs systematically from a particular hermeneutic of the Arab Christians' *Sitz im Leben*. According to this hermeneutic reading, the Christian Arabs "experience … all forms of humanitarian suffering" which, he suggests, drives them to "painstakingly interrogate the connotations of this suffering,

[178] Ibid., p. 278 and Ḥāyik, "al-ʿUrūbah Mushkilat al-ʿArab."

[179] Aoun, "al-Fikr al-ʿArabī al-Dīnī al-Massīḥī al-Muʿāṣir fī Taṣaūurihi lil-ʿUrūbah al-Mustaqbaliyyah," p. 279.

[180] Ibid., p. 282.

inspired by the content of the hope of the belief the Lord Jesus bestowed upon his disciples' testimonies in the Gospel's salvific attestations."[181] In principle, the Arab Christians perceive this situation and try on personal levels to connect it with their privative belief in the Gospel of Jesus Christ. However, on the broader communal level of Christianity's existence in the Orient, the public, general construct of the Arab theological reasoning, Aoun claims, "has been inflected with sagging, disintegration, and laxity."[182] Contemporary Arab Christianity regressed from the contemporary Arab Islam and its endeavours to revive Arabic thought. There were various reasons that drove the Arab Christians to deny, or dilute, the necessity of developing an Arab Christian religious thinking that would respond to the requirements of the recent existential suffering in their life-setting.[183]

Aoun perceives, and concedes, the realistic reasons that drove the Arab Christians to privatise the occupation with the existential, practical, and historical concerns over the interest in intellectual, theological origination. Nevertheless, if the Christians, Aoun believes, continued either abstaining from theologising altogether, or theologising by means of Western, foreign, non-Arabic terms and preconceptions, none of their perceptions or imaginations would serve the purpose of confronting the existential, historical experiences and overcoming their challenges.[184] Be that as it may, Aoun concludes, the Arab Christians must inevitably launch an attempt at drawing a preparatory theoretical (i.e. theological) framework for generating an Arab Christian intellectual stance on the reality of "this bad Arab political era." Such a theoretical attempt, he suggests, might be "one of the most dangerous civilizational tasks, which Arab Christianity must address at the beginning of the third millennium."[185]

What makes Aoun depart in his theological reasoning from a hermeneutical standpoint that reads the socio-cultural reality of the Christian Arab? Why this foundational starting point? Aoun offers us an answer to this methodological enquiry by stating the following:

> Theological thought is inevitably related to living reality. Therefore, it is required, first of all, to contemplate the reality of these Arab societies … and to anticipate the chances of conjuring up a theological imagination worthy of being intellectually implemented in addressing this reality responsibly.[186]

The second reason behind Aoun's point of departure is directly rooted in the Arab Christians' theological relatedness to the Arabic nature of their *Sitz im Leben.* Aoun realises that the Arab Christians have rather diverse, even

---

[181] M. B. Aoun, *al-Fikr al-'Arabī al-Dīnī al-Massīḥī* (The Arab Religious Christian Thought) (Beirut: al-Ṭalī'ah Press, 2007), p. 5.
[182] Ibid., p. 5.
[183] Ibid., p. 7. Some of the reasons behind this regression, according to Aoun, are: the historical position of the Arab Christians as a minority; the feeling of collective distortion; the perpetual tendency to desert the homeland; the fear of self-criticism, and the abstinence of the Arab theologians from renewing theology on the basis of granting a referential status to Arabic culture (ibid).
[184] Ibid., p. 8.
[185] Ibid., p. 9.
[186] Ibid., p. 63.

dispersed, stances on Arabism, primarily from theological perspectives. Aoun detects at least three primary theological stances on Arabism among contemporary Christians in his country, Lebanon.[187] Aoun's own stance on Arabism is shaped mainly after interrogation and anticipation, rather than after historical reactionism or momentary optimistic, pessimistic, or sceptical relatedness. His concern lies in exploring the potential of having, eventually, an interrogative relatedness to Arabism from a perspective that makes the Christians' theological reflection distinguished from the Muslims' religious approach to the same theme.[188] These are the two factors that make Aoun build on the socio-cultural reality of the Christian Arabs and nothing else.

The ensuing question is, how can the Arab Christians generate a Gospel-based theological reasoning that speaks in specific, and relates in particular, to the above-mentioned hermeneutical starting and reality-centred point of departure? Initially, Aoun confesses the severe difficulty of developing a theological discourse that simultaneously clarifies the structure of the Arab-Eastern reality on all its levels, and demonstrates the connotations and meanings of the belief in God's only Word and human incarnate Saviour, Jesus the Christ.[189] These two required elements, Aoun notices, "originate among each other tensional attraction and repulsion; the thing that leads the theological discourse we intend to compose into dangerous deadlock and perpetual aggravation."[190]

Aoun insists that the Christians have nothing other than theological reasoning and discourse to implement in living and conveying their core belief in a framework convenient to ready them to confront the path of death their communities live in.[191] It is because of this, Aoun argues (contrary to Ḥāyik), that the Arab-Eastern Christians cannot reject Arabism or exclude the Muslims who belong to it. This necessity, Aoun believes, is not just pragmatic or existential. It is significantly and primarily *theological* in nature. "Today's theological thought in the Arab-Eastern context needs to interact with any Arab thought that is genuine, contemporary, wholistic, and interpretative of the entire Arabic existence."[192] Any theological discourse must be developed to serve the good will of the Arab society in its totality, and to transform it into a place of progress and prosperity. It should not be a defensive theology that stands against the Arabism of that society, even if such Arabism means profound association with, and organic involvement in, the Muslim *Kultur* and *Weltanschuung*. One of the main means for achieving this goal, Aoun proposes, is "our

---

[187] Aoun, "al-Fikr al-ʿArabī al-Dīnī al-Massīḥī al-Muʿāṣir fī Taṣaūurihi lil-ʿUrūbah al-Mustaqbaliyyah," pp. 257–293. I have already offered a detailed analysis of these stances in Najib George Awad, *Umayyad Christianity*, pp. 405–415.

[188] Aoun, "al-Fikr al-ʿArabī al-Dīnī al-Massīḥī al-Muʿāṣir fī Taṣaūurihi lil-ʿUrūbah al-Mustaqbaliyyah," p. 258. The concern, Aoun suggests, must particularly be an attempt to discern a comprehensive Arab action that will innovate a contemporary Arabism befitting the human's dignity in Arab societies (ibid.).

[189] Aoun, *al-Fikr al-ʿArabī al-Dīnī al-Massīḥī: Muqtaḍaiyāt al-Nuhūḍ wa-Tajdīd wal-Muʿāṣarah*, p. 74.

[190] Ibid., pp. 74ff.

[191] Ibid., p. 76.

[192] Ibid., p. 77.

contemporaneous reading of the Gospel in the light of our faith experiences and our apprehension of the identity of the Arab-Eastern human person."[193]

In the ensuing parts of his proposal, Aoun points to the main theoretical prerequisites that the Arab Christians need to mind and uphold in order to successfully originate a theological discourse that speaks to his (Aoun's) proposed particular hermeneutical starting and methodological point of departure. Aoun pursues this by offering terminological clarification to every term in his proposed 'Arab Religious Christian Thought' phrase. This theology must be 'Arab,' because it needs to be rooted in the soil of the Arab civilisation. If 'Eastern' designates religious communality, 'Arab,' for Aoun, describes the cultural one.[194] Second, the aimed-at discourse in this content must be 'Christian' in the sense that it is "other than the Muslim discourse." It is derived from non-Muslim texts, sources, and traditions. However, by virtue of its cultural rootedness, this discourse maintains "one fateful epistemological partnership with the Arab Muslim discourse."[195] On the other hand, this thought is not just Christian, but also religious or theological. Aoun does not call for an Arab Christian political, economic, social, or cultural discourse. "The homogeneity of the Arab sufferance," he suggests, "necessitates a unified Arabic discourse."[196] And, when the Christians endeavour to contribute to such a unified discourse, the uniqueness of their contribution lies in none other than their religious experience and faith, which all the Arabs acknowledge as different from the Muslim religious experience and understanding. This different faith tradition is a source of enrichment to the Arab civilisation in the total sum of its dimensions, Aoun states.[197]

In the light of the above framework, Aoun proposes that only such a theological discourse can genuinely and fruitfully tackle three main dilemmas detectable in the Arab societies: the religious dilemma (the Christian–Muslim encounter and the reinforcement of religious plurality); the cultural dilemma (renewing the connotations of Arabism and counting it among the contributing prerogatives of universal modernism); and the social dilemma (attesting to human freedom and dignified life).[198] The interesting thing in relation to this framework is Aoun's proposed naming of this Christian theological discourse the 'theology of Arabism' (*Lāhūt al-'Urūbah*). For Aoun, this nomenclature illustrates the Arab Christians' endeavour to "rehabilitate the common cultural soil between Christianity and Islam, which is the soil of the Christian origination in the land of the Arab Orient."[199] The calling for a 'theology of Arabism,' Aoun stresses, does not mean amputating the Eastern Christian Syriac, Greek, and Coptic theological and cultural heritages from this Arab theological discourse.

---

193 Ibid., p. 81.
194 Ibid,, p. 90.
195 Ibid., p. 91.
196 Ibid., p. 91.
197 Ibid., p. 92.
198 Ibid., p. 106.
199 Ibid., p. 108. Therefore, Aoun continues, "the theology of Arabism must rehabilitate the Christian Arab theological mind in such way that fulfils the original Christian testimony in the Arab Orient's land" (ibid.).

It, rather, implements these traditions in the service of the theology of Arabism's call for liberating Arabic culture in its entirety from the risks of enclosure, seclusion, and isolation from international thought and civilisational cross-pollination.[200] Theology of Arabism, finally, is a theology of freedom. It guards the connotations of freedom, and it maintains freedom as the essential pillar of affiliation that liberates the human person from all forms of tyrannic intellectual, political, religious, and social oppression. 'Theology of Arabism' as a theology of freedom is, therefore, a theology of 'social resistance that aims at solidifying the allegiance to human rights and declaring it the ultimate, supreme referential stature."[201]

The final piece in the jigsaw puzzle of Aoun's theological project brings us full circle, back to where we started in analysing his mild secular theology. One of the pivotal items in Aoun's theological project, as we saw, is his understanding of Arabism and what he deems to be the precondition of accepting such a theological discourse like his by the Arab Muslims. Aoun believes that, for a theological voice like his to be embraced by the Arabic society in its entirety, and for it to be deemed by the Muslims as a genuine *Arabic* discourse, the Arab Muslims need to change their stance on, and to transform their understanding of, Arabism per se. The Muslims must realise that 'Arabism' exceeds Islam, and it does not define the Muslim tradition and faith alone: one can be an Arab without being a Muslim. In addition, the Muslims must concede an Arabism that is not confined to the past Arab-Muslim cultural and intellectual heritage of the early Islamic era. This, according to Aoun, requires allowing Arabic thought to exceed the boundaries of religious thinking. It demands that the theological reasoning *from* Arabism must be formed by the help of non-religious texts. This alternative, extra-religious literature, Aoun proposes, can only be found in the Western and international secularist heritages of the Enlightenment and modernity, which jettison religious dogmatism in favour of human-based values and hermeneutics.[202] Aoun argues that such a secularist modernist rationale is not against Islam, let alone religiosity in general, nor is it against Arabism. Arabism by nature, Aoun states, "is a state of interaction and cross-pollination among cultural identities and cultural alterities. One can even say that the Arab cultural identity was and still is like a continuous process of openness, communication, derivation, and formation."[203]

If Arabism was this dynamic and open in nature, Aoun concludes, it could then embrace the Arab Christians and their unique theological and cultural contributions that would certainly be different from those of the Arab Muslims. The Christian theological contributions' particularity would lie in their intellectual derivation from the secularist and modernist sources of knowledge

---

[200] Ibid., p. 109.

[201] Ibid., p. 110.

[202] On these non-religious sources and their humanist, modernist nature and origin, see the latest publications of Aoun, *Le Christ arabe. Pour une théologie chrétienne arabe de la convivialité* (Paris: Cerf, 2016), pp. 341–377 and Aoun, *Anthropologies croisées. Essai sur l'interculturalité arabe* (Paris: Cerf, 2017), pp. 43–83.

[203] Aoun, "al-Fikr al-ʿArabī al-Dīnī al-Massīḥī al-Muʿāṣir fī Taṣaūurihi lil-ʿUrūbah al-Mustaqbaliyyah," p. 290.

that were developed by the Christians in the West, Aoun believes. Such Western secular and modernist sources would enable the Christians to offer a theological discourse to Arabism that contains a unique perception of the universe, existence, human beingness, and history that are different from the ones offered by Islam.[204] What, therefore, challenges the Christians' 'theology of Arabism,' like the one Aoun conjures up, are the willingness and the ability of the Arab Muslims to tolerate an open Arabism willing to embrace secularist and modernist elements derived from a "genuine civilizational crosspollination between nations."[205] An Arab secular theology like Aoun's must first persuade the other Arabs in this particular *Sitz im Leben* that, if the Arab societies "maintained their rigidity and fixation, they will not gain an innovative overview of the connotations of human existence that can inherently be extracted from the heart of Arabism."[206] In his theology of Arabism, then, Mouchir Baseel Aoun seeks to offer a unique Christian Arab theological voice that contributes to the Arab multi-religious *Sitz im Leben* by means of allowing Western, secularist, and humanist modernism to inspire this theology's perspectives on the issues of identity, nationhood, social beingness and culture.[207]

Recently, we became able to see how Aoun takes his theological reflections on the Arab Christians' relation to their Arab context, and his assessment of their theological reasoning within this contextual framework, to its logical, final conclusion. This became possible after a major book of his was published in the English scholarly world. In this monograph, Aoun departs from a plausible critique of the contemporary theological reasoning of the Arab Christians in his country, Lebanon. Aoun claims that the theology that is being proliferated within the churches in the Arab Christian context tends to be "more in the nature of theoretical elements taken from imported theological experiences, rather than what has been learned through a living faith." This, he proceeds, makes Christian reasoning merely tangentially correspond to proper context-perceptive and context-sensitive theologisation.[208] Aspiring at remedying this defect in today's Arab-Lebanese theological reasoning, Aoun wrote his own book-length correction to this situation and published it in English under the title *The Arab Christ: Towards an Arab Christian Theology of Conviviality*.[209]

The primary motivator of Aoun's book was his conviction of the constitutive status religion occupies in the Arab self-consciousness and worldview. Aoun states that, though "religion may not display the full richness of Arabic identity," it, nevertheless, "distils the essence of it." When we probe the place of religion within the intellectual awareness of the Arabs – be that thought theological or not, and be these Arabs Christians or Muslims in identity – we discover,

[204] Ibid., p. 290.
[205] Ibid., p. 291.
[206] Ibid., p. 291.
[207] Ibid., p. 292.
[208] Mouchir Basile Aoun, *The Arab Christ: Towards an Arab Christian Theology of Conviviality*, Sarah Patey (trans.) (London: Gingko, 2022), p. 79.
[209] This volume was originally written in Arabic twenty years ago, before it appeared in a French version in 2016 under the title *La Christ arabe*, and now we have it published in an English translation.

according to Aoun, "an epistemological impasse in which ... Arab theological thinking is stuck ... [it is] prisoner of the *aporia* that has a general hold on the contemporary Arab thinking."[210] Aoun concedes, even confirms, the political, socio-cultural, and contextual nature of this crisis-breeding *aporia*. Yet he proposes in his book that the solution or the remedy for this crisis is nothing but essentially *theological* in nature: remedying a religiously founded identity (i.e. Arab) crisis by means of a politically responsible and context-rooted theology. He even goes as far as frankly stating that his proposal is a '*Lebanese* politico-contextual theology' par excellence. Aoun, nonetheless, surprisingly promotes his theological proposal as one that speaks as an '*Arab* Christian theology.' The claim of comprehensive, collectivist inclusivity is surprising from a subtle and attentive contextual thinker like Aoun: it is frankly puzzling to read Aoun claiming that Lebanon and Lebanese Christianity reductively define the entire Arab world and its vastly diverse contextual conditions and the entire, just as diverse, experiences of all the Christian communities living in it:

> Lebanon both reflects and sharply focuses key aspects of the challenges experienced by Christians within the Arab World. The life of Arab Christian communities in Lebanon crystallizes the experience of all Arab Christians: Their apprehension, their disillusionment, their hopes, and expectations, as they seek to give meaning to their present lives within their historic context ... the Lebanese experience can thus provide an invaluable hermeneutic key with which to understand other models of minority Christian existence.[211]

These strongly affirmative, far from context-sensitive terms can be easily misunderstood, as they invite the creation of a questionable, if not criticisable, image of the author which might be unfair, I like to believe. It images him as someone tangled intellectually with patriotic narcissism expressing itself via a highly superior, non-contextual perspective and Lebano-centric, essentialising favouritism (something reminiscent of Mitri Raheb's attitude toward Palestinian Christianity). It is my belief, nevertheless, that one must not assess Aoun's theological proposal from the narrow angle of this Achilles heel in his discourse. One can also tenably deem it a mere rhetorically saturated, not quite successful, justification of Aoun's restriction of his theological proposal to conditions, challenges, and questions exclusively rooted and detected in the specific context of Lebanon and Lebanese Christianity alone.

Apart from this glitch, Aoun is quite perceptive in his diagnosis of the core challenges that generate a crisis in Arab Christian theological discourses. He accurately spots the twofold problem in this theology when he states that it is "both where it comes from and how it affects the reality of people's lives in Lebanon and in the Arab World."[212] When it comes to unpacking the details of the crisis-related causes, Aoun counts such causes as follows: first, the expiration and obsolescence of the vocabularies the Arab Christians use to convey Christ's *kerygma* to their Arabic-Muslim context. Underpinning this is his preconceptual conviction that "any renewal in Arabic thinking, whether philosophical or

---

[210] Ibid., p. 100.
[211] Ibid., p. 10.
[212] Ibid., p. 101.

religious, must necessarily find expression within existing linguistic and conceptual structures in the language."[213] Second, there is the challenge of the variety of influences and multiplicity of forming references that impact on Arab Christian theology (although I am not sure why this is a cause of a crisis?). For Aoun, this multiplicity, though enriching in principle, is problematic because "it complicates [the situation], bringing over with it divergent and irreconcilable elements"; the thing, he opines, that makes "the path ahead seem fraught with danger."[214] The outcome of this, Aoun believes, is a dire lack of "internal coherence."[215] Third, there is the challenge of synchronisation between the "medieval, pre-conciliar" elements of Arab Christian theology and the "modern and post-conciliar" ones. This "major epistemological caesura," Aoun says, traps Arab Christian theology in a deep anachronistic, dichotomic abyss. Emancipation from this pit, Aoun believes, lies in identifying "the extremes of the divergence–convergence polarity" between the old and the contemporary.[216] Fourth, the challenge that stems from the previous dilemma lies in a split "between the content of the Gospel message and lived reality."[217] Contemporary Arab Christian theology, Aoun confirms, must seriously stay in touch "with the daily lives, both individual and collective, of the faithful," for this engagement will originate an "authentic encultured theology truly concerned to preserve an unbroken link between words and their meaning."[218]

How can we, then, conjure up an Arabic theological discourse that is free from the dilemmatic, aporetic ramifications of these four challenges? Aoun's answer to this enquiry consists of proposing a politico-contextual, theological discourse circling around "the theme of conviviality" and then approaching this theme from a hermeneutical perspective able to address the following: 1) The sociopolitical and sociocultural integration of the Christians into their Arabic *Sitz im Leben*. 2) The reinterpretation of the Christ Event in relation to the multi-faceted challenges of Muslim otherness. 3) the need for an evangelical praxis that fosters "fraternal solidarity; a collective spiritual quest and … political and moral engagement among all those living in the Arab World."[219] For Aoun, this is the only theology the Christians must develop if they want to salvage their country, Lebanon, from its serious, almost destructive, defects, like toxic confessionalism and its disastrous consequences; the extra-territorial religious allegiances; the sprawling intellectual tyranny.[220] The hermeneutical core of this theology must generate a consensual understanding "on major principles of common life, such as freedom, justice, peace, [and] solidarity."[221] This is what enables the Arab Christians, in Aoun's opinion, to live and to foster conviviality in the Middle East. Such conviviality will be seriously threatened in Lebanon

---

[213] Ibid., p. 102.
[214] Ibid., p. 103.
[215] Ibid., p. 103.
[216] Ibid., pp. 104–105.
[217] Ibid., p. 105.
[218] Ibid., p. 105.
[219] Ibid., pp. 1–2.
[220] Ibid., pp. 15–18.
[221] Ibid., p. 19.

and the Arab world as a whole if Arab Christianity's existence "is persistently overlooked ... if their existence diminishes, Arab conviviality will suffer severely. An imagined confessional homogeneity could devastate the Arab experience of plurality."[222]

How can the Lebanese confront this threat and secure conviviality? Aoun answers: "the Lebanese Christians must ensure their physical safety,"[223] so they are "called upon to reflect in theological terms on the magnitude of the political challenge they face." The Lebanese should do this without, however, spiritualising the Christians' political engagement. The need is, actually, for a hermeneutic of conviviality that is expressive of "a clear-eyed political theology."[224] Such clarity alone is capable of advocating for the Lebanese churches, whose present political theologised stances are accused of lack of credibility and ambiguity.[225] This can be remedied when the theology of Christian–Muslim conviviality is grounded in the Christian theology of the incarnation, for such theology lies in Jesus Christ's situatedness in history and His eternal travel through the centuries to meet the Arabs as well as other people.[226] This incarnational perception manifests in a conviviality-centred perspective when it unpacks societal plurality and "opens up communication and social entities."[227] After all, Aoun states, "the Christian faith operates in the context of interpersonal relationship," and it calls for "an open and bold attitude to human relationships."[228] Aoun sees this relational aspect as theologically rooted in the "trinitarian model." He points to the lack of a Trinitarian theology in Lebanon before he proposes that:

> A contextual Trinitarian theology in Lebanon could ... protect the Lebanese political sphere from the allure of confessional or community despotism ... if Lebanese political forces could align themselves with the spontaneous Trinitarian outpouring of life, it could lead to the healthy development of a better forum for communication, incarnation, and critical distancing within Lebanese society.[229]

Be that as it may, Aoun stipulates that the only relevant theology in Lebanon today is "one that is involved in politics and closely focused on liberty and interculturalism ... [one that works] in tandem with a new approach to Muslim–Christian interculturality and to practicing politics."[230]A proper political-contextual Arab theology of conviviality must stand on the tripod of "prayer, words, and actions." This tripod symbolises the existential nature of the Arab Christians' perception of the Gospel of Jesus Christ and their tendering of the

---

[222] Ibid., p. 24.

[223] Ibid., p. 37. "The human community of Lebanese Christians will always have had legal and constitutional protection for their physical safety in a region where people are recognised only in terms of their confessional adherence" (ibid.).

[224] Ibid., pp. 38–39.

[225] Ibid., pp. 51–52.

[226] Ibid., p. 52.

[227] Ibid., p. 55.

[228] Ibid., p. 70.

[229] Ibid., p. 71.

[230] Ibid., p. 75. In the context of Lebanon, this interculturality involves addressing the three subjects of "Islamism, Arab identity and Modernity," Aoun states (ibid., p. 85).

Gospel message's implications in their multi-religious (predominantly Muslim) context.[231] Methodologically speaking, Aoun suggests, such conviviality-centred theology "enables a dialectical tension between the transcendent notion of the evangelical imperative and the immanent notion of the human response."[232]

Aoun could easily end his book at this stage and tenably dispense with the ensuing 206 page-long second part. Attentive journeying through this lengthy second part of the volume demonstrates that it is an extensive survey of models of theologies of conviviality that already exist on the Lebanese scene. This might suggest that the title of the book misguides the reader about the content of the text. The main title, "The Arab Christ," is not indicative of the main theme of the book's two parts, since neither of them offers an Arabic theological interpretation of Jesus Christ's event or life, identity, and ministry, let alone reasoning theologically about Christology.[233] On the other hand, the book's subtitle of "Arab Christian Theology of Conviviality" in terms of '*towardness*' gives the impression that the author is inviting the readers to ponder the possibility of developing a theological discourse that has not been moved *towards* before and that the author is initiating, if not pioneering, this towardness. Far from being the case, the second part of the volume is stuffed with models of theologies of conviviality already developed by other Lebanese theologians, like Youākīm Moubārak (pp. 135–196); Michel Ḥāyek (pp. 197–221); George Khodr (pp. 223–310); and Gregoire Ḥaddād (pp. 311–341). A more appropriate and telling title for the book would be something like: "The Lebanese Christians: Models of a Politico-Contextual Theology of Conviviality."

The above notwithstanding, Mouchir Aoun's survey of the four Lebanese theologies of conviviality in the second part of the book invites us to glean that his proposed politico-contextual Lebanese theology hinges conspicuously upon George Khodr's theological hermeneutics of conviviality. He dedicates quite extensive, elaborate exposition to Khodr's discourse, skilfully and thoroughly unpacking its multi-dimensional and preconceptual constituents. Aoun adapts without further ado Khodr's advocation of a theology of conviviality that is based on "three forms of justification: the absolute liberty of God, the multifarious radiance of the Spirit, and the multiple places in which Christ revealed Himself."[234] What does this imply in the context of Christian–Muslim conviviality? Aoun responds, inspired by Khodr, by affirming that the Lebanese Christians must *love* their Arabic cultural tradition and identity, not just embrace it pragmatically and out of sheer utilitarian, survival-centred motivations.[235] This 'love stance' must prevail not just because the God of Jesus Christ is love per se,[236] but also because "Christian faith, in the context of the Arab World, can

---

[231] Ibid., p. 128.

[232] Ibid., p. 129.

[233] I rely on here my book review of Aoun's monograph in my review of it: Najib G. Awad, "*The Arab Christ: Towards an Arab Christian Theology of Conviviality*, by Mouchir Basile Aoun, trans. Sarah Patey, London: Gingko, 2022," in *Scottish Journal of Theology*, 2023, 76(4), pp. 394–396.

[234] Ibid., pp. 259–260.

[235] Ibid., pp. 286–287.

[236] Ibid., p. 294.

only become incarnate in Arab life itself, and can only find expression in the specific idioms of Arab culture."[237] Khodr's project of Christian–Muslim conviviality drives Aoun to state the following:

> Arab Christians are now called to recreate an authentically Arabic Christianity. Following the example of Arab theologians, who had to engage with courage and creativity in their first [historical] contacts with Islam, they will need to undertake a reinterpretation of the *Kerygma*. This will have a major impact on how they can influence contemporary Arab culture.[238]

Aoun realises that this task is yet to be fulfilled: the Christians in the Arab world have yet a mission to attend to, namely achieving a Christian–Muslim conviviality deeply rooted in the politico-contextual needs of the Arab world. The shared fate of the Christians and the Muslims in this context "enables them to witness to a spirit of solidarity … [it requires from them] constant vigilance and an unwavering openness to criticism and readiness to adjust and amend."[239] This solidarity manifests itself politically when the two communities "strip out of their political relationship the stench of intolerance and hegemony that has poisoned their past experiences."[240] Such healing of the political relationship would make the Muslims believe that the Arab Christians live with them a life of shared challenge and destiny: "Whatever affects the Arab World affects them even more viscerally."[241] On the other hand, this convivial solidarity also manifests itself culturally. Both Islam and Christianity in the Arab World are equally facing the challenge of confronting their shared Arab heritage.[242] The Arab Christians, thus, must avoid cultural self-alienation and the mistaken, reductionist, total identification of Arab identity with Islam: "Any dialogue between Muslims and Christians should help Arab Christians to become better aware of their Arab cultural identity."[243] Finally, convivial solidarity expresses itself theologically. Both Muslims and Christians in the Arab world must allow conviviality to motivate them to dare to question their usually static and deemed infallible belief systems. It invites them to re-think together about the following triad: "God, mankind and the hermeneutic of plurality."[244] Conviviality in the Arab political-contextual framework will benefit politically, culturally, and theologically "from a proper respect for the whole of Arab humanity."[245]

In conclusion, the future of the potential Arab theology of conviviality lies in finding its place in a religiously pluralist landscape, wherein only the language of love "will be able to express the distinctive, yet universal, characteristics of the Christ event in the context of contemporary Arab societies."[246] It will incarnate this life in reality by means of allowing all people to "experience

[237] Ibid., p. 291.
[238] Ibid., p. 299.
[239] Ibid., p. 345.
[240] Ibid., p. 348.
[241] Ibid., p. 351.
[242] Ibid., p. 352.
[243] Ibid., p. 353.
[244] Ibid., pp. 356ff.
[245] Ibid., p. 380.
[246] Ibid., p. 380.

justice, peace and the opportunity to flourish fully."[247] Aoun ends his display with the following, worth-citing words:

> Challenging their traditional fears for their own survival, Arab Christians now have the agonizing task of bringing together the interculturality and the universality of Christ into a fresh theological formulation; it needs to be one that might speak to the modern Arab mind in such a way that mature, responsible and respectful Arabs might want to engage with it in the hope of reaching abundant fulfillment.[248]

Interreligious Arab-Eastern Theology

The next trend of theological reasoning I would like to pause at is the theological discourse that is rooted in the keenness of Arab-Eastern theologians to dialogue with and interrelate to the religious belief of the Arab public majority, Islam. It is my belief that this trend of theological reasoning is one of the most important and unique theological discourses one can find on the Arab-Eastern Christian scene in today's Arab world. I have already demonstrated in this study that the Arabic-speaking Christians have never stopped interrelating to Islam and dialoguing with its faith ever since the first Muslim empire (Caliphate) of the Umayyad dynasty was established and based in the Fertile Crescent or the Greater Syria region. Early *Kalām*, as I showed, was the crown jewel of that interreligious cross-pollination that reached its peak during the second/eighth to fourth/tenth centuries. This acknowledged, the interreligious theology one can find in today's Christian Arab intellectual context is not actually a continuation of that old *Kalām* interreligious and inter-theological phenomenon. It is a totally new enterprise. The only similarity between it and the old one lies in the fact that the two dialoguing sides are still the very same followers of the two main Abrahamic religions in that region: the Muslims and the Christians. Other than that, all the subjects, the focuses, the motifs, the goals, and the methods of relating that one can detect in today's Christian interreligious theological discourses are expressive of a new theologisation deeply rooted in the contemporary social, political, cultural, contextual, existential, and anthropological circumstances of the Muslim and Christian inhabitants of the Arab world.

The number of the Arabic-speaking Christians who contribute to this theological genre is proportionately higher than the number of those who endeavour to offer theological voices on one of the previously displayed theological trends. This number has even increased, though slowly, since the beginning of the twenty-first century, as more and more generations of young Arab Christian postgraduate students found their way to the West, pursued higher academic training in interreligious studies and Christian–Muslim relations there, and then returned to their homelands to create an Arab indigenous voice on these areas of study and to foster the development of educational programmes on it in universities and religious seminaries. One can, therefore, find a good number of theological voices that merit being presented as examples

---

[247] Ibid., p. 381.

[248] Ibid., p. 383.

of this theological trend in the region (the author of this study is included in this group). I shall only pick up two demonstrative examples from the interreligious theology genre to give the reader some stimulating data that might encourage her to pursue broader study on this theological discourse and to look closely at other contributions made by other Arabic-speaking voices. The two voices I would like to briefly present here are Protestant and Orthodox ones. The Protestant is the voice of the Lebanese Baptist theologian Martin Accad, the associate professor of Islamic Studies at the Arab Baptist Theological Seminary, Lebanon. The Orthodox is the voice of the most prominent and influential Orthodox Antiochene theologian in the Arab world during the twentieth and the twenty-first centuries, Bishop George Khodr, the Metropolitan of Byblos' and Mount Lebanon's Orthodox, Antiochene Church.

Let me first start with Martin Accad's project.[249] Accad is one of the Arab Protestants who manifest a perceptive sensitivity to the Muslim-Arab context of the Near East, and who is ready to critically scrutinise the inappropriate, inimical, anti-Islam attitude which some American Baptist missionaries still come loaded with to the region to espouse fundamentalist beliefs, anti-ecumenism, and vilification against non-Christian faiths.[250] Accad seems to criticise this approach because he believes it threatens the credibility of the local Protestants' Arab identity before their local compatriots.

In a short article titled "Too Many Christian Books Fuel Paranoia about Islam," Accad deprecates the literature that depicts Islam in a stereotypical, overgeneralising, and essentialist manner, without paying sufficient objective attention to the inherent complexities of Islam. According to him, this binary-breeding literature fails in solving the potential conflicts between Christianity and Islam. Accad diagnoses the existence of such Christian literature on Islam in the following perceptive words:

> Unfortunately, it seems to meet the demands of a readership that books far-too-quick fix to life's complexities. Many today, when they approach a reality that frightens them, begin by turning it into a repelling caricature, and after dehumanizing it, set about to destroy it.[251]

Accad deems this stance as "neither Christian nor human." Far worse than that, he continues, "it is like the fight of an over-sized giant setting out to war against a quixotic enemy. Suddenly our giant is going to wake up, exhausted and knocked out by its fight against a gigantic windmill, its enemy, the product of its own imagination."[252]

---

[249] The following paragraphs on Martin Accad's stance on Islam are borrowed from my early study on the Protestants' presence and life in today's Syria and Lebanon. See Najib George Awad, *After-Mission, Beyond Evangelicalism*, pp. 125–130.

[250] Melanie E. Trexler, *Evangelizing Lebanon: Baptists, Missions and the Question of Cultures* (Waco, TX: Baylor University Press, 2016), p. 189.

[251] Martin Accad, "Too Many Christian Books Fuel Paranoia About Islam," in *www.ethicsdaily.com/too-many-christian-books-fuel-paranoia-about-islam-cms-7708* (consulted 7 June 2017).

[252] Ibid, p. 9.

Elsewhere, Martin Accad incarnates an Arab Protestant voice that is calling the Christians and the Muslims to do their best to rise above any conflict in their relationship. He tackles the clash-fostering mentality that generates a largely polarised take on Islam, "not the least within the church," as Accad maintains.[253] Departing from a critique of the conventional evangelical tendency to privatise faith and relegate it to the narrow realm of personal choice only, Accad accuses the Arabic-speaking evangelicals of imposing inaccurately the same understanding on Islam. He, then, invites them to try to understand Islam by *talking* to Muslims, rather than by just *reading* about Islam. He opines that it is the Christians' "duty and responsibility to seek a genuine, fair and balanced understanding of others in our [i.e., the Christians'] effort to relate to them as witnesses to the Gospel."[254] Lest he gets accused of proliferating an unfairly and unrealistically condemning judgement against the Christians, Accad concedes that "current wars causing immense suffering among Middle-Eastern peoples are doing nothing to encourage a moderate expression of Islam."[255]

In 2019, Martin Accad published a book titled *Sacred Misinterpretation* on the theme of Christian–Muslim dialogue. This latest monograph represents his, by far, most mature and complete discourse on the Christian–Muslim relations from an interreligious theology perspective.[256] Accad structures the thesis of his volume on a contextually driven motivation. He departs from his personal, first-hand experience of interrelating to Muslims and co-existing with other Christians in the predominantly Arab-Muslim context of Lebanon. While he himself reflects a very tolerant, embracive, and open-minded appreciation of his growth and life as Christian with Muslims in his birth-country, Lebanon (something the writer of this study has also experienced in a very similar way in his birth-land, Syria),[257] Accad concedes fully the, rather, globally detectable conviction that religions and their relations are a core component of conflict. Yet, in his book, Accad reveals (probably inspired and energised by his personal contextual experience) that the primary motivation and belief of his discourse on Christian–Muslim dialogue is "the idea that religious discourse can also contribute

---

[253] M. Accad, "Christianity and Islam Beyond Conflict," in *The Voice: Insert*, September 2009, pp. 6–10, p. 6.

[254] Ibid., p. 7.

[255] Ibid., p. 9.

[256] The following paragraphs are expanded elaborations on my review of Accad's book. See Najib George Awad, "Sacred Misinterpretation: Reaching Across the Christian–Muslim Divide," book review in *The Muslim World*, 10(2020), pp. 259–262. See also Najib G. Awad, "Interfaith Relations and Middle East Christianity: Beyond Dialogue, Toward Interrelationality," in *Levant, Cradle of Abrahamic Religions: Studies on the Interaction of Religion and Society from Antiquity to Modern Times*, Catalin-Stefan Popa (ed.) (Berlin: LIT, 2022), pp. 291–326. Recently, Martin Accad responded to my critique of his approach in Martin Accad, 'Deconstructing the Kerygmatic?" in *The Blog of Arab Baptist Theological Seminary*, 2 March 2003, https://abtslebanon.org/2023/03/02/deconstructing-the-kerygmatic/ (consulted on 13 March 2023).

[257] See, for instance, Najib G. Awad, "Kullunā Ka-Aiyyūb Naghsul Qurūḥ al-Istibdād wal-Qamʿ bi-māʾ al-Baḥr Dhātih" (We Are All Like Job, Washing the Blisters of Tyranny and Oppression by the Same Sea Water), in www.syria.alsafahat.net/-نصوص نوافذ-عن-المشرق-مسيحيين-ومسلمين [accessed 12.8.2021].

significantly in working towards peaceful relations between populations with rival ideologies."[258]

How can religions become part of the remedy's prescription instead of one of the conflict's ingredients? The transformation of the role of religious interrelations and communication in our living context, Accad suggests, lies in re-viewing and re-assessing the Christians' and Muslims' theological reasonings about each other: "Our theologies have been fundamental to our understanding of one another, and our murky relational history seems to indicate that our mutual perceptions have been largely negative."[259] It is this essential role of theologisation in the history of interreligious relation between Christianity and Islam that makes theology "a foundation of dialogue," Accad believes:

> Your *view* of Islam affects your *attitude* to Muslims; your *attitude*, in turn, influences your *approach* to Christian–Muslim interaction, and that *approach* affects the ultimate *outcome* of your presence as a witness among Muslims.[260]

Accad's following discussion and analysis become, then, a conglomeration of ideas and experiences that are assembled on the basis of the abovementioned premise to create what he calls "the SEKAP spectrum of Christian–Muslim interaction."[261] 'SEKAP' here abbreviates "syncretistic, existential, kerygmatic, apologetic, and polemical." From all these key-notional trends of interaction between the Christians and Muslims, Accad leaves those who relate to interrelationality (like syncretistic and existential) and focuses, instead, on the one that centres around the key-concept of 'kerygmatic.' He opts for what he calls the 'kerygmatic interaction' option, deeming it the most fruitful and peaceful alternative between the other two extreme options of 'syncretism' and 'polemics.' According to him, this option more than any other one in 'SEKAP' enables the exploration and finding of the most 'Christ-like' symptoms in Islam and the Muslims.[262] Accad opines that such an evangelistic stance is not conflictual but peaceful, because it maintains the distinction between 'kerygma' and 'apologia.' For him, however, the difference between 'kerygma' and 'apology' does not actually connote a distinction in terms of content or necessarily theological viewing. The difference between them merely lies in the communicational *attitude* or *manner* each delineates or pertains to. The distinction, he opines, "reflects [difference] between an apologetic defence of one's beliefs, on the one hand, and a positive proclamation of it, on the other."[263]

The above entails that Accad promotes in his book a Christian–Muslim interaction wherein the Christian seems to be expected to treat dialogue as a chance for evangelism and faith-promoting. What is emphasised here is the necessity of pursuing this evangelism role in the most peaceful, most inviting, and most transparent manner. Accad clarifies that what the evangelising

---

[258] Martin Accad, *Sacred Misinterpretation: Reaching Across the Christian–Muslim Divide* (Grand Rapids, Mich: W. B. Eerdmans Publishing Company, 2019), p. 6.

[259] Ibid., p. 7.

[260] Ibid., p. 7.

[261] Ibid., p. 8.

[262] Ibid., p. 7.

[263] Ibid., p. 9.

Christian invites the Muslim to do in this kerygmatic interaction is not to adopt the "religious system" of Christianity. It is, rather, an invitation to embrace "Christ himself," so that the dialogue, Accad proposes, "is removed entirely from the realm of institutionalized religious talk."[264] Does this kerygmatic approach allow for any recognition of some values in the other's religiosity as such? Accad suggests that the value of Islam's religiosity, from this kerygmatic perspective, lies in the fact that "Islam preserved many important and positive elements from the Judeo-Christian tradition."[265] Whichever value one bestows upon Islam or detects in the Muslim message or religious texts is determined and appreciated by virtue of its closeness to, or remoteness from, the divine revelation in Jesus Christ, as well as to Christ's life's and ministry's value-system.[266] Accad invites us to glean this understanding from his own words in the book, as he says, for instance:

> Followers of Jesus embracing the Kerygmatic approach will not shy away from theological engagement. And, as they do so, based on a thoughtfully developed framework and understanding of Islam, they will do so respectfully, with a genuine desire to learn through a mutual exchange or perceptions about God and faith. The kerygmatic person remains a Christ follower and therefore cannot be expected to compromise solid biblical truths. Dialogue at this level will therefore likely remain in a space that maintains disagreements. But, engagement with Islam at a kerygmatic level will almost certainly be enriching for all involved.[267]

Believing in this enrichment and its mutuality, Accad further states that "the engagement does not go merely in one direction," for "kerygmatic engagement creates an opportunity to listen to what Muslims have to say about religious issues as well, the opportunity to learn and stand corrected, rather than stick to our own perceptions of what they believe."[268]

What is Christian–Muslim dialogue within the framework of Accad's thesis? It is that sphere of theological correspondence, the success of which is determined by the Christian interlocutor's ability to be a smart and successful kerygma-conveyer. What are the things that enable the Christian kerygma-deliverer to excel in his or her performance in the dialogue? One of the basic elements Accad centres his book around in relation to this enquiry is a concern about finding an appropriate hermeneutic method to present the Scripture and to approach the Qur'ān before the Muslims. Accad states that his hope in his book is "to make a positive contribution to the development of a more comprehensive *biblical* understanding of Islam."[269] It is essential for the evangeliser, Accad believes, to realise when engaged in dialogue with Muslims vis-à-vis scriptural attestations that "just as Christians consider it illegitimate for people of other faiths or sects (even groups within Christianity) to interpret the Bible without paying due attention to the various contexts of a passage, Muslims also consider it illegitimate for people of other faiths to interpret the Qur'ān without paying

---

[264] Ibid., p. 10.
[265] Ibid., p. 11.
[266] Ibid., pp. 11ff.
[267] Ibid., p. 15.
[268] Ibid., p. 15.
[269] Ibid., p. 323. Italic is mine.

due attention to the various Islamic traditions that have accompanied the meaning and implications of the text through history."[270] What should be avoided in dialogue is falling into the common tendency that makes Muslims and Christians "read each other's sacred texts in the exact way that [they] do not wish [their] own scriptures to be read."[271] Avoiding this tendency is essential for the Christians and Muslims to interact theologically without falling into either syncretism or polemics. Interpretation of religious texts is here deemed the foundation of the proper kerygmatic theology. For, according to Accad, "interpretation is central to the development of any theological discourse." Also, "it is only by learning and applying the principles that each community considers as legitimate when approaching their sacred texts that interfaith dialogue can hope to be fruitful and eventually help to break out from the grasp of age-long conflicts."[272]

In his book, Accad argues that, in today's world, what drags the Christians and Muslims into a vicious circle of interaction is their opting for a 'dialogue of life' and their avoiding of dialogues on theological issues. Accad correctly states that the first model of dialogue helps Muslims to be more tolerant toward the Christians due to the friendship that common life experiences generate. However, Accad does not seem to be quite pleased with this, for he opines that, without the second model of dialogue, co-existence and friendship will not change the Muslims' theologically rejecting views against the Christians (that they are associators and not monotheists, for example).[273] The dialogue of life alone, Accad argues, will not suffice, for:

> Our history is burdened with conflicts and wars that have been legitimized by religion [i.e. theology]. It will take more than a few good interfaith friendships for Christians and Muslims to lay new foundations for the future that begins today, and for them together to set the tone for the history to come. If our past is riddled with mutual theological misconceptions, is our future not therefore in desperate need of a theological dialogue that will mend our mutual prejudices?[274]

Accad seems to be convinced that the mere dialogue of life will not pluck out the roots of conflict and potential clashes from the soil of Christian–Muslim relations without a biblically based theology. The dialogue of life will be a moment of meeting at the mercy of 'fluctuating feelings and moods, which tend to swing between highs and lows depending on the latest representations of Islam in the news media."[275] Only when we establish values like mercy, humility, and justice as a way of life on a bibliocentric theological understanding, Accad affirms, can these values truly "affect relationships between Jews, Christians and Muslims."[276] Only a theological perception of Islam in its reality and faith, on the basis of "a biblical understanding of divine revelation,"[277] can grant the

---

[270] Ibid., pp. 43–44.
[271] Ibid., p. 64.
[272] Ibid., p. 65.
[273] Ibid., pp. 67–68.
[274] Ibid., p. 68.
[275] Ibid., p. 323.
[276] Ibid., p. 342.
[277] Ibid., p. 323.

evangelicals, Accad says, the chance of having a "profound and balanced comprehension of Islam" and can breed an interfaith that goes beyond exposing Islam to either "slanderous caricaturing" or "idealized representation" tendencies.[278] The only option before Christians to protect themselves from the religious extremism and violent attitudes of Muslims lies in knowing these Muslims and their Islam "by moving toward them rather than retreating *from* them in judgment."[279]

Let me now move to the interreligious project of the Orthodox George Khodr. I believe it is quite fair to say that George Khodr is not just one of the most influential Christian theologians in the Arab world during the last four decades of the twentieth century and the first quarter of the twenty-first, but also "a leading figure in Christian–Muslim dialogue in the Arab world as well as the main interlocutor in theological and political matters for Muslim thinkers in Lebanon."[280]

Khodr did not produce a complete monograph on Christian–Muslim relations and dialogue. It is generally fair also to say that Khodr's writings do not present systematic and complete hermeneutic, but sporadic and diverse, approaches and arguments related to various theological and religious subjects.[281] As Khodr's apprentice, Assaad Elias Kattan, once said, "Georges Khodr has not developed a hermeneutical system" (*Georges Khodr hat kein hermeneutisches System entwickelt*).[282] Kattan explains this statement by relating that Khodr "has nowhere presented his theological thinking in a systematic way. This thinking is scattered, so to speak, in thousands of newspaper articles Khodr has published since 1962, many of which have the character of short occasional writings" (*sein theologisches Denken nirgendwo auf systematische Art und Weise dargelegt hat. Dieses Denken befindet sich sozusagen zerstreut in Tausenden von Zeitungsartikeln, die Khodr seit 1962 verfast hat und von denen viele den Charakter von kurzen Gelegenheitsschriften besitzen*).[283] A good collection of these essays was published in the year 2000, in one volume produced by al-Boulusiyyah Press in Lebanon. A careful systematic reading of the relevant

[278] Ibid., p. 342.

[279] Ibid., p. 343.

[280] Assaad Elias Kattan, "The Cross as 'Islam': George Khodr's Approach to Islam as a Paradigm of Contextual Theology," *Journal of Eastern Christian Studies*, 69(1–4), 2017, pp. 69–78, p. 70 and A. E. Kattan, *Shirā' fī 'Uyūn Mustadīrah: Dirāsāt fī Fikr al-Muṭrān George Khodr* (A Sail within Round Eyes: Studies on the Thought of Bishop George Khodr) (Beirut: al-Nūr Orthodox Cooperation, 2012), pp. 15–17.

[281] Mouchir B. Aoun, *The Arab Christ: Towards an Arab Christian Theology of Conviviality*, Sarah Patey (trans.) (London: Gingko, 2022), p. 306 and Assaad Elias Kattan, "Wort und Leib. Zur Hermeneutik Georges Khodrs in ihrem islamischen Kontext," in *Patrologie und Ökumene: Theresia Hainthaler zum 75. Geburtstag*, Peter Knauer, Andrea Riedl, and Dietmar W. Winkler (eds.) (Freiburg, Basel & Wien: Verlag Herder, 2022), pp. 295–308.

[282] Kattan, "Wort und Leib. Zur Hermeneutik Georges Khodrs in ihrem islamischen Kontext," p. 304.

[283] Ibid., p. 297. Kattan believes that this makes the studying of Khodr's theological thought a "labyrinthine task": "labyrinthisch die Aufgabe einer Studie ist" (ibid., p. 298).

essays in the mentioned volume, *Afkār wa-Ārā' fī al-Ḥiwār al-Masīḥī al-Islāmī wal-'Aiysh al-Mushtarak* (Ideas and Opinions on Christian–Muslim Dialogue and Co-existence), suggests that Khodr constructs his assessment of the Christian–Muslim dialogue on a hermeneutical appraisal of how the Christians and Muslims view each other in life, and what kind of interrelationality this mutual viewing generates. According to Khodr, the problem between human beings in general lies in the fact that each one of us synthesises (*yaṣṭani'*) the other and then reads him or her from the perspective of the image this synthesiser carves (*naḥataha 'anhu*). This negative tendency to abstract the other, Khodr continues, stems from our disregarding of the other's independence and distinctiveness. Instead of letting self-distinction invite harmony between two distinguished correlates, we try to suppress the other's distinction because we cognitively prefer hegemonic monism, and we tend to imagine an absolute and static humanity that descends from above and applies to all people.[284]

Khodr states that this synthesising attitude towards the other, and the reliance on it instead of relating to the other in her self-distinction, requires from us a critical anatomisation of our view of the other, and a realisation of the unfairness that could linger within it. This view of the other creates in society a state of injustice, the roots of which are nothing external, but rather intrinsic and inherent to our other-perception. The history of human relating and interrelating (the socialisation aspect), Khodr states, does not come from texts and records only. It is primarily generated by daily presumptions on and premeditated perceptions of the other.[285] In a paper on plurality and citizenship which he read in a regional panel held in 2011, Khodr speaks about the foundational status of the dialogue of life by invoking an old Latin-Roman saying, "primum vivere, deinde philosophare" (first, we live, then we philosophise), before he then states:

> We must, thus, exceed [differences], ally together, and exchange goods. And there needs to be doctors, scientists, solicitors, and a high-quality school and security forces for the person to rest and feel secure in the land he or she lives on ... Love compels you to tender all the inhabitants of the land equally, justly, and by means of equal extent of services. We can all convene together on the basis of all these matters.[286]

"No one lives alone," Khodr proceeds, "and none of us has a language for himself alone." Yes, he notes, Muslims and Christians have distinguished civilisational values (*qiyam ḥaḍāriyyah*) and each one of them derives views and ideas from the other according to their premeditated perception of each other's religious heritage. Yet, what makes this possible, Khodr states, is nothing other

---

[284] George Khodr, "Madkhal ilā al-Naḍrāt al-Mutabādalah" (An Introduction to the Reciprocal Views) in *Afkār wa-Ārā' fī al-Ḥiwār al-Masīḥī al-Islāmī wal-'Aiysh al-Mushtarak* (Ideas and Opinions on Christian–Muslim Dialogue and Co-existence), George Khodr (Jounieh: Boulușiyyah Bookshop, 2000), pp. 107–123, p. 107.

[285] Ibid., p. 108.

[286] G. Khodr, "al-ʻAyish al-Mushtarak bayn al-Taʻaddudiyyah eal-Mūwāṭanah" (Co-existence between Plurality and Citizenship), in *Al-'Ayish al-Mustarak wal-Waḥdah fī al-Tanaūw'* (Co-existence and Unity in Diversity), Jerome Shahin (ed.) (Beirut: The Platform of Development, Culture and Dialogue, 2011), pp. 120–127, p. 122.

than their factual co-existence (*al-'ayish al-mustarak*).[287] According to Khodr, this co-existence is what drives Muslims to view Christianity from the history of colonialism, and Christians to view Islam from the history of the Mamlukides' persecuting policies. This is, also, what prevents the teachings in the religious texts from shaping reality, and imposes, instead, the lived realistic conditions of the Christians and Muslims as the main factors that influence and dictate their reading of, and abidance with, the written faith.[288] Khodr relates that what colours the perspective of our view of each other is our condition and realistic status in relation to the other in our life-setting, "whether we are rulers or ruled, in the position of minority or the position of majority."[289]

Other factors that colour one's appraisal of the other, as well as one's self-perception in alterity with the other, are cultural circumstances and statuses. Khodr reveals that the Lebanese Christians, for instance, used to have a culturally superior view that made them, intellectually and socially, degrade the Muslims, who in turn developed sceptical and even treacherous views against the Christians and their intentions toward, and affiliation to, the Muslim world. The Christian superiority complex was the reason for a Muslim inferiority complex, and this vicious circle led to a sharply divisive tension and mutual intolerance and estrangement.[290] The Christian clings to an accusing and judgemental view, while the Muslim resorts to an apologetic and vindicatory stance.[291] The outcome of this is a lack of interrelation, an elimination of communication, a prohibition of meeting and correlation, and the prevalence of binarism, territoriality, or mere adjacence (*tajāuwr*).[292] Such territoriality divorces the socially lived reality from the religious views which one upholds and presumes that the other believes in.[293]

If the interreligious relationship is injured, the interreligious dialogue that is pursued on its basis would turn into a demonstration of violence generated from a conglomeration of pragmatist interests, political hauteur, and religious inspiration that are all implemented in the service of utilitarian agendas.[294] In the light of this, the noble and positively relational values and lessons, which one finds in the Christian religious Scripture, do not really have any tangible impact on the dialogue's process, content, or consequences. On the contrary, the Scriptures remain muffled and their content determined by the decisions and orientations of their believing followers. What would actually be communicated in the dialogue will not be the texts' contents, but the minds and sentiments of their readers. These readers may not be motivated or guided by a passion for

---

[287] Ibid., p. 126.

[288] Khodr, "Madkhal ilā al-Naḍrāt al-Mutabādalah" (An Introduction to the Reciprocal Views), pp. 108–109.

[289] Ibid., p. 109.

[290] Ibid., pp. 110–111.

[291] Ibid., pp. 114–115.

[292] Ibid., p. 122.

[293] Ibid., p. 123.

[294] Khodr, "al-Ḥiwār al-Islāmī al-Masīḥī" (The Muslim–Christian Dialogue), in *Afkār wa-Arā' fī al-Ḥiwār al-Masīḥī al-Islāmī*, pp. 59–86, p. 59.

truth, but haunted, instead, by their instinctive presumptions and historically rooted experiential injuries.[295]

Properly interrelational dialogue, Khodr opines, is one that results from the Christians' and Muslims' cooperation and co-creation of the contextual and social setting (or 'city/*madīnah*', in Khodr terms) that will be the abode, the habitat, of their interreligious communication. It is a true setting of societal coalition (*i'tilāf ijtimā'ī*), wherein "I can say 'I' and I can say 'you,' but also we can together say 'us'." An 'us', that is, which Christians and Muslims co-create on the basis of their common geography, history, and destiny.[296] This belief in the factuality of such co-generation, which makes the Muslims and the Christians speak about the 'us' that combines them, is what frames Khodr's reading of the history of the Christians' presence in, and their contributions to, the trajectory of originating an 'Arab culture' throughout the past centuries. For Khodr, the historical biography of cultural co-creation demonstrates that the Christians and Muslims did not walk on two parallel, binary cultural tracks, but ploughed together one, common cultural trajectory.[297]

Such an 'us-ness' perception, Khodr states, makes the 'other' "as necessary as breathing" (*ḍarūrī ḥatta at-tanaffus*) to the Christians.[298] Thus, it cannot be achieved if one of the two sides (the Muslim in this case) alone enjoyed power and prevailed socially, politically, and culturally over the other (the Christian in this case), and if this side, consequentially, used his or her religious belief and theology to sanctify and legitimise this hegemony. In such a situation, there is no true 'us-ness,' and there will not, thus, be genuine communication, even if there was a dialogue-like encounter. It will be a figurative and far from genuine dialogue because, according to Khodr, "we are here in a clash between two sides that have nothing in common and [who follow] two different understandings of God."[299] True 'us-ness' is possible only in democratic spaces, where freedom and equality are foundational and not subjected to, or pre-conditioned by, interpretations that are dictated by the tolerance or intolerance of the powerful and dominating side.[300] Only in such spaces do the Christians and the Muslims not only co-exist, Khodr says, but more essentially co-support "the foundations of living" (*usus al-'ayish*)[301] that are required for enabling both sides to exist in their full human dignity.

The needed dialogue, Khodr opines, is the dialogue wherein there is no disregard or subordination, where there is no 'original' (*aṣīl*) versus 'intruder' (*dakhīl*) and no one is under the state of *dhimmitude* in relation to the other, but

---

[295] Ibid., p. 62.

[296] Ibid., p. 63.

[297] G. Khodr, "Al-Ḥuḍūr al-Masīḥī fī al-Thaqāfah al-'Arabiyyah" (The Christian Presence in Arabic Culture), in *al-Ma'ārij Journal*, 24(173), 2014, pp. 65–76, p. 76.

[298] G. Khodr, "Qādirūn 'ala at-Talāqī" (Capable of Getting Together), in *Ma'ārij Journal*, 23(161), 2013, pp. 28–30, p. 30.

[299] Khodr, "al-Ḥiwār al-Islāmī al-Masīḥī" (The Muslim–Christian Dialogue), p. 66.

[300] Ibid., p. 67–68.

[301] G. Khodr, "Naḥn wal-Muslimūn" (We and the Muslims), in *Ma'ārij Journal*, 24(172), 2014, pp. 10–11, p. 10.

all religious groups are equal.[302] Here, Khodr interestingly stresses that this dialogue of life is not truly different from the dialogue of ideas. None of us has her or his ideas developed in separation from her or his lived experience, and no one can structure a rational view centred on truth unless one's own living, existential awareness is not historically injured by the other and their convictions.[303] One's own relatedness to daily or historically interreligious living with the other shapes, if not generates, one's own intellectual understanding and assessment of the idea of interreligious communication. Dialogue, thus, is not a chance to penetrate Islam and Christianity, but to delve into the historical experiential legacies that originated among the religious people from their communication together.[304]

Ultimately, Khodr believes that the dialogue of ideas is another form of the central and ultimate dialogue of life. On this dialogue he says: "the dialogue of life is the one we taste and experience every day. It is the good common life between the people of the two religions, especially the spiritual unity between the Arab Muslims and Christians."[305] The interreligious life of the Arab Muslims and Christians fuels their dialogue with the common aspirations they share about the renaissance of the Arab world, as much as with the fear and questions they have about the challenges that threaten their common destiny.[306] After all, the essence of dialogue for George Khodr is the pre-dialogue relationship that paves the way to it, for, as he says, "social intercourse (*mu'āsharah*) is the secret of convergence in actions."[307]

Khodr suggests that this *a priori* social intercourse would create true dialogue between the Christians and the Muslims. It would be a dialogue wherein each side penetrates the other and allows this penetration to become a chance of self-examination and a critical assessment of one's own history and belief expressions.[308] The fertile interreligious communication is the process where one endeavours to think *with* the other and *for* the other, so that both of them travel beyond the historical efforts to interpret one's own faith in isolation.[309] Maybe, then, the Christians and Muslims would launch an open dialogue and transparently confess before each other that the past interreligious history witnessed some failed moments of communication because the Muslims acknowledge the faith and the "ʿIsā of the Qur'ān's Naṣārā," but not the faith and "the Christ, the divine-*Logos*" of the Christians. On the other hand, the

---

302 Khodr, "al-Ḥiwār al-Islāmī al-Masīḥī" (The Muslim–Christian Dialogue), p. 69.
303 Ibid., pp. 72–73.
304 Ibid., pp. 78ff.
305 Khodr, "Maʿrifatnā Baʿḍunā li-baʿḍ Sharṭ min Shurūṭ al-Ḥiwār al-Islāmī al-Masīḥī" (Our Knowledge of Each Other is One of the Preconditions of Muslim–Christian Dialogue), in *Afkār wa-Arā' fī al-Ḥiwār al-Masīḥī al-Islāmī*, pp. 87–105, p. 90.
306 Ibid., 93.
307 Khodr, "Maʿ baʿḍ al-Muslimīn" (With Some Muslims), in *Afkār wa-Arā' fī al-Ḥiwār al-Masīḥī al-Islāmī wal-'Aiysh al-Mushtarak* (Ideas and Opinions on Christian–Muslim Dialogue and Co-existence), pp. 215–220, p. 216.
308 Khodr, "Ḥiwār al-Dīyānatayn fī ʿAmmān" (The Dialogue of the Two Religions in Amman), p. 152.
309 Ibid., p. 153.

Christians have always thought that recognising Islamic faith means giving up on Christian belief.[310] Be that as it may, a Christian–Muslim dialogue born from an interreligious life-setting would be a venue for dissipating the misunderstanding between the two sides and perceiving that the distance between them is far shorter than what many imagine (or even wish?). Dialogue departs from interrelation and aims at creating symbiosis (*mu'āyashah*) at all levels of existence.[311] The road towards reaching this destination is far ahead still. But, reaching the end of this path is not impossible, Khodr concludes.[312]

Khodr's logical departure from interrelationality towards dialogue, rather than the other way round, fairly deems him "a true theologian of conviviality,"[313] and not just of dialogue. Khodr's belief that the distance between Arab Muslims and Christians is shorter than they imagine is founded on his call for the Arabic-speaking Christians not to fuse 'Muslim' and 'Arab' identity-codes, but to dissociate them. He recognises that history demonstrates the indissoluble connectedness between Arab identity and Islam, yet he also emphasises that the Arab identity has also always been far greater, deeper, and broader than Islam.[314] The Arab Christians must, instead, embrace this common, encompassing identity and enjoy it as expressive of a non-monolithic culture open to plurality and diversity. The interrelational stance of the Arabic Christians would enable them to produce a dialogical engagement open to cultural diversity and deeply grounded in religiously sensitive and perceptive conviviality.[315] The Arab Christians, Khodr then states, are now called to recreate an authentic Christianity rooted in its Arabic history and context.[316]

The theological crux of this conviviality-centred approach lies in Khodr's belief that the foundation of the Christians' duty to commit to such an approach is no other than their belief that the God of Jesus Christ is 'love'; the thing that makes them a 'community of love,' rather than a 'confessional community.' The Christians are witnesses of love; love is their binding force and sole opportunity to make the Muslims perceive and experience human beingness. On this theological approach, Mouchir Basil Aoun perceptively comments by saying: "This is the direction taken by G. Khodr when he firmly and critically addresses all those who believe that they can preserve Christian truth by shutting themselves up in a homogenous and defended ghetto."[317] In this relation of love towards their companions in life and history, the Arab Christians, according to Khodr, need to study carefully the distinctive features and components of Arab identity, so that in the heart of this self-identification and conviviality context they can disclose before the Muslims the love of the God of Jesus Christ.[318] The

---

310 Ibid., p. 159.
311 Ibid., p. 156.
312 Ibid., p. 157.
313 M. B. Aoun, *The Arab Christ*, p. 286.
314 G. Khodr, "Le christianisme, l'islam et l'arabité," *Contacts*, III (110), 1980, p. 106.
315 Ibid., p. 97.
316 Ibid., p. 101.
317 Aoun, *The Arab Christ*, pp. 294–295.
318 Khodr, "Le christianisme, l'islam et l'arabité," p. 98; see also Aoun, *The Arab Christ*, pp. 296–297.

Christian task lies not, therefore, in a dialogue centred around proselytising and appropriation, but around communion and solidarity that makes Islam "the privileged beneficiary of the message [of Christ]."[319]

Probably one of the most interesting and intriguing aspects in Khodr's interreligious theology is his attempt at making Islamic thought accommodate the Crucifixion into its religious imagination. It is well known that the Islamic faith refuses the theological tenability of Christian soteriology that is centred on the belief that the Messiah of God was crucified and killed by other humans to atone for our sins. This rejection is harboured solidly in the Qur'ānic verses in *Surat an-Nisā'* 157–158, which states: "And their saying: We killed 'Īsa the Messiah, the Son of Mariam, the messenger of God. They killed Him not and they crucified Him not, but it was made to appear as so to them, and those who disagree on it are suspicious about it. They have no knowledge of it but only presumption and they did not kill Him certainly, but God raised Him up to Him, and God was glorious and prudent." The extant records of the old *Kalām* interlocutions between Christian and Muslim rationalists during the early Abbasid era inform us that the subject of Jesus's Crucifixion has always been one of the hottest subjects the Christians and Muslims debated.[320] In the contemporary Arab intellectual context, George Khodr is one among two rare scholars (the second is a Muslim[321]) who attempt at reappropriating the theology of the Crucifixion in such a manner that will make the Muslims conceive in the Cross of Jesus Christ a plausible and relevant understanding for religious belief.

One of the best interpretations of Khodr's understanding of the Cross in relation to Islam was offered by his student, the Lebanese Antiochene Orthodox scholar Assaad Elias Kattan, the professor of Orthodox Theology at Münster University, Germany, who published this study in the German language in 2008.[322] Kattan starts studying the Cross in Khodr's theology from realising the

[319] Aoun, *The Arab Christ*, p. 297.

[320] On this old *Kalām* on the crucifixion, see, for example, Najib George Awad, "If His Crucifixion Was Figurative As You Claim, Then So Be It": How Two Christian Mutakallims from the Abbasid Era Used An-Nisā' 4:157–158 in Dialogues with Muslims," in *Journal of Eastern Christian Studies*, 68(1–2), 2016, pp. 53–80; Todd Lawson, *The Crucifixion and the Qur'an: A Study in the History of Muslim Thought* (Oxford: Oneworld Publications, 2009); A. H. Mathias Zahniser, *The Mission and Death of Jesus in Islam and Christianity* (Maryknoll, NY: Orbis Books, 2008); Michael G. Fonner, "Jesus' Death by Crucifixion in the Qur'ān: An Issue for Interpretation and Muslim–Christian Relations," in *Journal of Ecumenical Studies*, 29 (1992), pp. 432–450.

[321] The other scholar who tries to make Islam accommodate the Cross within its religious thought and reconcile with its theological implications, is the late Muslim-Shi'ite Lebanese scholar Mahmoud Ayoub. On this, see Mahmoud Ayoub, *A Muslim View of Christianity: Essays on Dialogue by Mahmoud Ayoub*, Irfan A. Omar (ed.) (Maryknoll, NY: Orbis Books, 2007), pp. 156–179.

[322] Assaad E. Kattan, "Das Kreuz als Hingabe (islām) an den Willen Gottes. Zu den Besonderheiten der Kreuzestheologie Georges Khodrs im Blick auf ihren islamischen Kontext," in *Christlische Gotteslehre in Orient seit dem Aufkommen des Islams zur Gegenwart*, Martin Tamcke (ed.) (Wūrzburgh: Ergon Verlag, 2008), pp. 213–224. The same essay was later published in Arabic and then English versions. See A. E. Kattan,

central significance which the belief "Jesus of Nazareth, the crucified Messiah" occupies in Khodr's overall intellectual discourse. He then concludes that this centrality warrants the theology of the Cross a particular role and foundational value in Khodr's intensive commitment to the Christian–Muslim dialogue.[323] Whenever Khodr writes about the Cross, Kattan opines, the horizon of his critical discourse is always Islam. This is why his starting point is a consistent emphasis on the historicity of the Crucifixion, which is denied by most of the Muslim interpreters. Khodr departs from the affirmation of historicity before he afterwards develops a *theological* explanation of Jesus's death that will relate to Islam.[324]

According to Kattan, Khodr endeavours to link before the Muslims Jesus's birth (which is central to the Qur'ān's attestation in *Surat Mariyam* (N.3)), with His death. He achieves this by speaking about the union between the divine and the human in the ontological reality of Jesus Christ. Khodr does that because he knows that such an idea of a 'mystic union' (*unio mystica*) is also known in Muslim Sufism.[325] For Khodr, whoever acknowledges in her or his belief system the possibility of being contiguous to God (*mulāṣiq*) must be able to perceive the depth of union which the Cross represents: "Whoever says that we are called to be united with God [*mulāṣaqat Allah*] and that [God's] nature is to be united with us [*yulāṣiqunā*], has no problem with the Cross. It [i.e., the Cross] is the final word of Love."[326] What Khodr does in his Cross-focused interreligious theology is travel beyond questioning the Qur'ānic rejection of the historicity of the Crucifixion towards building, instead, bridges to Muslim Sufism and its understanding of the divine–human union. Khodr does this, Kattan notes, via a serious deconstruction of all the problematic Christian ideologies that lean on the idea of the Cross. He invites both the Christians and the Muslims to realise that the truth of the Cross contradicts all ideologies of crusadership, triumphalism, and self-flagellation. Khodr manifests this by skilfully and learnedly surveying texts and views from the Christian and the Muslim traditions alike, aiming thereby to show that the idea of the Cross is liberating from ideologisation for both Christianity and Islam.[327]

On the basis of the above, Khodr then develops his own conclusion on the core meaning of 'the Cross' from an interreligious perspective. The Cross becomes, for him, the hermeneutic key of the word '*islām*.' The Arabic term

---

"Al-Ṣalīb bi-Waṣfihi Islāman li-Mashī'at Allah: Khaṣā'iṣ Lāhūt al-Ṣalīb lada George Khodr fī Siyāqih al-Thaqāfī al-Islāmī" (The Cross as a Surrender to God's Will: The Characteristics of George Khodr's Theology of the Cross in its Islamic Cultural Context), in *Shirā' fī 'Uyūn Mustadīrah*, pp. 23–41 and A. E. Kattan, "The Cross as 'Islam': George Khodr's Approach to Islam as a Paradigm of Contextual Theology." In the above paragraphs, I present my reading of Kattan's analysis, relying on the Arabic version of this study.

323 Kattan, "Al-Ṣalīb bi-Waṣfihi Islāman li-Mashī'at Allah," p. 25.

324 Ibid., p. 26.

325 Ibid., p. 27.

326 George Khodr, *Maṭāriḥ Sujūd. 2* (Prostration Spots. 2) (Beirut: al-Nahār Press, 2001), pp. 17–18, p. 18.

327 Kattan, "Al-Ṣalīb bi-Waṣfihi Islāman li-Mashī'at Allah," p. 30.

'*aslama*,' Kattan proposes, is etymologically expressive of the Greek '*paradidomai*' (surrender), which is used in the liturgical texts to speak about Jesus's death. The liturgy says that, on the Cross, Jesus "surrenders His soul" (*aslama al-rūḥ*).[328] Kattan suggests that George Khodr is inspired by this specific liturgical language-game in his belief that the Cross is the perfect expression of the notion of '*islām*' (surrender), from which the name of the Muhammedan religion "al-Islam" is derived. For Khodr, if there is a state of '*islām*' in Christianity, it is deeply and primarily expressed in Jesus's surrendering (*taslīm*) of His soul on the Cross.[329] As the Qur'ān speaks about obeying God by means of surrendering (*islām/taslīm*) oneself unconditionally to Allah, Khodr suggests, the Christians are also called to become similarly '*musallimūn*' (surrenderers) by means of laying themselves down (*aslama*) before the crucified Jesus.[330]

In this sense, Jesus Christ is the ultimate '*musallim*' (surrenderer) in Christianity, who manifests the kernel of the Qur'ānic notion of 'Islām' in the very surrendering moment (*taslīm*) of His soul to God's hands on the Cross. Therefore, the Muslim interpreters' denial of the Cross negates, and tends to obscure, Jesus's surrender to God, or his '*islām*' to the almighty as God's prophet, messenger, and ultimately Word (*kalimah*), which the Qur'ān itself attributes to Jesus.[331] In this sense, Khodr corrects the Islamic understanding of the Cross by drawing the attention to the fact that Jesus's surrendering of His soul to God on the Cross is the ultimate Christian manifestation of '*islām*,' which the Qur'ān and the Muslim faith identify themselves with. Jesus's Cross as surrender (*taslīm*) reflects the state of surrendering to Allah (*islām*), which the religion of Islam is constituted by and is teleologically directed toward.

In the previous pages, I presented two examples of the Arab-Eastern intellectual voice that aims at theologising in close and direct interaction and interlocution with Islam. As I stated earlier, one can find other theological figures who travel on the very same interreligious track around the Arab world. The ones I presented here, however, are serious examples of such a theological endeavour. Both scholars, as I tried to demonstrate, are occupied with the primary concern about sparing the co-existing Christian and Muslim communities in that region the pitfalls and negative ramifications that have generated from their religious interaction in the past centuries. They both seek a reconciliatory and candidly filial language to address Islam and to present Christianity to the Muslims of today.

The Protestant example (M. Accad) displays before us a good case of an Arab Protestant scholar trying sincerely and conscientiously to reconcile his church's missiological and evangelistic legacy (which stands on the ground of

[328] Ibid., p. 35.

[329] Ibid., p. 36. Kattan says that the oldest text he could find in Khodr's legacy, wherein the latter conjures this idea for the first time, goes back to 1989. See George Khodr, "La communication du message en terre d'Islam," in *Études theologiques et religiouses*, 64(1989), pp. 373–391.

[330] Kattan, "Al-Ṣalīb bi-Waṣfihi Islāman li-Mashī'at Allah," p. 37 and Khodr, *Maṭāriḥ Sujūd. 1* (Prostration Spots. 1) (Beirut: al-Nahār Press, 2001), p. 141.

[331] Kattan, "Al-Ṣalīb bi-Waṣfihi Islāman li-Mashī'at Allah," p. 37 and Khodr, *Maṭāriḥ Sujūd. 2* (Prostration Spots. 2), p. 217.

Christianising, not just tolerating, the Muslim) with his belief in the openness towards, acceptance of, and co-existence with Islam. This is not an easy task to fulfil, indeed. It is one of the challenges the Protestants in the Arab Middle East have always confronted and found it challenging to deal with in a balanced and positive manner.

On the other hand, I presented probably the best Christian Orthodox theological voice one can find in the Arabic-speaking region in the modern time (G. Khodr). This voice belongs to someone who not only aims at co-existence between Christianity and Islam, but also at inviting the Christians to discern the fact that they are children of the very same civilisational womb of Islam and Arab heritage. It is an interreligious theology that aims at restoring Arabic-speaking Christianity and Islam alike and bringing them back to the common ground of self-perception they both belong to. The interreligious theology trend is still well in progress in the Arab-Eastern context of the Middle East. Its ultimate consequences and ramifications are yet open-ended. What is promising is that the group of the Arab-Christian theologians who are getting involved in such a theologisation attempt is growing larger in that region day after day.

Interrelational Arab-Eastern Theology

An overview of this trend of theological reasoning reveals noticeable similarities between its approach and the seventh theological approach I discussed above, *Interreligious Arab-Eastern Theology*. However, and contrary to what seems to be the case for the reader, there are also major methodological discrepancies between them that invite us to discern two trends, rather than one single trend, of theological reasoning in operation. Both trends pay attention to the relation with other religions in the *Sitz im Leben* of the Arab Middle East. Nevertheless, while the interreligious approach tends to seek commonality and endeavours to make it replace diversity among religions, the interrelational approach pays attention to plurality and tries to build upon it, rather than replace it. It achieves that by developing a symbiotic form of co-existence *by means of* plurality.

On the other hand, in the interreligious trend of theological reasoning, we have an emphatic, if not sometimes singular, centralisation of 'dialogue' as the primary, if not the sole, means for bringing followers of different religions together. On the contrary, the interrelational approach acknowledges the value and necessity of dialogue, yet it deems it only one means among equally essential others that are needed to create a symbiotic, co-existent state of being among the members of different faiths. This is why, methodologically and epistemologically speaking, while the interreligious approach considers 'relationality' and 'cross-pollination' the *goals*, the *outcomes*, the *results* of the life of dialogue among religions, the interrelational approach treats 'relationality' and 'cross-pollination' as the *foundations*, the *pre-requisites*, the *originators*, or even the *arche* of any possible dialogue among religions. Instead of theologising on the value and core importance of dialogue per se, therefore, the promoters of an interrelational theological reasoning endeavour to evolve a religious voice that invites the members of the different religions (specifically, Christianity and Islam, in the context of the Arab world) to ponder the deeply rooted, historical, and genuinely interrelational, cross-pollinating, multi-religious context of their living reality. They aspire to this upon believing that this realisation and no other will eventually *drive*, and consequentially *pave the way* for, these two religions' serious dialogue and interlocution over all aspects of existence and belief with the religiously different other.

In the ensuing paragraphs, I introduce two valuable examples of discourses from the interrelational Arab-Eastern theological trend of reasoning. I take the first example from the context of the Christian existence in Iraq; namely, the voice of the Patriarch of the Chaldean Catholic Church, Lūwīs Rūfā'īl Cardinal Sākū. The second example will be taken from the context of the Christian presence in Syria; namely, the prelate of the Syriac Orthodox Episcopate of Aleppo, Syria, Bishop Yūḥannā Ībrāhīm.

I have pointed out earlier that the arena of Arab-Eastern Christian theological reasoning in the Middle East is devoid of a specific, fully-fledged discourse on immigration theology, despite the dire seriousness of this challenge against the existence of Christianity in its historical birthplace. This notwithstanding, the patriarch of the Chaldean Church, the Iraqi Lūwīs Rūfā'īl Cardinal Sākū, touches indirectly upon this challenge when he develops a theological voice that is deeply concerned about, and existentially disturbed by, the radically persistent drainage of Iraq's historical Christian communities. Driven by his clerical role and his personal, profound adhesion to his homeland, Cardinal Sākū stresses the deep-rootedness of the ancestral family trees of the Iraqi Christians in the soil of historical Mesopotamia. Cardinal Sākū stresses this factor indirectly by criticising those Christians who associate their existential identity with a specific nationalist background: "Every now and then, someone comes out and declares that [all the Christians in Iraq] are Assyrians, or Chaldeans, or Syriac or Arameans."[332] For Cardinal Sākū, such nationalisation of certain ethnic or ecclesial nomenclatures is not useful to the Christians. It discloses their deviation towards radicalism and fanaticism. Such old traditional nomenclatures, he states, merely designate an ecclesial naming-style stemming from certain historical, not dogmatic, political, or ethnic, circumstances.[333]

Against this tendency, which he deems biased and totally inaccurate, Cardinal Sākū argues that there is a substantial difference between the ecclesial affiliation and identity, on one hand, and nationalist affiliation, on the other. The latter seeds a sense of belonging to certain group of people or a nation with specific language, land, history, and heritage, and it calls for serving designated political, economic, and social agendas. On the contrary, the former connotes a state of belonging to an inclusive, universal human and spiritual message that embraces all people, all languages, and all lands. To this deeply historical Church of the East that belongs to the entire Iraq and to everyone in it, Cardinal Sākū invites his Christian

---

[332] Lūwīs Rūfā'īl Cardinal Sākū, "Kanīsat al-Sharq wa-Maūḍū' al-Qawmiyyah" (The Church of the East and the Subject of Nationality), in www.abouna.org (consulted 20 July 2022).

[333] Sākū, "Al-Tasmiyāt?" (Nomenclatures?), in www.ankawa.com/forum/index.php/topic,315929.0.html , 94/07/2009 (consulted 17 April 2023).

compatriots to belong and to examine. The Church of the East, Cardinal Sākū confirms, primarily and referentially symbolises the co-existential and convivial natures of the life together of all the people of the land as one interrelated collective of humans. In the midst of the pluralist backgrounds and heritages of the people of Iraq stands the Church of the East as an expression of a plurality that exceeds all nationalistic boundaries and divisions; as one that has contained throughout its history Assyrians, Chaldeans, Persians, and Arab tribes from Ḥīra and the Gulf, as well as Afghanis, Indians, and Chinese.[334]

During their life under the Muslim Abbasid Caliphate, Cardinal Sākū proceeds, the churches of the East contained also Christians from all backgrounds: Syriac Orthodox, Melkite-Chalcedonian Orthodox, and others. This plurality and diversity notwithstanding, all these communities enjoyed prosperous life conditions, and they all interrelated in peace and security in the shadow of the Muslim rule. In such a historical context, Cardinal Sākū reminds the Iraqi Christians today, the Christians co-existed and convivially interrelated to their other Christian sister-churches and to the Muslim-majority society in openness and partnership; without, that is, clinging to, or shrinking back into, narrow, radically self-othering, nationalist, or ethnic identities (e.g., Assyrian, Syriac or Chaldean).[335] The exclusivist identity-formation strategy which cages Christians in a nationalist, self-otherising mentality is a modern phenomenon, Cardinal Sākū maintains. It contaminates the Christians of Iraq with a blind self-enclosure and fanaticism that militate against their solidarity and cooperation with the non-Christian co-inhabitants of the land and amidst the region's turmoil and crises. It is such a plurality-based, otherising nationalism, rather than a spiritually and existentially open, pluralist self-perception, Cardinal Sākū believes, that drives the Christians of Iraq and the region to emigrate and mistakenly abandon their homeland: the sense of defection from a radically contrasting, nationality-based, self-identification.[336]

We should not confuse Cardinal Sākū with an idealist or utopian Christian prelate and theologian. He knows that the contemporary Christian–Muslim relations in the Middle Eastern countries witness serious difficulties due to the rising of political Islam, religious fanaticism, and sectarian-confessionalist discrimination, especially in Iraq. He is fully aware that such an insufferable situation forces Christians to emigrate and to sustain dire numerical deterioration in the land.[337] Against this situation, Cardinal Sākū does not opt for a defensive or protectionist approach to plurality that aims at justifying the Christians'

---

[334] Sākū, "Kanīsat al-Sharq wa-Maūḍū' al-Qawmiyyah."

[335] Ibid.

[336] Ibid.

[337] Thus Sākū, "Al-Masīḥiyyūn al-'Irāqiyyūn: Makhāwif wa-Amāl" (Iraqi Christians: Fears and Aspirations), in *Masīḥiyyū al-Waṭan al-'Arabī: al-Tārīkh, al-Daūr, al-Mustaqbal* (The Christians of the Arab World: History, Role, Future), Jerome Shahin and Radwa Salah (eds.) (Beirut: The Arabic Team for Muslim–Christian Dialogue, 2013), pp. 221–225, p. 221. According to Cardinal Sākū, the Christians in the Arab countries represented 20% of the overall population. Yet, due to consistent conflicts and the deterioration of security after the USA's invasion of Iraq in 2003, they dropped down to something between 400–500 thousand only in Iraq (ibid., p. 221).

victimised self-imagery and their appeal to be salvaged from tyrannical monadism. He, rather, endeavours to remind the Christians, before the Muslims, that the Iraqi Christians are indigenous citizens and not a foreign community in an expatriate land who hailed from "another planet" (*kaūkab ākhar*): "They are as rooted in their land of origin as the rivers of Tigris and Euphrates. Iraq and Mesopotamia are their home and land since time immemorial."[338] What the Christians face today is a contemporary condition that is far from authentically expressive of their normal existence among Muslims. During the early Islamic empire, Cardinal Sākū confirms, the Christians enjoyed a considerable level of freedom, and they co-created the Arab-Islamic civilisation with the Muslims.[339] Plurality, that is, was not a cause of conflict and threat, but a basis of cross-pollination and correlation.

Be the above as it may, and in order to confront the challenges of religious radicalism and politicism, Cardinal Sākū calls the Christians to participate with the Muslims in transforming the situation and shifting the weight of the scale towards peace, conviviality, and co-existence and to turn plurality into a source of harmony, instead of friction.[340] Radicalism, Cardinal Sākū argues, is a threat to the wellbeing of the Christians and the Muslims alike, and all the people of the land pay the high price of fanaticism and violence in the name of religious identity.

For Cardinal Sākū, the beginning of the healing from religious fanaticism is theological-scriptural in nature. It starts from re-investigating and re-interpreting the founding religious texts by means of developing a new exegesis, in the case of Christianity, and a new approach to the "science of the Occasions of Ascension" (*'ilm asbāb al-nuzūl*), in the case of Islam. Both communities need to construct new readings and hermeneutics of their doctrines and theological perception of the scriptural attestations.[341] According to Cardinal Sākū, the depth of the messages of both the Bible and the Qur'ān lies evenly in their declaration that God created us to be diverse and different (*khalaqanā mukhtalifīn*). God's creatures are called to embrace this fact, not just as a circumstantial, inescapable, and sometimes threatening situation, but as an ontological, natural, defining norm and truth that require our belief, tolerance, and veneration.[342] It is such a theological interrelational perspective, Cardinal Sākū believes, that the religious leaders of both Christianity and Islam are obliged to seed in the minds and hearts of their communities' members. They are called to develop a theological, interrelational interpretation of plurality that encourages their communities to become "a positive force of change" (*qūwat taghyīr ījābī*). Instead of deserting their homeland and giving up on co-existence, the members of both beliefs are called to interrelationally develop their commonly shared society by a spirit of

338 Ibid., p. 221.
339 Ibid., p. 222.
340 Ibid., p. 223.
341 Ibid., p. 224.
342 Ibid., p. 224.

love and sincerity and by a genuine willingness to live together under the umbrella of one Arabic-Islamic culture.[343]

Cardinal Sākū seems to be developing a Christian reasoning which believes that interrelationality is the passageway towards transforming Iraq and the Arab world from a mono-religious into a pluri-religious expression of diversified co-existence. Such a transformation is not going to be successful, he maintains, nonetheless, unless this plurality is shaped after the following threefold awareness. First, that the Arab countries are not just pluri-religious, but also diverse in terms of people, ethnicities, cultures, languages, and sects. This is not an unfortunate reality in which people must strive to survive, but rather a privileged wealth from which all the communities must glean strength and belief. Second, that religious, Scripture-based faith traditions must avoid the inaccurate exegetical approach that is shaped after a belief in infallibility (*'iṣmah*), indoctrination (*talqīn*), and superiority (*faūqiyyah*).[344] Third, that the history of the people of the region must be re-read objectively and scientifically[345] in order to learn from the past, not just to invoke it; in order to transform the past's mistakes, not to transmit them; in order to learn from the past's achievements, not to idolise them.

Down-to-earth interrelationality, when constructed in tandem with these three factors, will then become one that is built on reason (*'aql*), not on sentiments (*'āṭifah*). Even if it was developed under the umbrella of Arab-Muslim civilisation (in the broader, not jurisprudential, sense of the word), such rational interrelationality would grant the non-Muslims security and rights. Then, such a rationalist approach, Cardinal Sākū suggests, would consequentially change education, including of the religious and societal types. It will remind the Muslims of the prophet's saying: "I have my religion, and you have yours … and our God and yours are one."[346] Cardinal Sākū believes that the new rationalist and historically responsible re-reading of religious scriptures and doctrines would produce a form of plurality that is moderate, intermediate in theological thinking, and verbalised in a manner relevant to, and congenial with, the human being of today and her contemporary circumstances and life-setting. So much so, that the Muslims would now live in accordance with the parable-like saying: "*al-Muslim man salima al-nāsu min lisānihi wa-yadih*" (the Muslim is the one who does not endanger other people by his tongue and hand). At the same time, the Christians would now give up their Islamophobia, integrate truly into their Arabic *Sitz im Leben*, and quit resorting to immigration.[347]

For Cardinal Sākū, this interrelational interpretation of plurality can only be *theological* in nature, because theological reasoning is by default an echo of the human condition as seen in the eyes and will of God. Theology, Cardinal Sākū

---

343 Ibid., p. 224.

344 Sākū, "Ī'timād al-Mūwāṭanah al-Wāḥidah wa-Damj al-Mūwāṭinīn fīhā" (Employing Unifying Citizenship and Incorporating Citizens Into It), in *Al-'Aysh al-Mushtarak wal-Waḥdah fī al-Tanaūw'* (Co-Existence and Unity in Diversity), Jerome Shahin (ed.) (Beirut: The Forum for Development, Culture and Dialogue, 2011), pp. 7–11, p. 7.

345 Ibid., p. 9.

346 Ibid., p. 9.

347 Ibid., pp. 10–11.

confirms, is a human endeavour that seeks to understand faith and express it in a language perceptible by, and meaningful to, the relevant spatio-temporal realities. Such theological talk, therefore, varies from one generation to another and one civilisation to another. Theological plurality is natural, a just right, and a civilisational phenomenon (*ḥaqq mashrūʿ wa-ẓāhira ḥaḍāriyyah*).[348] The interrelational theological reasoning Cardinal Sākū calls for, eventually, is one that frankly departs from a "historical perspective attentive to the meaning of events and the hermeneutic of persons in such a manner that drives people to fulfil God's call in the midst of their daily-life's circumstances, and one that focuses on the human dimension without undermining the divine aspect of salvific liberation and by means of emphasising the spiritual dimension."[349] Be that as it may, Cardinal Sākū's interrelational theological re-interpretation of plurality places centre-stage the civilisational, social, and economic reality of the people of the Orient, Christians included. It tries to construct a theological hermeneutic that takes into consideration the interrelational dynamics that are characteristic of the life of the down-to-earth Iraqi Christians, who used to be peasants, shepherds, or monks, and who rarely occupied power and authority positions, according to him. This anthropological-existential background historically made the Christians' theologisation fully vibrant, enthusiastic, and heartily sincere.[350] This theology, Cardinal Sākū adds, founds its interrelational character on the patristic heritage, the biblical-revelational attestations, the liturgical-spiritual practices of the church, the catechetical-homiletical legacy, the pastoral and counselling-centred practice, the apostolic perception of God, the apologetic-doctrinal demonstration, and the Sufist-mystical and monastic spirit.[351] For Cardinal Sākū, the essence of the interrelational nature of the theological reasoning on plurality is the spiritual-mystic correlation between the human being and God. This intimate relatedness to the divine in the Holy Spirit, Cardinal Sākū says, liberates plurality from becoming an expression of seclusion and self-enclosure, for it turns it into a venue for opening us up to interrelate with the world and others in the depth of normal, daily co-existence.[352]

Only such interrelationality, according to Cardinal Sākū, can salvage the Middle East from religious fundamentalism. It echoes a theological voice that demonstrates credibly and practically before the Muslims that the Christians are an indigenous component in the region's rich mosaic textile, and they are authentic members of its population, not aliens or a community of migrants in it. The interrelational symbiosis between the Christians and the Muslims conveys a theological message from the latter to the former: "We want to maintain our standpoint side-by-side with you … we venerate your religion as you represent it in your own terms. We believe that God is love, and God loves us all … we

---

[348] Sākū, *Khulāṣat Tārīkh al-Kanīsah al-Kaldāniyya* (The Summa of the History of the Chaldean Church) (Kerkuk: Beth Mardutho Press, 2006), p. 52.
[349] Ibid., p. 53.
[350] Ibid., p. 53.
[351] Ibid., pp. 53–56.
[352] Ibid., pp. 61–62.

also ask you to venerate us and our religion as we believe in it in our own terms."[353]

The symbiotic interrelatedness between the Christians and the Muslims in Cardinal Sākū's theological logic abides in an affirmative belief in correlationality and cross-pollination in terms of practical responsibilities and dialogical common co-contribution of the Muslims and the Christians to their own life-conditions, and in the same land of the Middle East. This correlationality and cross-pollinating logic is articulated by the Iraqi Cardinal in an essay he wrote to comment on *The Special Assembly of the Synod of Bishops for the Middle East*. This event took place in the Vatican, Rome, between 10 and 24 October 2010, and it conducted a discussion on Middle Eastern Christianity and its relation to other Christian churches and to Islam. In his comment on this synod, and the declaration-like message it originated, Cardinal Sākū pauses at the relation between Eastern Christians and Islam in the Middle East and rearticulates his interrelational theological perspective on this relation in reciprocity-centred terms that cannot be clearer. He expressed this correlation via divulging parallel proposals and invitations for the Christians and the Muslims alike. He called the Christians to help the Muslims "to modernize their religiosity and to be more integrated into modern society ... [and to] call themselves, and not only others, into question."[354] He, then, also affirmed that the Christians "have to find answers to the [Muslims'] questions and to give better witness to how the truths and values of the Bible really appear in [the Christians'] lives."[355] Cardinal Sākū expressed also his affirmative belief that such correlation must not be exclusively social, political, and cultural, but also frankly theological in perspective. He emphasises that the *theological* dialogue with Muslims is quite possible, contrary to what many people may believe. This theological dialogue is urgently needed to safeguard the interrelationality between Christians and Muslims in the Middle East, Cardinal Sākū maintains, because "Muslims want a clearer position from the Church on the Islamic Faith" as eagerly as "they are also waiting for an evaluation of morality in the subjects of family, economy, society, and political justice."[356] He believes that such a dialogue would profoundly ground interrelationality in a deep theological soil, because "our common faith is in a God who is almighty and loving for us and almighty and merciful for Muslims ... [therefore,] we can find a coherent comprehensible vocabulary to explain our faith."[357] Be that as it may, Cardinal Sākū concludes,

---

[353] Sākū, "Al-Masīḥiyyūn fī al-Sharq al-Awsaṭ. Bayn Islām al-Dawlah wal-Uṣūliyya" (The Christians in the Middle East. Between the State's Islam and Fundamentalism), in www.aramean-dem.org/Arabic/tarikh_skafe/luis_sako/3.htm,sept,22,2011 (consulted 17 April 2023).

[354] Cardinal Sākū, "The Synod and Christian–Muslim Relations: Personal Critical Evaluation, Results and Perspectives," in *Middle Eastern Christians Facing Challenges: Reflections on the Special Synod for the Middle East*, Dietmar W. Winkler (ed.) (Piscataway, NJ: Gorgias Press, 2019), pp. 134–139, p. 136.

[355] Ibid., p. 137.

[356] Ibid., p. 137.

[357] Ibid., p. 137.

> the Eastern churches should participate more explicitly in the Arab world, for they are an integral part of it; they should repudiate the ambiguous perception of some that they belong to the West ... Additionally, Christians should claim their full civil and human rights as equal citizens on the same level as others.[358]

I will move now to the second representative voice in this theological trend of reasoning: Yūḥannā Ībrāhīm, the bishop of the Syriac Orthodox Diocese of Aleppo, Syria. What the Chaldean Catholicos Lūwīs Rūfā'īl Cardinal Sākū's interrelational theological reasoning calls for in the context of Iraq, the Syriac Orthodox Bishop of Aleppo (who was abducted with Bishop Būlus Yazijī of the Roman-Antiochene Orthodox Diocese of Aleppo on 22 April 2013) tries also to construct a discourse about in the context of Syria by means of similar interrelational theological reasoning. Focusing on the Christian–Muslim co-existence and presence in Syria, Bishop Ībrāhīm also looks at the historical presence of the Christians in Syria, and he gleans a theological reading of the co-living with and relatedness to the Muslims and to Islam in the present era. His goal, like Cardinal Sākū, is not merely to call for dialogue, nor to solely focus on it. He, rather, wants to go beyond mere dialogue into historico-existential interactions. But, more essentially, He, like Cardinal Sākū, pays attention to what lies beneath, or what operates as a foundation for dialogue; namely, the interrelational conditions and potentials of the Christian Chaldean Catholic–Muslim co-existence. Any dialogical interreligious state of existence can take place on the basis of this Chatholic-Muslim co-existence, as well as it generates as one of the outcomes of this co-existence. Cardinal Sākū of Iraq did not construct a single, coherent, fully-fledged theological discourse on a called-for interrelational theology. Bishop Ībrāhīm of Syria, on the contrary, endeavoured to develop such a constructive theological reasoning, on which he published a monograph in Arabic in 2006. In the ensuing paragraphs, I will look in detail at this monograph. Yet before doing so, I shall pause at some other papers relevant to the same theological discourse, which Bishop Ībrāhīm developed in his yet insufficiently examined book.

In his attempt at highlighting the core value of the interrelational co-existence of Christians and Muslims, Bishop Ībrāhīm revisits the past centuries, focusing geographically on the history of his episcopal See's location, the Syrian city of Aleppo (which elsewhere he calls "the jewel of the Orient"[359]). The history of this city, he relates, clearly demonstrates that the pluralist social textile of Aleppo

---

[358] Ibid., p. 138.

[359] See Yūḥannā Ībrāhīm, "The Ecumenical Dimension of the Synod: Critical Evaluation, Results and Perspectives," in *Middle Eastern Christians Facing Challenges: Reflections on the Special Synod for the Middle East*, Dietmar W. Winkler (ed.) (Piscataway, NJ: Gorgias Press, 2019), pp. 56–71, p. 56. In 2012, Aleppo was encircled and mostly isolated, and later on it turned into a war zone between the opposition fighting factions and the Syrian regime's army and Shiite supporting militias during the revolution and then the war that damaged Syria starting from 2011. During that time Bishop Ībrāhīm remained in his diocese, with his parish, refusing to leave Aleppo and bravely sustaining the difficult and dangerous life conditions with the people of his beloved city, until his saddening obduction with his fellow Greek Orthodox prelate, Bishop Yazijī, by an unknown fighting side.

not only demonstrates throughout the centuries the side-by-side existence of diverse communities from various religions, cultures, ethnicities, and traditions without any disturbance. It more fundamentally manifests the active and profound correlational co-sharing of all the requirements and needs of life in the city, as well as co-confronting all the challenges together.[360] For Bishop Ībrāhīm, this closely affinitive interrelationality in the city of Aleppo exceeded the mere factual boundaries of religious and confessional plurality by preventing this diversity from turning into a source of schism, conflict, or disharmony. It, rather, made this plurality the foundation of what he calls 'patriotic cohesion' (*talāḥum waṭanī*) and a source of 'religious fraternity' (*īkhā' dīnī*). This interrelationality made the Christians and the Muslims equally contribute to, and participate in, the glorious history of the city and to work together towards solidifying plurality and correlation.[361] So much so that, when a foreign enemy stood at the historical walls of their city, trying to invade it (*al-firanjah*), both the Christian and Muslim inhabitants stood together as one population in its protection. The Christians did this disregarding the religious affiliation of the foreign enemy. The Christians of the land decided to stand with those whom they interrelated to, confronting those strangers who shared their own religious belief.[362] It is such interrelationality, Bishop Ībrāhīm concludes, that generates the depth of plurality or transforms it into "one of the treasures of humanity" (*kanz min kunūz al-īnsāniyyah*).[363]

If this was the past, the present situation in Aleppo and Syria is quite the contrary. This is what Bishop Ībrāhīm confirms in another work published amid the latest tragic Syrian crisis (that started in 2011 and is still existing today). Consistently attentive to the factor of plurality, and perceptively spotting that Syria's plurality was deprived of interrelationality during this crisis, Bishop Ībrāhīm raises the flag of danger, alarming the world and all the clerical authorities therein that the destructive Syrian crisis not only impaired all the relational ligaments that attach all the components of the Syrian mosaic to each other. It, more drastically, turned plurality into a devouring threat that forced Christians to escape and emigrate from their homeland. Bishop Ībrāhīm calls this immigration situation a "lethal plague" (*āfah fattāka*).[364]

As related earlier, Bishop Ībrāhīm's core theological reasoning is articulated in his 2006 monograph *Qubūl al-Ākhar* (Accepting the Other). Bishop Ībrāhīm's interrelational approach to existence with the different other is constructed above

---

[360] Yūḥannā Ībrāhīm, "Al-Ta'addudiyyah wa-Yanābī' al-Jamāl al-'Arabī" (Plurality and the Springs of Arabic Beauty), in *al-Ma'ārij Journal*, 23(161), 2013, pp. 17–20.

[361] Ibid., p. 20.

[362] Ibid., p. 19.

[363] Ibid., p. 20.

[364] Ībrāhīm, "Muqtaraḥāt li-Sinudūs al-Asāqifah" (Proposals to the Episcopal Synod), in *al-Ma'ārij Journal*, 24(173), 2014, pp. 187–188, 187. In another piece, which he read before the Grand 8 Summit, Bishop Ībrāhīm called for peace in Syria, before stating that he personally "is not with those who want to tumble the [Syrian] regime, yet at the same time, we join in the call for a reformation process against corruption and bribery" (*lasnā ma' man yurīd isqāṭ an-niẓām, wal-lakinanā, fīl-waqt dhātih, nunādī ma' masīrat al-iṣlāḥāt ḍid al-fasād wal-rishwa*): Ībrāhīm, "Sūriyyā unmudhaj lil-'Ayish al-Mushtarak" (Syria as a Model for Co-Existence), in *al-Ma'ārij Journal*, 24(173), 2014, p. 189.

placing 'interrelationality' against 'clash' (*ṣidām*). This manifests in his methodological departure from a frank rejection of the 'clash of civilisations' hypothesis. Bishop Ībrāhīm takes us back to the birthplace of this theory in the 1993 discourse of Samuel Huntington. According to Bishop Ībrāhīm, those who foster this 'clash of civilizations' approach (*ṣidām al-ḥaḍārāt*) stipulate that those civilisations "do not contest each other; they rather conflict with each other, and their conflict leads inevitably to one of them eliminating the other, or to one of them melting into another, or the emergence of one particular new civilization owning all the dominating and requisition capacities."[365]

Contrary to the 'clashing' thesis, Bishop Ībrāhīm argues that his theological reasoning on the Other departs from a specific stance on the acceptance or rejection of the 'clash of civilisations' claim.[366] Departing from a disapproval of the 'clash' presumption, Bishop Ībrāhīm proposes reading the history of human existence from a perspective other than the political one. He opines that reading this history from the angle of religious experience demonstrates the idea of 'accepting the Other' (*qubūl al-ākhar*) in various forms and its depiction in diverse models of interrelationality, which, despite differentiation and discrepancies, leads to dialogue and prevents the clash with the Other.[367] The alternative religious and interrelational readings of human history, Bishop Ībrāhīm relates, begin from looking at the religions' (Christian and Muslim) holy scriptures. All the religious texts and laws, he states, confirm:

> That the notions of tolerance, fraternity, and solidarity are what must prevail in societies to solidify justice and peace, and it is what connects people to each other. Lord Jesus Christ said: "So in everything, do to others what you would have them do to you" (Matt. 7: 12) … This harmonizes with what is said in the glorious Qur'ān in *Surat al-Naḥl* (16: 125): "Call unto the way of thy Lord with wisdom and fair exhortation," and also in *al-Naḥl* 16: 90: "Lo, Allah enjoineth justice and kindness" … [so] all the expressions of the idea of accepting the Other consensually concede, despite their diversity, that justice, safety, prosperity, and peace are of the most significant elements of a world suitable for human existence … therefrom stems the idea of accepting the Other as the primary foundation of a world dominated by justice.[368]

The framework of Bishop Ībrāhīm's theological reasoning is a faith-based worldview, wherein interrelationality and Other-acceptance are the cornerstone of a faith-based reading of existence. Now, if such is the foundational framework, and if the focus is on relatedness to human life, the human being becomes the focal point, the central attention of the theological reasoning that is interrelational and Other-concerning in nature. "The human being," Bishop Ībrāhīm states, "is the axial point in relation to the acceptance of the Other." This is why, he proceeds, both Christianity and Islam attach deeply their belief in God's revelation (*al-waḥī al-īlāhī*) to the endeavour to develop an anthropological perception of the essence of human identity (*jawhar hauwiyyāt*

---

[365] Bishop Ībrāhīm, *Qubūl al-Ākhar* (Accepting the Other) (Damascus: Qadmus Press, 2006), p. 13.

[366] Ibid., p. 14.

[367] Ibid., p. 16.

[368] Ibid., p. 17.

al-īnsān).[369] Both Christianity and Islam construct their interrelational hermeneutics of human identity, and their anthropological emphasis on 'Other-acceptance', on the attestations of the religious scriptures. Both learn from the Bible and the Qur'ān alike that being God's vicegerent means that the last thing the human needs is to invent conflicts between her and her sister in humanity.[370] The human being is the most important creature in God's eyes only because this creature was brought into being to interrelate, not to clash; to accept the Other, not to conflict with her: "The human's longing for his human sibling is the essence of the notion of 'Other-acceptance', which, in turn, is for the sake of human civility in society."[371]

Be that as it may, Bishop Ībrāhīm suggests that interrelationality and Other-acceptance not only confirm and celebrate plurality. They, more substantially, transform the nature of plurality, and they transport it beyond the boundaries of merely representing differences and diversity towards making plurality a factual interpretation of a more foundational, interrelational, and convivial symbiosis. They transform plurality by converting people's interrelation into a moment of co-realisation that what combines the Christians and the Muslims together, as both God's Creation, is far more than what places them asunder. Both need to cling to their faith's benevolent teachings and allow this to unite them in defending human dignity and in co-operating according to a common value-system. Interrelationality makes people realise that plurality in terms of opinions, ideas, and theories does not prevent co-operation, as long as each side accepts the other as equally God's Creation.[372]

Now, if in 2006 we happened to ask Bishop Ībrāhīm if he thought that such a theological utopia was applicable in reality, or was it just a theological call wrapping itself in an eschatological garment of hope, he would confirm that he personally encountered the factual potential of such an interrelational, Other-accepting theological promise genuinely shown in the interreligious life of his country, Syria.[373] In his book, Bishop Ībrāhīm pauses at a report made (then, in 2006, or earlier) by *The Economist*, which granted Syria '8/10' grade on the international scale of interreligious relations. Boasting about this accreditation, Bishop Ībrāhīm proceeds by saying that such a manifestation of interrelationality in Syria is not just a present phenomenon, "but a truth and a reality that is inherent to the history of Syria in the past and the present," and he affirms that the religious discourse in the country brings the Christians and the Muslims

---

[369] Ibid., p. 17.
[370] Ibid., p. 18.
[371] Ibid., p. 19.
[372] Ibid., p. 20.
[373] I personally heard the Bishop stating this conviction right in front of me, when in summer 2007 I had the chance to meet up with him in his episcopal office in Aleppo. At that time, the Bishop quite comfortably expressed his belief that our country, Syria, is an example second to none in the region for peaceful and secure interrelational co-existence among people from different backgrounds. Much of this has proven itself to be merely wishful thinking, as we all realised a few years later, as the ruling regime led the country into destruction and eliminated all features of peace and interrelationality in the land, and one of its militias abducted Bishop Ībrāhīm in 2013.

together, "regarding, in specific, citizenship and the combating against colonialism in all its forms."[374]

Aiming at demonstrating the inherence of this interreligious interrelationality in the long historical past of Syria, Bishop Ībrāhīm offers a tour de force exposition of the history of the Christian *ecclesia* in Syrian cities.[375] He highlights the social and educational work that the churches never ceased performing throughout Syrian cities, and he also praised their contributions to the building and fostering of the Arab-Muslim culture.[376] From surveying the past, Bishop Ībrāhīm moves forward into discerning the future of this interrelationality and the fate of Christianity in the land of Islam. From the very same standpoint of Cardinal Sākū, Bishop Ībrāhīm also stresses the indigeneity of the Arab-Eastern Christianity and its rootedness in the historical soil of the land and the human existence on it.[377] This invocation of the indigenous belongingness to history, as in Cardinal Sākū's writing, is Bishop Ībrāhīm's instrument for calling the Muslims to embrace the past and allow it to help them open their mind for the future. But, more importantly still, it is the backbone of his calling the Christians of the land to volitionally refuse denying their indigeneity and history and of his attempt at turning this indigeneity and history into sources of interrelatedness and rootedness. He wants the Christians to avoid clinging to a state of denial as a justification for abandoning their homeland. He sets upon himself the goal of reminding the Christians and the Muslims alike that interrelationality and its generated tolerance, conviviality, and cooperation have been tangibly experienced since the beginning of the Christian–Muslim co-existence, and despite all the dark historical moments of tension and self-otherising that the history of these two religions' co-existence is stained with.[378]

Is this historical anamnesis enough to guarantee the prevalence of a Christian–Muslim, theologico-anthropological belief in interrelationality and Other-acceptance in the future? Bishop Ībrāhīm predicts that this might be remotely the case. Like Cardinal Sākū, he pauses at the present threat of Muslim (but also generally religious) radicalism, and he warns of the radical demographic changes that stem from the Christians' emigration.[379] Nonetheless, he also calls 'narrow-minded' (*dhawī al-ʿuqūl al-ḍayyīqah*) those people among the Christians who proliferate the allegation that Christianity is in peril in the Muslim world. Against this phobic voice, Bishop Ībrāhīm emphasises the value of interrelational symbiosis, and he argues that "neither the Christian nor the Muslim can live secluded from each other."[380] For the Christians, he says, to have a future in their homeland, they need to embrace an interrelational, Other-accepting theology, and they must employ it in their attempts at living according to the teachings of the Holy Gospel. Only this, he maintains, can enable them to embody a true, Christian, faith-based anthropology that presents the follower of Christ as "a

---

374 Ibid., p. 21.
375 Ibid., pp. 23ff; 31ff.
376 Ibid., pp. 25–26ff.
377 Ibid., p. 30.
378 Ibid., p. 31.
379 Ibid., p. 36.
380 Ibid., p. 37.

good citizen living in a society of various religions and sects."[381] "If the Christians," he ends up saying, "become aware of their role as citizens, the image of Christian benevolent contribution would remain shining before the forthcoming generations."[382] For Bishop Ībrāhīm, after all, "there would be no fear or compromise for Christians … on the basis of demography or diminishing number if citizenship were the measuring stick and if the dignity of the human person, equality in rights and duties, and religious freedom … were enshrined in the psyche of citizens and were upheld by the law."[383]

Both Cardinal Sākū from Iraq and Bishop Ībrāhīm from Syria illustrate in their significant theological voices quite a valid and profoundly relevant theological reasoning in the heartland of that unique region called the Arab-Eastern Middle East. Both develop a from-below, or even from-within, theological reading of the Christians' life in that region, without stuffing their theological interpretation with metaphysical or abstract, purely theoretical, and dogmatic views. Instead of philosophising 'plurality' and find a doctrinal, systematic appreciation of it at all costs, they decide to anthropologise this notion by looking at its incarnation and ramifications in the depth of human life and conditions in the particular context of the Christian–Muslim existence. Therefore, they theologically realise that 'plurality' per se is neither good and virtuous nor evil or dangerous. The way it is applied, lived, and related to by those different communities and individuals in a particular setting is what decides whether plurality is a source of clash, conflict, and tension, or rather the expression of a profound interrelationality, symbiosis, and cross-pollination. Theologising plurality for them means turning it into a source of co-existence and symbiotic life based on accepting the Other and interrelating to her in peace, love, and equality. Theologisation here is a tool for conceptual liberation, for cognitive correction, while interrelationality, for them both, is the basic instrument for transforming plurality into a down-to-earth source of symbiotic co-existence, the absence of which, they both believe, would eliminate the Christian presence from its historical birthplace.

Second, the representative voices of the interrelational Arab-Eastern theological reasoning do not place all their eggs in the basket of dialogue alone. Interreligious dialogue for them is just one means of interaction and co-existence among other equally, if not more, substantial ones. They, rather, found any correlation and co-existence, dialogical or otherwise, on a more fundamental and pre-conditioning concept, namely 'interrelationality.' Among the various theological trends I discuss in this study, the interrelational theological trend seems to me to be the most balanced, promising, and relevant in the context of the Arab Middle East. I have already indirectly expressed my full vouching for such a theological approach when I stated elsewhere that

> in the beginning was not dialogue, but the discovering of inevitable interrelationality … realizing the *inevitability* of the involvement in interrelational existence is the 'big-bang,' the first *ex-nihilio* moment, that generates a dialoguing

---

[381] Ibid., p. 37.

[382] Ibid., p. 38.

[383] Ībrāhīm, "The Ecumenical Dimension of the Synod: Critical Evaluation, Results and Perspectives," p. 60.

> orientation and impregnates an interlocution event … discerning the interreligious affairs between the Christians and the Muslims in the Middle East requires traveling beyond the boundaries of narrating the story of their interlocution. It demands pondering, instead, these Christians' and Muslims' interrelationality and their perception of it, which eventually generates the awareness of the inevitability of engaging in continuous interreligious dialogue.[384]

Woman-Centred Arab-Eastern Theology

Since the last decade of the twentieth century, woman-centred theology has become a global intellectual phenomenon in contemporary Christian reasoning. The Christian library today contains texts on this theological genre composed by female, but also male, theologians hailing from all the continents and corners of the planet, as well as from all Christian churches and spiritual traditions. The Arab Middle East is not an exception in this regard. Some Arabic-speaking Eastern female theologians have also composed feminist theological discourses during the past two decades. One must say, nevertheless, that these compositions remain singular and sporadic, lacking any coherent framework and encompassing intellectual umbrella. The theological attempts at developing a Christian woman-centred discourse(s) in the Arab-Eastern context are still generally juvenile, and one cannot yet name a specific theologian who has developed a full-featured, comprehensive, and integral Arabic feminist theology project that one can study or anatomise. In other words, the Arab-Eastern theological scene has not yet given rise to a fully-fledged, coherent feminist theology like that of major Western woman theologians, such as Mary Daly, Rosemary Radford Ruether, Elisabeth Schüssler Fiorenza, Elizabeth Johnson, Sallie McFague, Dorothe Sölle, and numerous others.

In the ensuing lines, I shall introduce the readers not to Arab-Eastern feminist theologians proper, but to woman-centred single theological texts composed by a few Arabic-speaking female theologians from two different Christian denominations in the Middle East. It is not my purpose here (as it was not my purpose regarding the previous eight trends of theological reasoning) to invoke every text written on women by Arab-Eastern Christian female authors today. This is not a survey-like presentation. What I do is just invoke certain representative examples that model before the readers the particular trends of reasoning the female theologians in the Arab world follow in their writings on the situation of woman and her rights in that region. These female theological voices offer a valuable demonstration of the contextually determined theological, cultural, and social perspectives the Arabic-speaking female Christians generally pause at, depart from, and introduce when they speak about the situation of woman and defend, or critique, woman's conditions in a manner that is relevant to, and interactive with, the specific Christian *Sitz im Leben* they exist in. The reader will easily realise that I am invoking here female theological voices that, actually, develop binary stances on the situation of women and the woman's right

[384] Najib G. Awad, "Interfaith Relations and Middle East Christianity: Beyond Dialogue, Toward Interrelationality," p. 291.

of enjoying leadership status and decision-making roles within the Christian community.

The first exemplary model of a woman-centred Arab-Eastern theological discourse I will discuss is the voice of the Syrian-Lebanese Christian educator, and the former president of the Near East School of Theology, Beirut, Lebanon (the first Protestant theological seminary established by the American Missionaries in the Middle East), Mary Mikhael. Mikhael hails originally from a Roman (Antiochene) Orthodox churchly background, yet she has joined the Protestant Presbyterian community and was ordained a presbyter in this church in 1987, as well as pursuing all her higher theological education at Protestant schools of theology in Lebanon and the United States of America. Mary Mikhael is not known in the relevant local circles as a prolific scholar or author who has generated her own theological project or full-fledged discourse. This notwithstanding, throughout her entire professional career, she has been one of the strong and leading advocates of women's rights and equality within the circles of the evangelical churches in the Arab Middle East, especially in Lebanon and Syria.

In 2007, Mary Mikhael was invited to contribute a lengthy chapter on woman-centred theology for a one-volume anthology on contemporary Christian Arabic theological issues. This chapter was published in a volume titled *Naḥwa Lāhūt 'Arabī Mu'āṣir* (Toward a Contemporary Arabic Theology).[385] Twelve years later, the same anthology was published in the English language as well.[386] My presentation of Mary Mikael's chapter on women from a theological perspective will rely on the English translation in the 2019 version of the *Anthology of Arabic Christian Theology*.

It is worth noticing initially that Mikhael titles her chapter 'The *Christian* Woman,' instead of, for instance, the 'Middle Eastern Woman,' or the 'Arab Woman,' or even 'Woman in the Arab Middle East.' This is probably her way of informing her readers that her exposition does not aspire at offering a panoramic, comprehensive overview of the conditions of women in the Middle Eastern context: the non-Christian woman is not included in her discourse. On the other hand, Mikhael seems to be insisting that her approach is exclusively religious and particularly Christian in foundations, perspectives, and methods. This equally implies her belief that approaching the conditions of the Christian woman in the Arab world requires *Christian* strategies of reasoning (though she does not clarify exactly what would make a reasoning on women differently 'Christian' or what is 'Christian' in focusing theologically on the Christian woman alone), as well as suggesting her conviction that what the Christian woman seems to counter in her Arab-Eastern *Sitz im Leben* is unique, incomparable, and unilateral: only the *Christian* woman, among all other women in that context, faces certain challenges and lives under the designated, highlighted circumstances (which is highly questionable). One might also

---

[385] Mary Mikhael, "al-Mar'ah al-Massīḥiyyah" (The Christian Woman), in *Naḥwa Lāhūt 'Arabī Mu'āṣir* (Toward a Contemporary Arabic Theology), pp. 275–340.
[386] Andrea Zaki Stephanous (ed.), *Arabic Christian Theology: A Contemporary Global Evangelical Perspective* (Grand Rapids, Mich: Zondervan, 2019).

surmise that Mikhael is simply focusing on the Christian woman alone because her take on this female is going to be *theological and biblical* in nature, and she does not want to impose this, by default, Christian interpretation method on the study of non-Christian women.

At any rate, in her chapter, Mikhael departs briefly from a general, almost generic, discussion of women's rights in the Universal Declaration of Human Rights, before she narrows down to pondering primarily the Middle Eastern context and secondarily, and more microcosmically, the context of women's conditions within the Christian Church. Her point of departure becomes specifically ecclesiological in foundation:

> It is now time to look at the status of women in the church. What is the reality that they have endured for more than 2000 years, and what should it be, so that the Christian Church is able to embody the will of its Lord in its life and witness?[387]

For Mikhael, the Christian woman's primary challenge within the context of her ecclesial existence (but also her societal one, as Mikhael notes) lies in "leadership and [women's] participation in official services of the church." Mikhael eloquently articulates her deconstructive anatomisation of this challenge in the following elegant words:

> For close to twenty centuries, men have 'sung solos' before the curtains of the temple. Men spoke and women maintained a long silence ... throughout this time of men's talk and women's silence, no official dialogue took place within the Church regarding the supremacy of men and the inferiority of women with respect to the gifts of the Holy Spirit and abilities in leadership and service. The situation was more of a social contract than anything else.[388]

For Mikhael, sociologising the issue of women's rights is one of the conceptual impediments before the core problem that challenges the Christian woman, which is essentially theological and biblical in nature. Mikhael is sceptical about the hermeneutical validity of blaming the absence of women leaders in the Church "on cultural and social necessity."[389] She certainly concedes that, in the Middle Eastern Muslim context, the social, political, and religious are intertwined. The social factors' impact on the religious life is inescapably real, so the Church should naturally be affected by the societal and ideological situation around it, and it would prefer to lean towards complying with the prevailing leadership structures. This notwithstanding, Mikhael maintains that the core nature of the woman's situation in Christian circles is primarily, and more crucially, biblical and theological in *arche*, components, and *telos*: "It has also been claimed that the Bible declares that it is God's will that women not participate in church leadership, especially in the priestly capacity."[390]

When it comes to anatomising the biblical attestation in search of the origin of the theological interpretations that have deprived women of their leadership

---

[387] Mary Mikhael, "The Christian Woman," in *Arabic Christian Theology*, pp. 297–273, p. 298.
[388] Ibid., p. 299.
[389] Ibid., p. 299.
[390] Ibid., p. 300.

rights in the Church, Mikhael refers to the theological legacy of Paul the Apostle, and she deems the Pauline literature accountable for seeding in the mind of Christians throughout history that "women are quicker than men to fall into temptation." Aiming at tackling this clichéd, stigmatising teaching and to correct the hermeneutics of the Pauline legacy, Mikhael then asks: "But what if we were wrong in our understanding of what Paul meant and the circumstances he was addressing?" before she, afterwards, proposes her own answer to this question: "We need to learn how to read Paul and understand his intentions by studying the historical, social, and ecclesial context in which he wrote to various churches."[391]

The tripod of 'history–society–church' becomes Mikhael's primary hermeneutic instrument in the ensuing parts of her study. First, she pauses at the interpretation history of the Pauline literature, focusing on the Western exegetical trends that appeared from the second half of the twentieth century.[392] She then looks at the social reality that motivated the interpretation of Paul's discourse in a patriarchal manner. Here, Mikhael pauses specifically at the social context of the Christian woman in the Arab Middle East. She proposes that, in addition to the biological and tradition-based factors that entangle women globally, the Arab Christian woman in the Middle East "experience yet another stronger and deeper cultural pressure."[393] Being affiliated with the third Abrahamic religion besides the other two indigenous ones in the Middle East, Judaism and Islam, the Arab Christian woman find herself a victim of the Jewish and Islamic cultural rules and restraints.

When it comes to Islam, Mikhael notices the diversity of women's situations from one Arab country to another. Yet she points to a dilemmatic stance on women and their rights in traditional Islamic jurisprudential schools (*fiqh*), relating that:

> Though Islamic thinkers, both men and women, constantly reiterate that Islam gave women a dignity they had previously lacked, there are essential issues in which Islamic teaching undermines women's rights. These include issues of guardianship, marriage, social rights, polygamy, and women's political, legal, and economic rights.[394]

The Muslim societal context wherein the Arab Christian Church and its women exist, Mikhael concludes, presents "a male-dominated society in which women occupy a subordinate position and rarely share in decision-making."[395] In order to survive in such *Sitz im Leben*, Mikhael maintains, the Arab Christians were forced to embrace and accommodate the Islamic patriarchal cultural rules (I beg to differ and believe that the patriarchal mentality is equally inherent in the Arab-Eastern Christians' *habitus* and is not imposed on them from without). They even incorporate these rules of reasoning into their interpretation of the biblical attestations on women, including the ones in the Pauline literature.

---

391 Ibid., p. 300.
392 Ibid., pp. 301–302.
393 Ibid., p. 302.
394 Ibid., p. 305 (pp. 303–315).
395 Ibid., p. 316.

When it comes to Judaism, Mikhael also argues that the fact that the Church was historically "planted within a Jewish culture in which women did not enjoy equality with men" has forced the Church to embrace the Jewish rules of understanding women's rights and importing them to Christianity.[396] From surveying women's situation in Judaism, Mikhael gleans that "we can see many similarities between the lives of women in Arab Islamic cultures and in Judaism. Both cultures were patriarchal: in both, the roles of women were circumscribed and women lived in the shadow of men, with limited freedom."[397] Be that as it may, Judaism also, as in the present influence of Islam, forces Christianity in the Middle East to impose patriarchal exegetical readings of the Pauline stance on women in the Bible, according to Mikhael.

Mikhael opines that the above historical and social factors define for us the position of women in the Arab-Eastern Church today. Due to these surrounding, extrinsic factors, "Middle Eastern Christian women have suffered because of general attitudes toward women ... [and] the most difficult challenges they have faced came from within the Church, especially in regard to anything that has to do with positions of leadership and decision-making."[398] Mikhael here notices that during the past couple of decades an evolution occurred in women's participation and activism, as meetings and presentations calling for gender equality and promoting women's rights increased in the local churches. For Mikhael, this evolution provides "a good opportunity [for women] to reach out to the heads of churches in the Middle East to explain the evolution in these decades and to ask for assistance and real solidarity with women in each church."[399] Mikhael also pauses at the Protestant theological seminary the Near East School of Theology, where she was (by the time of writing her study) a professor and the president (she retired in 2010) and praises the status of woman in its context:

> In the Near East School of Theology in Beirut, for example, women have the same right as men to engage in theological studies and be qualified for service in the Church. There is open Biblical discussion about women's participation in decision-making and leadership.[400]

A careful consideration of Mary Mikhael's strategic arguing method indicates that, for her, the socio-historical dimension is the preconceived foundation of the hermeneutic-theological one. What demonstrates this in her chapter is the fact that her attending to the development of a new hermeneutic for the biblical attestations *follows* after or *results* from, and is shaped by, the outcomes that one can extract from the down-to-earth historical, social and ecclesial situation. In other words, the conditions and ramifications of the experiential contextuality grounds, pre-conditions, and determines the theological perception and the exegetical interpretation. Theology is not the starting premise. It is the preconditioned outcome.

---

[396] Ibid., p. 316 (pp. 316–319).
[397] Ibid., p. 319.
[398] Ibid., p. 320.
[399] Ibid., p. 321.
[400] Ibid., p. 323.

After unpacking the historical, social, and ecclesial conditions of the Arab Christian woman in the Middle Eastern context, Mikhael embarks on re-interpreting the biblical teachings and attestations on women in the Old and the New Testament. She performs this upon the belief that the recent developments in the real-life conditions in the Arab Middle East permit Christian women to bring about a different reading of the religious Christian text. This brings her full circle, back to where she started from: the Pauline stance on women in the church.[401] Her analysis of Paul's stances on women does not offer any unique or unprecedented theological re-interpretation that one can describe as specifically 'Arab-Eastern.' She, rather, relies on the exegetical suggestions available in Western, commonly studied, and known Christian commentaries that are available in Christian academic libraries all over the world. Mikhael's overall conclusion from her exegetical re-visiting of the New Testament becomes also the final call she makes in her woman-centred discourse:

> The Church today is called to read the New Testament with an uncovered face. When we [do this] … all the objections that prohibit women from participating in the service of the Church at all levels will be nailed to the Cross … if God calls a woman for his service, who dares to prevent her fulfilling this calling?[402]

The second example of an Arab-Eastern female Christian author who contributed in Arabic to woman-centred theology is the Lebanese, Roman (Antiochene) Orthodox member in the Orthodox Youth Movement, Emma Ghrayyib Khoury. In 2011, the Orthodox an-Nūr Press published a book-length study by Khoury titled *Al-Mar'a fī al-Kitāb al-Muqaddas* (Woman in the Bible). In this study, Khoury surveys Old and New Testament female figures and she uses them as central female contributors or role models in the history of salvation that is narrated in the Scriptures. She offers a sort-of feminine-centred *Heilsgeschichte* that lies basically in the roles, negative or positive, women played to manifest, or iconise, God's redemptive will in Creation.

Khoury starts her study with a contemplative introduction wherein she presents woman as such as a mystery, if not even an enigma, especially to the male, who fails to grasp her truly and to capture by any means imaginable the essence of woman's unique personality: "Man feels sometimes that he [has] perceived her secret and solved her mystery, and he thinks that he [has] painstakingly captured her essence. Yet, she immediately slips off his hands and vaporizes like smoke seeping through his fingers."[403] On the other hand, Khoury stresses, this enigmatic human being can outperform the male in sanctity and gifting (*al-'aṭā wal-qadāsa*), and she can sometimes stand behind the holiness and gifting of saintly men and teach them spiritual bravery. From this mysterious-saintly personality binary, Khoury concludes that inside the soul of every woman there are two contrasting natures: "One extracts its food from the senses, and the other longs for the food of the heart and the soul. One of these

[401] Ibid., pp. 344–353.

[402] Ibid., p. 371.

[403] Emma Ghrayyib Khoury, *al-Mar'a fī al-Kitāb al-Muqaddas: Min Ḥauwā' īlā Maryam* (The Woman in the Bible: From Eve to Mary) (Tripoli: an-Nūr Orthodox Press, 2011), p. 9.

natures can prevail over the other due to surrounding environment, nurturing, education, life-style, and internal and external factors."[404] It is this binary nature, Khoury suggests, that drove the church fathers to clash with woman, trying to tame the 'devil' in her and to bring about the 'angel' (*īnnahā malāk wa-īblīs fī ānin wāḥid*). However, it was for this very dualistic nature that God used woman as a major actor or medium in the divine salvation history, implementing woman's two natures in the fulfilment of this redemptive and atoning will. This is why, Khoury proposes, the biblical accounts of salvation history include Eve – who represents the dark side in the female, for Khoury – and the Virgin Mary – who models the bright, angelic, and saintly nature of the female, as one expects the case to be with an Orthodox believer – and the biblical attestations oscillate between different female models who mirror either the danger of Eve or the sainthood of Mary throughout the Old and the New Testaments.[405]

In her reading of the biblical accounts of women in her binary, dialectic nature, Khoury argues that the depictions of the female in the Old Testament (Hebrew Bible) are certainly male-made, and this is why they are not exactly positive or appreciative of her (*hya min rasm al-rajul wa-lidhalika lam-takun 'alā aḥsan wajh*).[406] There, woman is mostly depicted in a sceptical, negative manner, and she is only praised or appreciated positively on rare occasions. For Khoury, nonetheless, these depictions demonstrate nothing save what Khoury personally believes to be definitive of woman's binary nature as both the source of good and of evil, of righteousness and of sin, of Eve-like and of Mary-like personalities.[407]

The above is the preconceptual baseline of Khoury's reading of the scriptural attestations on women. Her woman-centred theological reasoning represents an Eastern Orthodox, Arab Christian mind that does not actually seem to be trying to apply a feminist hermeneutics to the Scripture that endeavours to deconstruct the patriarchal interpretational legacy of the historical Church. On the contrary, Khoury seems to be actually embracing such a patriarchal hermeneutical stance since she, in fact, accords with the patriarchal concept that woman is the source of sinfulness and darkness (she is 'Eve' in one of her two natures; thus, she needs always to be tamed). The impression Khoury divulges is of an author who tries hard not to displease the patriarchal, male-dominated ecclesial authorities of her church. Thus, she does not criticise the patristic discourses that lean towards degrading women, though she reveals her knowledge of this fact. She, then, just unpacks the biblical illustrations of women, in their negative and positive aspects alike, without actually endeavouring to challenge, question, or re-read them in a new exegetical manner different from the tradition of her Orthodox Church. It is known in the traditional biblical teaching of the Roman (Antiochene) Orthodox Church (but also other Arab-Eastern churches in general) that the character of Eve is demonised and portrayed as representative of the source of Original Sin, while the character of Mary represents the ideal female holiness and purity.

---

[404] Ibid., p. 10.
[405] Ibid., p. 10.
[406] Ibid., p. 10.
[407] Ibid., p. 11.

Khoury, in her text, seems to be playing strictly within the rigidly delineated boundaries of this churchly authoritative discourse. After all, her book would presumably not have been published by a churchly publisher like an-Nūr Press without first earning the '*nihil obstat*' stamp of the patriarchal ecclesial authority.

But let us go back to Khoury's text and point out that, in her exposition, the author pauses at the socio-cultural impacts of the stance on, and view towards, woman and her value within the predominantly Muslim, Arab-Eastern context. In the Orient, Khoury states, women lived mostly under suppression (*al-mar'a fī al-sharq 'āshat fī kabt ījmālan*). She then adds that the male's disdaining of woman is a Semitic phenomenon (*īḥtiqār al-rajul lil-mar'a ẓāhira sāmiyyah*), Jewish and Islamic alike.[408] On the other hand, Khoury seems to offer a justificatory excuse for the Eastern Church Fathers' negative stance and degradation of woman in the history of the Orient. During the Eastern Fathers' era, she suggests, it was the woman herself who cherished and fostered her negative, trivial, shallow, reckless, irresponsible, and impure nature at the expense of her other, saintly one. This drove the Fathers, Khoury advocates, who called for decency and self-composure, to impose strict and hostile measures over women and to excessively slander them (*yan'atūhā bi-shattā al-qabā'iḥ*). In this, the Church Fathers had a stance similar to the virtuous stance of the Muslim patriarchs (like 'Alī b. Abī Ṭālib, according to Khoury). So, the Fathers, Khoury argues, are forgiven for their cruelty and hostile stance towards women because they were 'suffering' (*'ānū*) from woman and they confronted this by interacting with her as a stumbling block on the way of faith (*'atharah fī ṭarīq al-īmān*). For Khoury, the fathers did not opt for this choice because women were females (*lam yataḥāmmalū 'alyihā li-annahā īmra'a*). They just happened to be surrounded in their churches with many women who were following the track of evil and sedition. So, their cruelty aimed at fulfilling an educational and disciplining goal.[409] Instead of constructing a conclusion related to the situation of women in the Eastern patristic history, Khoury extracts an apologetic alibi to defend the Orthodox patriarchs of the church. The Church Fathers' discourses on women became now expressive of these patriarchs' "wonderful knowledge of woman's psyche" (*ma'rifatahu al-rā'i'ah li-nafsiyyat al-mar'a*),[410] as she says.

What do the Church Fathers' lessons on women (in their very negative, degradational tone) teach the Eastern Christian woman today? According to Khoury, the woman of today is not different from the women of the patristic era, so the Church Fathers' warning and disciplining voices must be listened to by her today, too. The Fathers' negative voice is what is needed to challenge the impurity and decadence that Khoury seems to associate with women's life today, as she calls the Eastern women to alleviate the world's sinfulness.[411] Instead of calling the female to fight the sinfulness directed against her, Khoury urges women to acquire characteristics associated with masculinity in order for her to

---

[408] Ibid., p. 12.
[409] Ibid., p. 13.
[410] Ibid., p. 17.
[411] Ibid., p. 17.

enjoy what Khoury describes as "complete human beingness," since the human is male and female united (she does not call the male to also uphold feminine characteristics upon a belief in the same unity!). This is what, in her belief, enables the woman to protect and foster the positive and pure nature in the binarism of her femininity. The Arab woman today strives for her right. Khoury thinks that women do not need to be occupied with 'rights,' for God has already blessed her with rights that are more sublime than those the woman of today fights for. Khoury rejects the strife for women's independence, equality, and emancipation, and she declares her belief that women were created by God to exclusively play the role of mothers and housewives (which is a typical patriarchal conviction in the Arab world). This is what surfaces in Khoury's following words:

> Woman today demands her rights. Had not God granted her more sublime rights than the ones she calls for? Is not she a house keeper and a queen in her house? By means of her femininity, she gets all what she wants, so why does she need to desert her house and work outside it? ... I personally think that the collapse of the family foundations started from the moment woman demanded the right of working outside the house and became independent from the male financially and spiritually.[412]

In contrast to her Protestant compatriot, Mary Mikhael, who blamed Paul the Apostle and held him accountable for woman's degradation in today's Middle East, Emma Khoury resorts to the very same Pauline teaching to derive a theological and biblical legitimisation for her call to the Arab-Eastern Christian woman to quit appealing for equality with, and emancipation from, man. She recalls Paul's saying that "Man is the head of woman,"[413] before she afterwards raises the flag against women's participation in church services and clerical ordination. She also uses some attestations from the Gospels to argue that Jesus Christ only used women to convey the news of His resurrection, but He never asked women to preach, baptise, or evangelise with the disciples all over the world.[414] Khoury argues that the theological message of the Bible on this matter teaches her that "woman gains much from her modesty, silence, and concealing herself away. There is a sacrament of silence [woman] must fulfill; she is an instrument of inspiration and inspiring; a tool of sanctification and lust for perfection."[415]

Woman's perfection lies, for Khoury, in her silence, not in her speaking up; lies in her withdrawal, not in her activism and emancipation; lies in her exemplary submission, not in her free equality. This is what Khoury sees manifested in the biblical character of the Virgin Mary. Mary, for Khoury, is the iconic manifestation of God's will for woman to be the model of holiness and righteousness in silence, withdrawal, and passive presence: "The image of Mary is the supreme example for every female, and this example is inapplicable to the

---

[412] Ibid., p. 18.
[413] Ibid., p. 18.
[414] Ibid., p. 19.
[415] Ibid., p. 19.

image of the female priest."[416] Again, Paul the Apostle is used to support this view theologically and biblically. The Pauline teaching declares, for Khoury, that "the female in the church has a working domain and the male has another one ... she is ultimately a mother and a parent ... and her fate is attached to her children or to children in general, whether she is married or single."[417] Khoury's theological and biblical message to the Arab-Eastern Christian women, eventually, states the following:

> Let woman, then, remain on the trajectory of faith in every activity she conducts, and let her life be a testimony to Christ. And, if she adheres to the Christian life's battle, she must, first of all, kill Eve within her ... she must kill Eve as a means of seduction, possessiveness, hegemony, vigor, spurning, plotting, stubbornness, arrogance, money-craving, etc ... in order to rear Mary within her; that is modesty, love, sacrifice, self-denial, respect of freedom, etc.[418]

I have deliberately presented two starkly contrasting, woman-centred theological discourses from today's Arab-Eastern Christian context in order to give foreign readers the chance to encounter the peculiar and particular diversity of stances among Arabic-speaking females on the situation of Christian woman in the contemporary churchly and worldly contexts of the Arab Orient. I hope that the reader will appreciate the fact that studying the potential feminist theology's trends in today's Arab-Eastern Christian traditions means, if not also requires, pausing evenly at the existing pro-feminist *and* anti-feminist stances among the Arabic-speaking females of this Christianity.

It is also equally my hope that the readers will ponder the fact that, in the two voices we were exposed to, we have two female theologians similarly relying on the biblical attestation in principle, and on Pauline literature in specific, and employing it as a theological foundation for their discourses. However, each one of these two theologians implements this foundation in a contrasting and dialectically oppositional thesis and conclusion. The Protestant Mary Mikhael tackles Pauline literature, and the scriptural attestations in general, as a challenge to women's rights of leadership and decision-making in the church and society, and she believes that these Scriptural views need to be confronted, deconstructed, and re-interpreted in the service of woman's present struggles. Quite the opposite, Emma Ghrayyib Khoury uses the very same biblical materials in the service of apologetically advocating for the church's degrading, discriminative, and ontologically diminutive understanding of woman's value and role in the church and in God's Creation, both in the patristic era and the present era of the ecclesial establishment of the Arabic-Eastern Orthodox (Antiochene) Church. The very same theologico-biblical presumptions are equally invested in the service of two totally contrasting discourses.

One has here, I reckon, to point out that though Mikhael and Khoury belong to, and exist in, the very same Arab-Eastern *Sitz im Leben*, the stark discrepancy in their woman-centred theological reasoning has also to do with the discrepancies between the two ecclesial circles of existence they operate within.

---

416 Ibid., p. 20.
417 Ibid., p. 20.
418 Ibid., pp. 21–22.

Though she hails from a Roman Orthodox background and upbringing, Mary Mikhael affiliated to the Protestant, Reformed Church quite early, and she did all her theological training at Protestant schools and universities. Had she been still belonging to the Orthodox tradition, the clerical institution of this tradition would not have allowed her to publish, or at least would have not granted her study the approval it needed to be published by an Orthodox publishing house. One has to say here that there is a recognised margin of free-thinking and critical reasoning allowed within the Protestant circles of the Arab Middle East, especially in Syria, Lebanon, and Palestine, and far more tangibly than one can find (at least regarding the issue of women's rights) within the Arab-Eastern Orthodox campaign. I specify Syria and Lebanon in Mikhael's case because the Protestants in other Arab countries today may still lean towards a rather conservative stance on women. In today's Presbyterian/Reformed Synod of Syria and Lebanon (which Mary Mikhael is also a member of, as I was once in my past, on the institutional level), one can meet at least three or four female ordained pastors (two of whom were my study colleagues in the past). One can also find two other ordained female pastors in the Congregationalist Church of Beirut and the Lutheran Church of Palestine.

This is far from being the case, however, in the Protestant/Reformed Synod of the Nile in Egypt, where we have the largest presence of Arabic-speaking Protestants in the entire region. The Synod of the Nile has opened the door for an open discussion of women's rights to leadership and ordination in the church. It now has also female theologians, elders, and educators serving actively in its churches and institutional body, just like the Protestant Synod of Syria and Lebanon. The difference between the two Synods lies in the fact that the former has not yet officially opened the door for ordaining females for clerical ministry. One must here keep in mind that the broader Muslim-majority society in Egypt is still strongly sceptical about, if not even inimical towards, the feminist discourses that call for gender equality and women's rights in the Arab-Muslim world. There are still male authors in Egyptian society who proliferate anti-feminist discourses and offensive statements against feminist thought. There are authors who speak about feminist thought as "contemporary heathenism" (*wathaniyya jadīda*); as a thought that "destructs society from within" (*takhrīb min al-dākhil*), and "an intellectual treachery" (*īḥtiyāl fikrī*); or as "a new cultural colonialism" (*īsti'mār thaqāfī jadīd*).[419] The Christian community of Egypt finds itself striving to maintain its own unique stance on women and their rights, yet the Egyptian Christians are, after all, part and parcel of Egyptian society and they hold the very same cultural, societal, and anthropological value systems and webs of meaning that are embraced by their Muslim co-citizens. One can find that manifested, for instance, in the fact that, when one looks for books on feminism and woman-centred thought among Egyptian intellectual publications, one finds many more texts on women's issues written by males than by

[419] See, for instance, al-Haytham Za'fān (ed.), *al-Ḥaraka an-Nasauwiyya wa-Khalkhalat al-Mujtam'āt al-Īslāmiyyah; al-Mujtama' al-Maṣrī 'Unmūdhajan* (The Feminist Movement and the Raping of the Muslim Societies, the Egyptian Society as a Case-Study) (Cairo: al-Bayān Book, 2006).

females.[420] At any rate, an author like Mary Mikhael, composing a woman-centred theological discourse, capitalises on the relatively privileged, open atmosphere in which Protestant Christianity exists in Syria, Lebanon, and Palestine.

The above is not the privilege or prerogative of the Lebanese Orthodox author Emma Ghrayyib Khoury. She would not be able to develop as critical, deconstructive, and confrontational a discourse as Mary Mikhael in her writing about women in the Eastern Christianity of the Arab world, even if she was personally a genuine advocate for a stance similar to Mikhael's (which Khoury is not, as we saw). When it comes to woman's rights of leadership and decision-making *ex cathedra*, the Arab-Eastern Orthodox traditions (like Orthodox Christianity almost everywhere) is still stiffly conservative, protectionist, and clinging to an old patristic, rather degrading and hostile, stance on women. Obeying the 'Orthodox' ruling, a purely patriarchal, authoritative *credo* is a normative criterion that any Orthodox author, male or female, must abide by in order for his or her writing to be approved and allowed publication on behalf of the establishment. The situation is even more dire in the context of the Orthodox Coptic tradition in Egypt. In the Antiochene Orthodoxy of Syria, Lebanon, Palestine, and Jordan, one can find female authors discussing critically and calling for women's rights in church service and leadership. In Egypt, the stance on women's ordination and role is more radically negative and the door is still closed on discussing this matter.

It is within this peculiar and particular context that some female Christian theologians endeavour to match the bravery of the Muslim and non-religious female scholars and authors, to mimic their feminist intellectual movement, and to create a Christian version of it inside the circles of Arab-Eastern Christianity. It is the hope that a younger generation of female Christian theologians and authors has started lately to surface throughout the Arab world. It is the aspiration that through the contributions of these young females we will witness not just a growth in the number of publications on woman-centred theological reasoning, but also celebrate the birth of a fully-fledged, self-sufficient legacy called 'Arabic Christian Feminist Theology.' In the ensuing pages, I would like to extend my exposition of this trend of theological reasoning in the Arab-Eastern Christian context by presenting three examples of such young female theological voices I am pointing to here.

In 2021, the Arabic online Christian intellectual magazine for West Asia and North Africa, *TELOS*, produced an issue on women's rights and gender equality in the Arab-East. In it, three young female theologians from Syria, Lebanon, and Egypt, and from the Antiochene Orthodox Church, the Maronite Catholic

---

[420] See, for example, Kyrillus ʿAbdulmasīḥ Ḥannā, *'An al-Mar'a wa-Ghiṭā' al-Ra's* (The Woman and the Head Scarf) (Cairo: The Coptic Bookshop, n.d.); Mattā al-Miskīn, *al-Mar'a: Ḥuqūqahā wa-Wājibātihā fī al-Ḥayāt al-Ijtimā'iyya wad-Dīniyya fī al-Kanīsa al-'Ulā* (The Woman: Her Rights and Duties in Social and Religious Life in the Early Church) (Shehet Desert: Anba Maqqar Monastery, n.d.); and Saʿīd Ḥakīm Yaʿqūb, *Makānat al-Mar'a fī al-Khidma al-Kanasiyya wal-Ḥayāt al-Nuskiyya* (The Woman's Status in Churchly Service and Monastic Life) (Cairo: The Orthodox Center for Patristic Studies, n.d.).

Church, and the Protestant Reformed Church, divulged opinions on woman's rights and roles in the Arabic-speaking Christian contexts of their countries. In what follows, I summarise these three female authors' stances. I display each author's text as a sample of the young generation of female voices articulating a woman-centred theological discourse. I hope these short samples will offer a valuable sketch of the potential theological women's scene we might witness in the future of the Arab world.

I shall start with the essay of Anne Zaki, a Protestant Reformed theologian from Egypt. In this piece of writing, Zaki starts with a generic description of the stance on woman in Egyptian society in general:

> The societal, Egyptian mentality and rational perception of woman is paradoxically confused and flustered. On one hand, it wants to protect woman from the society. On the other hand, it wants to protect the society from woman. Woman intimidates it, yet [this mentality] does [simultaneously] fear for woman's body, dignity, relations, financial status, and future – it fears for woman even from herself.[421]

Zaki suggests that this broader, societal perception of woman influentially colours the Egyptian female's self-perception, and it imposes on her a negative, paradoxical, and self-demeaning appreciation of her role and worth. It leaves Egyptian woman, according to Zaki, fragmented into three segments: a woman who impersonates (*tataqammaṣ*) the character of a subdued female longing for the male's support and aid; a woman who resorts to the radical opposite option of impersonating the character of a liberated woman emancipated from societal restraints; and, finally, a third group of women, who end up paying the highest price for this societal dilemma because they find themselves stuck astride the two other radical extremes, confused about which one they must opt for.[422] Zaki maintains that the third segment represents the dominant majority of Egyptian women (it is interesting that Zaki considers the stance of liberation and emancipation an extreme option, and not the necessary one, as conventional feminist discourse usually states).

Zaki believes that the essence, or the crux, of woman's suppression in society lies ultimately in the general culturally and intellectually pressurising atmosphere (*al-manākh al-thaqāfī al-'ām*) which determines woman's social and anthropological statuses, as well as her legislative and constitutional rights.[423]

---

[421] Anne Zaki, "Al-Dhukūriyya al-Nā'ima fī Maṣr," (Soft Masculinity in Egypt), in *TELOS Magazine*, 4(2021), pp. 15–17, p. 15, www.telosmagazine.org/uploads/2/5/5/6/25561514/3-anne_zaki-telos_issue_no4.pdf (consulted 1 February 2024). Zaki's other recognised publications do not touch upon woman-centred theological reasoning, but upon public and practical theologies in general. See, for example, Anne Zaki, "Shall We Dance? Reflections on the Nairobi Statement on Worship and Culture," in *Worship and Mission for the Global Church: An Ethnodoxology Handbook*, James R. Krabill, Frank Fortunato, Robin P. Harris, and Brian Schrag (eds.) (Pasadena, CA: William Carey Library, 2012) and A. Zaki, "Public Theology and the Middle Eastern Church" in *Surviving Jewel: The Enduring Story of Christianity in the Middle East*, Mitri Raheb and Mark A. Lamport (eds.) (Eugene, OR: Cascade Books/Wipf & Stock Publishers, 2022).

[422] Zaki, "Al-Dhukūriyya al-Nā'ima fī Maṣr," p. 15.

[423] Ibid., p. 15.

Zaki argues that the masculinising trends of woman's cultural degradation are not restricted to public imagination and legislation. Far more dangerously sinister than these explicit manifestations, she suggests, are the implicit features of what she calls 'soft masculinity' (*dhurkūriyya nā'ima*). According to Zaki, this *incognito* masculinity is every male-centred attempt at degrading woman's value, image, or rights in such a manner that is embraced and endorsed socially (*ayyi amr fīhi taqlīl min sha'n, ṣūrat, qīmat auw ḥaqq al-mar'a bi-shakl layssa maqbūl mujtama'iyyan*).[424]

Zaki's article is unfortunately too short and slightly simplistic. It neither offers any proposal for attending to this gender situation in Egypt, not even with regards to Christian women, nor does she touch upon the religious or theological aspects of this 'soft masculinity' phenomenon. One cannot say that there is truly a woman-centred *theological*, or even analytical, discourse in her text. This is, nevertheless, a good example of the particular contextual conditions that influence these female authors' attempts at speaking about women's rights and situation in the Arab-Eastern *Sitz im Leben*. The existence of Zaki in the closed, conservative societal context of Egypt is what probably detains churches, the Protestant ones included, from theorising, even theologically, freely or critically about women's rights, as I pointed out earlier. This notwithstanding, Anne Zaki is an example of a potential future female theological voice on woman-centred theology in the Arab world, especially now that she occupies an academic position in the evangelical theological seminary in Cairo.

The second example presented in *TELOS*'s designated issue is the Maronite Catholic Lebanese scholar Pamela Chrabieh. Chrabieh contributes a sort-of autobiographical sketch of what she deems her "journey towards gender equality." She turns her personal self-perception narrative into the underpinning benchmark of her stance on women's status in her *Sitz im Leben*. What injects a religious perspective into Chrabieh's discourse is her self-identification strategy: she roots herself in the soil of the Maronite Church's tradition, insinuating that her journey towards gender equality awareness is harboured in her experience as a Christian Maronite woman hailing from, and still standing within, the circle of that particular ecclesial context. She also suggests that her support of gender equality was reared in the lap of her family's "culture of conviviality and inclusivity," which meant her parents "never missed a chance to talk about dialogue and fight against gender-based discrimination, and by so doing, they set an example of openness to 'otherness' and to gender equality."[425]

---

424 Ibid., p. 16.

425 Pamela Chrabieh, "A Journey towards Gender Equality," in *TELOS Magazine*, 4(2021), pp. 23–28, p. 23. www.telosmagazine.org/uploads/2/5/5/6/25561514/5-pamela_charabieh-telos_issue_no4/pdf (consulted 1 February 2024). Chrabieh's essay is written in the English language. This author wrote numerous texts in Arabic and English touching upon women's situation in the Middle East and the Arab world. See, for example, P. Chrabieh, *al-Mar'a fī Āsiya al-Gharbiyya: Riḥla īlā al-Māḍī* (The Woman in Western Asia: A Journey to the Past) (Beirut: al-Mashriq Press, 2013); P. Chrabieh and Nadia Wardeh, "Against the Current: Rethinking Gender, Religious Authority and Interreligious Dialogue," in *Middle Eastern Women: The Intersection of Law, Culture and Religion*, Mitri Raheb (ed.) (Bethlehem: Diyar Press, 2020), pp. 153–191.

Like Zaki, Chrabieh points to the patriarchal context she experienced in society and school, which rivalled the gender equality experience she lived in her family home. This binary situation continued surfacing also in her education years at university. There, too, Chrabieh encountered the "tradionalism and even conservatism" of the Maronite and Greek-Orthodox teachers and learning curricula and their difference from the rather liberal views she was exposed to by her Western teacher, Fr. Antoine Lammens. This teacher, in specific, seeded in her young mind the belief that she could excel in fulfilling what she trained to become, not just as a skilful practitioner, but also as a woman.[426] She reveals, gloves-free, that her intellectual upbringing of believing in gender equality was intimately associated with witnessing her Western teacher Fr. Lammens's deconstructive strife against the perception of woman, not merely in the broader society, but primarily in local religious communities, especially the Maronite and Greek-Orthodox institutions and their discourses and practices. This educational upbringing shaped Chrabieh's adult personality as a fighter "against sexism, sectarianism, and other sorts of -isms as an activist and an artist."[427] Her activism experience went through her own career's journey as a professor in Lebanese Catholic universities, where she was told "if [you] had a beard and were wearing the male monastic robe, it would have been easy to obtain tenure."[428] In her teaching career, Chrabieh encountered the Middle Eastern male students' and colleagues' opposition to "questioning gender traditional and patriarchal institutions."[429]

In her scholarly writing on the history of women in Western Asia and North Africa, Chrabieh not only studies women's ancient history in these regions and how other feminists have interpreted it. She also aims at drawing the attention of her readers to what she deems "often forgotten foundations of many contemporary cultures and religions in this region concerning womanhood, especially as they apply to men and women today."[430] Chrabieh bluntly unpacks what she believes to also be the defect in the Christian ecclesial existence in the Arab-East, not just in its societies and academic schools:

> Most religious institutions and grassroots interfaith initiatives in South-Western Asia and North Africa are attributed to men, leadership continues to be predominantly male, and it is to be expected that women appear absent or underrepresented in official dialogues between religions. This invisibility ... is acute in our region, particularly when it comes to the decision-making circles within and across religiously/sectarian borders.[431]

---

[426] Ibid., p. 24. On Lammens' views, Chrabieh says: "Lammens believed in the role of the church in welcoming and embracing the development and full participation of women in Christian communities, the Lebanese society, and the Levant region in general ... I still remember how he used to be supportive of women's perspective, and how he argued with other priests and bishops about the urgency of affirming that human rights are at the core of humanity and of Christianity" (ibid.).

[427] Ibid., p. 24.

[428] Ibid., p. 25.

[429] Ibid., p. 25.

[430] Ibid., p. 26.

[431] Ibid., p. 27.

Chrabieh suggests that this gender inequality situation in the church is rooted in "the relation between religious authority and tradition," before she proposes a critical reformation of this relation on the basis of her conviction that "'tradition' itself is not a fixed atemporal entity ... the concept of tradition should be analyzed in relation to the question of cultural continuities/discontinuities, cultural interpretations, and invention."[432] Chrabieh believes that male-dominant interpretation manifests in the practice of "complementarianism" in the Church. This is what she detects in the case of priesthood and ordination:

> When it comes to the Maronite Church, complementarianism is the official position in gender matters. Priesthood/ordination for example is tied to men's roles/responsibilities, and women can [only] be prayer leaders outside the context of a mass, ministries of the word, and giving of holy communion previously consecrated by a priest.[433]

Overall, Chrabieh concedes that feminist theologians are still "a rare breed" in the Maronite Church of Lebanon, and, if they exist, they would rather avoid tackling openly religious authority from gender perspectives. They deem this a taboo, and they focus only on the legal and socio-political aspects of the matter.[434] Chrabieh thus openly declares that the Arab-East context still lacks a frank, coherent, and fully-fledged *theology* of gender relations that "addresses the brokenness in the relationships between genders."[435]

In the Egyptian Protestant theologian's voice, we heard a diagnosis of woman's situation and appraisal on the down-to-earth, societal, soft masculinity-centred *Sitz im Leben*. On the other hand, in the Lebanese Catholic theologian's voice, we met a female author who not only anatomises woman's status in society, but also diagnoses surgically her situation in the Church; something we saw being similarly pursued in the case of the Syrian, older-generation female theologian, Mary Mikhael. Both, Chrabieh and Zaki, nonetheless, do not delve theologically deep in their woman-centred discourse towards challenging the degraded female status embedded in the Church's theological reasoning, and they do not offer a fully-fledged feminist religious remedy to it (though they are correct in their conviction that the roots of the problem extend from the religious context into culture and society). In other words, they describe and diagnose; and Chrabieh, more than Zaki, offers some considerable suggestions and proposals. Yet, neither of the two theologians develop a substantial feminist *theological* cure.

The promise of such a feminist reconstructive theology in the future of the Arab-Eastern Christian context might manifest in the last woman-centred voice I would like to introduce to the reader. This voice is heard within the community of the Roman (Antiochene) Orthodox Church. Beyond mere diagnosis and description, the young female Syrian theologian Maria Qabbara demonstrates a very promising surgical, deconstructing and re-constructing feminist-like theology. Chrabieh and Zaki have already started on their professional

---

432 Ibid., p. 27.
433 Ibid., p. 27.
434 Ibid., p. 28.
435 Ibid., p. 28.

theological career trajectories. Qabbara is still in the process of doing so fully, as she still pursues her doctoral studies at Aristotle University of Thessaloniki, Greece. Despite her youth, Qabbara has written various texts in Arabic that bravely and openly anatomise and critique woman's role and status in her Church tradition.[436] If her fellow church member, Emma Ghrayyib Khoury, whom we looked at earlier, tries to justify and advocate for her church's reading and stance on the patristic, negative views on woman, Maria Qabbara courageously challenges the Church's male-centred and patriarchal reading of the patristic tradition, and she constructs her own innovative, critical, and scrutinising reading of patristic and biblical trends of reasoning alike. Whatever the theme it covers, theological discoursing must not merely be descriptive and diagnostic. It should also be surgically probing and reconstructively therapeutic. This is what Qabbara's discourse aspires to be.

Qabbara contributed also to the previously mentioned issue on women's rights and gender equality produced by *TELOS Magazine*. Compared to the other two examples of her colleagues, Zaki and Chrabieh, Qabbara's discourse is the most approximate to what we know of feminist theological discourse in academic theological circles. Her approach almost hints that, in Maria Qabbara, the Arab Antiochene Orthodox Church might witness the birth of an Arabic version of Elisabeth Schüssler Fiorenza. In her *TELOS* article, Qabbara embarks on arguing in defence of women's rights to clerical, priestly ordination and service, in a manner reminiscent of Fiorenza's '*ekklēsia*-logy' approach and re-interpretation of biblical and patristic traditions.[437] Presumably walking in the footsteps of Fiorenza, Qabbara also adopts a revisional hermeneutic methodology that (in the postcolonialist Homi Bhabha's fashion) reinterprets the patristic heritage, instead of either antagonising or vindicating it, by basically flipping over the centre–margin equation. In the present circles of reasoning in the Arab-Antiochene Orthodox Church, there is a tendency to misunderstand the ideas of 'reservation' and 'transmission' as opposed to 'innovation' and 'revision' in studying patristic legacy. The tendency is to mechanically and passively transmit this tradition and to glorify, defend, and vindicate its teaching, no matter how negative and unfair it might be towards women and their role in the Church. This is, for instance, what we saw Emma Ghrayyib Khoury staunchly abide by earlier in her argument. In this vindicating circle, the patristic, male-dominant

---

436 In addition to the text I shall be studying below, one can read many of Qabbara's articles in the Arabic language on an online platform. See, for example, Maria Qabbara, "Azmat al-Khiṭāb ad-Dīnī al-Masīḥī al-Qadīm wal-Jadīd: Rafḍun Ṣarīḥ li-ʿAdam Tamkīn al-Marʾa fī al-Kanīsa al-Urthūdhuksiyya" (The Crisis of the Old and New Christian Religious Discourse: An Explicit Rejection of Empowering Woman in the Orthodox Church) in www.kalimat.one/maria-kabara, 12/10/2022; M. Qabbara, "Ṣūrat wa-Makānat al-Marʾa fī al-ʿAhd al-Jadīd" (Woman's Image and Status in the New Testament), in www.kalimat.one/maria-kabara, 7/31/2022; M. Qabbara, "Marthā am Maryam? Makānat al-Marʾa wa-Daūruhā fī al-Kanīsa al-Urthūdhuksiyya" (Martha or Mary? Woman's Status and Role in the Orthodox Church), in www.kalimat.one/maria-kabara, 2/18/2021 (all these articles were consulted on 2 February 2024).

437 See the authoritative work of Elisabeth Schüssler Fiorenza, *Discipleship of Equals: A Critical Feminist Ekklēsia-logy of Liberation* (New York: Crossroads, 1993).

centralisation of the patriarchal identity of priesthood becomes central and far more referential than the positive and supportive stances on women's role in the Church, which one can also find, in fact, in the very same patristic tradition. This attention to the women's role therefore becomes marginal and peripheral. Against this strategy, and like Schüssler Fiorenza before her, Qabbara endeavours to turn the equation and to swap its two sides. For her, this is achieved by bringing the Bible's and the Church Fathers' positive appreciation of woman's role in the Church right into the centre of the historical and theological stage and then moving their male-biased voices into the periphery, so that the patristic traditions' hermeneutics will not simply be '*ekklesio-*' but also '*ekklēsia*-logical' in nature and perspectives.

In her *TELOS* article, Qabbara departs from realising that women's rights is the most permanent issue in today's Church around the world. She notices that the permanence of this subject has generated major developments in the global Church on the front of gender equality and women's eligibility for clerical ordination. This worldly evolution notwithstanding, the issue of women's rights is not even yet touched upon in, or at all listed on, the agenda of the Antiochene Orthodox Church in the Arab world. This total absence, Qabbara states, "is primarily due to the total negligence and indifference of the Church's prelates to this issue, [as] the reality of the Orthodox Church still cages woman and captures her in some of the taboos that are derived from [the Bible]." So much so, Qabbara adds, that one can perceive in churchly thought "the tensional contrast between woman's freedom in Christ's teaching and the patriarchal religious institutions' tacit condemnation of woman."[438]

Against this contextual factor, Qabbara launches a hermeneutic re-reading of the biblical, mainly Pauline, attestations and patristic tradition. She starts with re-highlighting particular aspects in the Pauline literature that were kept in the shadows in the service of centralising the male-centred emphasis on aspects in Paul's teaching that order woman to remain silent in the Church and forbid her to practise priestly services like the male. Qabbara flips over the centre–margin equation in the hermeneutics of the Pauline legacy by arguing that just as central in Paul's letters is his acknowledgement of the existence of female presbyters (*presbutera*) and deacons (*diakonissa*) in the churches he established. Qabbara finds such attestations in Romans 16:1 and Timothy I 3:11,[439] before she then suggests that the Pauline literature has two parallel and intertwined traditions, not just a single one: one tradition is male-oriented, and another tradition is actually supportive of the female's service and role in the community of faith. What led eventually to the prevalence of one tradition of interpretation over the other was not historical evidentiality or exegetical legitimacy, but domination-oriented patriarchal hegemony.

---

[438] M. Qabbara, "al-Shammāsāt, Sharṭūniyyat al-Nisā' fī al-Taqlīd al-Līṭūrjī al-Urthūdhuksī: Nuṣūṣ min Ta'līm al-Rusul al-Ithnay 'Ashar wal-Qawānīn al-Kanasiyya" (Deaconesses, Women's '*Cheirotonia*' in the Orthodox Liturgical Tradition: Texts from the *Didache* and the Apostolic Rules), in *TELOS Magazine*, 4(2021), pp. 32–36, p. 32, www.telosmagazine.org/uploads/2/5/5/6/2556114/7-maria_kabara-telos_issue_no4.pdf (consulted on 2 February 2024).

[439] Ibid., pp. 32–33.

Qabbara believes that the same power-game was applied to the reading of the patristic literature and its exegesis. She retreats to the earliest extant patristic and apostolic documents and endeavours to similarly twist the centre–margin equation, pinpointing in this literature specific teachings and ecclesial rules that demonstrate and support, in her opinion, woman's service as deaconess in the Church. In her re-exegesis of the *Didache*, Qabbara notices that "the deaconesses are mentioned not just as a segment of females distinguished from widows and virgins, but as one of the apparatuses of the ecclesial liturgical services that has clearly defined pastoral and liturgical duties."[440] Qabbara, then, looks at the apostolic rules in the *Didache*, and she pauses at the ones that suggest that deaconship was a specific churchly, though not a clerical, role and position and many women were appointed to practise it. Here, Qabbara notices that these women were appointed without "laying hands on their heads," the sign that later became one of the ritualistic signs that are designated for priestly ordination. On this, Qabbara suggests that 'laying hand on the head' in the earliest Church was not necessarily associated with clerical ordination. It, rather, meant general consecration for a specific role.

From this new perspective, Qabbara proposes, one can conclude that, in the era of the *Didache*, female deacons, like male pastors, were both consecrated for certain duties without exerting on them any gender-discriminating gesture, like the one expressed by the particular ritual of 'laying hands on the head.'[441] Qabbara even refers to some other reports in the *Didache* on different Church Fathers, in whose churches women were *ordained* as deaconesses (*ḥuṣūl rasāmah lil-murashshaḥāt īlā al-shumūsiyya*).[442] Qabbara concedes the existence of other apostolic and patristic stances and incidents wherein the ordination of female deaconess was totally forbidden, yet she argues that such historically questionable accounts must not be centralised or advocated. They should, rather, be relegated to the margin when counteracted with other, more historically reliable accounts, like the apostolic rules of the Council of Chalcedon in 451 A.D., which states that women can be ordained as deaconesses when they become forty years old.[443]

In one of her other writings, Qabbara pauses at the negative and degrading image of women in the patristic tradition, and she unpacks the destructive ramifications of some Church Fathers' stances on woman's role in, and contribution to, the clerical life of the church.[444] She pauses particularly at John Chrysostom's negative description of women in some of his homilies, and his belief that the female is not *imago Dei* like the male because women, Chrysostom states, are not only incapable of performing like men, but also have a physical nature that is different from the male's.[445] According to Qabbara, such views contradict starkly Jesus Christ's teaching. On the other hand, Qabbara also

[440] Ibid., p. 33.
[441] Ibid., p. 33.
[442] Ibid., p. 33.
[443] Ibid., p. 34.
[444] M. Qabbara, "Azmat al-Khiṭāb ad-Dīnī al-Masīḥī al-Qadīm wal-Jadīd: Rafḍun Ṣarīḥ li-ʿAdam Tamkīn al-Marʾa fī al-Kanīsa al-Urthūdhuksiyya," pp. 15–17.
[445] Ibid., p. 16.

realises that, in his other writings and treatises, John Chrysostom reflects a different stance on woman and her service in the church. In a letter he wrote to the deaconess Olympias, Chrysostom expresses his genuine admiration and appreciation of this deaconess's service in the church. She also points to other texts Chrysostom wrote, wherein he states that woman is capable of living according to Christ's teaching and to His ministry, just like males.[446]

Such binary views of woman and her role in the church, Qabbara notices, are frequent in various patristic texts, and they demonstrate that one should not reduce the patristic view to one overview, because the patristic stance on women is complex and multifaceted. What determined, nevertheless, which dimension of the patristic view was to be emphasised and followed in the history of the Church was the male-dominant clerical, referential will, not theological or textual evidentiality. Qabbara realises that, from the end of the fifth century onwards, the historical and contextual circumstances changed and societies became more predominantly patriarchal in the Oriental Christian world. She adopts the belief that during that period, and later with the arrival of Islam to the scene, the church embraced the Jewish and Muslim, as well as the Byzantine church-state mentality, and masculinised its ecclesial rules and regulations. This led eventually to the degradation of women's status and role in the Church and to the total, reductionist association of woman with physical and biological impurity, which made the patriarchs prevent her from entering behind the '*iconostases*' into the offertory.[447]

In today's Orthodox Antiochene Church, this shift in the churchly orientation towards imposing a male-centred understanding of ecclesiology and clericalism is rather intensified and consolidated, according to Qabbara. In the patriarchal pastoral epistles to the Church today, Qabbara notices an explicit marginalisation of women from so many aspects related to roles in the family or the church, and she realises that woman's voice is hardly heard in decision-making circles.[448] According to Qabbara, the reductionist reading of the patristic tradition is officiated and authorised by means of a simplistic exegesis of the biblical attestation, specifically of Paul the Apostle's literature and the forbidding stance against women's ministerial service in some parts of his epistles.[449] Against this one-sided reading of Pauline literature, Qabbara advocates for discerning the multi-faceted views on woman in the Pauline literature and calls us to pause at the contradictions between them, as some Church Fathers already did in antiquity, like Gregory of Nyssa and Gregory Nazianzus.[450] Against this reliance on Pauline literature, and in an attempt at avoid its contradictions, Qabbara advocates for discerning and centralising Jesus Christ's stances and teaching in

---

446 Ibid., p. 16.
447 Ibid., p. 35.
448 Ibid., p. 19.
449 Ibid., p. 14.
450 Ibid., pp. 14–15. See also M. Qabbara, "Kahnūt an-Nisā' ka-Mushkila Lāhūtiyya Maskūniyya" (Female Clergies as an Ecumenical Theological Problem), in www.telosmagazine.org/blog_arabic/1794900 (consulted on 06/02/2024). There, Qabbara pauses at Gregory Nazianzus's saying, "men are the legislators of rules against woman."

the Synoptic Gospels. Qabbara, nevertheless, realises that in the Orthodox Church's and patristic tradition's histories of biblical exegesis, an exegetical reductionism was also exerted on the Gospel traditions and on the attestation on Jesus's life and views therein.

In order to demonstrate this reductionism, Qabbara visits in one of her writings the story of Jesus's visit to two women called Maryam and Martha (Luke. 10: 38–42). This Lukan story represents two women with two distinguished characters: one is Martha, the traditional woman who abides by the conventional Eastern role of housekeeping that is assigned exclusively to the females. The other woman, Maryam, in Qabbara's view, represents an emancipated woman who refuses to abide like her sister by the conventional role assigned to women, who searches for knowledge, and decides to spend her time learning from Jesus. According to Qabbara, Jesus's reaction to Maryam's decision and his defence of it before her complaining sister reveals Jesus's liberationist and revolutionary stance on women and their role and status in society.[451] More significantly still, Qabbara suggests that the present Orthodox Church parts ways with Jesus's liberationist gender-equality perspective when it endorses the example of Martha, while Jesus backs up the example of Maryam (*yabdū ann Yasū' al-Masīḥ waqbal daūr Maryam, baynamā al-Kanīsa tufaḍḍil daūr Martha*).[452] On this favouritism towards Martha and the marginalisation of Maryam, Qabbara states the following:

> Despite the [occasional] praising of Maryam's role, the role of Martha enjoyed growing significance throughout the ages, gaining a parallel importance within the trajectory of the church's institutionalization. On the theological and skills-centered levels, there is an acknowledgement of the equal value of the Maryam-like woman in the churchly society. Yet, on the institutional and societal levels, the praised Martha-like woman is merely appointed for strictly limited roles that are mostly discriminative, marginalized, and degradable in nature. Such roles have been institutionalized and embraced widely in the church's institution.[453]

From this re-reading of the church patristic legacy from an '*ekklēsia*-logical' hermeneutic perspective, Qabbara concludes that women's churchly service and ministry tradition were not actually non-existent. They were, rather, deliberately suppressed, doomed into oblivion, and neglected throughout the years. Reviving this genuine Christian tradition and bringing it from the margin into the centre is "a positive response to so many needs and requirements in the contemporary churchly world." "We do know," Qabbara continues, "that refusing to concede males and females equality is nothing but a rejection of the teachings of Jesus

---

[451] Qabbara, "Martha am Maryam? Makānat al-Mar'a wa-Daūrahā fī al-Kanīsa al-'Urthūdhuksiyya."

[452] Ibid.

[453] Ibid. Again, the resemblance between Qabbara's woman-centred hermeneutical approach and that of Elisabeth Schüssler Fiorenza is uncanny. See, for example, E. Schüssler Firoenza, *But She Said: Feminist Practice of Biblical Interpretation* (Boston: Beacon Press, 1993), pp. 57–68 and E. Schüssler Fiorenza, *Theological Criteria and Historical Reconstruction: Martha and Mary, Luke 10: 38–42*, Herman C. Waetjen (ed.) (Berkeley, CA: Center for Hermeneutical Studies in Hellenistic and Modern Culture, 1987), pp. 1–12.

Christ and of the righteous church fathers, who did not discriminate between the male and the female in terms of their createdness in the image of God."[454]

Maria Qabbara, Pamela Chrabieh, and Anne Zaki are three young (Orthodox, Catholic and Protestant, respectively), Arabic-speaking, female theologians who echo a very promising woman-centred theological voice for the coming decades in the Arab world. None of them has yet presented to us a fully structured, coherently systematised, and completely definable feminist theological theory. Yet, out of the three, Maria Qabbara is showing strong signs that her intellectual contributions might quite seriously and potentially aspire towards creating the first Arabic-Eastern feminist theology in the coming years or decades.

---

[454] Qabbara, "al-Shammāsāt, Sharṭūniyyat al-Nisā' fī al-Taqlīd al-Lītūrjī al-Urthūdhuksī: Nuṣūṣ min Ta'līm al-Rusul al-Ithnay 'Ashar wal-Qawānīn al-Kanasiyya," p. 36.

6. Arab-Eastern Theology: Characteristics and Potential Revisions

Before I share my assessment on the trends of Arabic-speaking, Eastern Christian theological reasoning studied in this book, I would like to draw the attention of the reader to a valuable general appraisal of theological reasoning in the context of the Middle East that was made elsewhere. In 2018, the Protestant Lebanese theologian George Sabra contributed a piece on theology in the context of Arab-Eastern Christianity. In his essay-long exposition, Sabra suggests that surveying the Christian publications in the Middle East between 1950 and 1990 reveals, according to him, that "the majority of writings were of a devotional or homiletical nature, and that very little had been produced in the area of systematic reflection on contemporary issues of thought and life." Sabra then immediately confirms that "this is still more or less the case in the second decade of the third millennium, but with an increase in historical and liturgical theological writings."[1] In principle, Sabra's observation conveys a partial truth about the textual productions on theology in the Middle Eastern context; something I have also already expressed in my own terms in this volume. This conceded, I do believe that the trends of theological reasoning discussed in the fifth chapter of this monograph question seriously the sweeping and essentialising tone of Sabra's appraisal in their broad and far from narrowly devotional or homiletical perspectives and focus. They question the overgeneralisation of his claim, especially in regard to the theological reasoning during the last quarter of the twentieth century and the beginning of the third millennium alike.

The above critique notwithstanding, I would concur with Sabra's conclusive belief that the theological discourses in that region are far from representing "scholarly undertakings of Christian faith reflecting on its object (God) and its situation in the contemporary world – namely the task of Systematic Theology."[2] I have already reflected a similar conviction when I pointed out that what we have in the Arabic-speaking Christian context is not 'theology' in the sense of 'God-talk,' but theology-like voices. On the other hand, Sabra is also right, I believe, in his opinion that "theological reflection in the Middle East is not so much inspired or challenged by Christian faith's conversation with philosophy and the sciences, nor primarily by the need to clarify and interpret the gospel to the church. It is, rather, prompted by political, social, and interreligious questions

---

[1] George F. Sabra, "Theology," in *Christianity in North Africa and West Asia*, Kenneth R. Ross, Mariz Tadros, and Todd M. Johnson (eds.) (Edinburgh: Edinburgh University Press, 2018), pp. 325–334, p. 325.

[2] Ibid., p. 326.

and issues that arise from the context of the life of the churches in that region of the world."[3]

What I beg to differ on with George Sabra is his narrow restriction of the thematic orientation of theology in the Arabic-speaking Middle East to two main subjects: 1) existence in the world of Islam and 2) the Arab–Israeli conflict. The numerous trends of theological reasoning which I discuss in this study demonstrate that the spectrum of the issues and challenging questions these theological discourses address is much broader than these two subjects, no matter how basic and fundamental they are. On the other hand, I would hesitate seriously to read the theological attempts in the region as solely, or necessarily, developed and divided after denominational, ecclesial distinctions. The diverse trends of theological thought I discuss in this monograph clearly show that the interests, focuses, methods of reasoning, and goals of the various Arabic-speaking Orthodox, Catholic, and Protestant theologians conspicuously and deeply overlap and intertwine across the dividing borders between the denominations. I have mentioned, in almost every trend of theological discourse I have introduced, exemplary voices that belong to different churchly denominations. This shows, I believe, that the map is far more sophisticated, trans-denominational, and multi-layered than Sabra is seemingly willing to acknowledge.

It is my belief that the trends of theological reasoning one finds in the Arab-Eastern context can be placed validly under the rubric of theologies that are developed by Christian theologians and scholars who belong to the non-Western, non-Northern American and Non-European worlds (even if some of them live and pursue their careers in these geographical locations). Recently, such theological forms of reasoning were called theologies from 'the Global South' (I place this category between quotation marks because I have some conceptual reservations about it!). Such a nomenclature-like category started to proliferate in contemporary theological scholarship. In 2023, Mitri Raheb and Mark Lamport produced a large anthology on various trends of theological reasoning that have emerged from the southern hemisphere. In their introduction to the anthology, the two editors offer a general characterisation of these non-Western, southern-eastern theological trends. According to them:

> Theologies from the Global South tend to be ecumenical in nature and focus more on the suffering of local people due to the socio-economic and political context rather than on denominational doctrinal differences. Theology from the Global South had to relate to the multireligious context in which they existed … This religious plurality influenced many of the theologies of the Global South to be interreligious in nature.[4]

Raheb and Lamport proceed by suggesting three main characteristics expressive of how theologians from the Global South develop theological

[3] Ibid., p. 326.

[4] Mitri Raheb and Mark A. Lamport, "The Interpretative Challenge for Grace and Peace in the Global South: A Hermeneutical Perspective," in *Emerging Theologies from the Global South*, M. Raheb and M. A. Lamport (eds.) (Eugene, OR: Cascade Books, 2023), pp. 7–18, p. 10.

reasoning and discourses within the above-formulated epistemological framework. They call these features "three macro-factors," and they describe them as follows:

> First, Christianity is related to the social conditions among the culture in which it exists ... Second, Christianity tends to be mingled into some measure of relationship with the national consciousness of the culture in which it exists ... Third, Christianity adapts and responds to contemporary issues when a society experiences rapid change.[5]

I must admit that I do have methodological and conceptual reservations about how Raheb and Lamport present what they call "theologies from the Global South." I do not concur with their methodological strategy of placing this so-called 'Global South's theologies' in an oppositional, dialectic binarism with other Christian theological forms of reasoning which they call 'Global Northern European/American.' This binary, otherising-by-contrasting approach presumes that the theological reasoning of the Northern hemisphere is the traditional, primary defining '*thesis*' of Christian thought. This makes the theological trends of reasoning that come from this imagined 'Global South' an '*antithesis*,' and even antithetical to what is actually a *constructed* formula, not a realistic one. Such an oppositional, dialectically binary logic presumes an existing 'clash' and 'alterity in contrariety'[6] (inescapably reminiscent of the 'clash of civilisations' hypothesis and clearly manifested in Raheb's and Lamport's speaking of 'North Atlantic imperial-colonial enterprise'), which might not truly or evidently be there in the first place. On the other hand, dialectic thesis–antithesis logic relates, in both its Platonic and Hegelian trends, that the 'antithesis' is conjured up to primarily defy and counterpart the 'thesis' and, more crucially, to *replace* it. Be that as it may, Raheb and Lamport present the so-called 'Global South theologies' as an 'antithesis' to *replace* what they conceive as the old predominant and past-prevailing 'Global North theologies.'

I believe such a dichotomic, binary point of departure is questionable, for at least three reasons. First, who decided that the theological reasoning of the 'Global North' was dominant over the Christian intellectual history, whether in antiquity, medieval times, or even modernity? Theological voices, at least from the eastern parts of the Roman/Byzantine world, let alone from central Asia, never ceased evolving and impacting Christianity throughout the past centuries, even if its ability to spread around the globe and to cross dividing geographical boundaries was not as effective (due to historical, political, and cultural circumstances) as the theological traditions that originated in the western parts of the Roman/Latin world.

Second, who said that the demographic shift which Christianity witnesses today, due to the concentration of the largest Christian populations in Latin America, Africa, and Asia, indicates that the Christian theologians who come from these parts of the world develop theological reasoning that is totally self-otherising and antagonistically different from the theological reasoning that is

---

[5] Ibid., pp. 13–14.

[6] On this 'alterity in contrariety' in religious self-awareness, read, for instance, N. G. Awad, *After-Mission, Beyond Evangelicalism*, pp. 99–108.

being developed in Northern America and Europe? Demographic shifts are not necessarily an automatic demonstration of a seismic shift in *theological* reasoning. Raheb and Lamport jump too rapidly, I reckon, to this conclusion without paying sufficient attention to the fact that, upon a careful reading of the theological discourses of theologians from Africa, Asia, Latin America, and other places that are considered parts of the 'Global South' (something which I did regularly between 2010 and 2021, when I used to teach a course on contextual and non-Western theological trends of reasoning), one almost immediately realises that these theologians do not actually construct their theologies in stark contrast to those one finds in the discourses and writings of North American and European theologians. They, rather, use the theologies of the latter scholars and converse with them openly, if not often build upon their epistemic reconstruction, systematic cognition, and methodological options. Even the various authors Raheb and Lamport present as voices illustrative of the underpinning hermeneutics of their conjured 'Global South theologies' use methods of reasoning, exegetical approaches, cognitive analytical strategies, and theological arguments that are commonly used by theological scholars from the Christian demographic entities that belong to the so-called 'Global North.'

Third, I fully agree with Fernando Segovia, whom Raheb and Lamport invite to reflect critically on their project (something they are to be credited for, indeed), in his critical assessment of the jargon of 'theologisation from the Global South.' Segovia, I believe, is quite right in his argument that "the term 'the Global South' is neither self-evident nor determinate."[7] Segovia goes on to demonstrate that such a term has a "flowing nature" with respect to its objectives, which makes its description "not as keenly drawn and discussed as one might wish."[8] He then points out that some scholars tried to delineate particular meanings and definitions for the 'Global South' term, deeming it either 'metaphorical' or 'geographical' in signification, or treating it either as a 'structural' or 'subaltern' hermeneutic tool.[9] Segovia himself suggests that such signification attempts merely tell us that the nomenclature is of what Segovia describes as a 'flexible' nature with 'epistemic' connotations. All these defining attempts tell us that the term 'Global South' is a fuzzy and ambiguous phrase, used unreservedly and un-forensically to speak about Christian theological trends in contrast with presumed and equally constructed 'Global North' theological others. After all, Segovia has a point in his opinion that "a recourse to the 'Global South' as substitute represents but a futile exercise in political correctness: an attempt to preserve the geographical signification via a cleaner term, yet one that skirts the change in political realities and that maintains the

---

[7] Fernando F. Segovia, "Theologizing from the Global South," in *Emerging Theologies from the Global South*, pp. 19–33, p. 20.

[8] Ibid., p. 21.

[9] On the first use, see Sinah Theres Kloß, "The Global South as Subversive Practice: Challenges and Potentials of a Heuristic Concept," in *The Global South*, 11(2017), pp. 1–17. And, on the second use, see Nina Schneider, "Between Promise and Skepticism: The Global South and Our Role as Engaged Intellectuals," in *The Global South*, 11(2017), pp. 18–37. See also an assessment of both Kloß's and Schneider's approaches in Segovia, "Theologizing from the Global South," pp. 21–27.

focus on economic development … the term continues the various shortcomings inherent in the 'Third World.'"[10]

It is certainly not my purpose here to present a comprehensive or detailed critique of Raheb's and Lamport's 'Global South theologies' project. All I want to bring to the reader's attention is that my positive appraisal of their discourse *does not* aim to make Arab-Eastern theological reasoning an example of so-called 'Global South theologies.' I merely realise, however, that the above-quoted elements that are definitive and characteristic of the so-called 'Global South theologies' on the *macrocosmic* level of observation (as Raheb and Lamport discuss in their anthology) are fairly applicable to, and manifested in, the theological trends of reasoning I find in the Arab-Eastern Christianity's context. This conceded, one can go beyond the 'macro' level of observing, which Raheb and Lamport resorted to in their attempt at being as comprehensive and inclusive as possible in their exposition. One ought to aim at detecting the particular *micro*-factors that are characteristic of the Arab-Eastern trends of theological reasoning as they were discussed in this monograph.

Be the above as it may, let me now move to my own assessment of the Arabic-speaking theological endeavours in today's Middle East. The previously surveyed main trends of theological reasoning or discourses in today's Arabic-speaking Eastern Christianity invite us to pause at the following characteristics and defects that commonly characterise them:

1. Save for the protectionist and self-enclosed approach, these theological voices are overtly *politicised* in nature, foundation, and outcomes. They all exceed the boundaries of their theological applicability to the public affairs (*politia*) of human existence in the Arab Middle East. They all, rather, tend to allow the crudely political *a priori* postulates and concerns to predetermine their theologised reasoning. So much so, that their theology-like discourses are played in accordance to modus operandi rules, language-games, and hermeneutic strategies that are all dictated and pre-meditated by political pre-conditioning presumptions, determining challenges, and tailored expectations. Instead of a theological enterprise that is sensitive to the politically affected aspects of the human condition and life-settings, we end up encountering variations of overwhelmingly politicised religiosity, which aims at advocating, justifying, redeeming (sometimes in a populist manner), and even apologising for ready-made views and convictions by means of employing the religious texts in their service.

Once, the South Korean theologian and associate professor of Ecumenical Theology at Union Theological Seminary, Chung Hyun-Kyung, stated a thought-provoking view on the relation between the religious text and the lived context in the following, postcolonially influenced terms: "*We are the text*, and the Bible and tradition of the Christian church are the context for our theology."[11] Hyun-Kyung wants by this provocative statement to reverse the hermeneutical and exegetical equation by making the readers and their contextual reality

---

[10] Ibid., p. 22.

[11] Chung Hyun-Kyung, *Struggle to be the Sun Again: Introducing Asian Women's Theology* (Maryknoll, NY: Orbis, 1990), p. 11.

determine what the scriptural attestation conveys and how it ought to be interpreted and used to relate to one's own aspirations, hopes, struggles, worldviews, and conditions from a religious perspective. It seems to me that the overwhelming tendency of the contemporary trends of Arab-Eastern theological reasoning reflects the very same logical and hermeneutic methodology delineated in Hyun-Kyung's dictum. This, however, is far from a theology that prophetically confronts the political condition by questioning it from the angle of God and God's revelation in the radical and challenging ministry of Jesus Christ and the textual attestation to this revelation in the Bible and the Church's traditions. It is, rather, a theological orientation which, despite its pluriformity, aspires monolithically at offering the God of Jesus Christ and presenting His Gospel as an *answer*, as a mere satisfactory, if not pleasing, *response* to the political questions and crisis-breeding conditions which the Arab-Eastern Christians' broader society demands from their theologians.

The danger of playing such an intellectual game in a context like the Arab world lies in the fact that the Christians therein live in a broader societal and religious context that is predominantly Muslim by nature and extension. In the mainline, institutional, and popular Muslim imaginations, political awareness and involvement are substantially inherent to one's religious self-perception, worldview (*Weltanschauung*) and self-awareness (*selber Bewusstsein*). Why this is the case? Because the belief is deeply sunk in the consciousness of the Muslims that Islam is 'religion and state' (*Dīn wa Daūlah*). Be that as it may, in the Arab world's context, the religious is overwhelmingly over-politicised by default and presumption. Religiosity often serves the state and the power games related to it, rather than religion being the vigilant critic and corrector of the performance and quality of political engagement in the affairs of the state.

Now, the Christians who co-exist in this context belong anthropologically, sociologically, and culturally to the very same setting. So, they tend, consciously or unconsciously, to fall into imagining Christianity to be as rooted in the 'religion and state' mentality. Therefore, they might easily turn the religious or theological rationale into an instrument in the service of granting the Christians a political role and foothold in the power-struggle or state-affairs arena. This makes the Christians, like their Muslim compatriots, dictate, mould, and manipulate the religious or theological perception according to the conditions and expectations of state politics. A proper revolutionary and truly liberating theological discourse in such a particular context like the Middle East would be one that theologically questions and exposes the pitfalls of a 'religion and state' mentality, instead of (maybe unconsciously) playing according to its rules and consequentially (maybe unintentionally) fostering and consolidating it further. In his description of the particular nature of world Christian theologies, Peter Phan relates that the role of global theologians must be the following:

> The theologian's task is to mediate between faith and culture, and the goal is to express the contents of the faith in categories that are understandable to the people of a particular time and place, and, if necessary, to jettison the traditional, even ecclesiastically sanctioned, formulations of Christian beliefs and practices to meet the needs of the age ... [nevertheless] the main task of theology is [also] to critique – and, when necessary, resist and reject – cultural trends that are judged to be

inimical to the Christian faith, rather than seeking ways to accommodate it to culture.[12]

It seems to me to be the case that today's Arab-Eastern theologians are content with developing theological discourses that express faith in categories acceptable by the broader societies of the Middle East and that speak to this broader public's time and place in such a manner that makes the Christians of that region primarily, but also narrowly, concerned about meeting the needs of their Muslim-majority life-setting. This is indeed part of the main task of the theologians, as Peter Phan eloquently states. However, it seems to me that this is being achieved more successfully on the account of Phan's other emphasis; namely, that it is also the duty of the theologian to critique, resist, and reject, as Phan says, the cultural trends that are inimical to the Christian faith, and not to seek ways to accommodate his or her theological reasoning to culture.

2. The second central characteristic of these trends is the general tendency of these Arabic-speaking theologians, each in his or her own way, to treat religiosity or religious affiliation as an '*identity*.'[13] I have already written on the common phenomenon among the Christians, Muslims, and Jews in the Arab world of treating religion as a defining, if not *the* primary and central, self-identifying criterion. In that earlier piece, my argument was basically the following: shaping identity after religiosity would actually strip religion of its real and actual nature. Religion by nature is not an instrument for self-definition. Statements like 'I am Christian' or 'I am Muslim' do not actually say anything specific or definitive of me or myself. If the term 'Christian' or 'Muslim' defines the 'me' or the 'myself' truly, this will make one's own 'self' the subject and the object, that is, the sole content, of the thing that is called 'Christianity' or 'Islam.' This means that the person is the content of his or her very own religion, when, at least in Christianity, the religious discourse that is *theo*-logy is basically 'God-talk,' not 'human-talk.' Making the core subject of religious discourse a 'human-talk' implies that the person worships him/herself, that he or she is the core focus of one's own self, as much as it would follow that the terms 'Christian' and 'Muslim' would be reduced to the self of the one who defines him/herself by means of them.

When religion is used as an identity-formation criterion, or a criterion to identify not just humans, but everything related to human existence, intellect, and awareness,[14] religion becomes, in fact, a tool for otherising and contrariety.

---

[12] Peter C. Phan, "Doing Theology in World Christianities: Old Tasks, New Ways," in *Relocating World Christianity: Interdisciplinary Studies in Universal and Local Expression of the Christian Faith*, Joel Cabrita, David Maxwell, and Emma Wild-Wood (eds.) (Leiden & Boston: Brill, 2017), pp. 115–142, p. 126.

[13] See Najib George Awad, "Democracy without Democrats, Identity-Formation and Religions: The Challenge of Cross-pollinating Self-perception in the post-Arabic Spring Contexts," *Journal of Philosophy & Social Criticism*, XX(10), 2021, pp. 1–12. The ensuing lines in this section are all directly borrowed from this essay.

[14] A good example of those who have followed this trend of thought in the Arab world since the beginning of the twentieth century up till today are the radical Islamist movements of Islamic revivalism. They tend to call for Islamising every scientific or intellectual sector of knowledge and experience in the life of the Arabs, claiming that

It becomes an expression of confrontational and contrasting alterity, which only states that oneself is categorically, ontologically, and hierarchically different from the self of others. When I depart in my co-existence and perception from a normative statement like 'I am Christian,' or 'I am a Muslim,' etc., what I depart from does not actually designate anything about who I am. It only makes the others realise what I am *not*: I am not Muslim, Jew, Buddhist, Hindu, atheist, non-religious, agnostic, etc., etc. 'I am Christian' does not aim at making my identity known to others. It rather says "I am not the other'; it does not say who I am, but that I am not what the others are. Be that as it may, defining who I am in terms of a religion does not say anything about me, and it eventually fails to specify anything about the connotations and meaning of the Christianity and Islam I define myself with.

Turning religion into an identity follows a Hegelian dialectic that presumes that the self cannot be itself except in a binary contrast with a conjectured 'other,' whose otherness is often imaginary, pre-constructed, and far from realistic. This is exactly what we practise in our harmful and dangerous relation with religiosity in the Arab world today. Rather than becoming one of the incentives of inter-culturation or cross-pollination, the identity-formation experience become a process of othering, wherein self-identification turns into an act of exclusion of otherness. Here, clinging to an a priori constructed religious awareness centred around contrariety mutilates differentiation by transforming it from a mere expression of self-distinction into a dangerous state of excluding divisiveness, especially when the religiously defined subject considers the religiously perceived 'other' a potential contaminating threat to oneself and one's own religious superiority. This antagonistic binarism drives both subjects into violently negating each other.[15] The religiously founded, otherising self-perception I talk about here is not an idea or a mere theoretical speculation. It is a down-to-earth *action*, a factual, strategised modus operandi, a practised, behavioural *habitus* that is granted the status of a defining and categorising process. It is an intellectual and cognitive process of self-defining by binarily categorising the other in such a manner that not only emphasises 'who I am,' but also presumes premeditatedly and pre-conceptually that the 'other' cannot, let alone is allowed to, be 'the *same* as I am.' The other is not entitled to be looked

---

this will not only salvage the Arab-Muslim nation from its backwardness and defeat, but will also liberate sciences in general from their crypto-scientific and pseudo-knowledge status. See, for instance, on this discourse: Mohamed 'Amārah, *Islāmiyyat al-Ma'rifah: Madhā Ta'nī* (The Islamicity of Knowledge: What Does it Mean?) (Cairo: Nahḍat Maṣr, 2007) and Mohamed 'Amārah, *Maqām al-'Aql fil-Islām* (The Status of *'Aql* in Islam) (Cairo: Nahḍat Maṣr, 2008).

[15] J. Kruger, "Christian Identity in an Age of Difference," in *Christian Identity*, Eddy van der Borght (ed.) (Leiden: Brill, 2008), pp. 119–132. See also the forthcoming study by Najib George Awad, "Deciphering the *Genome* of 'Crisis' in the Syrian 'Refugee Crisis': Toward a *Hermeneutic Tripod*," in *Church and Migration: Global (In)Difference*, Darren Dias, Jaroslav Skira, Michael Attridge, and Gerard Mannion (eds.) (New York: Palgrave MacMillan, 2020).

at and appreciated as one who stands with me on the same level of existence, nature, value, and rights.[16]

The discussed trends of theological reasoning do reflect to various degrees and extents a potential drift into the snare of such a mentality. The driving motif behind such a possibility seems to be suggested in a noticeable occupation with survival and combating extinction in the Arabic-speaking Christians' homeland. One cannot but pause at the urgency and profound concern that drive these Arabic-speaking theologians to construct theological discourses fixated on the question of the Christians' conditions, roles, and destinies in a direly unstable, turbulent, and dangerous life-setting like the Middle East. What might be ringing an alarm bell in this, rather genuine, life-concern is what seems to manifest a sort of excessive clinging to one's own religious affiliation and then treating this as the primary source of identity and self-awareness. Such a tendency might end up breeding the reverse effect, and it might send the wrong, far from intended, message to the different, non-Christian, co-existing other.

The need in the Arab Middle Eastern context, I reckon, is for a theological discourse that demonstrates the call of the God of Jesus Christ to *all* the human beings in the context of the Middle East; one that conveys the divine, healing Grace of the Holy Spirit that overshadows *all humans* regardless of their religious affiliations. There is a need for a theology that counterparts the self-otherising policy by showing that "*all* are one in Christ Jesus" (Galatians 3:28). Reducing religiosity down to an 'identity' only fosters what the broader Muslim context is grounded in; namely, treating 'Islam' not just as a belief or a state of affiliation, but as an ontologically defining foundation that otherises binarily, qualitatively, and tangibly those who are called 'the Nation of Islam' (*Ummat al-Islam*) from other communities. The needed theology is one that, on the contrary, invites Muslims and Christians alike to travel beyond the narrow circles of otherising identity-formation processes into a more inclusivist, pluralist, and non-otherising self-perception that lies in the theological belief that we are all created by one divine Creator.

3. The discussed trends of theological reasoning are also predominantly symptomatic of a religious thinking that is excessively and exhaustively *socio-cultural* in nature. They invite us to pause at the form of relationality such trends manifest between their theological reasoning and the question of (inter)contextuality. Ever since (inter)contextual theology appeared in the field of theological studies, so many theologians, especially those who live in, and belong to, the non-Western Christian sphere, became keen on developing (inter)contextual theological discourses rooted in their indigenous *Sitz im Lebens* and expressive of their life-settings' enquiries and rules of cultural perception. The most intriguing factor in this endeavour was that these theologians often departed in their projects from the belief that such newly created (inter)contextual theology is made to replace, if not to displace, the classical,

---

[16] Richard Rorty, "Human Rights, Rationality and Sentimentality," in *On Human Rights: The Oxford Amnesty Lectures 1993*, Stephen Shute and Susan Hurley (eds.) (New York: Basic Books, 1993), pp. 111–134; Sune Qvotrup Jensen, "Preliminary Notes on Othering and Agency," in *Sociologisk Arbejdspapir*, 27, 2009, pp. 1–36.

usually deemed Western, genre of theological reasoning called systematic/dogmatic/constructive theology. In the theological voices I discussed above, it seems that we encounter theologians, each in his or her own particular and distinguished manner, trying to pursue, explicitly or implicitly, the same goal and to enact a similar replacement/displacement strategy. As if any Arabic-speaking theological discourse that can be conjured up must represent an (inter)contextual voice that stands, not just socio-culturally, but also theologically, against the systematic/dogmatic/constructive theology of non-Eastern Christianity.

Can one truly develop (inter)contextual, or (inter)contextualised, theology without relating it to Christian dogmatics, and should (inter)contextuality be placed in binary contradistinction with systematic/constructive reasoning in theology? I would like to reflect briefly on these questions in the ensuing paragraphs. I shall do this by critically anatomising the conceptual and methodological presumptions behind the (inter)contextualisation attempts of the above discussed Arabic-speaking theological trends and then showing the shortcomings and mistakes of such attempts.

Principally speaking, I have already attended to the discussion of the validity of 'contextual theology' as an alternative to 'dogmatic theology' in an essay I published in 2013.[17] In this essay, I noticed a paradigm shift in the writing *habitus* of today's theological circles, where an enquiry like 'what is theology?' is now replaced with 'who is the theologian?'[18] This new *habitus* originated from a growing attention to contextuality and socio-cultural conditions. Theology is now examined as a pure contextual phenomenon; that is, from "a personal, autobiographical perspective that treats theology as a poetic of testimony."[19] The question I raised in the face of this was "if the theologian [opted only for doing theology exclusively from her own specific context,] would she still be doing theology in the real Christian sense of the word? Is speaking about one's theological context, and how one deals with the theological scholarship in relation to her specific culture, reflective of the nature and subject of theology, or of what the theologian personally finds herself tackling as a Christian in a certain life-setting by means of the theological methods of intellectual inquiry?"[20]

---

[17] Najib George Awad, "What Has the Jerusalem of Dogmatics to Do with the Athens of Context, or How Should One Do Contextual Theology?" in *PLURA: Revista de Estudos de Religião*, 2(3), 2013, pp. 198–221.

[18] Ibid., p. 199. See also on the notion of *habitus* as well as the shift in theological writing: Pierre Bourdieu, *The Logic of Practice* (Stanford, CA: Stanford University Press, 1990) and Graham Ward, *Cultural Transformation and Religious Practice* (Cambridge: Cambridge University Press, 2005).

[19] Awad, "How Should One Do Contextual Theology?" p. 199. See also Rebecca S. Chopp, "Theology and the Poetics of Testimony", in *Converging on Culture: Theologians in Dialogue with Cultural Analysis and Criticism*, D. Brown; S. G. Davaney and K. Tanner (eds.) (New York & Oxford: Oxford University Press, 2001), pp. 56–70.

[20] Awad, "How Should One Do Contextual Theology?" p. 199. A similar Enquiry has also been raised in Gerhard Sauter, *Gateways to Dogmatics: Reasoning Theologically*

It is well known in the field that the question which (inter)contextualised theological discourses depart from, and are epistemologically shaped after, is "how can theology be done … to sufficiently respond to its context?"[21] It is undoubtedly essential to keep in mind that theology is a humanly originated affair: it is the child of the intercourse of the human theologian's socio-cultural, existential, anthropological, and historical conditions. Remembering this fact is even more crucial for the Christians in the Arab world. There, the Christian lives in the world of Islam, which conventionally treats and practises religious understanding as an absolute, a-historical, a-temporal, and God-given truth. The Qur'ānic text and its interpretations and the Islamic belief and its jurisprudential (*fiqh*) and theological hermeneutics are equally treated as *given*, as divinely bestowed upon the believers, as equally meta-historical, meta-contextual. In such a context, it is necessary for the Christians to remember the human-made creatureliness of theology.

The above fully conceded, nevertheless, the overwhelming emphasis on conveying a purely contextualised theological voice that is dogma-free and totally shaped after, and pre-meditated by, these Arabic-speaking theologians' socio-cultural conditions ends up presenting a theology that is "defined as merely talk about the human and her needs."[22] In such an approach, "the possible dangerous consequences of over-emphasising the human subjectivity at the expense of God's self-existing reality seems to be inescapable," for God here becomes the "mere cultural idea of a linguistic expression that is used, without any reservations or exceptions, in the service, and under the preconditioning rules, of the human context."[23] Here, theology as a discourse is used by these Arabic-speaking theologians for the sole purpose of restrictively contextualising the Christian God per se before their Muslim context by applying the idea of this deity to every indigenous, predominantly Muslim, metaphor, model, or concept that are pertinent to the particular socio-cultural context of the Arab Middle East.

One certainly wonders, in light of this centralisation of (inter)contextuality (rather than just attending to it), "whether or not theology remains the Christian discourse on God and God's relationship to Creation if the epi-centre and core-subject of faith becomes the human condition."[24] It is, in my belief, crucial for any Arab-Eastern theological discourse out there to discern seriously the essential conceptual difference, which Gerhard Sauter once pointed at, between 'mirroring the context,' on one hand, and 'reflecting upon the context,' on the other.[25] Yes, theology must reflect the theologians' solidarity and occupation with particular human conditions that pertain to these theologians' socio-cultural

---

for the Life of the Church (Grand Rapids, USA/Cambridge, UK: W. B. Eerdmans Publishing Company, 2003), p. 254.

[21] Awad, "How Should One Do Contextual Theology?" p. 207 and G. Sauter, *Protestant Theology at the Crossroads: How to Face the Crucial Tasks for Theology in the Twenty-First Century* (Grand Rapids, USA/Cambridge, UK: W. B. Eerdmans Publishing Company, 2007), p. 96.

[22] Awad, "How Should One Do Contextual Theology?" p. 207.

[23] Ibid., p. 208.

[24] Ibid., p. 209.

[25] Ibid., p. 209 and Sauter, *Protestant Theology at the Crossroads*, p. 114.

context. However, the theological reasoning must not be purely induced from the private, situational conditions and occupations, and these should not become the source and the criterial basis of the theological discourse. After all, there needs to be a theological differentiation between "God's acting in the human historical context, on one side, and the course of this historical context *per se*, on another."[26] Otherwise, contextualising theology morphs into a theologised contextual perception.

There is nothing wrong with pursuing contextual perception and description. Yet associating this pursuit with a language-game that includes vocabularies like 'God,' "Christ,' 'Gospel,' 'Faith,' etc., does not automatically make it 'theology' proper, or even 'theology' as such. Reducing the theological discourse to a mere echo of the cultural voice, or to a mirror of the narrow conditions of a specific socio-cultural concern, strips off theology's core nature. This reductionism traps theology in a pit of "*syncretistic indigenisation*", forcing the Christian message to turn into a manifestation of a certain cultural, religious, and spiritual tradition that is restrictively and narrowly relevant to, and definitive of, a specific timely context and a present existential condition.[27] This deprives the Gospel of Jesus Christ of its dialogical and correlational nature. It turns it into an apologetic instrument, or even an ideological manifesto, that aims to show that God's message echoes what is deemed by a specific cultural-social setting to be the true and normative constituents of religious and socio-cultural identity or self-perception.

It seems to me, ultimately, that the trends of Arab-Eastern theology I discussed do not demonstrate a subtle perception of the substantial difference between 'contextualisation' and 'indigenisation.' The crucial discrepancy between these two concepts marks a foundational systematic difference between "making the local culture and the religious context the criterion of the meaning and interpretation of the Christian Gospel, on one hand, and letting the truth of the Christian Gospel or faith speak to the human condition in its particularity and then seeing how God speaks to the human being in a specific historical moment and space, without reducing God's truth into the by-product of this specific condition, on another."[28] It is because of this that the excessively socio-cultural voices of today's Arabic-speaking theologians need to be reconciled with, and grounded in, a systematic and dogmatic theological reasoning. It is this latter reasoning that helps the contextualised Arabic theological trends to reflect on the socio-cultural context, instead of mirroring it; and to contextually correlate the Gospel with their context without indigenising it. Systematic/dogmatic/constructive theology would remind these theologians that the core subject of theology is primarily God, not the human condition, and that theology is 'faith seeking understanding,' not 'context seeking religious legitimisation.'

Theology as '*fides quaraens intellectum*' means reflecting on, and analysing, the rationality and plausibility of the core message of faith. It does not seek the

---

[26] Awad, "How Should One Do Contextual Theology?" p. 210.
[27] Ibid., p. 215.
[28] Ibid., p. 216.

legitimisation of a certain context used for the demonstration of this faith's rationality. Theology, thus, as Aaron Langenfeld correctly notes, "can be understood as a systematic elaboration of the contents of a certain religious belief," which means that theology "has to face the task of justifying the rationality of the fundamental Christian belief that God has revealed Himself in the person of Christ Jesus."[29] It is indeed essential to pursue this rationalisation in relation to, and correlation with, a socio-cultural context, and not in a nebulous abstraction. Yet the danger lies in turning theology into a task for rationalising that mediating socio-cultural context to such an extent that theology turns from '*fides quaraens intellectum*' into '*contextus quaraens intellectum.*'

4. These models of theological voices are mostly *amnesiac* in perception. By 'amnesiac,' I mean that the contemporary trends of Arab-Eastern theological voices, which I discussed in the previous chapter, are not rooted in any kind of connectedness to the old traditions of theological reasoning that emerged and existed in the past history of Eastern Christianity, which once dominated the region that is now known as 'the Middle East and Northern Africa' (MENA region). We do not have here new theological discourses that endeavour to re-model the Arab-Eastern Christians' presence and witness in their homeland according to their historical, anthropological, existential, intellectual, and cultural affinity to, and rootedness in, Eastern Christianity and its theological (patristic) history. These recent voices hardly echo any discourse that is related to the theological legacies of either the Eastern Christianity of the early Islamic era, or to the theological, authoritative patristic theological legacies of antique and late antique Eastern Christianity. They are theological voices without memory, without *anamnesis*; thus, voices without a historical depth.

I have already touched upon the possibility of re-forming theological reasoning in the Middle East via understanding theologisation as an 'act of remembrance' (anamnesis).[30] I highlighted the tendency in the area of Religious Studies to deem 'religious remembrance' a practical endeavour both to correct the memory of the past and as a corrective to the present.[31] I then called for applying the same appreciation of 'remembrance' to the territory of theological reasoning in the Middle East. I argued that theology not only has memory. Theology itself *is* memory: it is a state of anamnesis (remembrance). From the anamnesis perspective, theology becomes "a chain of memory, that is, a form of

---

[29] Aaron Langenfeld, "The Moment of Truth: Comparative and Dogmatic Theology," in *How to Do Comparative Theology*, F. X. Clooney, S.J., and K. von Stoch (eds.) (New York: Fordham University Press, 2018), pp. 59–71, p. 60.

[30] See Najib George Awad, *After-Mission, Beyond Evangelicalism*, pp. 178–226.

[31] Ibid., p. 209. See also on this, Jakub Urbaniak, "Religion as Memory: How Has the Continuity of Tradition Produced Collective Meanings? – Part One," *HTS Teologiese Studies/Theological Studies*, 71(3), 2015, Art. 2815, pp. 1–8, p. 2. http://dx.doi.org/10.4102/hts.v71i3.2815. See also on memory, Paul Ricoeur, *Memory, History, Forgetting*, Kathleen Blamey and David Pellauer (trans.) (Chicago & London: The University of Chicago Press, 2004); Kurt Danziger, *Making the Mind: A History of Memory* (Cambridge and New York: Cambridge University Press, 2008); and Jacob H. Climo, Maria G. Catell et. al. (eds.) *Memory and History: Anthropological Perspectives* (Walnut Creek, CA: AltaMira Press, 2002).

collective memory and imagination based on the sanctity of tradition."[32] 'Theology as remembrance' designates this state of continuity of a shared historical engagement with reality that "manifests itself in the essentially religious act of recalling a past which gives meaning to the present and contains the future."[33] What the discussed Arabic-speaking theological trends lack is the development of theology by practising theological reasoning as "a medium of remembrance and anamnesic engagement with a hermeneutic process, which a particular community of faith pursues to re-view, re-read, and re-interact critically and epistemologically with its theology, historical narrative, and identity-formation from the perspective of its historical collective memory."[34]

Lacking any detectable connectedness to the past memory of the theological history in the Middle East indicates that today's Arab-Eastern theologians find it unnecessary to acknowledge, and be attentive to, "the central value in Christian faith of remembering where we come from theologically." This, consequentially, not only causes 'amnesia,' but also conflicts the contemporary theological voices with "historical *myopia*."[35] What current attempts at developing theological voices in the Arab Middle East need is a serious rooting of the theological understanding of today's context and challenges in the soil of a hermeneutical practice that is deeply founded on an engagement with a process of historical anamnesis. Such anamnesic hermeneutics would offer a theologising practice characterised by interaction and reciprocation, wherein the Christians discover "who they were called by God to become," not just "who they were," on the basis of a connection to those previous Christians who faced this same experience of self-awareness, or self-identification, through remembrance of them.[36]

I believe that one can find an explanation for the contemporary Arabic-speaking theologians' prioritisation of reasoning theologically on the present context and life challenges over any other form of cognitive enquiry. The dire and tormenting conditions of the Arab world today force the Christians, along with other communities, to focus rather singularly on the present and postpone any reflection on the past, or even any attempt to anticipate the future. This notwithstanding, the present conditions of the Arab Middle East are deeply grounded in the soil of this region's past historical complications, theological or non-theological, and narratives, whether secular or religious. Therefore, a relevant and effective theological reasoning in that particular region and *Sitz im Leben* cannot be constructed by means of a theological and historical detachment from 'what was before.' One cannot truly address the present by means of an

[32] Urbaniak, "Religion as Memory," p. 2. See also Danièlé Hervieu-Léger, *Religion as a Chain of Memory*, S. Lee (trans.) (New Brunswick: Rutgers University Press, 2000), pp. 4, 101.

[33] Urbaniak, "Religion as Memory," p. 2 and Hervieu-Léger, *Religion as a Chain of Memory*, p. 125.

[34] Awad, *After-Mission, Beyond Evangelicalism*, p. 209.

[35] Ibid., p. 210. See also Stefana D. Laing, *Retrieving History: Memory and Identity Formation in the Early Church* (Grand Rapids, MI: Baker Academic, 2017), pp. 2–11.

[36] Awad, *After-Mission, Beyond Evangelicalism*, p. 212. See also Laing, *Retrieving History*, pp. 20–25.

amnesiac theology. Only when theological reasoning is rooted in *anamnesis* can it have a liberating and salvific impact on the life of those who created it.[37] Attachment to collective theological memories will not only affect the Arabic-speaking Christians' connectedness to their present life-setting and contextual self-awareness. It will also deeply impact their understanding of the Bible, the theological traditions, and the spiritual heritage which they develop to relate to their life and context.[38] So far, such an attachment to memory and a systematised implementation of it in theological construction are noticeably lacking in the arena of theological reasoning in Arab-Eastern circles.

5. These trends of Arabic-speaking theological discourses are *multi-religious* and *Christian–Muslim* in orientation, whether they address Christian–Muslim relations as the central subject of the theological reasoning, or they have inter-religiosity as one of the driving presumptions in the theological reasoning's backdrop. In the contemporary Arab-Muslim context of the Arab East, the attention to the interreligious co-existence of the Christians and Muslims occupies centre stage.[39] Many Arab Christian theologians are deemed prominent in the dialogical undertaking in the Arab Middle East, like, for example, Adel Theodore Khoury, Paul Khoury, Mouchir Aoun, Kirillus Bustros, and Tarek Mitri, just to name a few.[40] Since the last two decades of the twentieth century, this attention has generated numerous local and international conferences, panels, workshops, and meetings on the ramifications and orientations of interreligious relations in that region. Some examples one can mention of the activities and outcomes that were generated for reflecting on, and fostering, interreligious relations in the region are the "Colloquium on Mutual Views and Changing Relations between Christians and Muslims" (University of Balamand, Lebanon, 27–29 August 1997); "Consultation on Cooperation in Christian–Muslim Studies" (Middle East Council of Churches [MECC], Beirut, 29–31 August 1997); "Charter for Dialogue of Life and Common Action" that was produced by the Arab Working Group on Muslim–Christian Dialogue (Cairo, Egypt, 20 December 2001); *Marqab al-'aych al-Mushtarak fī Lubnān* (The Observatory of Christian–Muslim Relations in Lebanon); International Conference on Muslim–Christian Dialogue entitled "Sustainability of Peace and Consolidation of National Unity" (Khartoum, Sudan, 4–6 July 2007); international conference entitled "Religion and the Rule of Law in the Near East" by the Royal Scientific Society (RSS) (Amman, Jordan, 27–28 February 2008);

---

[37] Awad, *After-Mission, Beyond Evangelicalism*, p. 213. See also on the salvific value of memory in theology, Miroslav Volf, *The End of Memory: Remembering Rightly in a Violent World* (Grand Rapids, MI and Cambridge: W.B. Eerdmans Publishing Company, 2006).

[38] Awad, *After-Mission, Beyond Evangelicalism*, p. 217.

[39] I derive the ensuing lines and ideas of this point from my previous writing on interreligious relations in the northern Mediterranean coasts and the western end of Asia. See Najib George Awad, "Inter-Religious Relations," in *Edinburgh Companion to Global Christianity: Christianity in North Africa and West Asia*, Kenneth R. Ross, Mariz Tadros, and Todd M. Johnson (eds.) (Edinburgh: Edinburgh University Press, 2018), pp. 383–393.

[40] These names are mentioned in George Sabra, "Theology," p. 329.

and the "Colloquium of Religion and Civil Society" organised by Royal Institute of Inter-Faith Studies (RIIFS) (Amman, Jordan, 18–20 May 2009).[41]

This attention to interreligious relations from the dimension of *dialogue* between faiths is undoubtedly important and central to any interreligious relationality. What might, however, be a weakness that we ought to beware of and to avoid as much as possible is reducing interreligious relationality into mere dialogues exclusively focusing on discussing the co-existence issue and no other. The theologians I mentioned above under the category of interreligious theology do try to take the interreligious dialogue in the Arab East beyond the narrow boundaries of the concern about co-existence by trying to root this dialogical connectedness in constructive theological reasoning on inter-religiosity as such. Yet this frank *theological* approach is still more promising and young compared with other, far more prevalent, trends in the Arab Middle East. It tends to foster Christian–Muslim dialogue not just to pursue an interreligious theological perception of the Christians and the Muslims in the region, but also to guarantee a state of peaceful and tolerant symbiosis between the communities of the two Abrahamic faiths. In the other trends of theological reasoning, we detect the overriding of the dialogical and procedural over the interrelational and symbiotic. This appears in the fact that the main enquiry that was addressed in the abovementioned religious dialogical conferences was the following: side-by-side with their religious claim of owning *alone* 'the truth,' do Christians and Muslims believe that a societal and political plurality is tenable in their co-existence and on the basis of each religion's acknowledgement of other religious communities' equal rights and upon a common willingness to cooperate in achieving ultimate good for all people?

Probing the core content of this enquiry reveals that the principal and notional perspective of this question exclusively centres on finding in the dialogical approach a space for securing from the other a filial, tolerant, and peaceful co-existence pledge in such a complex multi-religious context. The ultimate driving force behind the interlocution between religions becomes primarily existential, societal, and pragmatic (sometimes even implicitly kerygmatic) in nature, rather than interrelational, epistemological, or correlatively analytical-critical in orientation. Rather than meeting around a theologically, epistemologically, or intellectually driven interrelation, the dialogical inhabitants of this context often busy themselves with making the Christian–Muslim dialogue an instrument in the service of creating a possible state of co-existence that is capable of allowing people to live together in dignity, justice, accountability, and openness.[42] Such an orientation impoverishes any attempt at developing an interreligious *theology*, because it makes this attempt one-sided in nature: it focuses on 'praxis-ology' at the expense of 'theology' and on 'how to exist in a truce with the other' at the expense of 'what existence in relationship with another as such means for me and the other.' Such concentration may enable the Muslims and Christians to survive and live in parallel and side-by-side. However, it does not per se guarantee that these two religious communities understand truly each other's

---

[41] Awad, "Inter-Religious Relations," p. 386.

[42] Ibid., p. 387.

core identity and mindset that make each one of them who they are and not the other. Such an epistemic dimension is capable of transforming the existence of these two religious communities from a state of 'islands co-existing in one ocean' into a state of 'communities existing in a *symbiosis*': communities in mutual interaction and reciprocally influential interrelationality.[43]

The endeavour of some Arabic-speaking theologians to develop an interreligious *theological* discourse on Christian–Muslim relations and dialogue alike is one of the most valuable and appropriate moves the Christians opt for in the context of the Arab Middle East. In their attention to the central role theological reasoning plays in religions, these theological voices invite us to consider their conviction about the following fact: dialogical interrelationality derives its constituents and purposes from the theological understanding, which the religious person relies on to construct his or her view and interpretation of interrelation as '*inter*-religious relation' and of dialogue as '*inter*-relational dialogue.' If, for example, the religious person departed from an exclusivist/discriminative approach that denies any trace of divinity or truth in other religions, she or he will then get involved in a controversial debate and confrontational relation with the religious other. She or he will be focusing solely on casting suspicion on the other's cultural, ethical, and societal worth, let alone proving the falsehood of the other's belief system and endeavouring to win eventually this other into her or his own belief circle in a proselytising strategy. Such an interreligious interaction will not be dialogical, and it will fail in creating a symbiotic interrelationship, if not even threaten any already existing peaceful, tolerant state these religious communities survived together within. Even if the terminology, the manner of communication, the conversation strategies and rules of such an interaction were peaceful, reconciliatory, embracive, filial, and charitable, they will fail in availing the presumptive rationale that underpins these communication means and skills. In this case, what avails the potential for symbiosis will be the two sides' equal willingness to co-assess and co-scrutinise critically the theological understandings that bring them into the interreligious relation or dialogue with exclusivist and conflictive mentalities.[44]

6. It has been perceptively said that "religion is relation … theology revolves around relations: to oneself as other, to the other as other, and to God as the radical other." Theology, that is, is an affair immersed in "relational anxiety" and "experiences of alterity."[45] In the trends of Arab-Eastern Christian theological reasoning I expose in this study, one witnesses ideal examples of the understanding of theology's relational nature within the framework of the notions of 'relational anxiety' and 'experiential alterity' that depicts a vibrant, diverse, but also far from simplistic, 'black-versus-white' binary stance on the

---

[43] Ibid., p. 387.

[44] Ibid., p. 388.

[45] Ulrich Schmiedel, "(Instead of the) Introduction Open to the Other: The Dynamics of Difference in Werner G. Jeanrond's Hermeneutical Theology," in *Dynamics of Difference: Christianity and Alterity: A Festschrift for Werner G. Jeanrond*, Ulrich Schmiedel and James M. Matarazzo, Jr. (eds.) (London & New York: Bloomsbury T&T Clark, 2016), pp. 1–16, p. 1. See also Werner G. Jeanrond, *Call and Response: The Challenge of Christian Life* (New York: Continuum, 1995).

'other' within oneself and the 'other' against it alike. Each group of the Arab-Eastern theologians I introduce displays in his or her theological discourse a particular relational awareness of his or her Christian identity and existence in an anxious, sometimes alarmed, alterity stance on otherness and the different religious other in the heart of the Arab-Eastern existence and co-existence circles. For these Arab-Eastern theologians, this other is predominantly Islam and the Muslims, sometimes the Jews (but not necessarily 'Judaism': the attention to the Jews is solely connected to the Palestinian–Israeli conflict). Yet this 'other' is not (or not any more, in today's Arab world) the different Christian other. Alterity with the Christian other (e.g., the other Protestants and Catholics for the historically more indigenous Orthodox Christians of the land) is no longer a source of relational, theological anxiety as once it was during the nineteenth and the first half of the twentieth centuries, when Protestant and Catholic missionary workers from Europe, the UK, and the USA were still present and construed as a foreign threat to the mother ecclesial traditions (Orthodox Chalcedonian and non-Chalcedonian) of the land.

In today's contemporary Arab-Eastern theology, it is Islam and the Muslim-majority reality of the region that presents the source of experiential alterity and relational anxiety in today's Arab-Eastern theology. The majority of the Arab-Eastern theologians, male and female, more or less demonstrate in their discourses their consensual concurrence with the conviction that "Christianity is not interpreted as the restoration of tradition, but as the creation and re-creation of tradition through communication with the other [or, with the non-Christian other]."[46] The question for them here is, how can the theologian transform the anxiety towards the other's alterity from a source of hostility and threat into a motivating instrument for communication and understanding?

One of the primary features of these Arab-Eastern theologians' methods of pursuing this transformation task surfaces in their refusal to view or consider the non-Christian other they co-exist with as foe, binary antithesis, contrasting rival, or alien foreigner. The Muslim other and his or her Islam for them is just a completing other, a partnering other, a neighbour, an interlocutor in a dialogue, not in a polemic–apologetic binarism. Each one of the theological trends of reasoning we encountered (even the protectionist and self-enclosed one, though in its particular manner and terms) echoes in its own way and strategies of interpretation a belief once voiced by Hans-Georg Gadamer; namely, that the event of understanding happens through dialogue.[47] On this dialogical nature of theological understanding of/from the other, David Tracy perceptively relates:

> Ontologically, dialogue is a particular kind of game. As in any game, the conversation is destroyed if controlled by the self-consciousness of the players. A self-conscious actor, like any self-important player in any game, destroys the game

[46] Schmiedel, "(Instead of the) Introduction Open to the Other…," p. 9. See also Werner G, Jeanrond, "Belonging or Identity? Christian Faith in a Multi-Religious World," in *Many Mansions? Multiple Religious Belonging and Christian Identity*, Catherine Cornille (ed.) (Maryknoll: Orbis Books, 2002), pp. 106–120.

[47] H. G Gadamer, *Truth and Method*, pp. 362–379.

> by refusing or being unable to enter any game with others since he or she is trapped in the only game he or she knows – his or her own ego drama.[48]

The Arab-Eastern theologians studied here do not endeavour to control or hegemonise self-consciously the dialogue-game with the co-existing other. They do not at all refuse to enter the game with the other. They are not caged behind the bars of a Christian 'ego drama.' They openly dialogue with their Muslim-majority, existential reality, even when the circumstances of this reality are not characteristic of a game he or she already knows. They embrace the risky factor in theologising while the other is dialogically always present, consciously or unconsciously, explicitly or implicitly, in the mind: "In dialogue, the self is not in control; the other … must be in control … the self experiences understanding (*logos*) only through (*dia*) the dialogical event of understanding the other … the other [that is] as a genuine alterity to the self, not as a projected other posed by the self."[49]

What enables these Arab-Eastern theologians to pursue theological reasoning by means of, and not despite, the abovementioned risk is the fact that they neither treat the Muslim and his or her Islam as a foreign reality; nor do they deem themselves, and their Christianity, a foreign entity in the land of Islam. In their theological discourses, these theologians discern, or envision, a Christianity living side by side with Islam and aspiring at reaching a "successful co-existence in which everyone stays who they are, nobody is assimilated, and nevertheless an exchange happens in which the dignity of the other is respected and reinforced."[50] In their theological reasoning with otherness and alterity in perspective, these theologians understand 'foreignness' in the senses of 'difference' and 'distinction,' not in the senses of 'alienation' and 'antagonism.' So, the Muslim other's foreignness (that is, particularity) and the Christian self's foreignness (that is, individuation) are neither negated after a model of equality and assimilation that deems difference intolerable; nor are they morphed into a starkly binary form of alterity and self-othering, where the foreignness of the other means "there is no possibility of recognition … [and] this radical other can provoke fear or fascination, but he or she cannot prompt mutual respect."[51] Here, foreignness is indeed still a challenge in these theologians' reasoning. Yet, it is a positively motivating and inspiring challenge. Theologising becomes a

---

[48] David Tracy, "The Other of Dialectic and Dialogue," in *Dynamics of Difference*, pp. 105–114, p. 109.

[49] Ibid., p. 110.

[50] Achieving a theoretical understanding of the fulfilment of this possibility was aspired at in 1935 in Theo Sundermeier, *Den Fremden Verstehen: Eine praktische Hermeneutik* (Göttingen: Vendenhoeck und Ruprecht, 1996). See also on this project Pierre Bühler, "Foreignness as Focal Point of Otherness," in *Dynamics of Difference*, pp. 153–159, pp. 154–156.

[51] Bühler, "Foreignness as Focal Point of Otherness," p. 155. See also Pierre Bühler, "Ricoeur's Concept of Distinction as a Challenge for Theological Hermeneutics," in *Paul Ricoeur: Poetics and Religion*, Joseph Verheyden, Theo L. Hettema, and Peter Vandecosteele (eds.) (Leuven: Peeters, 2011), pp. 151–165.

fortunate space wherein "the confrontation with one's own foreignness has to be inspired and instigated by a foreignness which is not one's own."[52]

This substantial and organic symbiosis of Arab-Eastern theological foreignness with that of Islam does not mean that the Arab-Eastern theologians necessarily echo the voice of a community who deems itself powerless before its co-existing partner and, therefore, submissive to it. It just indicates that these Christians never consider themselves a group of alien outsiders in faith and culture striving to survive in a foreign land and in a society full of enemies. They, rather, volitionally accept the dependence factor that acknowledges one's principal, *a priori* need for 'the other.'[53] From the angle of this sense of dependence, theological reasoning, as Glenn Morrison succinctly suggests, "unfolds as a gift of passivity [that is, having a heart for the other]. Passivity, then, is an essential component of otherness."[54] In their theological thinking, these contemporary Arab-Eastern theologians do not primarily treat the non-Christian, Middle Eastern other (especially the Muslim) as someone 'opposite' to, or someone 'like' them, but as "someone different."[55]This is a blunt manifestation of the fact that, contrary to the Western imagination of binary, dialectical, and a survival-obsessed, parallelism state of existence (see chapter three), the Arab-Eastern Christians live, perceive themselves, and think theologically of a Christianity inherent to the Arab-Muslim world and part and parcel of its self-understanding, experiences, and circumstances.

Finally, the overview of the nine displayed trends of theological reasoning in this study are all pregnant with the *potential* of representing coherent, fully-fledged, complete *theologies*. Yet, as they are right now, they are still *prospectively* 'theologies' in nature and content. Theology per se is, in fact, far from a static block of statements, ideas, and views related to a particular religious belief. 'Theology' by nature is a *process*, an *activity*, a *journey*. A particular discourse and discoursing trajectory related to, and grounded in, a particular religious belief, or *Weltanschauung*, can *become* 'theology' when it succeeds in articulating the fundamental components of a certain faith and interpreting them in such a manner that corrects, clarifies, and expands the meaning, implications, and applications of these faith elements. The potential becoming-theology enterprise, therefore, is a process determined by temporality: it *happens* as "a process of discernment and reflection [that is] guided by purpose and a sense of mission"; a process that "necessarily must also face the maturation of time and test [its] relevance and reflection."[56] Be that as it may, these nine trends of Arabic-Oriental theological reasoning are still experiments in progress, quests in the making, sojourners on the trajectory towards *becoming* a 'theology.' It is my

[52] Bühler, "Foreignness as Focal Point of Otherness," p. 156. This is something that has been highlighted also in Paul Ricoeur, *Oneself as Another*, K. Blamey (trans.) (Chicago: University of Chicago Press, 1992), pp. 297–356.

[53] Anne-Louise Eriksson, "The Other on the Cross," in *Dynamics of Difference*, pp. 173–180, p. 176.

[54] Glenn Morrison, *A Theology of Alterity: Levinas, von Balthasar and Trinitarian Praxis* (Pittsburg, Penn: Duquesne University Press, 2013), p. 2

[55] Eriksson, "The Other on the Cross," p. 178.

[56] Morrison, *A Theology of Alterity*, p. 2.

humble belief that they will become so if they heed the above stated corrections and assessments I propose in this chapter, and if they maintain their already positive and valuable rootedness in the notions of 'relationality,' 'otherness,' and 'alterity' that make them directly and indirectly always reflect theologically on the Arab-Eastern Christian existence in its specific *Sitz im Leben* and in an awareness of otherness that is genuinely related to the factual, not imaginary, and real, not wished-for, non-Christian other. Will they manage to *become* 'theology' eventually? This is yet to be seen upon the horizon of their future, as these theological voices continue moving forward towards maturity.

Concluding Remarks

In this study, I endeavoured to demonstrate that the driving motif and ruling rationale behind the various forms of theological reasoning in the contemporary Arab-Eastern Christian context are, in fact, far from just theological, or faith-centred, in nature or focus. Tarek Mitri, the Lebanese Antiochene/Roman Orthodox scholar and statesman, is not far from truth when he realises that "the specific nature and limitation of [the] interpretation of the history of Christians in the contemporary Arab East resides in the fact that it plows ahead between the general political, social, and cultural spheres, on the one hand, and the ecclesiastical domain, on the other."[1] Mitri goes further in arguing that the challenges the Arabic-speaking Christians face in their homeland exceed the alarming decline of their numbers and the swelling of their emigration rate. The more radical challenge they face, Mitri relates, is "the ever-widening expression of concern about Christian participation in politics and culture and with apprehension about the future."[2] There was a time during the nineteenth century when the Christians had their elite groups and voices that enabled them to pioneer a substantial and influential role of liberation and progress in the Arab Middle East. This role shaped the Christians' life as well as the life of their Muslim co-citizens. This achievement bestowed upon the Christians the chance to regain "an effective role which they had already played in the period of the establishment of Islamic Arab civilization."[3] Yet, according to Mitri, this privileged situation started to regress consistently throughout the second half of the twentieth century. What the Christians in the Arab Middle East were left with, due to this recession, is the restricted potential of playing a societal role primarily, if not exclusively, through religious thinking. Mitri eloquently articulates this outcome in words that merit full citation:

> The contribution of Christians in the cultural, social, and political life was not specifically of a 'Christian' reference except to a very limited extent … the 'Christian' role of Christians and its influence in public life appears in a special way through religious thought and its responsiveness to the needs of society as a whole in the face of the challenges of the contemporary world.[4]

It is such a context like the one perceptively diagnosed by Tarek Mitri that lingers beneath the various discourses of Arabic-speaking Christians, which they dress with the garment of 'theology' and no other. 'Theology' here is just a language game, an expression and communication style that hides beneath it a

---

[1] Tarek Mitri, "Christians in the Arab East: An Interpretation of Contemporary History," in *Christianity: A History in the Middle East*, Habib Badr, et. al. (eds.) (Beirut: The Middle East Council of Churches, 2001), pp. 851–869, p. 851.

[2] Ibid., p. 856.

[3] Ibid., p. 857.

[4] Ibid., p. 858.

far more essential socio-political, cultural, existential, and interreligious concerns and motifs rooted in an attempt at regaining the ability to play an influential and meaningful role in the excessively religious context of the Arab world. Conjuring up specifically *theological* thought to play a role in their homeland is these Christians' endeavour to express before the broader Muslim-majority environment a genuine keenness to identify with the recent circumstances, conditions, expectations, and crises of the Arab world, and to obtain the strength they need to attend to its requirements and expectations.[5] These Christians, thus, try to develop Arabic-speaking theological voices in order to say to their Muslim co-citizens, in a language comprehensible to them, "we exist here, we belong here, and we want to give whatever this 'here' needs to survive."

Be the above as it may, it is quite a perceptive and realistic decision from the Arabic-speaking Christians to try to play a role in the Arab Middle East via religious thought and to develop *theological*, or theology-like, discourses on their living context, rather than purely political, social, cultural, or secular ones. Opting for the creation of Arabic-speaking Eastern-Christian theology is the more relevant and needed discourse, particularly in light of the aftermath of the 'Arab Spring' experience within the Arab countries. The 'Arab Spring' wreaked havoc on the region, caused a resurgence of religiosity, and renewed the role of the religious webs of meaning and worldviews in the transitional process which both the societies and the states are going through in the Arab world.[6] This is so despite the perpetual declaration of all sides therein, the Islamists included, that they dream of establishing civil, pluralist, democratic, and human rights-based states and societies. Such an Arab Spring aftermath indicates, as I noticed elsewhere, that "the socio-political re-building process is inevitably exposed to a 'theologisation' attempt and its being clothed with religious garbs."[7]

It seems to me that all the theologians discussed in this study reflect serious attention to, and concern about, the fact that "the Arab Christians find themselves living in a specific setting, wherein one's religious background inevitably shapes, even dictates, the other's reception and perception of whatever one contributes to society, whether the contributor personally wanted to act in society from a sober, deliberate emphasis on his or her religious affiliation and beliefs

---

[5] Ibid., pp. 863–865.

[6] Najib G. Awad, *And Freedom Became a Public Square*, pp. 135–139. See also on the Arab Spring's religious ramifications, Jason Browless, Tarek Masoud, and Andrew Reynolds, *The Arab Spring: Pathways of Repression and Reform* (Oxford: Oxford University Press, 2015); Tariq Ramadan, *Islam and the Arab Awakening* (Oxford & New York: Oxford University Press, 2012); Marc Lynch, *The Arab Uprising: The Unfinished Revolutions of the New Middle East* (New York, NY: Public Affairs, 2012); James L. Galvin, *the Arab Uprisings: What Everyone Needs to Know* (Oxford & New York: Oxford University Press, 2012); Tom Henghan, "Arab Spring and the Rise of Political Islam," in www.muslimvillage.com, 1 November 2011 [accessed 12.2.2024]; Patrick Seal, "The Rise of Political Islam," in www.gulfnews.com, 28 October 2011 [accessed 12.2.2024]; and Ahmad H. al-Rahim, "Whither Political Islam and the 'Arab Spring'?" in *The Hedgehog Review*, Fall 2011, pp. 8–22.

[7] Awad, *And Freedom Became a Public Square*, p. 135.

or not."[8] This situation necessitates the development of clear and definable theological discourses, right from the outset. Such theological attempts cannot but rationalise about, and offer hermeneutics on, the political, social, cultural, anthropological, and existential thinking of the Arabic public spheres. By developing such theological trends, the Christians would be "calling for freeing the religious element of the Arab's identity from any magical world-view or naïve understanding of the relationship with the different religious other."[9]

The challenge that any contemporary Arabic-speaking Eastern theology, from any perspective, is yet to theologically tackle, think about, and interpret is the 'Arab Spring' itself and its ramifications and consequences. None of the Arabic-speaking theologians (save for the author of this study) has yet seriously paused at the Arab Spring per se and tried to develop a theological hermeneutics *from*, *within*, and *about* the Christians' situation, self-perception, and worldviews in the framework of that pivotal historical moment. Would such a theologisation ever happen inside the realm of the Arab world? What kind of theological voices would we hear the Arabic-speaking Christians echoing on this in the coming years, if such a theology was ever created? These questions, and many relevant others, remain totally open to all the possible answers the future may bring forth.

One can, nevertheless, pause at the overall post-Arab Spring situation in the Arab Middle East and ponder the Christians' conditions in their homeland in its aftermath. I would be deluding the reader if I said that the overall picture of the Arab world at the moment is less than pitch black and devastating. After the administration of the American president Barack Obama co-signed the nuclear agreement with Iran, a new catastrophic era was inaugurated in the Arab Middle East. The Iranians were granted the permission to dominate over that region and to oversee it unreservedly. For the Iranians, this meant reviving the old historical Sasanian, imperial hegemony over the region, except this time the ancient imperial dream was implemented in the service of proliferating the staunchly religious and sectarian Khomeini's Shi'ite Revolution to the pre-dominantly Sunnite-majority Arab region and, if possible, Shi'itising the adjacent Arab countries as radically as possible. In order to achieve this dream, the Iranians decided to shake the foundations of the Arab countries from within. It pursued this by, first, supporting the hegemonic usurpation of the Muslim Brotherhood (the Sunnite equivalent of the Shi'ite pan-religious and theocratic Iranian Revolution ideology) of the Arab Spring revolutions and then endorsing their subsequent power seizure in Tunisia, Egypt, and Libya. Then, second, and as the central instrument for fulfilling its expansionist and despotic dream, the Iranian Mulla's regime spread an ideology called "Alliance of Minorities" (*ḥilf al-aqalliyyāt*). This ideological discourse called all the minorities in the Middle East, like Shi'ites, Christians, Jews, Kurds, Copts, etc., to unite and form one confrontational front to balance the scale of the prevalent presence and role of the Muslim Sunnite community in the region.

Those among the Arab-Eastern Christians who rejected this 'Alliance of Minorities' project and withstood it intellectually and existentially, remember in

---

[8] Awad, *And Freedom Became a Public Square*, p.136.

[9] Ibid., p. 137.

sadness that there were Christian factions and groups who, rather, embraced this call and joined this alliance at full scale. This took place in Iraq, Lebanon, and Syria (the central Arab countries within the Iranian 'Shi'ite Crescent' project in the heart of the Arab Middle East). Little, so it seems, had these Christians known that such an alliance project would be doomed to catastrophic failure and fall into irreparable peril. In Lebanon, the Shi'ite militia, *Ḥizbullah*, allied with the radical rightist Christian party, 'The National Free Party' (*al-Taiyyār al-Waṭanī al-Ḥurr*), which granted this latter party's Maronite leader, Michael Aoun, the chance to become the president of the country. As of today, this 'Alliance of Minorities' case in point in Lebanon led the country into total collapse, so much so that Lebanon today is a frank example of a 'failed state' situation and the Christians of Lebanon started to react to this catastrophic situation by calling for the application of a crude federal system in the country and the separation of the Christians' living zones from those of the Muslims. Segregation and division are what the Christians ended up calling for, instead of the 'Alliance of Minorities'' delusional call for unity and cohesion.

In Iraq, the situation of the Christians on the post-Saddam Iraqi scene is disastrous on all fronts (given the fact that Iraq also is in a 'failed-state' situation and all communities in the country from all backgrounds are suffering, save the Shi'ites, who are full servants of the Iranian agenda). Some of the Christian communities in that country decided to also join an 'Alliance of Minorities' with the now dominating and sweeping Shi'ite communities and factions (who declare explicitly and wholeheartedly their allegiance to Iran and to the Shi'ite Imamate ideology), hoping thereby to guarantee themselves survival, security, and a relativelu peaceful life in the heart of the new situation of the country. As of today, this alliance attempt too has drastically failed, as the Sunnites of Iraq reacted very aggressively and negatively to it by threatening the lives of the Christians and forcing hundreds of thousands of them to pursue internal migration inside the country and overseas immigration into the West. Most recently, the Patriarch of the Chaldean Catholic Church of Iraq (the largest Christian community in the country), Lūwīs Rūfā'īl Cardinal Sākū, was forced into exile from his patriarchal seat in Baghdad due to pressures exerted on him personally and an attempt from some powerful sides to confiscate the properties of the church. The prelate was forced to resort to one of the monasteries in the environs of Arbil, the capital of Iraqi Kurdistan. Prior to this, the churches in Baghdad and in other parts of Iraq were frequently the victims of radical Muslim suicide-bombing incidents. Again, the 'Alliance of Minorities' project did not save the Christians of Iraq from becoming scapegoats in a sectarian, Shi'ite–Sunnite clash, which they have no part to play in and cannot be held accountable for.

On the dire situation of the Christians in post-September 11 Iraq, Lūwīs Rūfā'īl Cardinal Sākū spoke in the *Pro Oriente* conference of 2010. The Cardinal related that Iraq suffered from radical transformation that had turned the land into a haven of terrorism in the aftermath of the invasion of Iraq. First, the radical Islamists who flooded into the land were foreigners and they formed sporadically dispersed pockets. However, the Cardinal proceeded, they were now (in 2010) in control of various locations inside the country, and striving to establish a

Muslim caliphal state. This, Cardinal Sākū affirms, threatens the existence of Christians and Jews, as these radicals preach one religion and one culture, namely (their own version of) Islam.[10] On the Iraqi Christians' situation, Cardinal Sākū stated the following:

> Christians have become a specific target, and the conditions have deteriorated at an increasing pace, and it is sometimes hard to quantify the extent of the persecution in some cities like Baghdad and Mosul, where we witness kidnappings, ransom, torture, and executions. The armed extremists threatened to kill the Christians if they did not convert to Islam … Christians have to convert immediately to Islam or to consign their property and leave the country, or to pay a monetary tribute (*djiziya*) to the Jihad if they want to avoid their death.[11]

Cardinal Sākū's proposed response to this situation centres around his appeal to the moderate Muslims, who are the majority, to start promoting 'religious harmony and tolerance' in society and to prove praxically and factually to the world that Islam is not a religion of hatred and killing of innocent civilians.[12] By voicing out such a call, the Iraqi prelate is stressing that moderation and tolerance are the predominant stances characteristic of Islam and the majority of the Muslims in his country. He is not, that is, invoking the tragic conditions of the Christians in the development of a radical, totally condemning, and demonising discourse against Islam. He, rather, states that it is the duty of the persecuted Christians, and because of their persecution not despite it, to "bridge for and push forward the culture of dialogue, peace, and conviviality"[13] in the present Iraq. "This is our task" and no other, despite everything we suffer from, insists Cardinal Sākū candidly and admirably. He points to some positive examples of conviviality and tolerance experienced between the Christians and the Muslims in some parts of today's Iraq, like the region of Kirkuk. On this experience, Cardinal Sākū says: "In Kirkuk we have [a] nice relationship. We meet often with the imams. We offer a dinner to Muslims and political leaders during Ramaḍan. We respect Muslims as they are and, on the other hand, they should respect us as we are."[14]

Finally, the same "Alliance of Minorities" strategy was marketed and proliferated among the Christians and the Alawites in Syria during the decade-or-more-long revolution against the Asadi-Baathist regime in the country. The Iranians, the staunch allies and patrons of the al-Assad regime since the rule of al-Assad senior, fully supported the regime in its mass-elimination campaign against the Syrian public, and it deployed tens of militarised phalanges into Syria (besides the tens of billions of US dollars it invested in the country) to protect the regime. The Iranian regime justified its meddling in the Syrian scene by claiming that it protects the rule of a minority from the atrocities and inimical

---

[10] Lūwīs Rūfā'īl Cardinal Sākū, "Relations between Christians and Muslims in Iraq – A Brief Statement," in *Syriac Churches Encountering Islam: Past Experiences and Future Perspectives*, Dietmar W. Winkler (ed.) (Piscataway, NJ: Gorgias Press, 2010), pp. 219–221, p. 219.

[11] Ibid., p. 220.

[12] Ibid., p. 220.

[13] Ibid., p. 220.

[14] Ibid., pp. 220–221.

attempts of the Sunnite majority. In order to recruit the public's support for its presence within the Syria territories, the 'Alliance of Minorities' propaganda was employed to lure the Christians toward embracing the Alawite regime and refusing to join the revolution. This was backed up with the allegation that it is exclusively a 'Sunnite' revolution against the other minorities in the country.

Today, and after thirteen years of the conflict, the Christians' percentage in Syria dropped radically down from 10% before the revolution into hardly 3–5% today, and it is our anticipation that in the coming decade or so, the percentage will possibly drop down to 1% or even 0.5%.[15] Most of the Christians, especially the quiescent majority who implicitly refused to support al-Assad's despotic, corrupt, and criminal regime, painstakingly found a way to flee from their homeland either into the neighbouring countries, like Turkey, Lebanon, Egypt, and Jordan, or towards Europe and other parts of the world. Those among the Syrian Christians (especially the clerical leadership of all the denominations), who embraced the 'Alliance of Minorities' agenda and stood behind the regime, ended up creating an unbridgeable gap between them and the remaining Sunnite majority in the country. They are looked at – at least by the 12 million Syrian refugees who were uprooted and forced to resort to camps and cities outside the country – as no longer compatriotic siblings, but as strange, foreign others and far from trustworthy counterparts.

In 2010, in the same *Pro Oriente* conference where Cardinal Sākū spoke about the present situation of Iraq, Mor Yūḥannā Ībrāhīm, the bishop of the Syriac Orthodox Diocese of Aleppo, Syria, spoke also about the present situation of the Christians in pre-revolution/war Syria (the revolution kicked off in March 2011). In his paper, Bishop Ībrāhīm leaned heavily on the positive Christian–Muslim co-existence that characterised the history of the Christians' existence and role in the past times of the Muslim-majority Middle East. He seemed to be building on this positive history his hope and aspirations about the present and the future, despite the difficulties and challenges inflicted on the life of the people of the region in the present.[16] In contrast to the dark picture of the Christians' present life in Iraq, the picture Bishop Ībrāhīm presented of Syria, especially in Aleppo (the seat of his episcopal diocese), emphasised ecumenism, dialogue, and tolerance, not just among Christians and Muslims, but also among the various Christian denominations in the country. He related that these various communities and faith groups concentrate in today's Syria (the one of 2010) on dialogues of "practical, applicable nature: Dialogue of Life, Dialogue of Work, Dialogue of Experience; and they call for enhanced understanding of the applicable culture of co-existence that is an every-day reality."[17] Bishop Ībrāhīm

[15] In a demographic study published in 2018, it was estimated that the Christian population in North Africa and West Asia declined from 7% (12 million) of the Arab population in 1970, down to 5% (25 million) of the overall population in 2015. See: Gina A. Zurlo, "A Demographic Profile of Christianity in North Africa and West Asia," in *Christianity in North Africa and West Asia*, Kenneth R. Ross, Mariz Tadros, and Todd M. Johnson (eds.) (Edinburgh: Edinburgh University Press, 2018), pp. 3–14.

[16] Mor Bishop Ībrāhīm, "Culture and Coexistence in Syria," in *Syriac Churches Encountering Islam*, pp. 222–228, pp. 223–224.

[17] Ibid., p. 226.

did not convey to his audience a picture of Christians experiencing an insufferable persecution from radical Muslims, as we saw in the report of the Catholic Cardinal from Iraq. He merely emphasised the principal significance of the culture of co-existence as necessary and vital for carrying the mission of the Church, not only in Syria, but in the entire region. He uttered this emphatically, affirming that "Christians in Syria are neither strangers nor allies. They are the people of the land and citizens of the state."[18]

Let us here remember what I earlier pointed out, that this testimony was made before the beginning of the revolution and the ensuing war in Syria, which led to the abduction of Bishop Ībrāhīm himself, whose fate remains totally unknown to this day. The Syrian people in general, and the Christians among them, suffer today from incredibly inhumane living conditions and a bleak forecasted future. What one can realise from the above testimonies of the two prominent church prelates from Syria and Iraq are the noticeable discrepancies between how each one of them experiences the situation of his Christian community in his homeland and living environment. This demonstrates quite realistically the broad diversity of the present life-conditions and existential circumstances the Arab-Eastern Christians live in and survive under, each in his or her particular *Sitz im Leben*. One must not, therefore, approach this Christianity as single, monolithic, and statically amassed entity. One must rather discern the multiplicity, plurality, multiformity, and pluri-contextuality of these Christians' existence, not just politically, socially, and culturally, but also theologically.

I have waited till the end of this study to speak about this direly catastrophic situation which the Christians, but also all other communities in the region, suffer from to the core of their existence because there is not yet any considerable, coherent, and fully-fledged *theological* discourse developed by the Arabic-speaking Christian theologians of the region on their present diverse situations. All these various catastrophic circumstances can be deemed consequences of the post-Arabic Spring context (though this is not meant to mean that the drastic, catastrophic life-conditions and deadly experiences are recent in the region; they are much older and far more complex than one single scenario or narrative). Throughout the past couple of years, I have produced various writings in Arabic and English to analyse, deconstruct, and interpret this context from different interdisciplinary perspectives. What is still unachieved is a fully-fledged theological reasoning on the 'Arabic Spring' and 'Alliance of Minorities' phenomena. The Arab-Eastern Christians need to engage seriously in a meticulous, candid, piercing, and critical thinking on the nature, impact, validity, ramifications, and stances of such phenomena from a frank and direct *theological* perspective rooted in their Christian faith, history, and role in their homeland.

The core issue here is not whether or not the Arab-Eastern Christians produce writings on the situation in the Middle East, but whether what they produce is *theological* in nature and orientation or not. It is unfortunate that, so far, the signs point almost fully towards the first option instead of the second. Most recently, the Palestinian Lutheran theologian Mitri Raheb edited yet another anthology on Christianity in the Middle East, this time aiming at displaying the Arab-Eastern

[18] Ibid., p. 227–228.

Christians' situation in the twenty-first century. When one reads the contributors' essays in this anthology, one easily notices the absence of any conspicuous, targeted, and intended analyses of the situation from any theological perspective. Raheb himself introduces the entire volume with an interesting, comprehensive exposition of all the political, social, and economic challenges and circumstances the Christians (and the Muslims) of the region experienced during the past two decades. He starts with the Israeli atrocities against the Palestinian territories, moves into 11 September 2001 and the war against terrorism in Iraq, to the situation in Lebanon, to the situation in the Arab countries after the Arab-Spring era down to Syria's revolution (which he mistakenly calls 'civil war,' something actually far from reality). He correctly states that "the events of the Arab Spring presented a huge challenge for the people of the Middle East, and particularly for the Christians of the region."[19] Raheb does not pause just at the microcosmic situations of the Christians in every Arab Middle Eastern country. He also looks at the bigger, macrocosmic picture of the geopolitical context of the region, and he proposes a number of challenges that are facing the Arab-Eastern Christians of the region in the foreseeable future. He founds his anticipated challenges on the *Arab Human Development Report* of 2022 and its statistics and calculations regarding the population's rate. Therein, he highlights the refugees' situation to be the primary challenge the Christians face in the foreseeable future, with the Palestinian and Syrian refugees constituting "the largest number of refugees globally with over six million each."[20]

Raheb moves into naming dire circumstances that jeopardise the life and existence of the Arab-Eastern Christians in the Middle East. He refers to the fact of these Christians' existence in "countries with [a] high risk of conflict" and in living environments paralysed by an almost totally demolished infrastructure.[21] He then refers to the demographic explosion in the MENA region, with one of the highest birth rates in the world within the Muslim populations. "Lower birth rates among the Middle Eastern Christians," Raheb maintains, "and the migration patterns that have resulted from the brain drain or wars, unrest, and occupation … have resulted in a steady decline in their total percentage of the population."[22] Raheb adds to these factors the challenge of the region's access to water, since this zone has only "1.4 percent of global water resources" and "over two hundred million people are exposed to water stress that puts increased pressure on groundwater sources."[23] The problem of militarisation also finds its way into Raheb's list of crises, as "five of the top ten most militarised countries globally are found in the Middle East … Ranked by military spending per capita, six of the seven top countries are found in the Middle East."[24] Another challenge

---

19 Mitri Raheb, "Introduction," in *In the Eye of the Storm: Middle Eastern Christians in the Twenty-First Century*, Mitri Raheb (ed.) (Eugene, OR: Pickwick Publications, 2023), pp. 1–12, p. 6.

20 Ibid., p. 7.

21 Ibid., p. 7.

22 Ibid., p. 8.

23 Ibid., p. 9.

24 Ibid., p. 9.

Raheb points to is the region's vulnerability to climate change, "as it is one of the world's driest and most water-scarce regions with [a] high dependency on climate-sensitive agriculture."[25] Raheb, then, ends his report by pointing to the challenge of "a huge divide between the oil-exporting countrics ... and oil-importing countries" in thc region. His conclusion from this survey is the following:

> Geopolitically speaking, Christians in the twenty-first century Middle East are not major players and have seldom been the immediate target of regional politics. Yet, like their Muslim compatriots, they are directly affected by the overall geopolitical context ... Nevertheless, Christians have repeatedly proven themselves to be a resilient community despite all the challenges, and capable at times not only of surviving but of thriving.[26]

Reading the introductory pages and the ensuing essays of this mentioned volume leave the serious reader, who seeks depth and analytical engagement with critical and hermeneutical rigor, disappointed and even puzzled. Almost all the information the volume divulges to the reader is exhaustively descriptive and hardly analytical in nature. It is written in an almost journalistic manner, rather a than forensic, scholarly one. In today's telecommunication era, one can easily collect the very same information and data which Raheb and his volume's co-contributors offer, directly from the internet. One does not need a whole anthology to do so. On the other hand, Raheb is a 'theologian' and 'church servant' in specialisation. We do not need him to play the journalist's or reporter's role, but to benefit, instead, from his bright and piercing theological mind. One can understand that this new anthology on the Christians in the Middle East is just one of many popular, or even populist, publications that are liked by the lay readership in the United States of America and the Western context as a whole, where people prefer to have what they seek to know, especially about the global south-eastern world, served to them in light portions. And Raheb has been skilfully preparing such portions for the American readership in the 'reader-digest' publications he has been producing for American publishers in the past few years.

Back in 2018, the Lebanese Protestant theologian George Sabra contributed an essay on theology in the Middle East to an anthology on Christianity in North Africa and West Asia produced by Edinburgh University Press. In this essay, Sabra tackles precisely the question of the presence of theological reasoning, its nature and characteristics, and the potentials of its creation in the Middle Eastern Christian context. He departs from a generic preconception of 'theology' as a reflection on Christian faith and the relations of this to different dimensions of intellectual, social, and political life in the context of the contemporary Middle East. Sabra's survey of the Christian publications that were produced in that region between 1950 and 1990 drives him to conclude that "the majority of writings were of a devotional and homiletical nature and that very little had been produced in the area of systematic reflection on contemporary issues of thought

[25] Ibid., p. 10.

[26] Ibid., pp. 10–11.

and life."[27] He maintains that this is still more or less the case, with a noticeable increase in the "historical and liturgical theological writings," as well as the apologetical ones that emerged as a response to the suffering and persecution experiences of the Christians in the region. Sabra correctly notices that theology in the Middle East is predominantly inspired "by issues arising from society," rather than issues arising from the academy (like philosophy and the sciences) or from the necessity of interpreting the Gospel of the Church.[28] Drawn by the societal and contextual factors of their life in the world of Islam and with Muslims, the Christians in the Middle East develop theological discourses, the subjects of which are deeply rooted in the challenges Christians encounter in their co-existence with Muslims: being treated as a minority in a land dominated by another religion. So, the theologians of that region try to make theological sense of the role of Christianity in the world of Islam and to develop discourses on how Christianity can incorporate Islam into its own religious perception.[29] Another niche of theological reasoning on, and in contact with, Islam which Sabra notices circles around the theme of Christian–Muslim dialogue,[30] and also a theological reasoning on Christian identity and cultural heritage from the perspective of the question of what does it mean to be a Christian in the larger Islamic world?[31] Sabra does not also forget the Arab–Israeli conflict and its impact on the life of the Middle Eastern Christians, so he also points to some historical milestones on the road of the theological efforts that were made to deal with this conflict after the 1967 war.[32] Overall, Sabra concludes from his survey that the Arab-Eastern Christian theology today circles around, and must remain circling around, two orbits: the world of Islam, and the world of the Arab–Israeli conflict. Sabra notices simultaneously that the focus on the first orbit must be the dominant one. Towards the end of his essay, Sabra points to some contemporary theological efforts made by the recent generation of different Arab-Eastern theologians who are trying to attend to the composition of theology today in the region, stating that:

> Some theologians are just beginning to reflect on and study the recent events in the Arab Middle East, especially the rise to power and prominence of Islamist groups in many countries, and the effects on Christians and what a Christian theological response ought to be (Najib [George] Awad on Syria; Andrea Zaki on Egypt; Mitri Raheb on Palestine and elsewhere). The presence, role and fate of Middle Eastern Christians again form a topic of reflection and discussion in many Christian and inter-religious circles in the Middle East. These attempts are still in their beginning stages, but they clearly indicate that Christians in the Middle East are again confronted by the world of Islam...[33]

---

[27] George F. Sabra, "Theology," in *Christianity in North Africa and West Asia*, pp. 325–334, p. 325.
[28] Ibid., p. 326.
[29] Ibid., pp. 326–327.
[30] Ibid., pp. 329–330.
[31] Ibid., pp. 330–331.
[32] Ibid., pp. 331–332.
[33] Ibid., p. 334.

George Sabra's conclusion demonstrates his concurrence with the concluding observation I am trying to end this study with: what we still lack in the theological adventure of Arab-Eastern Christianity is a serious engagement with the challenges the people of the Arab Middle East face (like the ones Raheb reported on and Sabra is implying) from a frank and deliberate *theological* perspective that would, at least, explain to us Raheb's insistence on associating the long list of challenges in the Middle East with the *Christian identity* (but also Muslim one) of those who suffer, and will suffer further still, from these challenges. What exactly has the Christian identity of these Arab-Christian people to do with their suffering from the aforementioned political, economic, social, environmental, and infrastructural, let alone militaristic, challenges? Raheb concedes that what the Christians suffer from is very similar to what the Muslims in the region suffer from too. But, why then speak about the population that suffers from the very same conditions in terms of their *religious* and faith-based affiliations and self-perception? What difference does it make to speak about the '*Christians* and the *Muslims*' who suffer from dire geopolitical situations instead of simply speaking of the '*Arab-Easterners*' who suffer from such a geopolitical context? Such questions cannot be answered save from the perspective of the cognitive and preconceptual perceptions of what makes the members of the Christian community '*Christians*' and not '*Muslims*' in their own faith-based self-identification and self-awareness. The dimension of reasoning that usually deals with this perspective is the area of reasoning the Christians call 'theology.' Thus, the need for a seriously committed and consciously based theological reasoning on the past, present, and future of the Arab-Eastern Christians is not an intellectual luxury, but an inescapable necessity.

To be fair to Mitri Raheb and George Sabra, they are sharp and admirable theological minds who indeed read the Christians' situation in the heart of context and historicity, and they try, each in his own way, to shed light on the down-to-earth, realistic factors that drive the Christians in the Middle Eastern region to act, or abstain from acting, in the way they do. In the epilogue he produced for the previously mentioned anthology, Raheb pauses at the Christian churches and leaders in specific to assess a transformation in their stances on the situation and the potential future outcomes in the region. According to Raheb, the optimism and enthusiasm that has characterised the churches' attitude since the fall of the Berlin Wall (1989), the release of Nelson Mandela from prison (1990), the Arab–Israeli Madrid Peace Conference (1991), the Oslo Accords between Israel and PLO (1993), and the peace treaty between Jordan and Israel (1994) have almost completely faded away during the twenty-first century.[34] Raheb does not endeavour to reflect critically and analytically upon the rationale that drove the churches to lose optimism in light of the changes that have impacted the region during the past twenty years. He settles, instead, with briefly reporting on four churchly statements related to Jerusalem, which the Chistian religious leaders of Palestine and other Arab countries issued to express the

[34] Raheb, "Epilogue: Middle Eastern Christian Thought in the Twenty-First Century," pp. 169–185, pp. 169–172.

Christians' stances on particular political crises. Raheb's conclusion from his brief report on the four statements is the following:

> What these documents clearly demonstrate is that the twenty-first century has seen the rise of contextual theologies, first in Palestine and later in the region, with Christian leaders who care for their societies and churches, analyze the changing contexts, and are committed to engaging in the shaping of the future of the region.[35]

Raheb correctly concludes that the Christians of the Middle East have long ago realised that "they have no option but to get involved in the national and regional struggle for social and political transformation ... Even when Middle Eastern Christians find themselves in the eye of the storm, they do not give up easily. Based on their faith in their Lord who stills the storm, they stay alert, engaged and faithful to their call."[36] Again, Raheb does not, it seems, find it necessary to unpack what the 'rise of contextual theologies' means exactly in the rationales and conceptual presumptions that were jotted down in any of the four statements he discusses. There are various forms of 'contextualisation' that one can theologically pursue and apply. Which contextualisation method and perspective are the Christians of the Arab Middle East opting for in their theological take on their situation? What makes these Christians' stances on the region, in these statements or elsewhere, 'contextual,' but more crucially, 'theological'? Raheb is right in stating that the Arab-Eastern Christians realised the inescapable demand of their involvement in the dream of transformation in their homeland. Yet, his ensuing concluding remarks and appraisal of this realisation sounds more homiletical and euphoric than actually revelatory of any guidance or hint about how these Christians are going to truly "stay alert, engaged faithful to their call." What is that 'call'? Is it a general call for all the populations of the region? Is it a trans-religious, trans-confessional, trans-sectarian call, or is it a call particularly related to these Christians' *Christianity*? And, if the latter option is the case, have this alertness and faithfulness any *theological* foundations and implications?

It is certainly not the responsibility of Mitri Raheb or George Sabra alone to offer answers to all these crucial questions. It is the responsibility of every Arab-Eastern Christian specialised in the field of reasoning called Christian theology. The shortcomings of this latest anthology, which are not unique or unprecedented at all, can be, therefore, taken as an *invitation* for the Arab-Eastern theologians of the region to embark seriously not just on getting involved in the "regional struggle for social and political transformation" – something Mitri Raheb and George Sabra in the region try sincerely to get involved in – but also, if not primarily, carry the intellectual Cross of trying to develop a contextually particular *theological* involvement in this struggle and in critically assessing it as well.

The above invitation *must* primarily and dominantly be carried out by the *local* Arabic-speaking Eastern theologians before any other theologian from around the world. There are today Western Christian, ecclesial organisations and bodies that embrace the invitation I pointed to above and work hard to help the

---

[35] Ibid., p. 183.

[36] Ibid., pp. 183–184.

Christians in today's Middle East to survive and enjoy a peaceful and secure presence and role in their homeland. An exemplary case in point of such a Western initiative is the work pursued by *Pro Oriente*, a Christian organisation founded in 1964 by the Catholic Cardinal of Vienna, Franz König, to build and foster the fraternal connections between the Catholic Church and the Orthodox Oriental churches. On the work of *Pro Oriente* towards fulfilling its mission for Eastern Christianity, Dietmar Winkler once said the following:

> *Pro Oriente* might not be able to contribute to immediate peace-making [in the Middle East], which has to be a political task, but we may contribute substantially to peace-keeping, to support peaceful co-existence by developing ideas, prospects, and chances. Reflecting on achievements, developing perspectives and visions for the future, not only in theory but also in practice, giving political impulses, and lobbying for a peaceful living together is the very task of *Pro Oriente*.[37]

Winkler is quite candid and accurate in relating that the primary responsibility of attending to the fulfilment of a peaceful existence for the Arabic-speaking Eastern Christians lies essentially on the shoulders of the local Christians in the Arab Middle East. It is not the duty of the Western or worldwide Christian Church, who can gratefully and valuably contribute to the *maintaining* of such peaceful co-existence when it is achieved on the ground. However, I tried in this study to expose the reader to a group of contemporary Arabic-speaking Eastern theologians, whose unique focuses of theological reasoning frankly inform us that the creation of a state of peaceful co-existence between all the communities, traditions, factions, sects, cultures, and ethnicities in the Arab Middle East is *not merely a political task*. For these theologians, it is equally, if not primarily, a *theological task* and a theology-centred responsibility. The attempts at developing *theological* answers to enquiries related to existence with other faiths (specifically Islam) and existence with other communities and cultural entities (differently Christian and non-religious alike) is for these Arab-Eastern theologians the foundation for achieving a peaceful co-existence with the different Other. Theology, for them, must not be avoided as an intimidating clash- and enmity-breeding factor, as many others used to believe, and thus intended to replace theological dialogue with dialogues over political, social, and co-existential pragmatic matters. Theology is not a scarecrow – it is not supposed to scare the other and push her away. It is rather an inspirational, generative source for possible, imaginable co-existence in the unknown, and rather black, future of that troubled and tormented region.

---

[37] Dietmar W. Winkler, "Reflections on a Culture of Co-Existence in Pluralistic Societies," in *Towards a Culture of Co-Existence in Pluralistic Societies*, pp. 1–6, p. 2.

Bibliography

Abdel-Haleem, Muhammad. "Early *Kalām*," in *The Routledge History of Islamic Philosophy*, Oliver Leaman and Sayyid H. Nasr (eds.). Abingdon: Routledge, 1995, pp. 71–88.

Abdel-Malek, Anouar. "*al-Istishrāq fī Azmah*" (Orientalism in Crisis), Ḥasan Qubaysī (trans.), in *Al-Fikr al-'Arabī Journal*, 33(5), 1983, pp. 70–93.

ʿAbdulmasīḥ, Magī. "Lāhūt al Taḥrīr: Asʾilah Mutajaddidah" (Liberation Theology: Renewed Inquiries), in *Lāhūt al-Taḥrīr: Rū'iyah 'Arabiyyah Islāmiyyah Masīḥiyyah* (Liberation Theology: An Arab, Muslim-Christian View), William Sidhum, S.J. (ed.). Cairo: A. R.S.E/C.R.E.M.E.D., 2005, pp. 29–36.

ʿAbdulwāḥid, Muḥammad Ḥilmī (ed.). *al-'Urūbah wal-Qarn al-Wāḥid wal-'Ishrīn* (Arabism and the 21st Century). Beirut: Arab Scientific Publishers, 2009.

Abū Qurrah, Theodore. *Mayar fī Wujūd al-Khāliq wal-Dīn al-Qawīm* (Maymar on the Existence of the Creator and the Right Religion), Ignace Dick (ed.). Jounieh: Librairie St. Paul/ Rome: The Papal Oriental Institute, 1982.

Accad, Martin. "The Gospels in the Muslim Discourse of the Ninth to the Fourteenth Centuries: An Exegetical Inventorial Table (Part I)," in *Islam and Christian–Muslim Relations*, 14 (2003): pp. 67–91.

. "The Ultimate Proof-Text: The Interpretation of John 20.17 in Muslim–Christian Dialogue (Second/Eighth–Eighth/Fourteenth Centuries)," in *Christians at the Heart of the Islamic Rule*, David Thomas (ed.). Leiden: Brill, 2003, pp. 199–214.

. "Too Many Christian Books Fuel Paranoia About Islam," in *www.ethicsdaily.com/too-many-christian-books-fuel-paranoia-about-islam-cms-7708*

. "Christianity and Islam Beyond Conflict," in *The Voice: Insert*, September 2009, pp. 6–10.

. *Sacred Misinterpretation: Reaching Across the Christian–Muslim Divide*. Grand Rapids, Mich: W. B. Eerdmans Publishing Company, 2019.

. "Deconstructing the Kerygmatic?" in *The Blog of Arab Baptist Theological Seminary*, 2 March 2003, https://abtslebanon.org/2023/03/02/deconstructing-the-kerygmatic/ (consulted on 13 March 2023).

Acton, Lord. "Döllinger's Historical Work," in *English Historical Review*, 5(1890), pp. 700–744.

Aksoy, Anna, James E. Montgomery, and Peter E. Pormann (eds.). *Islamic Crosspollinations: Interactions in the Medieval Middle East*. Exeter: Gibb Memorial Trust, 2007.

ʿAmārah, Mohamed. *Islāmiyyat al-Ma'rifah: Madhā Ta'nī* (The Islamicity of Knowledge: What Does it Mean?). Cairo: Nahḍat Maṣr, 2007.

. *Maqām al-'Aql fil-Islām* (The Status of *'Aql* in Islam). Cairo: Nahḍat Maṣr, 2008.

Anastassiadis, Anastassios (ed.). *Visionages fragiles: les relations interconfessionnelles dans le Sud-Est européen et la Méditerranée orientale 1854–1923: Contraints Locales et enjèux internationaux*. Athens: Ecole francaise d'Athèns, 2013.

Aoun, Mosheer Basil. *Al-Fikr al-'Arabī al-Dīnī al-Masīḥī: Muqtaḍayāt al-Nuhūḍ wal-Tajdīd wal-Mu'āṣarah* (The Christian Arab Religious Thought: The Prerequisites of Resurgence and Renewal and Contemporaneity). Beirut: Dār al-Ṭalīʿah, 2007.

. *The Arab Christ: Towards an Arab Christian Theology of Conviviality*, Sarah Patey (trans.). London: Gingko, 2022.

. "Al-Fikr al-ʿArabī al-Dīnī al-Massīḥī al-Muʿāṣir fī Taṣaūurihi lil-ʿUrūbah al-Mustaqbaliyyah" (The Contemporary Arab Religious Christian Thought in its Conception of the Futural Arabism), in *al-'Urūbah wal-Qarn al-Wāḥid wal-'Ishrīn* (Arabism and the 21st Century), Muḥammad Ḥilmī ʿAbdulwāḥid (ed.). Beirut: Arab Scientific Publishers, 2009, pp. 257–293.

. *Le Christ arabe. Pour une théologie chrétienne arabe de la convivialité*. Paris: Cerf, 2016.

. *Anthropologies croisées. Essai sur l'interculturalité arabe*. Paris: Cerf, 2017.

Argyriou, Asterios. "Christianity in the First Ottoman Era (1516–1650)," in *Christianity: A History in the Middle East*, Habib Badr, et. al. (eds.). Beirut: Middle East Council of Churches, 2001.

Armanios, Febe. *Coptic Christianity in Ottoman Egypt*. Oxford and New York: Oxford University Press, 2011.

Ateek, Naim S. *Justice and Only Justice: A Palestinian Theology of Liberation*. Maryknoll, NY: Orbis Books, 1989.

. *A Palestinian Theology of Liberation*: *The Bible, Justice and the Palestinian–Israeli Conflict*. Maryknoll, NY: Orbis Books, 2017, pp. 31–40.

Awad, Najib George. *After-Mission, Beyond Evangelicalism: The Indigenous 'Injīliyyūn' in the Arab-Muslim Context of Syria-Lebanon*. Leiden & Boston: Brill, 2021.

. *Orthodoxy in Arabic Terms: A Study of Theodore Abu Qurrah's Theology in Its Islamic Context*. Berlin: De Gruyter, 2015.

. *Umayyad Christianity: John of Damascus as a Contextual Example of Identity Formation in Early Islam*. Piscataway: Gorgias Press, 2018.

. *And Freedom Became a Public Square: Political, Sociological and Religious Overviews on the Arab Christians and the Arabic Spring*. Berlin & Vienna: LIT Verlag, 2012.

. "Is Christianity from Arabia? Examining Two Contemporary Arabic Proposals on Christianity in the Pre-Islamic Period," in *Orientalische Christen und Europa: Kulturbegegnung zwischen Interferenz, Partizipation und Antizipation*, Martin Tamcke (ed.). Wiesbaden: Harrassowitz Verlag, 2012, pp. 33–56.

.“Arab Orthodox Christianity,” in *Oxford Islamic Studies Online*, 2018, http://www.oxfordislamicstudies.com/article/opr/t343/e0265?hi=1&-pos=1#mat

. “Al-Mujādalah in al-Mā’mūn’s Court: When Could it Have Been Composed? Reflecting on Historicity vis-à-vis Socio-Cultural Data,” in *Oriens Christianos*, 103(2020), pp. 144–169.

. “‘Understanding the Other from Within’: The Muslim Near East in the Eyes of Duncan Black Macdonald,” in *The Muslim World*, 106(3), 2016, pp. 523–538.

. “‘Min al-ʿAql wa-laysa min al-Kutub’: Scriptural Evidence, Rational Verification and Theodore Abū Qurrah’s Apologetic Epistemology,” in *Exegetical Crossroads: Understanding Scripture in Judaism, Christianity and Islam in the Pre-Modern Orient*, George Tamer, Regina Grundmann, Asaad Elias Kattan, and Karl Pinggéra (eds.). Berlin & Boston: De. Gruyter, 2017, pp. 95–118.

. “*Creatio ex Philosophia*: *Kalām* as Cultural Evolution and Identity-Formation Means in the Early Abbasid Era,” in *The Muslim World Journal*, 4(109), pp. 510–534.

. “Sacred Misinterpretation: Reaching Across the Christian–Muslim Divide,” book review in *The Muslim World*, 10(2020), pp. 259–262.

. “Kullunā Ka-Aiyyūb Naghsul Qurūḥ al-Istibdād wal-Qamʿ bi-māʾ al-Baḥr Dhātih” (We Are All Like Job, Washing the Blisters of Tyranny and Oppression by the Same Sea Water), in www.syria.alsafahat.net/-نصوص-نوافذ
عن-المشرق-مسيحيين-ومسلمين

. “If His Crucifixion Was Figurative As You Claim, Then So Be It”: How Two Christian Mutakallims from the Abbasid Era Used An-Nisā’ 4:157–158 in Dialogues with Muslims,” in *Journal of Eastern Christian Studies*, 68(1–2), 2016, pp. 53–80.

. “Democracy without Democrats, Identity-Formation and Religions: The Challenge of Cross-pollinating Self-perception in the Post-Arabic Spring Contexts,” *Journal of Philosophy & Social Criticism*, XX(10), 2021, pp. 1–12.

. “Deciphering the *Genome* of ‘Crisis’ in the Syrian ‘Refugee Crisis’: Toward a *Hermeneutic Tripod*,” in *Church and Migration: Global (In)Difference*, Darren Dias, Jaroslav Skira, Michael Attridge, and Gerard Mannion (eds.). New York: Palgrave MacMillan, 2020.

. “What Has the Jerusalem of Dogmatics to Do with the Athens of Context, or How Should One Do Contextual Theology?” in *PLURA: Revista de Estudos de Religião*, 2(3), 2013, pp. 198–221.

. “Inter-Religious Relations”, in *Edinburgh Companion to Global Christianity: Christianity in North Africa and West Asia*, Kenneth R. Ross, Mariz Tadros, and Todd M. Johnson (eds.). Edinburgh: Edinburgh University Press, 2018, pp. 383–393.

. “Is ‘Post-Christendom’ a Relevant Hermeneutical Framework to the Situation of the Christians in Greater Syria? Towards a Critical Appraisal,” in *Post-Christendom Studies*, 1(2016), pp. 31–76.

. "Interfaith Relations and Middle East Christianity: Beyond Dialogue, Toward Interrelationality," in *Levant, Cradle of Abrahamic Religions: Studies on the Interaction of Religion and Society from Antiquity to Modern Times*, Catalin-Stefan Popa (ed.). Berlin: LIT, 2022, pp. 291–326.

. "*al-Kalām al-Mu'tazilī bi-Ṣifatihi 'Ābiran lil-Adiyān: fī al-Baḥth Taṭālu'iyyan wa-Siyāqiyyan 'an Tawajjüh Mu'tazilī Masīḥī*" (Muʿtazilite *Kalām* as Cross-religious: In Search Crosspollinationally and Contextually for a Christian Muʿtazilite Orientation), in *Ostour Journal*, 20 (2024), pp.31–55.

. "*The Arab Christ: Towards an Arab Christian Theology of Conviviality,* by Mouchir Basile Aoun, trans. Sarah Patey, London: Gingko, 2022," book review in *Scottish Journal of Theology*, 2023, 76(4), pp. 394–396.

Ayoub, Mahmoud. *A Muslim View of Christianity: Essays on Dialogue by Mahmoud Ayoub*, Irfan A. Omar (ed.). Maryknoll, NY: Orbis Books, 2007.

al-Azmeh, Aziz. *The Emergence of Islam in Late Antiquity: Allah and His People*. Cambridge & New York: Cambridge University Press, 2014.

Badr, Habib; et. al. (eds.). *Christianity: A History in the Middle East*. Beirut: Middle East Council of Churches, 2001.

Bailey, Betty Jane and J. Martin Bailey (eds.). *Who Are the Christians in the Middle East?* Grand Rapids, USA/Cambridge, UK: W. B. Eerdmans, 2003.

Baur, Ferdinand Christian. *Church and Theology in the Nineteenth Century*, Peter C. Hodgson (ed.), Robert F. Brown and Peter Hodgson (trans.). Eugene, OR: Cascade Books, 2018.

Beaumont, Mark I. *Christology in Dialogue with Muslims: A Critical Analysis of Christian Presentations of Christ for Muslims from the Ninth and Twentieth Centuries*. Eugene, OR: Wipfe & Stock, 2005.

. "ʿAmmār al-Baṣrī's Apology for the Doctrine of the Trinity," in *Orientalia Analecta*, 218(1982), pp. 169–191.

. "Early Christian Interpretation of the Qur'ān," in *Transformation*, 22 (2005): pp. 195–203.

. "Muslim Readings of John's Gospel in the 'Abbasid Period," in *Islam and Christian–Muslim Relations*, 19 (2008), pp. 179–197.

Becker, Christian H. "Christliche Polemikund islamische Dogmenbildung," in *Zeitschrift für Asseriologie und verwandle Gebiete*, 26 (1912), pp. 175–195.

Bediako, Kwame. *Christianity in Africa*. Edinburgh: Edinburgh University Press/Maryknoll: Orbis Books, 1995.

Betts, R. B. *Christians in the Arab East: A Political Study*. Athens: Lycabettus Press, 1975.

Bhabha, Homi K. *The Location of Culture*. London: Routledge, 1994.

Biesterfeldt, Hinrich (ed.). *Keleine Schriften by Josef van Ess*. Leiden & Boston: Brill, 2018.

Bodine, Jermain. "The Legacy of Duncan Black Macdonald," in *Occasional Bulletin of Missionary Research*, 4(4), 1980, pp. 162–164.

Bourdieu, Pierre. *The Logic of Practice*. Stanford, CA: Stanford University Press, 1990.

Bowersock, G. W., P. Brown, and O. Grabar (eds.). *Interpreting Late Antiquity: Essays on the Postclassical World.* Cambridge, USA/London, UK: Belknap Press/Harvard University Press, 2001.

Browless, Jason, Tarek Masoud, and Andrew Reynolds. *The Arab Spring: Pathways of Repression and Reform.* Oxford: Oxford University Press, 2015.

Brown, D., S. G. Davaney, and K. Tanner (eds.). *Converging on Culture: Theologians in Dialogue with Cultural Analysis and Criticism.* New York & Oxford: Oxford University Press, 2001.

Buber, Martin. *I and Thou*, Walter Kaufmann (trans.). New York: Simon and Schuster, 1970.

Bühler, Pierre, "Foreignness as Focal Point of Otherness," in *Dynamics of Difference: Christianity and Alterity: A Festschrift for Werner G. Jeanrond*, Ulrich Schmiedel and James M. Matarazzo, Jr. (eds.). London & New York: Bloomsbury T&T Clark, 2016, pp. 153–159.

. "Ricoeur's Concept of Distinction as a Challenge for Theological Hermeneutics," in *Paul Ricoeur: Poetics and Religion*, Joseph Verheyden, Theo L. Hettema, and Peter Vandecosteele (eds.). Leuven: Peeters, 2011, pp. 151–165.

Bulliet, Richard W. *Conversion to Islam in the Medieval Period: An Essay in Quantitative History*. Cambridge, MA: Harvard University Press, 1979.

Carlson, Thomas A. "Contours of Conversion: The Geography of Islamization in Syria, 600–1500", in *Journal of the American Oriental Society*, 135(4), 2015, pp. 791–816.

Casiday, Augustine (ed.). *The Orthodox Christian World.* London: Routledge, 2012.

Cheikho, Louis. *'Ulamā' al-Naṣrāniyyah fī al-Īslām, 622–1300* (The Scientist of Christianity in Islam, 622–1300), Kamīl Ḥushaymih (ed.). Rome: Pontifical Oriental Institute/Jounieh: al-Maktabah al-Buluṣiyyah, 1983.

. *Wuzarā' al-Naṣrāniyyah wa-Kuttābuhā fī al-Īslām, 622–1517* (The Ministers of Christianity and its Scribes in Islam, 622–1517), Kamīl Ḥushaymih (ed.). Rome: Pontifical Oriental Institute/Dhūq Mikhail: Arab Christian Heritage/Jounieh: al-Maktabah al-Buluṣiyyah, 1987.

Chrabieh, Pamela, "A Journey towards Gender Equality," in *TELOS Magazine*, 4(2021), pp. 23–
28, p. 23. www.telosmagazine.org/uploads/2/5/5/6/25561514/5-pamela_charabieh-telos_issue_no4/pdf

. *al-Mar'a fī Āsiya al-Gharbiyya: Riḥla īlā al-Māḍī* (The Woman in Western Asia: A Journey to the Past), Beirut: al-Mashriq Press, 2013.

. et. al., Nadia Wardeh. "Against the Current: Rethinking Gender, Religious Authority and Interreligious Dialogue," in *Middle Eastern Women: The Intersection of Law, Culture and Religion*, Mitri Raheb (ed.). Bethlehem: Diyar Press, 2020, pp. 153–191.

Chopp, Rebecca S. "Theology and the Poetics of Testimony," in *Converging on Culture: Theologians in Dialogue with Cultural Analysis and Criticism*, D. Brown, S. G. Davaney, and K. Tanner (eds.). New York & Oxford: Oxford University Press, 2001, pp. 56–70.

Ciggar, K. and H. Teule (eds.). *East and West in the Crusader States III*. Leuven: Uitgeverij Peeters, 2003.

Climo, Jacob H., Maria G. Catell et. al. (eds.). *Memory and History: Anthropological Perspectives*. Walnut Creek, CA: AltaMira Press, 2002.

Clooney, F. X., S.J., and K. von Stoch (eds.). *How to Do Comparative Theology*. New York: Fordham University Press, 2018.

Cook, David. "Syria and the Arabs," in *A Companion to Late Antiquity*, P. Rousseau and J. Raithel (eds.). Chichester: Blackwell Publishers, 2009, pp. 467–478.

. "New Testament Citations in the Ḥadīth Literature and the Question of Early Gospel Translations into Arabic," in *The Encounter of Eastern Christianity with Early Islam*, Emmanouela Grypeou, Mark Swanson, and David Thomas (eds.). Leiden: Brill, 2006, pp. 185–224.

Cook, Michael. "The Origins of *Kalām*," in *Bulletin of the School of Oriental and African Studies*, 43(1980), pp. 32–43.

Cragg, Kenneth. *The Arab Christian: A History in the Middle East*. Louisville; Westminster/John Knox Press, 1991.

Danziger, Kurt. *Making the Mind: A History of Memory*. Cambridge and New York: Cambridge University Press, 2008.

Davies, Noel and Martin Conway. *World Christianity in the Twentieth Century*. London: SCM Press, 2008.

Dawn, C.E. *From Ottomanism to Arabism Essays om the Origin of Arab Nationalism*. Chicago & London: University of Illinois Press, 1973.

Dias, Darren, Jaroslav Skira, Michael Attridge and Gerard Mannion (eds.). *Church and Migration: Global (In)Difference*. New York: Palgrave MacMillan, 2020.

Ebied, Riffat and Herman Teule (eds.). *Studies on the Christian Arabic Heritage*. Leuven: Peeters, 2004.

Eck, Diana L. "Dialogue and Method: Reconstructing the Study of Religion," in *A Magic Still Dwells: Comparative Religion in the Postmodern Age*. Kimberley C. Patton and Benjamin C. Ray (eds.). Berkeley, Los Angeles & London: University of California Press, 2000, pp. 131–149.

Elsässer, Sebastian. "The Copts in the January Revolution of 2011," in *Copts in Context: Negotiating Identity, Tradition and Modernity*, Nelly van Doorn-Harder (ed.). Columbia, SC: University of South Carolina Press, 2017, pp. 21–33.

Endress, Gerhard. *The Works of Yaḥyā Ibn 'Adī: An Analytical Inventory*. Wiesbaden: Reichert, 1977.

Eriksson, Anne-Louise. "The Other on the Cross," in *Dynamics of Difference: Christianity and Alterity: A Festschrift for Werner G. Jeanrond*, Ulrich Schmiedel and James M. Matarazzo, Jr. (eds.). London & New York: Bloomsbury T&T Clark, 2016, pp. 173–180.

Eutychius of Alexandria. *The Book of Demonstration*, W. Montgomery Watt (trans.). Louvain: Peeters, 1960.

al-Fārābī, Abū Naṣr. *Īḥṣā' al-'Ulūm* (Enumerating the Sciences). Beirut: *al-Īnmā'* Nationalist Center, 1991.

Fiey, Jean Maurice. *Chrétiens syriaques saus les Abbasides surtout à Baghdad (749–1258)*. Louvin: Secrétariat du Corpus SCO, 1980.

Fonner, Michael G. "Jesus' Death by Crucifixion in the Qur'ān: an Issue for Interpretation and Muslim–Christian Relations," in *Journal of Ecumenical Studies*, 29 (1992), pp. 432–450.

Fowden, E. Key. *The Barbarian Plain: Saint Sergius between Rome and Iran.* Berkeley, CA: University of California Press, 1999.

Frank, Richard M. *Beings and Their Attributes: The Teaching of the Basrian School of the Mu'tazila in the Classical Period.* Albany: State University of New York Press, 1978.

Fück, Johann. *Die arabischen Studien in Europa bis in den Anfang des 20. Jahrhunderts*, Leipzig: Otto Harrassowitz, 1955.

Gadamer, Hand-Georg. *Truth and Method*, Joel Weinsheimer and Donald G. Marshall (trans.). London & New York: Continuum, 2004.

Galvin, James L. *The Arab Uprisings: What Everyone Needs to Know*. Oxford & New York: Oxford University Press, 2012.

Gervers, Michael and Ramzi Bikhazi (eds.). *Conversion and Continuity: Indigenous Christian Communities in Islamic Lands*. Toronto: Pontifical Institute of Medieval Studies, 1990.

Gibson, Margaret Dunlop (ed.). *An Arabic Version of the Acts of the Apostles and the Seven Catholic Epistles with a Treatise on the Triune Nature of God.* London: Cambridge University Press, 1899.

Goldziher, Ignaz. *Vorlesungen über den Islam*. Heidelberg: Carl Winter Universitätsbuchhandlung, 1910.

Graf, Georg. *Die arabischen Schriften des Theodor Abu Qurra, Bishofs von Ḥarrān (Ca. 740–820)*. Paderborn: Ferdinand Schöningh, 1910.

Griffith, Sidney H. *The Beginnings of Christian Theology in Arabic: Muslim–Christian Encounter in the Early Islamic Period.* Aldershot: Ashgate/Variorum, 2002.

. *Arabic Christianity in the Monasteries of Ninth-Century Palestine*. Aldershot and Bloomfield: Ashgate/Variorum, 1992.

. *The Church in the Shadow of the Mosque: Christians and Muslims in the World of Islam*. Princeton, NJ: Princeton University Press, 2008.

. *The Controversial Theology of Theodore Abū Qurrah (C.A.D. 750–C. 820): A Methodological Comparative Study in Christian Arabic Literature*, PhD. Diss. Washington: The Catholic University of America/Ann Arbor, Mich: University Microfilms, 1978.

. *Theodore Abū Qurrah: The Intellectual Profile of an Arab Christian Writer of the First Abbasid Century*. Tel Aviv: Tel Aviv University Press, 1992.

. *The Bible in Arabic: The Scriptures of the "People of the Book" in the Language of Islam*. Princeton, NJ: Princeton University Press, 2015.

. "'Ammār al-Baṣrī's *Kitāb al-Burhān*: Christian *Kalām* in the First Abbasid Century," in *The Beginnings of Christian Theology in Arabic: Muslim–Christian Encounter in the Early Islamic Period.* Aldershot: Ashgate/Variorum, 2002, pp. 145–181.

. "The Concept of *al-Uqnūm* in 'Ammār al-Baṣrī's apology for the Doctrine of the Trinity", in *Actes du premier congrès international d'ètudes arabes*

Chrètiennes, Samir Khalil Samir (ed.). *Orientalia Christiana Analecta 218*. Rome: Pontificum Institutum Studiorum Orientalium, 1982, pp. 169–191.

. "'Malkites,' 'Jacobites' and the Christological Controversies in Arabic in the Third/Ninth-Century Syria," in *Syrian Christians under Islam: The First Thousand Years*, David Thomas (ed.). Leiden & Boston: Brill, 2001, pp. 9–55.

. "From Aramaic to Arabic: The Languages of the Monasteries of Palestine in the Byzantine and Early Islamic Periods," in *Dumbarton Oaks Papers*, 51(1997), pp. 11–31.

. "The Qur'ān in Arab Christian Texts: The Development of an Apologetical Argument; Abū Qurrah in the Mağlis of al-Ma'mūn," in *Parole de l'Orient*, 24 (1999): pp. 203–233.

. "Between the Cross and the Crescent: Co-Existence, Clash of Theologies and Interreligious Dialogue," in *Towards a Culture of Co-Existence in Pluralistic Societies: The Middle East and India*, D. W. Winkler (ed.). Piscataway, NJ: Gorgias Press, 2020, pp. 9–42.

Grypeo, Emmanouela, Mark Swanson, and David Thomas (eds.). *Christian-Muslim Relations: A Bibliographical History, Volume 1 (600-900)*. Leiden: Brill, 2006.

Gutas, Dimitri. *Greek Thought, Arabic Culture: The Graeco–Arabic Translation Movement in Baghdad and Early Abbasid Society 2nd-4th/8th-10th Centuries)*. London: Routledge, 1998.

HaCohen, Ruth. "Intercontextual Musical Currents and Performative Traditions in Twentieth-Century Palestine/Israel and Germany," in *Comparative Studies in the Humanities*, Guy Stroumsa (ed.). Jerusalem: Israel Academy of Sciences and Humanities, 2018, pp. 15–39.

Haddad, Robert M. *Syrian Christians in Muslim Society: An Interpretation*. Princeton, NJ: Princeton University Press, 1970.

Hage, Wolfgang. *Das orientalische Christentum*. Stuttgart: Verlag W. Kohlhammer, 2007.

Hainthaler, Theresia. *Christliche Araber vor dem Islam: Verbreitung und konfessionelle zugehörigkeit Eine Hinfürung*. Leuven & Paris & Dudley, MA: Peeters, 2007.

Ḥannā, Kyrillus ʿAbdulmasīḥ. *'An al-Mar'a wa-Ghiṭā' al-Ra's* (The Woman and the Head Scarf). Cairo: The Coptic Bookshop, n.d.

Hasan, S.S. *Christians Versus Muslims in Modern Egypt: The Century-Long Struggle for Coptic Equality*. Oxford & New York: Oxford University Press, 2003.

Hathaway, Jane, and Karl K. Barbir. *The Arab Lands under Ottoman Rule, 1516–1800*. London & New York: Routledge, 2013.

Ḥāyik, M. *al-Masīḥ wa-Lubnān wa-Filasṭīn* (Christ, Lebanon and Palestine). Beirut: al-Karmah Press, n.d.

. "al-ʿUrūbah Mushkilat al-ʿArab" (Arabism is the Arab's Problem), in *al-Nahar Newspaper*, 5 November 1979.

. "Kal-Masīḥ Kunnā Rahā'inan lil-Ummam Ḥatta al-Aqrabīn" (Like Christ, We Were the Nation's Hostages, Even the Close Ones), in *al-Nahar Newspaper*, 22 April 2000.

Henghan, Tom. "Arab Spring and the Rise of Political Islam," in www.muslimvillage.com , 1 November 2011.

Hervieu-Léger, Danièlé. *Religion as a Chain of Memory*, S. Lee (trans.). New Brunswick: Rutgers University Press, 2000.

Heyberger, Bernard. "Eastern Christians, Islam and the West: A Connected History," in *International Journal of Middle Eastern Studies*, 42(2010), pp. 475–478.

. *Middle Eastern and European Christianity, 16th–20th Century: Connected Histories*, A Girard, C. Santus, V. Kontouma, and K. S. Summerer (eds.). M. Robitaille-Ibbett (trans.). Edinburgh: Edinburgh University Press, 2023.

Hitti, Philip K. *A History of the Arabs from the Earliest Time to the Present*. New York & London: St. Martin's Press, 1970.

Hodgson, Peter C. *The Formation of Historical Theology: A Study of Ferdinand Christian Baur*. New York: Harper & Row, 1966.

Hourani, Albert. *Arabic Thought in the Liberal Age, 1798–1939*. Cambridge & New York: Cambridge University Press, 1983.

Hoyland, Robert. *Arabia and the Arabs: From the Bronze Age to the Coming of Islam*. London: Routledge, 2001.

. *In God's Path: The Arab Conquests and the Creation of an Islamic Empire*. New York & Oxford: Oxford University Press, 2015.

. "Epigraphy and the Linguistic Background to the Qur'ān," in *The Qur'ān in its Historical Context*, Gabriel Said Reynolds (ed.). London & New York: Routledge, 2008, pp. 51–70.

Hunter, Erica C. D. (ed.). *The Christian Heritage of Iraq: Collected Papers from the Christianity of Iraq I-V Seminar Days*. Piscataway, NJ: Gorgias Press, 2009.

Hurvitz, Nimrod, Christian C. Sahner, Uriel Simonson, and Luke Yarbrough (eds.). *Conversion to Islam in the Premodern Age: A Source Book*. Oakland, CA: University of California Press, 2020.

Hyun-Kyung, Chung. *Struggle to be the Sun Again: Introducing Asian Women's Theology*. Maryknoll, NY: Orbis, 1990.

Ībrāhīm, Yūḥannā, *Qubūl al-Ākhar* (Accepting the Other). Damascus: Qadmus Press, 2006.

. "Al-Taʿaddudiyyah wa-Yanābīʿ al-Jamāl al-ʿArabī" (Plurality and the Springs of Arabic Beauty), in *al-Maʿārij Journal*, 23(161), 2013, pp. 17–20.

. "Muqtaraḥāt li-Sinudūs al-Asāqifah" (Proposals to the Episcopal Synod), in *al-Maʿārij Journal*, 24(173), 2014, pp. 187–188.

. "Sūriyyā unmudhaj lil-ʿAyish al-Mushtarak" (Syria as a Model for Co-Existence), in *al-Maʿārij Journal*, 24(173), 2014, p. 189.

. "The Ecumenical Dimension of the Synod: Critical Evaluation, Results and Perspectives," in *Middle Eastern Christians Facing Challenges: Reflections on the Special Synod for the Middle East*, Dietmar W. Winkler (ed.). Piscataway, NJ: Gorgias Press, 2019, pp. 56–71.

. "Culture and Coexistence in Syria," in *Syriac Churches Encountering Islam: Past Experiences and Future Perspectives*, Dietmar W. Winkler (ed.). Piscataway, NJ: Gorgias Press, 2010, pp. 222–228.

Isaac, Munthir. *Arḍ al-Mi'ād: Qirā'ah lāhūtiyyah Ḍimn as-Siyāq al-Filasṭīnī* (The Promised Land: A Theological Reading within Palestinian Context). Bethlehem: Bethlehem Bible College, 2021.

. ed. *Madkhal ilā al-Lāhūt al-Filasṭīnī* (An Introduction to Palestinian Theology). Bethlehem: Dyar Press, 2017.

. *From Land to Lands, From Eden to the Renewed Earth*. London: Langham Monographs, 2015.

Janosik, Daniel J. *John of Damascus: First Apologist to the Muslims*. Eugene, OR: Pickwick Publications, 2016.

Jeanrond, Werner G. *Call and Response: The Challenge of Christian Life*. New York: Continuum, 1995.

. "Belonging or Identity? Christian Faith in a Multi-Religious World," in *Many Mansions? Multiple Religious Belonging and Christian Identity*, Catherine Cornille (ed.). Maryknoll: Orbis Books, 2002, pp. 106–120.

Jenkins, Philip. *The Next Christendom: The Coming of Global Christianity*, rev. ed. Oxford & New York: Oxford University Press, 2007.

Jensen, Sune Qvotrup. "Preliminary Notes on Othering and Agency," in *Sociologisk Arbejdspapir*, 27, 2009, pp. 1–36.

Jessup, Henry H. *Syrian Home-Life*, Isaac Riley (ed.). New York: Dodd & Mead Publishers, 1874.

Kachouh, Hikmat. *The Arabic Versions of the Gospels: The Manuscripts and their Families*. Berlin & New York: De Gruyter, 2012.

Karalis, Vrasidas. "Greek Christianity after 1453," in *The Blackwell Companion to Eastern Christianity*, Ken Perry (ed.). Oxford, UK/Malden, USA: Blackwell Publishers, 2010, pp. 156–185.

Kassis, Riad. "Mafhūm al-'Ahd fī al-Fikr al-Īnjīlī wa-Ta'thīrih fī Wāqi' al-Sharq al-Awsaṭ: Dirāsah Tārīkhiyyah, Kitābiyyah, Lāhūtiyyah wa-Akhlāqiyyah" (The Concept of Covenant in Protestant Thought and its Impact on the Middle East's Reality: A Historical, Biblical, Theological and Ethical Study), in *Naḥwa Lāhūt 'Arab' Mu'āṣir* (Toward a Contemporary Arabic Theology), Andrea Zaki (ed.). Cairo: Al-Thaqāfah Press, 2007, pp. 39–94.

. *al-Arḍ fī al-Kitāb al-Muqaddas* (The Land in the Bible). Damascus: Alif Bā' al-Adeeb, 1990.

Kattan, Assaad Elias. "The Cross as 'Islam': George Khodr's Approach to Islam as a Paradigm of Contextual Theology," *Journal of Eastern Christian Studies*, 69(1–4), 2017, pp. 69–78.

. *Shirā' fī 'Uyūn Mustadīrah: Dirāsāt fī Fikr al-Muṭrān George Khodr* (A Sail within Round Eyes: Studies on the Thought of Bishop George Khodr). Beirut: al-Nūr Orthodox Cooperation, 2012, pp. 15–17.

. "Das Kreuz als Hingabe (islām) an den Willen Gottes. Zu den Besonderheiten der Kreuzestheologie Georges Khodrs im Blick auf ihren islamischen Kontext", in *Christlische Gotteslehre in Orient seit dem Aufkommen des Islams zur Gegenwart*, Martin Tamcke (ed.). Wūrzburgh: Ergon Verlag, 2008, pp. 213–224.

. "Al-Ṣalīb bi-Waṣfihi Islāman li-Mashī'at Allah: Khaṣā'iṣ Lāhūt al-Ṣalīb lada George Khodr fī Siyāqih al-Thaqāfī al-Islāmī" (The Cross as a

Surrender to God's Will: The Characteristics of George Khodr's Theology of the Cross in its Islamic Cultural Context), in *Shirā' fī 'Uyūn Mustadīrah: Dirāsāt fī Fikr al-Muṭrān George Khodr* (A Sail within Round Eyes: Studies on the Thought of Bishop George Khodr). Beirut: al-Nūr Orthodox Cooperation, 2012, pp. 23–41.

. "Wort und Leib. Zur Hermeneutik Georges Khodrs in ihrem islamischen Kontext" in *Patrologie und Ökumene: Theresia Hainthaler zum 75. Geburtstag*, Peter Knauer, Andrea Riedl, and Dietmar W. Winkler (eds.). Freiburg, Basel & Wien: Verlag Herder, 2022, pp. 295–308.

Keating, Sandra T. *Defending the "People of Truth" in Early Islamic Period: The Christian Apologies of Abū Rā'iṭah*. Leiden & Boston: Brill, 2006.

. "Ḥabib Ibn Khidmah Abū Rā'iṭah al-Takrītī's 'the Refutation of the Melkites Concerning the Union [of the Divinity and Humanity in Christ] III," in *Christians at the Heart of Islamic Rule*, David Thomas (ed.). Leiden: Brill, 2003, pp. 39–54.

Kennedy, Hugh. "Islam", in *Interpreting Late Antiquity: Essays on the Postclassical World*, G. W. Bowersock, P. Brown, and O. Grabar (eds.). Cambridge, USA/London, UK: Belknap Press/Harvard University Press, 2001, pp. 219–237.

Kerr, David A. "A Western Christian Appreciation of the Eastern Christianity," in *Who Are the Christians in the Middle East?* Betty Jane Bailey and J. Martin Bailey (eds.). Grand Rapids, USA/Cambridge, UK: W. B. Eerdmans, 2003, pp. 3–11.

Khalidi, R. "Arab Nationalism: Historical Problems in the Literature," in *American Historical Review*, 96(5), 1991, pp. 1363–1373.

Khlayfāt, Saḥbān (ed.). *Maqālāt Yaḥyā b. 'Adī al-Falsafiyyah* (Yaḥyā b. ʿAdī's Philosophical Essays). Amman: Jordanian University Press, 1988.

Khodr, George. "Madkhal ilā al-Naḍrāt al-Mutabādalah" (An Introduction to the Reciprocal

Views) in *Afkār wa-Arā' fī al-Ḥiwār al-Masīḥī al-Islāmī wal-'Aiysh al-Mushtarak* (Ideas and Opinions on Christian–Muslim Dialogue and Co-existence). George Khodr, Jounieh: Bouluṣiyyah Bookshop, 2000, pp. 107–123.

. "al-Ḥiwār al-Islāmī al-Masīḥī" (The Muslim–Christian Dialogue), in *Afkār wa-Arā' fī al-Ḥiwār al-Masīḥī al-Islāmī wal-'Aiysh al-Mushtarak* (Ideas and Opinions on Christian–Muslim Dialogue and Co-existence). George Khodr, Jounieh: Bouluṣiyyah Bookshop, 2000, pp. 59–86.

. "Maʿrifatnā Baʿḍunā li-baʿḍ Sharṭ min Shurūṭ al-Ḥiwār al-Islāmī al-Masīḥī" (Our Knowledge of Each Other is One of the Preconditions of Muslim–Christian Dialogue), in *Afkār wa-Arā' fī al-Ḥiwār al-Masīḥī al-Islāmī wal-'Aiysh al-Mushtarak* (Ideas and Opinions on Christian–Muslim Dialogue and Co-existence). George Khodr, Jounieh: Bouluṣiyyah Bookshop, 2000, pp. 87–105.

. "Maʿ baʿḍ al-Muslimīn" (With Some Muslims), in *Afkār wa-Arā' fī al-Ḥiwār al-Masīḥī al-Islāmī wal-'Aiysh al-Mushtarak* (Ideas and Opinions on Christian–Muslim Dialogue and Co-existence). George Khodr, Jounieh: Bouluṣiyyah Bookshop, 2000, pp. 215–220.

. *Maṭāriḥ Sujūd. 2* (Prostration Spots. 2). Beirut: al-Nahār Press, 2001, pp. 17–18.

. "La communication du message en terre d'Islam," dens *Études theologiques et religiouses*, 64(1989), pp. 373–391.

. *Maṭāriḥ Sujūd. 1* (Prostration Spots. 1). Beirut: al-Nahār Press, 2001.

. "al-ʿAyish al-Mushtarak bayn al-Taʿaddudiyyah eal-Mūwāṭanah" (Co-existence between Plurality and Citizenship), in *Al-'Ayish al-Mustarak wal-Waḥdah fī al-Tanaūw'* (Co-existence and Unity in Diversity), Jerome Shahin (ed.). Beirut: The Platform of Development, Culture and Dialogue, 2011, pp. 120–127.

. "Al-Ḥuḍūr al-Masīḥī fī al-Thaqāfah al-ʿArabiyyah" (The Christian Presence in Arabic Culture), in *al-Ma'ārij Journal*, 24(173), 2014, pp. 65–76.

. "Qādirūn ʿala at-Talāqī" (Capable of Getting Together), in *Ma'ārij Journal*, 23(161), 2013, pp. 28–30.

. "Naḥn wal-Muslimūn" (We and the Muslims), in *Ma'ārij Journal*, 24(172), 2014, pp. 10–11.

. "Le christianisme, l'islam et l'arabité", *Contacts*, III (110), 1980.

Khoury, D. *State and Provincial Society in the Ottoman Empire: Mosul, 1540–1834*. Cambridge: Cambridge University Press, 1997.

Khoury, Emma Ghrayyib. *al-Mar'a fī al-Kitāb al-Muqaddas: Min Ḥauwā' īlā Maryam* (The Woman in the Bible: From Eve to Mary). Tripoli: an-Nūr Orthodox Press, 2011.

Kilpatrick, Hilary. "'Exotic' Christianity as a Translation Problem," in *Orientalismo. Exotismo y Traducción*, Gonzalo F. Parrilla and Manuel C. F. García (eds.). Cuenca: de Castilla-La Mancha, 2000, pp. 217–228.

Kloß, Sinah Theres. "The Global South as Subversive Practice: Challenges and Potentials of a
Heuristic Concept," in *The Global South*, 11(2017), pp. 1–17.

Kruger, J. "Christian Identity in an Age of Difference," in *Christian Identity*, Eddy van der Borght (ed.). Leiden: Brill, 2008, pp. 119–132.

Kuhn, Mike. "Conquest and Christian–Muslim Relations during the Islam Era (Seventh to Eleventh Centuries)," in *Surviving Jewel: The Enduring Story of Christianity in the Middle East*, Mitri Raheb and Mark A. Lamport (eds.). Eugene, OR: Cascade Books, 2022, pp. 19–35.

Laing, Stefana D. *Retrieving History: Memory and Identity Formation in the Early Church*. Grand Rapids, MI: Baker Academic, 2017.

Lamport, Mark A. and Mitri Raheb (eds.). *Surviving Jewel: The Enduring Story of Christianity in the Middle East*. Eugene, OR: Cascade Books, 2022.

. *Emerging Theologies from the Global South*. Eugene, OR: Cascade Books, 2023.

Langenfeld, Aaron. "The Moment of Truth: Comparative and Dogmatic Theology," in *How to Do Comparative Theology*, F. X. Clooney, S.J., and K. von Stoch (eds.). New York: Fordham University Press, 2018, pp. 59–71.

Lawrence, T.E. *Seven Pillars of Wisdom*. Hertfordshire: Wordsworth, 1997.

Lawson, Todd. *The Crucifixion and the Qur'an: A Study in the History of Muslim Thought*. Oxford: Oneworld Publications, 2009.

Lazarus-Yafeh, Hava, M. R. Cohen, S. Somekh, and S. H. Griffith (eds.). *The Majlis: Interreligious Encounters in Medieval Islam*. Wiesbaden: Harrassowitz, 1999.

Leaman, Oliver and Sayyid H. Nasr (eds.). *The Routledge History of Islamic Philosophy*. Abingdon: Routledge, 1995.

Leitzmann, H. and H. Hilgenfeld. *Das Leben des heiligen Symeon Stylites*. Leipzig: Hinrichs, 1908.

Levtzion, Nehemia. "Conversion to Islam in Syria and Palestine and the Survival of Christian Communities," in *Conversion and Continuity: Indigenous Christian Communities in Islamic Lands*, Michael Gervers and Ramzi Bikhazi (eds.). Toronto: Pontifical Institute of Medieval Studies, 1990, pp. 289–311.

Limor, Ora and Guy Stroumsa (eds.). *Christians and Christianity in the Holy Land: From the Origin to the Latin Kingdom*. Turnhout: Brepols, 2006.

Lumbard, Joseph E. B. "Decolonizing Qur'ānic Studies," in *Religions*, 176(13), 2022, pp. 1–14.

Lynch, Marc. *The Arab Uprising: The Unfinished Revolutions of the New Middle East*. New York: Perseus Books, 2012.

Makdisi, Usama. *Artillery of Heaven: American Missionaries and the Failed Conversion of the Middle East*. Ithaca: Cornell University Press, 2008.

Masters, Bruce. *Christians and Jews in the Ottoman Arab World: The Roots of Sectarianism*. Cambridge & New York: Cambridge University Press, 2001.

McGukin, John A. *The Orthodox Church: An Introduction to its History, Doctrine and Spiritual Culture*. Oxford, UK/Malden, USA: Blackwell Publishing, 2008.

. ed. *The Encyclopedia of Eastern Orthodox Christianity*. Oxford, UK/Malden, USA: Blackwell Publishing, 2011.

Medina, Jose. *Speaking from Elsewhere: A New Contextualist Perspective on Meaning, Identity and Discursive Agency*. Albany, NY: State University of New York Press, 2006.

Mikhael, Mary. "al-Mar'ah al-Massīḥiyyah" (The Christian Woman), in *Naḥwa Lāhūt 'Arabī Mu'āṣir* (Toward a Contemporary Arabic Theology), Andera Zak (ed.). Cairo: Al-Thaqāfah Press, 2007, pp. 275–340.

al-Miskīn, Matta. *al-Kanīsah wal-Daūlah: al-Ṭā'fiyyah wal-Ta'aṣṣub* (The Church and the State: Confessionalism and Radicalism). Naṭrūn Valley: St. Fr. Maqqār Monastery Press, 1969/2009.

. *Maqālāt Bayn al-Siyāsah wal-Dīn* (Essays between Politics and Religion). al-Natrun: Dār Majallāt Marqus, 1977.

. *al-Mar'a: Ḥuqūqahā wa-Wājibātihā fī al-Ḥayāt al-Ījtimā'iyya wad-Dīniyya fī al-Kanīsa al-'Ulā* (The Woman: Her Rights and Duties in Social and Religious Life in the Early Church). Shehet Desert: Anba Maqqar Monastery, n.d.

Mitchell, Margaret M and Frances M. Young (eds.). *The Cambridge History of Christianity*. Cambridge & New York: Cambridge University Press, 2006–2014.

Mitri, Tarek. "Christians in the Arab East: An Interpretation of Contemporary History," in *Christianity: A History in the Middle East*, Habib Badr, et. al. (eds.). Beirut: The Middle East Council of Churches, 2001, pp. 851–869.

Moffett, S.H. *A History of Christianity in Asia, Vol. 2: 1500 to 1900*. Maryknoll, NY: Orbis Books, 2005.

Monferrer-Sala, Juan Pedro. "An Arabic-Muslim Quotation of a Biblical Text: Ibn Kathīr's al-Bidāya wa-l-Nihāya and the Construction of the Ark of the Covenant," in *Studies on the Christian Heritage: In Honour of Father Prof. Dr. Samir Khalil Samir, S.I. at the Occasion of His Sixty-Fifth Birthday*, Rifaat Ebied and Herman Teule (eds.). Leuven: Peeters, 2004, pp. 263–278.

. ed., *Eastern Crossroads: Essays on Medieval Christian Legacy*, Piscataway, NJ: Gorgias Press, 2007.

Monier, Elizabeth. "Spatial Practices of 'Retreat' Among Egyptian Christians: Isolating or Empowering?" in *The International Journal of Levant Studies*, 2(2020), pp. 5–28.

Montgomery, James E. "Islamic Crosspollination," in *Islamic Crosspollinations: Interactions in the Medieval Middle East*, Anna Aksoy, James E. Montgomery, and Peter E. Pormann (eds.). Exeter: Gibb Memorial Trust, 2007, pp. 148–193.

Morrison, Glenn. *A Theology of Alterity: Levinas, von Balthasar and Trinitarian Praxis*. Pittsburg, Penn: Duquesne University Press, 2013.

Murquṣ, Samīr. "Tajribat Lāhūt al-Taḥrīr" (The Experience of Liberation Theology), in *Lāhūt al-Taḥrīr: Rū'iyah 'Arabiyyah Islāmiyyah Masīḥiyyah (Liberation Theology: An Arab, Muslim-Christian View)*, William Sidhum, S.J. (ed.). Cairo: A. R.S.E/C.R.E.M.E.D., 2005, pp. 99–125.

Murre-van den Berg, Heleen. "Chaldaeans and Assyrians: The Church of the East in the Ottoman Period," in *The Christian Heritage of Iraq: Collected Papers from the Christianity of Iraq I-V Seminar Days*, Erica C. D. Hunter (ed.). Piscataway, NJ: Gorgias Press, 2009, pp. 146–164.

. "The Patriarchs of the Church of the East from the Fifteenth to the Eighteenth Centuries," in *Higoye: Journal of Syriac Studies*, 2:2 (1999b) http://syrcom.cua.edu/Hugoye/index.html

Nasr, Seyyed H. *Islamic Life and Thought*. London & New York: Routledge, 1981.

Nassif, Bassam A. "Religious Dialogue in the Eighth Century: Example from Theodore Abū Qurrah Treatise," in *Parole de l'Orient*, 30(2005), pp. 333–340.

Neander, J. August. W. *Antignostikus: Geist des Tertullians und Einleitung in dessen Schriften. Eine Monographie als Beitrag zur Geschichte der Glaubens- und Sittenlehre in den ersten Jahrhunderten*. Berlin: F. Dümmler, 1825.

Pacini, Andrea. *Christian Communities in the Arab Middle East: The Challenge of the Future*. Oxford: Clarendon Press, 1998.

Pahlitzsch, Johannes. *Graeci und Suriani im Palästina der Kreuzfahrerzeit*. Berlin: Dunker und Humboldt Verlag, 2001.

Panchenko, Constantine A. *Orthodoxy and Islam in the Middle East: The Seventh to the Sixteenth Century*. Brittany Pheiffer Noble and Samuel Noble (trans.,). Jordanville, NY: Holy Trinity Publications/Holy Trinity Seminary Press, 2021.

Pannenberg, Wolfhart. *Theology and the Philosophy of Science*. Francis McDonagh (trans.). Philadelphia: Westminster/John Knox Press, 1976.

Parry, Kenneth. *The Blackwell Companion to Eastern Christianity*. Malden USA/Oxford, UK: Blackwell Publishing, 2007.

Pattai, Raphael. "Introduction: 'The Great Goldziher,' a Psychological Portrait," in *Ignaz Goldziher and His Oriental Diary: A Translation and Psychological Portrait*, Raphael Pattai (trans. & ed.). Detroit, MI: Wayne State University Press, 1987.

Patton, Kimberley C. and Benjamin C. Ray (eds.). *A Magic Still Dwells: Comparative Religion in the Postmodern Age*. Berkeley, Los Angeles & London: University of California Press, 2000.

Peacock, A.C.S. (ed.). *Islamization: Comparative Perspectives from History*. Edinburgh: University of Edinburgh Press, 2017.

Pelikan, Jaroslav. *The Christian Tradition: A History of the Development of Doctrine*. Chicago, IL: University of Chicago Press, 1975–1991.

Périer, Augustin (ed.). *Petits Traités Apologétiques Yaḥyā Ben 'Adī*. Paris: J. Gabalda Editeur/ Paul Geuthiner Editeur, 1920.

Phan, Peter C. "Doing Theology in World Christianities: Old Tasks, New Ways," in *Relocating World Christianity: Interdisciplinary Studies in Universal and Local Expression of the Christian Faith*, Joel Cabrita, David Maxwell, and Emma Wild-Wood (eds.). Leiden & Boston: Brill, 2017, pp. 115–142.

Pines, Shlomo. "A Note on an Early Meaning of the Term *Mutakallim*," in *Israel Oriental Studies*, 1(1971), pp. 224–240.

Platti, Emilio. *Yaḥyā b. 'Adī, Theologien Chrétien et Philosophé arabe*. Leuven: Department of Orientalistiek, 1983.

. "Islam et Occident: *Choc de theologies*?" in *Mélanges*, 24(2000), pp. 347–379.

Poggi, Vincenzo, S.J. "Christians in the Second Ottoman Era (17th Century)," in *Christianity: A History in the Middle East,* Habib Badr, et. al. (eds.). Beirut: Middle East Council of Churches, 2001, pp. 655–674.

Pratt, Mary Louis. *Imperial Eyes: Travel Writing and Transculturation*, 2nd ed. New York & London: Routledge, 2008.

Qabbara, Maria. "al-Shammāsāt, Sharṭūniyyat al-Nisā' fī al-Taqlīd al-Līṭūrjī al-Urthūdhuksī:

Nuṣūṣ min Ta'līm al-Rusul al-Ithnay 'Ashar wal-Qawānīn al-Kanasiyya" (Deaconesses, Women's '*Cheirotonia*' in the Orthodox Liturgical Tradition: Texts from the *Didache* and the Apostolic Rules), in *TELOS Magazine*, 4(2021), pp. 32–36, p. 32, www.telosmagazine.org/uploads/2/5/5/6/2556114/7-maria_kabara-telos_issue_no4.pdf

. "Azmat al-Khiṭāb ad-Dīnī al-Masīḥī al-Qadīm wal-Jadīd: Rafḍun Ṣarīḥ li-'Adam

Tamkīn al-Mar'a fī al-Kanīsa al-Urthūdhuksiyya" (The Crisis of the Old and New Christian Religious Discourse: An Explicit Rejection of Empowering

Woman in the Orthodox Church) in www.kalimat.one/maria-kabara, 12/10/2022.

. "Ṣūrat wa-Makānat al-Marʾa fī al-ʿAhd al-Jadīd" (Woman's Image and Status in the New Testament), in www.kalimat.one/maria-kabara, 7/31/2022.

. "Marthā am Maryam? Makānat al-Marʾa wa-Daūruhā fī al-Kanīsa al-Urthūdhuksiyya" (Martha or Mary? Woman's Status and Role in the Orthodox Church), in www.kalimat.one/maria-kabara, 2/18/2021.

Qāshā, Souhayl. *Ṣafaḥāt min Tārīkh al-Masīḥiyyīn al-'Arab Qabl al-Īslām* (Pages from the History of the Arab Christians before Islam). Jounieh: al-Maktabah al-Buluṣiyyah, 2005.

al-Rabīʿī, Fāḍil. *al-Masīḥ al-'Arabī: al-Naṣrāniyyah fī al-Jazīrah al-'Arabiyyah wa al-Ṣirā' al-Bīzanṭī al-Fārisī* (The Arab Christ: Christianity in Arabia and the Byzantine–Persian Conflict). Beirut: Rīāḍ al-Rayyīs, 2009.

Raheb, Mitri. "Shifting Identities: The History of Christianity in the Modern Middle East," in *Shifting Identities: Changes in the Social, Political and Religious Structures in the Middle East*, Mitri Raheb (ed.). Bethlehem: Diyar Publisher, 2016, pp. 9–39.

. *Shifting Identities: Changes in the Social, Political and Religious Structures in the Middle East*. Bethlehem: Diyar Publisher, 2016.

. "Sailing Through Troubled Waters: Palestinian Christians in the Holy Land," in *Dialogue: A Journal of Theology*, 41(2), 2002, pp. 97–102.

. *Sailing Through Troubled Waters: Christianity in the Middle East*. Bethlehem: Diyar Publisher, 2013.

. *Faith in the Face of Empire: The Bible Through Palestinian Eyes*. Maryknoll, NY: Orbis Books, 2014.

. et. al., Mark Lamport. *Emerging Theologies from the Global South*. Eugene, OR: Cascade Books, 2023.

. ed., *In the Eye of the Storm: Middle Eastern Christians in the Twenty-First Century*. Eugene, OR: Pickwick Publications, 2023.

. "Toward a New Hermeneutics of Liberation: A Palestinian Christian Perspective," in *The Biblical Text in the Context of Occupation: Towards a New Hermeneutics of Liberation*, Mitri Raheb (ed.). Bethlehem: Diyar Publishers, 2012.

. *The Biblical Text in the Context of Occupation: Towards a New Hermeneutics of Liberation*. Bethlehem: Diyar Publishers, 2012.

. "Educational Co-Operation among Christians, Muslims and Jews in the Middle East," in *British Journal of Religious Education*, 18(1), 2014, pp. 59–62.

. *I Am a Palestinian Christian*, Ruth C. L. Gritsch (trans.). Minneapolis: Fortress Press, 1995.

. "Mission in the Context of Fragmentation," in *International Review of Mission*, LXXXVI/343, 1997, pp. 393–398.

. et. al., Mark A. Lamport. "The Interpretative Challenge for Grace and Peace in the Global South: A Hermeneutical Perspective," in *Emerging Theologies from the Global South*, M. Raheb and M. A. Lamport (eds.). Eugene, OR: CASCADE Books, 2023, pp. 7–18.

Raheb, Viola. "Middle Eastern Theologies," in *Emerging Theologies from the Global South*, Mitri Raheb and Mark A. Lamport (eds.). Eugene, OR: Cascade Books, 2023, pp. 259–272.

al-Rahim, Ahmad H. "Whither Political Islam and the 'Arab Spring'?" in *The Hedgehog Review*, Fall 2011, pp. 8–22.

Ramadan, Tariq. *Islam and the Arab Awakening*. Oxford & New York: Oxford University Press, 2012.

Reiss, Wolfram. *Erneuerung in der Koptisch-Orthodoxen Kirche*. Muenster: LIT Verlag, 1998.

Retsö, Jan. *The Arabs in Antiquity: Their History from the Assyrians to the Umayyads*. London & New York: Routledge, 2003.

Ricks, Thomas W. *Early Arabic Christian Contributions to Trinitarian Theology*. Minneapolis: Fortress Press, 2013.

Ricoeur, Paul. Memory, History, Forgetting, Kathleen Blamey and David Pellauer (trans.). Chicago & London: The University of Chicago Press, 2004.

. *Oneself as Another*, K. Blamey (trans.). Chicago: University of Chicago Press, 1992.

Robson, Laura. "Recent Perspectives on Christianity in the Modern Arab World," in *History Compass*, 9/4(2011), pp. 312–325.

Roggema, Barbara. "A Christian Reading of the Qur'ān: the Legend of Sergius-Baḥīrā and its Use of Qur'ān and Sīra," in *Syrian Christians under Islam, the First Thousand Years*, David Thomas (ed.). Leiden: Brill, 2001, pp. 57–74.

Rorty, Richard. "Human Rights, Rationality and Sentimentality," in *On Human Rights: The Oxford Amnesty Lectures 1993*, Stephen Shute and Susan Hurley (eds.). New York: Basic Books, 1993, pp. 111–134.

Rousseau, P. and J. Raithel (eds.). *A Companion to Late Antiquity*. Chichester: Blackwell Publishers, 2009.

Rowe, Paul S. "The Middle Eastern Christian as Agent," in *International Journal of Middle Eastern Studies*, 42(2010), pp. 472–474.

Sabra, George. "A Response to 'Christianity in a Culture Marked by Islam': Facts and Visions," in *Theological Review*, 35(2014), pp. 145–148.

. "Theology," in *Christianity in North Africa and West Asia*, Kenneth R. Ross, Mariz Tadros, and Todd M. Johnson (eds.). Edinburgh: Edinburgh University Press, 2018, pp. 325–334.

Sahas, Daniel J. *Byzantium and Islam: Collected Studies on Byzantine–Muslim Encounters*. Leiden & Boston: Brill, 2022.

Sahner, Christian C. *Christian Martyrs under Islam: Religious Violence and the Making of the Muslim World*. Princeton, NJ: Princeton University Press, 2018.

. *Among the Ruins: Syria Past and Present*. Oxford & New York: Oxford University Press, 2014.

Sākū, Lūwīs Rūfā'īl Cardinal. *Khulāṣat Tārīkh al-Kanīsah al-Kaldāniyya* (The Summa of the History of the Chaldean Church). Kerkuk: Beth Mardutho Press, 2006.

. "Kanīsat al-Sharq wa-Maūḍū' al-Qawmiyyah" (The Church of the East and the Subject of Nationality), in www.abouna.org

. "Al-Tasmiyāt?" (Nomenclatures?), in www.ankawa.com/forum/index.php/topic,315929.0.html.

. "Al-Masīḥiyyūn al-'Irāqiyyūn: Makhāwif wa-Amāl" (Iraqi Christians: Fears and Aspirations), in *Masīḥiyyū al-Waṭan al-'Arabī: al-Tārīkh, al-Daūr, al-Mustaqbal* (The Christians of the Arab World: History, Role, Future), Jerome Shahin and Radwa Salah (eds.). Beirut: The Arabic Team for Muslim–Christian Dialogue, 2013, pp. 221–225.

. "Ī'timād al-Mūwāṭanah al-Wāḥidah wa-Damj al-Mūwāṭinīn fīhā" (Employing Unifying Citizenship and Incorporating Citizens into it), in *Al-'Aysh al-Mushtarak wal-Waḥdah fī al-Tanaūw'* (Co-Existence and Unity in Diversity), Jerome Shahin (ed.). Beirut: The Forum for Development, Culture and Dialogue, 2011, pp. 7–11.

. "Al-Masīḥiyyūn fī al-Sharq al-Awsaṭ. Bayn Islām al-Dawlah wal-Uṣūliyya" (The Christians in the Middle East. Between the State's Islam and Fundamentalism), in www.aramean-dem.org/Arabic/tarikh_skafe/luis_sako/3.htm (consulted on 22 September 2011).

. "The Synod and Christian–Muslim Relations: Personal Critical Evaluation, Results and Perspectives," in *Middle Eastern Christians Facing Challenges: Reflections on the Special Synod for the Middle East*, Dietmar W. Winkler (ed.). Piscataway, NJ: Gorgias Press, 2019, pp. 134–139.

. "Relations between Christians and Muslims in Iraq – A Brief Statement," in *Syriac Churches Encountering Islam: Past Experiences and Future Perspectives*, Dietmar W. Winkler (ed.). Piscataway, NJ: Gorgias Press, 2010, pp. 219–221.

Ṣalībī, Kamāl. *al-Baḥth 'an Yasū': Qirā'ah Jadīdah fī al-Anājīl* (The Search for Jesus: A New Reading in the Gospels). Amman: Dār al-Shurūq, 1999.

Ṣāliḥ-al'āyib, Salwā Balḥāj. *Al-Masīḥiyyah al-'Arabiyyah wa-taṬawurātihā: Min Nash'atihā īlā*

al-Qarn al-Rābi' al-Hijrī/al-'āshir al-Milādī (Arab Christianity and its Evolvements: From its Birth till the 4th/10th Century). Beirut: Dār al-Ṭalī'ah, 1998.

Samir, Samir Khalil (ed.). *Actes du premier congrès international d'ètudes arabes Chrètiennes*, in

Orientalia Christiana Analecta 218. Rome: Pontificum Institutum Studiorum Orientalium, 1982.

. *Alphonse Mingana 1878–1837 and His Contribution to Early Christian–Muslim Studies*. Birmingham: Selly Oak Colleges, 1990.

. "Lāhūt al-Sharq al-Adna al-Ḥadīth fī al-Ṣilah bayn al-Hawiyyah wal-Ghayriyyah" (The Theology of the Modern Near East. On the Connection between Identity and Othering), in *al-Mashriq*, 75(1), 2001, pp. 25–56.

. *Daūr al-Masīḥiyyīn al-Thaqāfī fī al-'Ālam al-'Arabī* (The Christians' Cultural Role in the Arab World). Beirut: al-Mashriq Press, 2004.

Sauter, Gerhard. *Gateways to Dogmatics: Reasoning Theologically for the Life of the Church*. Grand Rapids, USA/Cambridge, UK: W. B. Eerdmans Publishing Company, 2003.

. *Protestant Theology at the Crossroads: How to Face the Crucial Tasks for Theology in the Twenty-First Century*. Grand Rapids, USA/Cambridge, UK: W. B. Eerdmans Publishing Company, 2007.

Schadler, Peter. *John of Damascus on Islam*. Leiden & Boston: Brill, 2018.

Schmidtke, Sabine (ed.). *The Oxford Handbook of Islamic Theology*. Oxford: Oxford University Press, 2014.

. "The Muslim Reception of Biblical Materials: Ibn Qutayba and His *A'lām al-Nubuwwa*," in *Islam and Christian–Muslim Relations*, 22(2011), pp. 249–274.

Schmiedel, Ulrich. "(Instead of the) Introduction Open to the Other: The Dynamics of Difference in Werner G. Jeanrond's Hermeneutical Theology," in *Dynamics of Difference: Christianity and Alterity: A Festschrift for Werner G. Jeanrond*, Ulrich Schmiedel and James M. Matarazzo, Jr. (eds.). London & New York: Bloomsbury T&T Clark, 2016, pp. 1–16.

. et. al.; James M. Matarazzo, Jr. (eds.). *Dynamics of Difference: Christianity and Alterity: A Festschrift for Werner G. Jeanrond*. London & New York: Bloomsbury T&T Clark, 2016.

Schneider, Nina. "Between Promise and Skepticism: The Global South and Our Role as Engaged Intellectuals," in *The Global South*, 11(2017), pp. 18–37.

Schüssler Fiorenza, Elisabeth. *Discipleship of Equals: A Critical Feminist Ekklēsia-logy of Liberation*. New York: Crossroads, 1993.

. *But She Said: Feminist Practice of Biblical Interpretation*. Boston: Beacon Press, 1993.

. *Theological Criteria and Historical Reconstruction: Martha and Mary, Luke 10: 38–42*, Herman C. Waetjen (ed.). Berkeley, CA: Center for Hermeneutical Studies in Hellenistic and Modern Culture, 1987.

Seal, Patrick. "The Rise of Political Islam", in www.gulfnews.com (consulted on 28 October 2011).

Segovia, Fernando F. "Theologizing from the Global South," in *Emerging Theologies from the*

Global South, M. Raheb and M. A. Lamport (eds.). Eugene, OR: Cascade Books, 2023, pp. 19–33.

Shahid, Irfan. *The Martyrs of Najran*. Brussels: Soc. Des Bollandistes, 1971.

. *Byzantium and the Arabs in the Sixth Century: Ecclesiastical History*. Washington, DC: Dumbarton Oaks Research Library and Collection, 1995, I/2.

Shahin, Jerome and Radwa Salah (eds.). *Masīḥiyyū al-Waṭan al-ʿArabī: al-Tārīkh, al-Daūr, al-Mustaqbal* (The Christians of the Arab World: History, Role, Future). Beirut: The Arabic Team for Muslim–Christian Dialogue, 2013.

Shahin, Jerome (ed.). *Al-ʿAysh al-Mushtarak wal-Waḥdah fī al-Tanaūwʿ* (Co-Existence and Unity in Diversity). Beirut: The Forum for Development, Culture and Dialogue, 2011.

Shahin, Jerome. *al-Masīḥiyyūn al-'Arab: al-Taḥaddiyāt al-Rāhina wa-Khayārāt al-Maṣīr* (The Arab Christians: The Contemporary Challenges and the Choices of Destiny). Beirut: an-Nūr Orthodox Press, 2008.

Sharkey, Heather J. *American Evangelicals in Egypt: Missionaries Encounters in an Age of Empire*. Princeton, NJ: Princeton University Press, 2008.

Sharp, Andrew. *Orthodox Christians and Islam in the Postmodern Age*. Leiden & Boston: Brill, 2012.

al-Sharqāwī, Bāsim Samīr (ed.). *Madkhal īlā 'Īlm at-Turāth al-'Arabī al-Masīḥī* (An Introduction to the Science of Arabic Christian Tradition). Cairo: Franciscan Cultural Center (C.C.F.), 2017.

Sidhum, William, S.J. (ed.). *Lāhūt al-Taḥrīr: Rū'iyah 'Arabiyyah Islāmiyyah Masīḥiyyah* (Liberation Theology: An Arab, Muslim-Christian View), Cairo: A. R.S.E/C.R.E.M.E.D., 2005.

. "Ishkāliyāt al-Maṣāḍir al-Falsafiyyah li-Lāhūt al-Taḥrīr" (The Problems of the Philosophical Sources of Liberation Theology), in *Lāhūt al-Taḥrīr: Rū'iyah 'Arabiyyah Islāmiyyah Masīḥiyyah (Liberation Theology: An Arab, Muslim-Christian View)*, William Sidhum, S.J. (ed.). Cairo: A. R.S.E/C.R.E.M.E.D., 2005., pp. 17–21.

Smith, Wilfred Cantwell. *The Meaning and End of Religion*. New York: Macmillan, 1963.

Stroumsa, Guy (ed.). *Comparative Studies in the Humanities*. Jerusalem: Israel Academy of Sciences and Humanities, 2018.

Stroumsa, Sarah. "Comparison as a Multifocal Approach: The Case of Arabic Philosophical Thought," in *Comparative Studies in the Humanities*, Guy Stroumsa (ed.). Jerusalem: Israel Academy of Sciences and Humanities, 2018, pp. 133–151.

Sundermeier, Theo. *Den Fremden Verstehen: Eine praktische Hermeneutik*. Göttingen: Vendenhoeck und Ruprecht, 1996.

Swanson, Mark. "Some Considerations for the Dating of *Fī Tathlīth Allah al-Wāḥid* (Sinai Ar. 154) and *al-Jāmi' fī Wujūh al-Imān* (London British Library Or. 4950)," in *Parole de l'Orient*, 18(1993), pp. 117–141.

. "Beyond Proof-texting: Approaches to the Qur'ān in Some Early Arabic Christian Apologies," in *The Muslim World*, 88(1998), pp. 297–319.

. "Apologetics, Catechesis and the Question of Audience in 'On the Triune Nature of God' (Sinai Arabic 154) and Three Treatises of Theodore Abū Qurrah," in *Christians and Muslim in Dialogue in the Islamic Orient of the Middle Ages*, Martin Tamcke (ed.). Beirut: Oriental Institute, 2007, pp. 113–134.

Tadros, Mariz. "The Undesirables of Egypt: A Story of Persecution and Defiance," in *Copts in Context: Negotiating Identity, Tradition and Modernity*, Nelly van Doorn-Harder (ed.). Columbia, SC: University of South Carolina Press, 2017, pp. 34–51.

Tamcke, Martin (ed.). *Christians and Muslim in Dialogue in the Islamic Orient of the Middle Ages*. Beirut: Oriental Institute, 2007.

. *Christlische Gotteslehre in Orient seit dem Aufkommen des Islams zur Gegenwart*. Wūrzburgh: Ergon Verlag, 2008.

Tamer, George, Regina Grundmann, Asaad Elias Kattan, and Karl Pinggéra (eds.). *Exegetical Crossroads: Understanding Scripture in Judaism, Christianity and Islam in the Pre-Modern Orient*. Berlin & Boston: De. Gruyter, 2017.

Teule, Herman. "Middle Eastern Christians in the Ottoman Empire and its Relationship with the West: The Case of the East-Syrians in the Diyarbakir Region between the 16th and the Early 18th Century," in *Towards a Culture of Co-Existence in Pluralistic Societies: The Middle East and India*, D. W. Winkler (ed.). Piscataway, NJ: Gorgias Press, 2020, pp. 43–58.

Thomas, David (ed.). *Syrian Christians and Islam*. Leiden: Brill, 2001.

. et. al. (eds.). *Christian–Muslim Relations: Bibliographical History; Volume 1 (600–900)*. Leiden & Boston: Brill, 2009.

. "Arab Christianity," in *The Blackwell Companion to Eastern Christianity*, Ken Perry (ed.). Oxford, UK/ Malden, USA: Blackwell Publishers, 2010, pp. 1–22.

. *Christians at the Heart of Islamic Rule*. Leiden: Brill, 2003.

. *Christian Doctrines in Islamic Theology*. Leiden & Boston: Brill, 2008.

. "Introduction," in *Christian–Muslim Relations: Bibliographical History; Volume 1 (600–900)*, D. Thomas, B. Roggema, J.P. Monferrer Sala, J. Pahlitzsch, M. Swanson, H. Tuele, and J. Tolan (eds.). Leiden & Boston: Brill, 2009, pp. 1–19.

. "The Bible in Early Muslim Anti-Christian Polemic," in *Islam and Christian–Muslim Relations*, 7(1996), pp. 29–38.

. *Anti-Christian Polemic in Early Islam: Abū 'Īsā al-Warrāq*'s *'Against the Trinity.'* Cambridge & New York: Cambridge University Press, 1992.

Tracy, David. "The Other of Dialectic and Dialogue," in *Dynamics of Difference: Christianity and Alterity: A Festschrift for Werner G. Jeanrond*, Ulrich Schmiedel and James M. Matarazzo, Jr. (eds.). London & New York: Bloomsbury T&T Clark, 2016, pp. 105–114.

Treiger, Alexander. "Origins of *Kalām*," in *The Oxford Handbook of Islamic Theology*, Sabine Schmidtke (ed.). Oxford: Oxford University Press, 2014, in: https://www.oxfordhandbooks.com/view/10.1093/oxfordhb/9780199696703.001.0001/oxfordhb-9780199696703-e-001

. et. al., Samuel Noble (eds.). *The Orthodox Church in the Arab World 700–1700: An Anthology of Sources*. DeKalb, IL: NIU Press, 2014.

Trexler, Melanie E. *Evangelizing Lebanon: Baptists, Missions and the Question of Cultures*. Waco, TX: Baylor University Press, 2016.

Trimingham, J. S. *Christianity among the Arabs in Pre-Islamic Times*. London: Longman, 1979.

Troupeau, G. "Le livre de l'unanimité de la foi de ʿAlī ibn Dāwud al-Arfādī", in *Melto*, 5(1969), pp. 197–219.

Urbaniak, Jakub. "Religion as Memory: How Has the Continuity of Tradition Produced Collective Meanings? – Part One", in *HTS Teologiese Studies/Theological Studies*, 71(3), 2015, Art. 2815, pp. 1–8, http://dx.doi.org/10.4102/hts.v71i3.2815.

Vagelpohl, Uwe. *Aristotle's Rhetoric In the East: The Syriac and Arabic Translation and Commentary Tradition*. Leiden & Boston: Brill, 2008.
van Doorn-Harder, Nelly (ed.). *Copts in Context: Negotiating Identity, Tradition and Modernity*.
Columbia, SC: University of South Carolina Press, 2017.
van Ess, Josef. *Anfänge muslimischer Theologie: Zwei Antiqadaritische Traktate aus dem ersten*
Jahrhundert der Higra. Wiesbaden: Feranz Steiner Verlag, 1977.
. "Disputationspraxis in der islamischen Theologi. Eine vorläufege Skizze," in *Keleine Schriften by Josef van Ess*, Hinrich Biesterfeldt (ed.). Leiden & Boston: Brill, 2018, Vol. 2, Pt. V, pp. 911–947.
Volf, Miroslav. *The End of Memory: Remembering Rightly in a Violent World*. Grand Rapids, MI and Cambridge: W.B. Eerdmans Publishing Company, 2006.
Von Kremer, Alfred. *Culturegeschichte des Orients: Unter den Chalifen*. Wien: Wilhelm Braumüller, 1875.
Wadīʿ the Franciscan, Fr. *Dirāsah 'an al-Mu'taman b. al-'Assāl wa-Kitābih "Majmū' Uṣūl ad-Dīn" wa-Taḥqīqih* (A Study on al-Mu'taman b. al-ʿAssāl and a Critical Edition of His 'The Summa of Religious Foundations'). Cairo & Jerusalem: The Franciscan Friars Press, 1997.
Walbiner, Carsten-Michael. "Christian Arabic Studies in Germany during the Last 150 Years: A Short Survey," in *Proceedings of the Arabic and Islamic Sections of the 35th International Congress of Asian and North African Studies (ICANAS), II*, A. Fodor (ed.). Budapest: Eotvos Lorand University/Csoma de Koros Soceity, 1999, pp. 239–247.
. "Die Entwicklung der Christlich-Arabischen Studien in Deutschland: Ein Kurzer Überblick," in *The Journal of Eastern Christian Studies*, 58(3–4), 2006, pp. 253–263.
Ward, Graham. *Cultural Transformation and Religious Practice*. Cambridge: Cambridge University Press, 2005.
Webb, Peter. *Imagining the Arabs: Arab Identity and the Rise of Islam*. Edinburgh: Edinburgh University Press, 2017.
Wickens, G. Michael. "Western Scholarship on the Middle East," in *Comparative Civilizations*
Review, 13(13/6), 1985, pp. 62–72.
Wilde, Clare E. "*Lingua Sacra*? Some Reflections on Christian Discussions of *Faḍā'il al-Suryāniyya* and *I'jāz al-Qur'ān*," in *Eastern Crossroads: Essays on Medieval Christian Legacy*, Juan Pedro Monferrer-Sala (ed.). Piscataway, NJ: Gorgias Press, 2007, pp. 61–82.
Winkler, Dietmar W. (ed.). *Middle Eastern Christians Facing Challenges: Reflections on the Special Synod for the Middle East*. Piscataway, NJ: Gorgias Press, 2019.
. ed.; *Towards a Culture of Co-Existence in Pluralistic Societies: The Middle East and India*. Piscataway, NJ: Gorgias Press, 2020.
. ed. *Syriac Churches Encountering Islam: Past Experiences and Future Perspectives*. Piscataway, NJ: Gorgias Press, 2010.

———. "Reflections on a Culture of Co-Existence in Pluralistic Societies," in *Towards a Culture of Co-Existence in Pluralistic Societies: The Middle East and India*, D. W. Winkler (ed.). Piscataway, NJ: Gorgias Press, 2020, pp. 1–6.

Wolfson, Harry A. *The Philosophy of the Kalām*. Cambridge, Mass & London, UK: Harvard University Press, 1976.

Wood, Philip (ed.). *History and Identity in the Late Antique Near East*. Oxford & New York: Oxford University Press, 2013.

Wright, Christopher J. H. *An Eye for An Eye: The Place of Old Testament Ethics Today*. Downers Grove, IL: InterVarsity Press, 1983.

Yaʿqūb, Saʿīd Ḥakīm. *Makānat al-Mar'a fī al-Khidma al-Kanasiyya wal-Ḥayāt al-Nuskiyya* (The Woman's Status in Churchly Service and Monastic Life). Cairo: The Orthodox Center for Patristic Studies, n.d.

Ye'or, Bat. *The Decline of Eastern Christianity under Islam*. Madison, NJ: Fairleigh Dickinson University Press, 1996.

———. *Islam and Dhimmitude: Where Civilizations Collide*. Madison, NJ: Fairleigh Dickinson University Press, 2002.

Zaʿfān, al-Haytham (ed.). *al-Ḥaraka an-Nasauwiyya wa-Khalkhalat al-Mujtam'āt al-Īslāmiyyah; al-Mujtama' al-Maṣrī 'Unmūdhajan* (The Feminist Movement and the Rapping of the Muslim Societies, the Egyptian Society as a Case-Study). Cairo: al-Bayān Book, 2006.

Zahniser, A. H. Mathias. *The Mission and Death of Jesus in Islam and Christianity*. Maryknoll, NY: Orbis Books, 2008.

Zaki, Andrea. "al-Thaqāfah wal-Hauwiyyah" (Culture and Identity), in *Naḥwa Lāhūt 'Arabī Mu'āṣir* (Toward a Contemporary Arab Theology) (Arabic), Andrea Zaki (ed.). Cairo: al-Thaqafah Press, 2007), pp. 487–531.

———. *al-Massīḥ wal-Naqd al-Tārīkhī: Qiṣṣat al-Ṣirā' bayn al-Kirāzah wal-Taghiyyīr al-Ijtimā'ī* (Christ and Historical Criticism: The Story of the Struggle between Evangelism and Social Change) (Arabic). Cairo: al-Thaqafah Press, 2002.

———. *Min Lāhūt al-Shafāfiyah ila Lāhūt al-'Ayish al-Mushtarak: al-Kanīsah wal-Mas'ūliyyah al-Mujtama'iyyah* (From the Theology of Transparency into Theology of Co-existence: The Church and Societal Responsibility). Cairo: Dār al-Thaqāfah, 2021.

———. "Al-Daūr al-Tajdīdī lil-Masīḥiyyīn al-ʿArab" (The Renewing Role of the Arab Christians), in *al-Ma'ārij Journal*, 24(173), 2014, pp. 78–84.

———. ed. *Arabic Christian Theology: A Contemporary Global Evangelical Perspective*. Grand Rapids, Mich: Zondervan, 2019.

Zaki, Anne. "Al-Dhukūriyya al-Nāʿima fī Maṣr," (Soft Masculinity in Egypt), in *TELOS Magazine*, 4(2021), pp. 15–17, www.telosmagazine.org/uploads/2/5/5/6/25561514/3-anne_zaki-telos_issue_no4.pdf

———. "Shall We Dance? Reflections on the Nairobi Statement on Worship and Culture" in *Worship and Mission for the Global Church: An Ethnodoxology Handbook*, James R. Krabill, Frank Fortunato, Robin P. Harris, and Brian Schrag (eds.). Pasadena, CA: William Carey Library, 2012.

. "Public Theology and the Middle Eastern Church" in *Surviving Jewel: The Enduring Story of Christianity in the Middle East*, Mitri Raheb and Mark A. Lamport (eds.). Eugene, OR: Cascade Books/Wipf & Stock Publishers, 2022.

Zubaida, Sami. "Islam and Secularization," in *Asian Journal of Social Science*, 33/3(2005), pp. 438–448.

Zurlo, Gina A. "A Demographic Profile of Christianity in North Africa and West Asia," in *Christianity in North Africa and West Asia*, Kenneth R. Ross, Mariz Tadros, and Todd M. Johnson (eds.). Edinburgh: Edinburgh University Press, 2018, pp. 3–14.